The Passion for Happiness

The Passion
for Happiness

Samuel Johnson and David Hume

ADAM POTKAY

CORNELL UNIVERSITY PRESS

Ithaca and London

This book has been published with the help of a grant from the College of William and Mary.

First published 2000 by Cornell University Press

Printed in the United States of America

Library of Congress Cataloging-in-Publication Data

Potkay, Adam, b. 1961
  The passion for happiness : Samuel Johnson and David Hume / Adam Potkay.
     p. cm.
  Includes bibliographical references and index.
  ISBN 0-8014-3727-x
    1. Johnson, Samuel, 1709–1784—Contributions in concept of happiness.   2. Hume, David, 1711–1776—Contributions in concept of happiness.   3. Happiness—History—18th century.   I. Title.
BJ1481.P56 2000
170—dc21   99-052777

Cornell University Press strives to use environmentally responsible suppliers and materials to the fullest extent possible in the publishing of its books. Such materials include vegetable-based, low-VOC inks and acid-free papers that are recycled, totally chlorine-free, or partly composed of nonwood fibers. Books that bear the logo of the FSC (Forest Stewardship Council) use paper taken from forests that have been inspected and certified as meeting the highest standards for environmental and social responsibility. For further information, visit our website at www.cornellpress.cornell.edu.

Cloth printing   10 9 8 7 6 5 4 3 2 1

*Omnis auctoritas philosophiae . . . consistit in beata
vita comparanda; beate enim vivendi cupiditate
incensi omnes sumus.*

Cicero, *De Finibus Bonorum et Malorum* 5.86

For my wife, Monica Brzezinski Potkay, editor sans pareil,
and for our son Aaron, now learning to read.
Also for Steven Scherwatzky, Johnsonian and friend.

Contents

Acknowledgments

I was first introduced to Johnson by John Lavia, an inspiring teacher always ready to have a frisk with us young dogs. My first forays into pairing Johnson and Hume were generously encouraged by John Richetti. Dorothy Coleman put me on the road to becoming a responsible Humean.

Working alongside Robert Maccubbin, king of good fellows and wale of senior colleagues, has contributed immeasurably to my sense of eighteenth-century life. Other colleagues, students, and friends at The College of William & Mary who have been particularly helpful during the course of writing this book are Paula Blank, Michael Blum, Chris Bongie, Chandos Brown, Sandy Burr, Loren Council, Tom Heacox, Joel Schwartz, Tolly Taylor, Kim Wheatley and Peter Wiggins. The wonderfully animated students in my spring 1995 graduate seminar on Johnson and Hume honed my sense of how to put these authors in dialogue with each other; Lawrence Becker's 1996 seminar on Stoic ethics cast light on what I've come to see as one of the chief topics of their dialogue. The college's Social and Political Philosophy Discussion Group provided a valuable forum for some of the ideas worked out in the later chapters of this book.

I'd like also to thank the scholars and friends far and wide who've provided sage council, timely advice, and rich opportunities: Laurence Bongie, Robert DeMaria, Nicholas Hudson, William Hutching, Paul Korshin, Donald Livingston, Jack Lynch, Anne McDermott, Bruce Merrill, Brad Morrison, David Raynor, and William Walker. Special thanks to my two anonymous readers for Cornell University Press, whose detailed reports greatly assisted in preparing the final draft of this book, and to my editor, Bernie Kendler, for all of his support.

Acknowledgments

The bulk of this book was first drafted during a year-long research leave, 1996–97, provided by The College of William & Mary. We lived that year in a variety of houses in and around Seaside Park, New Jersey—a locale that cheered my spirits, as did cavorting with the Jetties and the rest of the Jersey gang during the interstices of literary labor. In the fall of 1997 my wife and I traded places with Robin and Liz Gilmour of Aberdeen, Scotland, and of its fine university. My work on this book proceeded apace in Robin's cozy garret study, and at the university's Queen Mother Library and King's College Special Collections. Back home since 1998, I am as ever indebted to the Earl Gregg Swem Library of The College of William & Mary.

"The Spirit of Ending in Johnson and Hume," an early version of Chapter 10, appeared in *Eighteenth-Century Life* (16:3), pp. 153–66, © 1992 by The Johns Hopkins University Press. An early version of Chapter 3 appeared in *The Age of Johnson: A Scholarly Annual* 9 (1998), pp. 165–86. I am grateful to the editors for permission to reprint that material here. I would also like to thank the Conway Library of the Courtauld Institute of Art for permission to reproduce a likeness of the statue of Samuel Johnson located in St. Paul's Cathedral.

A. P.

Abbreviations

David Hume

Dialogues = *Dialogues concerning Natural Religion.* Ed. Norman Kemp Smith. London: Thomas Nelson & Sons, 1947.

ECHU & ECPM = *Enquiries concerning Human Understanding and concerning the Principles of Morals.* Ed. L. A. Selby-Bigge, rev. P. H. Nidditch. Oxford: Clarendon, 1975.

Essays = *Essays Moral, Political, and Literary.* Ed. Eugene F. Miller. Indianapolis, Ind.: Liberty Classics, 1985.

History = *The History of England.* 6 vols. Ed. William B. Todd. Indianapolis, Ind.: Liberty Classics, 1983.

LG = *A Letter from a Gentleman to His Friend in Edinburgh.* Edinburgh, 1745. Rptd. with an intro. by Ernest C. Mossner and John V. Price. Edinburgh: Edinburgh University Press, 1957.

HL = *The Letters of David Hume.* 2 vols. Ed. J. Y. T. Greig. Oxford: Clarendon, 1932.

NHL = *New Letters of David Hume.* Ed. Raymond Klibansky and Ernest C. Mossner. Oxford: Clarendon, 1954.

NHR = *The Natural History of Religion.* Ed. H. E. Root. Stanford: Stanford University Press, 1956.

T = *A Treatise of Human Nature.* Ed. L. A. Selby-Bigge, rev. P. H. Nidditch. Oxford: Clarendon, 1978.

Samuel Johnson

Dictionary = *A Dictionary of the English Language.* 2 vols. First Edition. London, 1755.

English Law = *A Course of Lectures on the English Law Delivered at the University of Oxford 1767–73 by Sir Robert Chambers . . . And Composed in Association with Samuel Johnson.* 2 vols. Ed. Thomas Curley. Madison: University of Wisconsin Press, 1986.

JL = *The Letters of Samuel Johnson.* 5 vols. Ed. Bruce Redford. Princeton: Princeton University Press, 1992–1994.

Lives = *The Lives of the Most Eminent English Poets.* 3 vols. Ed. G. B. Hill. Oxford: Clarendon, 1905.

Major Works = *Samuel Johnson: A Critical Edition of the Major Works.* Ed. Donald Greene. Oxford: Oxford University Press, 1984.

Plan = *The Plan of a Dictionary of the English Language.* London, 1747.

Poems = *The Complete English Poems.* Ed. J. D. Fleeman. New Haven: Yale University Press, 1982.

Prefaces = *Samuel Johnson's Prefaces and Dedications.* Ed. Allen T. Hazen. New Haven: Yale University Press, 1937.

Works = *The Works of Samuel Johnson, LL.D.* Ed. Arthur Murphy. 12 vols. London: 1806.

From *The Yale Edition of the Works of Samuel Johnson.* New Haven: Yale University Press, 1958– :

Diaries = Vol. 1: *Diaries, Prayers, Annals,* ed. E. L. McAdam, with Donald and Mary Hyde (1958).

Idler & Adventurer = Vol. 2: *The Idler and The Adventurer,* ed. Walter J. Bate, John M. Bullitt, and L. F. Powell (1963).

Rambler = Vols. 3–5: *The Rambler,* ed. Walter J. Bate and Albrecht B. Strauss (1969).

Shakespeare = Vols. 7–8: *Johnson on Shakespeare,* ed. Arthur Sherbo, with an intro. by Bertrand Bronson (1968).

Journey = Vol. 9: *A Journey to the Western Islands of Scotland,* ed. Mary Lascelles (1971).

PW = Vol. 10: *Political Writings,* ed. Donald Greene (1977).

Sermons = Vol. 14: *Sermons,* ed. Jean H. Hagstrum and James Gray (1978).

Rasselas = Vol. 16: *Rasselas and Other Tales,* ed. Gwin J. Kolb (1990).

Principal Biographies

Early Biographies = *Early Biographies of Samuel Johnson.* Ed. O. M. Brack and
Robert E. Kelley. Iowa City: University of Iowa Press, 1974.

Life of Hume = Ernest C. Mossner. *The Life of David Hume.* Edinburgh:
Thomas Nelson, 1954.

Life of Johnson = James Boswell. *The Life of Samuel Johnson, LL.D.* 6 vols.
2d. ed. Ed. G. B. Hill, rev. L. H. Powell. Oxford: Clarendon, 1934–64.

Miscellanies = *Johnsonian Miscellanies.* 2 vols. Ed. G. B. Hill. New York:
Harper & Brothers, 1897.

Tour = James Boswell. *The Journal of a Tour to the Hebrides, with Samuel Johnson, LL. D.: Now First Published from the Original Manuscript.* Ed. Frederick
A. Pottle and Charles H. Bennett. New York: The Literary Guild, 1936.

The Passion for Happiness

Moral Writing in an Enlightened Age

Pairing the names of Samuel Johnson (1709–84) and David Hume (1711–76) in the title of a book might at first seem paradoxical. What two intellectual figures of the eighteenth century could appear more opposed, or opposed in more various ways? The Christian doctor contrasts the pagan sceptic; the venerable *senex* frowns on the enfant terrible; the sparkling conversationalist seems out of place alongside the substantial philosopher.

Yet once we move beyond familiar clichés and inspect in tandem Johnson's and Hume's bodies of writing in their entirety, a very different picture emerges. The received notion of the two men as contrastive figures derives from an undue focus on two books, one by Hume and one about Johnson: book 1 of *A Treatise of Human Nature* (1739) and James Boswell's *The Life of Samuel Johnson, LL.D.* (1791). Generalizations about either Johnson or Hume drawn primarily from these books are bound to be seriously flawed.

In the first place, Johnson's well-known antagonism toward Hume is not to be found in his own writings, but in Boswell's *Life*, a record—actually, a creative representation—of Johnson's conversations, largely those of his last ten years. Here we find the topic of Hume introduced time and again by Boswell, who consistently misrepresents Hume's philosophical positions to Johnson and encourages Johnson's misconceptions insofar as they inflame his oratory. Thus, when Boswell assures Johnson that a certain acquaintance of theirs was, although an infidel, "a benevolent good man," the stage is already set for Johnson's hearty remonstrance. "We can have no dependence upon that instinctive, that constitutional goodness which is not founded on principle. . . . Hume, and other sceptical innovators, are vain men, and will gratify themselves at any expence. Truth will not afford sufficient food to their vanity; so they have betaken themselves to errour. Truth, Sir, is a cow which will yield such people no more milk, and so they are gone to milk the bull" (*Life of Johnson* 1:443–44).

Hume, for his part, had little relish for being thought "a sceptical innovator" and went to great lengths to avoid being tarred with this brush, even to renouncing late in life his youthful *Treatise of Human Nature* after its metaphysics had been so effectively caricatured by James Beattie. Hume wished to be identified not as a purveyor of Zenolike paradoxes, but rather as a polished writer of general history and a moral philosopher who might ground virtue on principle.[1] Hume's ambition, which he arguably achieved, was to be the Livy of English history and the Cicero of English philosophy. Hume's mature scepticism consisted of little more than reclaiming Cicero's epistemological modesty. Hume opposed the claims of both rationalism and dogmatism; positively, he advanced probabilistic claims about matters of fact according to the quantity and quality of evidence at hand.

Both these facets of Hume's scepticism are to be found in Johnson's writings. Hume, perhaps sensing this affinity, could be more generous toward Johnson than Johnson tended, in conversation, to be toward him. According to the memoirist William Shaw (1785), Hume "mentioned [Johnson's periodical] the Rambler . . . with respect; and only regretted there should be so much cant and so much pedantry, in a performance replete with taste, erudition, and genius" (*Early Biographies* 163). As I hope to show, the taste, erudition, and genius of Johnson and of Hume are largely in accord; when not in unison, they are contrapuntal, related but independent voices contributing to a greater whole.

I. Toward Reclaiming "Literature"

Mutual disregard now separates most academic Johnsonians from most Humeans, but the literary world was of course less fragmented in John-

---

[1] Among contemporary philosophers, Donald Livingston has perhaps done most to salvage Hume's oeuvre as a whole from the restricted epistemological concerns of academic Anglo-American philosophy. Livingston notes, "[V]ery little of Hume's writings, taken as a whole, are devoted to epistemological subjects. Over half of what he wrote was in history, and most of the rest of it was in ethics, aesthetics, philosophy of religion, and what today would be called the social sciences" (Introduction to *Hume as Philosopher of Society, Politics and History* x). Metaphysics may or may not have been Hume's first love: sensitive readers still disagree about how to weigh book 1 of the *Treatise* against its latter two books (is it crucial, or a mere portico to the moral and cultural concerns of books 2 and 3?). But metaphysics were certainly not the love of his life. Were they his sole claim to fame, Hume would fare badly in the new philosophical world ushered in by Ryle and Wittgenstein—witness, for example, Anthony Kenny's savaging of Hume in the recent *Oxford History of Western Philosophy* (158–66).

son's and Hume's own day. Given the two writers' prominence in that world, they hardly could neglect to take one another into account. Hume's personal library contained nine volumes of Johnson's writings as well as a three-volume set of *The Adventurer,* a periodical to which Johnson contributed.[2] And there is ample evidence that Johnson knew at least parts of Hume's oeuvre—in Boswell's *Life of Johnson* he comments freely on Hume's style in general, and on the philosophical essay "Of Miracles" in particular; elsewhere, he expresses a preference for Hume's *History of England* over Robertson's histories (*Miscellanies* 2:48). Johnson and Hume worked with the same London publishers (Andrew Millar, William Strahan); their literary coteries overlapped, and their British and American audiences were largely identical.

Two hundred odd years later, eighteenth-century Britain's two leading men of letters command the respect of largely separate and mutually indifferent audiences. What Johnson and Hume would simply have called "literature," or "the learned world," finds itself divided into several academic disciplines, each contending with ever-increasing bodies of specialized knowledge and moving further away from an acquaintance with other fields. As long ago as 1926, J. B. Black expressed nostalgia for the eighteenth century, when "the globe of human knowledge was still intact and fairly safe from the ravages of specialism; and writers moved about freely among the arts and sciences, with an easy gaiety and a sureness of step, that seem, by contrast with the laboured progression of today, little short of marvellous" (15). Today's academic, who professes still narrower fields of specialization, may justly lay claim to the virtuoso's self-vindication before the goddess of Dullness: "I meddle, Goddess! only in my sphere" (Alexander Pope, *The Dunciad* 4:432).

A basic aim of this book is to evince the wholeness of the eighteenth-century world of letters that contained both Johnson and Hume: to situate Hume alongside Johnson within eighteenth-century literature for the benefit of philosophers and historians of philosophy, and to evince Johnson's engagement with philosophy for students of literature. The activity of reading them alongside each other is illuminating. In bringing into focus the traits they share, we may see much that philosophers would not ordinarily appreciate about Hume, and that literary scholars would not notice about Johnson. My hope is to usher in a true dialogue between the disciplines—or, more modestly, between the numerous members of the International Hume Society and those of the various national and regional Johnson societies across the world. I hope as well to draw in a wide range of *dix-huitiemistes* who are preoccupied neither with Johnson nor

---

[2] According to David Fate Norton's reconstruction (*The David Hume Library,* 106), Hume owned Johnson's *The Rambler,* 4 vols. (London, 1763); *The Idler,* 2 vols. (London, 1763); *Miscellaneous and Fugitive Pieces,* 3 vols. (London, 1774).

with Hume, but interested in the history and contours of Enlightenment thought. And finally, I write these days with the sense of yet another audience looking over my shoulder—my book-reading friends outside the academy who, unprejudiced by the often unreal concerns of those of us cloistered "in colleges and cells," are ever looking for something at least modestly enjoyable and applicable to life. I find some reassurance in the fact that a good number of my nonacademic friends (who, admittedly, tend toward artsiness) have read and admired Johnson's philosophical tale, *Rasselas,* and bits and pieces of Hume's philosophical essays.

Which is in effect to say that my friends outside the university know more about Johnson than most philosophy professors, and little less about Hume than most literature professors. Philosophers, historians, political scientists, and economic historians seem hardly to know of Johnson save perhaps as a large blustery fellow given to pontificating in Boswell's presence. At best, he is thought a loveable old bear of a man with more than enough conversational quirks to flesh out a Dickens character: he has tavern repartee, Christian piety, Tory cant, late Latin pedantry, and the curious habit of prefacing his peremptory remarks with the term of address "Sir." As a footnote to the history of philosophy, Johnson is known as the person who kicks a stone to refute Berkeley's idealism. When some years ago I first mentioned the idea of a book linking Johnson and Hume to a friend, colleague, and prominent member of the International Hume society, she smiled with good-natured incredulity.

All this only mirrors, of course, the neglect—or, until quite recently, the largely uncomprehending admiration—afforded Hume in circles of Johnsonians, or literary critics in general. The reigning wisdom of the 1960s may be summed up in the words of the eminent Johnson biographer James Clifford, spoken to a graduate student—now himself an eminent professor of eighteenth-century literature—who proposed to write a dissertation on Johnson and Hume: "There is nothing to say about them, and there's an end of it." Today, the world of English literature history admits more light, and many people in literature departments are well acquainted with Hume's corpus; indeed, several of them were the first to introduce me to *le bon David.* However, many in English departments no doubt still share Professor Clifford's judgment. And while others have come to conclude, to the contrary, that Hume is of signal importance for the understanding of English literary history, a good number of these critics share a misunderstanding of Hume based on a cursory reading of selected portions of book 1 of the *Treatise.* (In my extreme youth I numbered among them.) To these critics, Hume revealed personal identity to be a fiction, and—depending on one's point of view—either freed or condemned Johnson, Boswell, and others to fashion their own "succession of perceptions" into ductile, provisional, pragmatic, rhetorical selves. According to this interpretation, Hume's inquiry into human understanding afforded his contemporaries, to borrow a phrase from Wallace Stevens, notes toward a supreme fiction.

Typically, then, Hume and Johnson have been viewed as antagonists; or as incommensurate figures; or as secret sharers in, to use some currently fashionable terminology, an epistemological crisis of the eighteenth century, before which people thought of themselves, if at all, as subsistent selves, and after which they felt, for better or for worse, like spectators in the theaters of their own minds.

My own insight is that David Hume and Samuel Johnson share a great deal of common ground, not as part of some existential quandary, but rather as moral philosophers who inherited similar terms and concerns from Hellenistic philosophy and especially from the eclectic Stoicism of Cicero's dialogues. In the eighteenth century, moral philosophy still aimed at directing people to their own good, or flourishing, or happiness; at the very least, it would show people the way to self-preservation. Johnson and Hume set forth largely compatible visions of human happiness that, while rooted in Cicero, draw as well on "modern" authors: they share common debts to Locke's empiricist psychology and Addison's art of the polite essay; Mandeville's naturalistic account of "selfish" society and Butler's reconciliation of self-love with benevolence. Johnson and Hume respond similarly to other aspects of their historical moment: both, for example, trace the humanistic implications of the new science and the commercial revolution. Still more important, both draw the same cautionary lesson from the course of English history after Elizabeth: they agree that the greatest threat to public happiness is "enthusiasm" in religion and, a fortiori, politics. As an antidote to the enthusiast's claim to divine authority—as well as to the rationalist's claim to know the truth about the way the world is—Johnson and Hume each cultivates the Ciceronian method of open-ended dialogue as the surest source in this world of truths we can live by.

Johnson and Hume share manners of writing that foster ethical complication, a both/and rather than either/or way of viewing situations and decisions; their most powerful works aim to derail the blinkered perspective of the partisan or the peremptory reader. Their best writings seek to shape an ideal reader not blinded by religious or political faction or prejudice, a reader who might boast the relative "impartiality" that is, for both writers, the sine qua non not only of reading but of all ethical judgment. Johnson and Hume encourage us imaginatively to assess the evidence and emotion that underlie, or ought to underlie, any moral or metaphysical conclusion or commitment—especially any religious belief.

I would be "milking the bull" myself to deny the religious differences between the two men. Yet even these differences are greatly diminished when one focuses, as I shall do, on the writings each author chose to publish in his own lifetime, bracketing—although we cannot, and need not, altogether disregard—what specialists now know about each man's life and private writings (correspondence, diaries, prayers). I will, in other words, attempt to read Johnson and Hume as they asked in their own day to be read. And they asked to be read as the polished authors of "an enlightened age."

II. The Enlightenment

In this book I survey the terrain shared by Hume and Johnson as students of human nature—as moral philosophers and as practical moralists—in an attempt to reclaim that terrain as the core of a period concept of the Enlightenment in Britain.[3] The lives and work of Johnson and Hume offer sometimes harmonious and sometimes contrapuntal themes in the larger unity of an age both saw as "enlightened." Hume, of course, holds a secure place in any account of the Enlightenment—Scottish, British, French, or European. Johnson, however, is still excluded from Enlightenment studies by almost all non-Johnsonians. He is scarcely to be found in the pages of the various surveys or readers titled *The Enlightenment* that have appeared in recent years.[4] A partial exception is Roy Porter's *The Enlightenment,* which adduces Johnson's *Rasselas* but only as a foil to *Candide,* in order to suggest that we should not "see *all* the writings of the eighteenth-century . . . as expressions of the Enlightenment" (63–64). It appears that the last European intellectual of stature to place Johnson in the Enlightenment was Paul Hazard (15, 19); by the time Peter Gay attempted his own grand synthesis, Johnson was admitted only to have "the Enlightenment style" of sceptical inquiry despite his best intentions (21).

Although perhaps not crucial to my argument about Johnson's place in this era, it seems worth noting that Johnson thought of himself as living in, and contributing to, an "enlightened age"—indeed, *the* enlightened age. Virgil, at the court of Augustus, was "enlightened with all the learning of one of the brightest ages" (*Rambler* 3:200); Louis XIV presided over "an age more enlightened" than that of the Roman emperors (4:193). John-

---

[3] In this I am inspired by an article written some years ago by Jeffrey Barnouw:

"By concentrating on texts of authors who might be considered marginal or opposed to the Enlightenment on the basis of a narrow conception, we may arrive at a more adequate idea of what 'the age' in fact considered enlightenment to be. . . . In my view the work not only of Hume but of Samuel Johnson . . . should be given prime consideration in any construction of the character of the age." (189–90)

[4] See my bibliography for works by Ulrich Im Hoff, Isaac Kramnick (*The Portable Enlightenment Reader*), Sergio Moravia, and Dorinda Outram. *The Blackwell Companion to the Enlightenment,* ed. John Yolton et al., is exceptional in its generous inclusion of Johnson.

son's scattered comments suggest a familiarity with Voltaire's claim that Europe had seen four great ages of Enlightenment, the greatest yet being the age of Louis XIV;[5] Johnson will not, however, concede superiority to even the recent past, much less to the mantle of a French king. "Our age," though susceptible to reform, is "enlightened beyond any former time" (*Idler* 2:12). The Johnson of Boswell's *Life* is ever impatient of hearing the past praised at the expense of the present; like Hume in his essay "Of the Populousness of Ancient Nations,"[6] Johnson is a debunker of the then-popular notion that Europe was once more populous—and thus more virtuous and prosperous—than it was at present (*Journey* 97–99). (The concepts of overpopulation and environmental "carrying capacities" were then as yet undreamed of.)

Johnson's voyage to the highlands of Scotland in 1773 gave him ample opportunity to meditate on the scale of enlightenment: "The ancient rigour of puritanism is now very much relaxed [in the Kirk], though all are not yet equally enlightened" (*Journey* 104); "second sight"—the power of seeing events other than those that appear before the eye—"is ascribed only to a people very little enlightened" (109); the Hebridean islands are full of many an "unenlightened ploughman" who would be amazed to hear of modern Newtonian physics (142). Johnson could also, as in *Idler* no. 6, refer to the present as "a more enlightened age" in a clearly ironic manner—as one "which considers profit the end of honour; and rates the event of every undertaking only by the money that is gained or lost" (2:20)—but the ability to consider a proposition from competing viewpoints is a salient part of the decorum of enlightened writing.

It would seem that the only impediment to considering Johnson as part of the Enlightenment is a misrepresentative and outmoded notion of what constitutes it, either as movement or as period. In the image bequeathed to us by Edmund Burke's *Reflections on the Revolution in France* (1790) and by French counterrevolutionary writers such as Louis de Bonald and Joseph de Maistre, the Enlightenment is chiefly associated with a small group of French *philosophes* whose supposed gospel of egalitarianism and pagan virtue bore fruit in the anarchy of the French Revolution. Peter Gay's influential revision of the Enlightenment legacy also centers on a small group of French *philosophes,* whose battle cry is liberty and Voltaire's

---

[5] See Voltaire's *Siècle de Louis XIV* (1751, rev. 1753), chap. 1. (Here, as in other cases where my bibliography lists untranslated French works, the translations are my own.) Voltaire's "four happy ages" include democratic Athens, late Republican and Augustan Rome, Renaissance Italy, and finally the age of Louis, in which "human reason in general reached perfection." While Voltaire's discussion of the later seventeenth century centers on France, he concedes that on account of London's Royal Society one could also call this "the age of the English, as well as that of Louis XIV" (chap. 31); all in all, "in the past century, men acquired more enlightenment from one end of Europe to the other than in all preceding ages" (chap. 34).

[6] See also Hume's *History* 1:12, 103.

"écrasez l'infame" (code for "wipe out the Church"); in Gay's tale, the Enlightenment leads not to the excesses of the French Revolution but, happily, to constitutional democracy and the modern secular state. Gay is also innovative in giving Hume, whom he deems "the complete modern pagan," an honorary pride of place among the French *philosophes*.

If such is the tide of Enlightenment, Johnson is clearly out of the swim. But recent scholarship questions most of what Gay took for granted, not least of which is the Francocentric nature of Europe's Enlightenment or, still more decentered, its several national and local Enlightenments. But even were we to look to France as exemplary, we might ask, Was the first wave of *philosophes*—before, say, 1770—"progressive" and "egalitarian"? "We have never pretended to enlighten shoemakers and servants," Voltaire wrote to D'Alembert. Excepting Rousseau, at once the most democratic and most egomaniacal of French writers, the *philosophes* sought rather a spectrum of solutions to French and other continental political ills, a palette that ran from Montesquieu's admiration for the English constitution to Voltaire's praise of enlightened despots—Frederick the Great, Tsar Peter I, the Emperor Yung-Cheng. And were the *philosophes* hostile to religion? One must expect criticism of both church and state by men who routinely experienced censorship and persecution by ecclesiastical and civil courts (the *parlements*). Yet when Voltaire, late in life, set about enlightening the village of Ferney, he sought to fortify the religious beliefs of the villagers, convinced of the salutary effects of Catholicism on humble people; indeed, he regularly received communion in the parish church he had rebuilt.

Finally, however, we need to ask the more fundamental question: Are a group of French *philosophes*, however prolific, an appropriate focus to the study of European Enlightenment? Scholarship subsequent to Roy Porter and Mikulas Teich's *The Enlightenment in National Context* (1981) has tended to concentrate on the distinctive national or local incarnations of what may only loosely be called *an* Enlightenment. And in most countries other than France, the philosophers, scientists, and men of letters who considered themselves and were recognized as "enlightened" were not only Christian but often clerics or the sons of clerics. Richard Sher has demonstrated the extent to which Scotland's Enlightenment, in particular, took place within the institutional settings of church and university. Moderate clergymen of the Church of Scotland—including the men of letters Hugh Blair, Alexander Carlyle, and William Robertson—numbered among Hume's closest friends.

By working within a wider European context, John Cannon has recently situated Johnson, with his standard of social utility and his distrust of all cant and dogma, "in the middle of the Enlightenment" (197–98). Cannon proceeds to identify the Enlightenment not only with a particular style or manner of thinking, but—implicitly following Jürgen Habermas—with a broadly public *process* of formulating and disseminating knowledge, of creating and nurturing a public capable of understanding and debating questions of ethical and political importance. According to Habermas's model, the twin engines of the Enlightenment were, on the one hand, a growing number of metropolitan and provincial newspapers, magazines, periodicals, and pamphlets, and on the other, the urban spaces that allowed for spirited conversation—the tavern, the coffeehouse, the club, the lodge, the salon.

Given this understanding of the Enlightenment, Johnson lies, with Hume, at its very heart. To Johnson we owe the word "clubable," used to distinguish those with social and conversational habits from those without; London's "The Club," founded by Joshua Reynolds and Johnson in 1764, was to become the most distinguished intellectual forum qua dinner club in all Britain. Edinburgh, however, teemed with newly founded conversational spaces of its own: Hume alone belonged to its Philosophical Society (from 1737), its Select Society (1754–63), and its more informal Poker Club (from 1762). And in Paris, Hume partook of both the sociable discussions offered by the salons, and the philosophical discussions available at Baron d'Holbach's, Rue Royale. Additionally, Johnson and Hume were both men of the century's burgeoning print culture. Late in life Hume joked to Adam Smith that his only excuse to Charon for not being ready to cross over the Styx was the need to correct and revise successive editions of his printed works. Johnson's entire life, in turn, revolved around the press: emblematically, he was born in the house of a bookseller and died in the house of a printer.

Of course, both Johnson and Hume had rather restricted ideas about just who constituted their proper audience. Not as many people read or read as widely then as do today. But making allowances for the fact that I live on the far side of industrial and technological revolutions that have transformed any eighteenth-century notion of franchise, I nonetheless firmly believe in what I understand to be the central values bequeathed to us by the Enlightenment. For we find in Johnson and Hume not only clubability and sense of place, but also a cosmopolitan respect for the reasonable passions of all peoples.[7]

---

[7] In a valuable study of eighteenth-century historiography, Karen O'Brien defines cosmopolitanism as "an attitude of detachment towards national prejudice . . . and an intellectual investment in the idea of a common European civilisation" (2). I would offer the qualification that while Enlightenment authors addressed a European *audience,* they often conceived of a common *world* civilization—even if its perceived commonalities ultimately reflected European concerns. Thus Voltaire feels a kindred bond to China and Confucianism; thus Johnson sets his most popular philosophical tale in Ethiopia and Egypt, amidst Coptic Christianity. For a sympathetic discussion of Johnson's "principled universalism," see Clement Hawes's essay in *The Cambridge Companion to Johnson,* ed. Clingham, 114–26; the essay stumbles only in its use of Hume as a foil, painting him quite hastily as a proto-"Romantic-racialist" (115 and n. 9).

Sadly, this last claim may require some defense. Since Thomas Schlereth's masterly essay (1977) on the nature and limits of cosmopolitanism in the eighteenth century, the cosmopolitan ideal has for many fallen out of favor. Lawrence Lipking is representative of much current wisdom: "Cosmopolitanism does not revoke nationalism but serves as its product or supplement, an illusion of common discourse that nations foster to show how much they can absorb" ("M. Johnson and Mr. Rousseau" 113). Behind cosmopolitanism some are quick to detect and assail hidden political agendas, presumably oppressive ones. Katie Trumpener's recent book contains a long and particularly colorful screed against Samuel Johnson's "cosmopolitan and imperial" travelogue, *A Journey to the Western Islands of Scotland,* which is condemned not so much for what it does as for what it does not set out to do: namely, it "fails to discuss the work of the Scottish Enlightenment," or "to characterize Scotland as a whole"; it fails to acknowledge Trumpener's belief that Scotland's was a "nationalist enlightenment" (though what Trumpener might mean by this unlikely proposition is never explained); and, worst of all, it is demonstrably unsympathetic to the untruths or half-truths fostered by "nationalist sentimentality" (68–70). Trumpener's professed norms of irrational nationalism and tribalism, and her armchair sympathy for vernacular calls "[t]o battle speed" (74), recall the spirited politics of her favorite Highland bard, James Macpherson, of whom Hume commented, "He would have all the Nation divided into Clans, and these clans to be allways fighting" (Boswell, *Private Papers* 1:128).

By contrast to the idea of the cosmopolite as secret imperialist, let us hear in its simplicity the Stoic ideal of the cosmopolis: "[T]he universe . . . is a city or state of which both men and gods are members . . . from which it is a natural consequence that we should prefer the common advantage to our own" (Cicero, *De Finibus* 3.19). This sentiment is echoed by most every writer we associate with the Enlightenment as a movement, and with a great many more who lived during the period. Was this ideal tarnished by our experience of its ideological abuse over the past two centuries by a variety of imperial endeavors? Let us recall that it was the British of the early nineteenth century, at the dawn of a military empire on which the sun has only recently set,[8] that first criticized Hume and Johnson for not being "English" enough; for having neglected the supposed Saxon purity of their language and its genius; for being members of no country, but a "republic of letters"; in a word, for being cosmopolitan. Cosmopolitan

---

[8] Anthony Pagden usefully distinguishes two British empires (1–10): the first, which arguably is not properly speaking an "empire" at all (130), consisted chiefly of American settlements sanctioned though only loosely regulated by the metropolis; it ended by 1780. The second, rooted in the 1730s but only taking hold in the 1780s, is the British Empire as we have come to think of it: militarily potent, hierarchically administered, and based on the exploitation of native populations in Asia, Africa, and the Pacific.

Left: Samuel Johnson, in St. Paul's Cathedral, by John Bacon. Photo courtesy of the Conway Library, Courtauld Institute of Art.
Right: David Hume, outside Edinburgh Sheriff Court, by Sandy Stoddart. Photo by the author.

were what the Britons who forged an empire were not; and surely an ideal should not suffer through association with those who denounced it.

Among the lesser evils of romantic nationalism, yet a crucial one here, is its tendency to divide portions of Hume's and of Johnson's respective audiences—or at least their tribes of well-wishers—north and south of the Tweed. Thanks to Boswell's *Life,* Johnson came in the nineteenth century and to some degree continues to be admired as the quintessential London conversationalist, brimming with English frankness, English prejudices (particularly anti-Scottish ones), English piety, and English beef. As William Rees-Mogg proudly proclaimed upon the bicentenary of Johnson's death: "Samuel Johnson was one of the greatest of Englishmen . . . Samuel Johnson was English of the English" (in Yung et al., 7). English culture—even, to some extent, its popular culture—accepts Johnson as a national icon; the marble index of the man has stood in Lichfield Market Place, directly opposite his birthplace, since 1838, and in London, in the churchyard of St. Clement Danes, Strand, since 1910.[9]

Rather more belatedly, Scots have grown proud to claim David Hume as their own. Edinburgh University Press's commitment to the rediscovery and scholarly reevaluation of Hume and his Scottish contemporaries paved the way, to some degree, for the recent erection of Sandy Stoddart's

[9] On monuments of Johnson, see Appendix I, *Life of Johnson* 4:464–72.

monumental statue of Hume outside the city's Sheriff Court, across the street from St. Giles Cathedral. Hume has, it seems, been welcomed home. Yet the statue is not to the liking of those academics and passers-by alike who would see Hume as a peculiarly Scottish figure. Stoddart classicizes Hume, draping a muscular version of his large frame with only a loose toga. The statue differs significantly from the monuments of Johnson erected on English soil in the nineteenth and twentieth centuries, in which Johnson's stout figure appears in eighteenth-century plain dress. Stoddart's Hume recalls instead the classicized statue of Johnson by John Bacon that stands in St. Paul's Cathedral, commissioned by the members of Johnson's Club, and opened to the public in 1794. But placed in the open air, Stoddart's Hume is still more emphatically in, though not of, Edinburgh—a distinction colorfully blurred by a passing local who complained to me as I stood by the statue one chilly November day, "A man dressed like that in weather like this? An intellectual? An idiot, more like it, an eighteenth-century idiot."

III. Medicine of the Mind

However much locals may harp on the material fact that Hume's statue sits in Edinburgh, it is clearly intended to embody an ideal of transcending time and place—even if that ideal is itself grounded, ironically, in the Roman world that first promulgated it. In this book, I will allow both Hume and Johnson to appear, as I believe both would have wished to appear, in Roman dress.

The burden of this book is that Hume and Johnson are not properly understood outside of the eudaimonism of ancient philosophy, and particularly of Roman philosophy. They concur that happiness or human flourishing is the proper aim not only of ethical precept but also of descriptive psychology, and that its attainment depends partly on political and economic conditions, but primarily on an inner economy, the proper management or regulation of the passions that propel us. Working within a Hellenistic tradition, both Johnson and Hume think of philosophy as analogous to medical therapy and correspondingly think of themselves as offering their readers, as Johnson put it, "physick of the mind" (*Rambler* 3 : 12).[10] Hume also employs this metaphor, speaking at one point in his *Essays* of philosophy as "the *medicine of the mind*" (169).

[10] Cf. *Rambler* 3 : 351, 4 : 94, 5 : 33. On the pervasive analogy between philosophy and medicine in the Hellenistic schools, see Martha Nussbaum, chapter 1, "Therapeutic Arguments." On Cicero's strong commitment to seeing philosophy as therapy, see *Tusculan Disputations* 3.1–7, and Andrew Erskine, "Cicero and the Expression of Grief," in *The Passions in Roman Thought and Literature*, ed. Braund, 36–47. John Immerwahr, in "Hume on Tranquillizing the Passions," clearly sets Hume's therapeutic aims in the context of Hellenistic philosophy.

Yet neither Johnson nor Hume considers philosophy a cure-all. Indeed, both men vacillate—with a double-mindedness we shall find characteristic of them—between affirming and questioning the efficacy of argument in our emotional lives. We may see Johnson do so, for example, in two anecdotes from Boswell's journal of their tour of the Scottish Highlands. In the first, Boswell, recalling a night of bad accommodations at Glenelg, confesses, "I was uneasy and almost fretful. Mr. Johnson was calm. I said he was so from vanity. 'No,' he said, ' 'tis from philosophy.' It was a considerable satisfaction to me to see that the Rambler could practice what he nobly teaches" (*Tour* 112). When Johnson uses "philosophy" in this way, he means not only moral philosophy as therapy, but something more nearly synonymous with *Stoic* therapy. The usage is a common Renaissance one, seen, for example, in the exchange between a distraught Romeo and a unavailing Friar Laurence:

> *Fri. L.* I'll give thee armor to keep off that word,
> Adversity's sweet milk, philosophy,
> To comfort thee, though thou art banished.
> *Rom.* Yet "banished"? Hang up philosophy!
> (*Romeo and Juliet* 3.3.54–57)

Johnson inherits not only Shakespeare's usage of "philosophy" but also his ability to recognize that "adversity's sweet milk" is not always or not wholly efficacious. So, when Johnson and Boswell visit the latter's father, the laird of Auchinleck, himself a professed believer in philosophy's curative power, "Dr. Johnson told me that he owned to him" (the pronominal references are ambiguous) his persuasion that the *animus aequus,* the calm or level mind, "was in a great measure constitutional, or the effect of causes which do not depend on ourselves, and that Horace boasts too much when he says, '*Aequum mi animum ipse parabo*' " (*Tour* 374)—"I will supply myself with a level mind"(Horace, *Epistles* 1.18.112).

With comparable qualification, when Hume speaks of philosophy as "the medicine of the mind" he does so through the fictive character of "The Sceptic," whose larger point is that not all of us, and none of us completely, are curable by philosophy's therapy. But in a further irony, Hume in propria persona responds to the Sceptic in a lengthy footnote in which he offers a broad affirmation of the therapeutic value of philosophy. After the Sceptic has argued for "the imperfection, even of the best of these philosophical topics of consolation"—reflection on the shortness of life, and comparison of our own condition with that of others—Hume counters: "The Sceptic, perhaps, carries the matter too far, when he limits all philosophical topics and reflections to these two. There seem to be others, whose truth is undeniable, and whose natural tendency is to tranquillize and soften all the passions." Hume then lists twelve such reflections, including "Custom deadens the sense both of the good and the ill, and levels every thing," and "Expect not too great happiness in life. Human nature admits it not." He concludes by urging "a frequent perusal of the entertaining moralists," including Plutarch, Lucian, Cicero, Seneca, Montaigne and Shaftesbury (*Essays* 176–79).[11]

Were it not for the decorum of modesty, Hume would no doubt include himself in this list, for he sought to be a painter as well as anatomist of the moral life. The consolatory or "entertaining" elements of Hume's writings were appreciated by Boswell, who sought to alleviate his dejection on the day of Hume's funeral by reading "some parts of his *Essays:* of his "Epicurean," his "Stoic," his "Sceptic"" (*Boswell in Extremes* 27). It was probably the same essays that soothed Louis XV's only son on his deathbed, although reports do not specify which of Hume's philosophical works the dauphin had in mind when pronouncing, "This reading is most consoling in the state that I am in" (*Life of Hume* 484).

The chief difference between Johnson and Hume concerns the role of religion in the therapy of desire. Johnson's therapy includes the consolation of religion—specifically, the inculcation of belief in a future state of justly distributed rewards and punishments. Hume's therapy does not feature this consolation, or at least does not feature it prominently. But in practice, the difference between them is not as significant as it at first might seem. There are two reasons why this is so. First, as a public moralist Johnson is less quick to offer religious consolation, and far more apt to dwell on this-worldly therapy, than those who chiefly know of him through Boswell's *Life* might suspect. In his periodical essays and his philosophical tales, Johnson largely confines himself to moral questions that are independent of religious belief. It is primarily in his role as a public moralist, rather than as diarist or biographical subject or the anonymous author of sermons written for a friend, that I shall examine Johnson. In looking back over his *Rambler,* Johnson informs us, "The essays professedly serious, if I have been able to execute my own intentions, will be found exactly conformable to the precepts of Christianity" (*Rambler* 5:320); of course, had anything distinctively Christian been more in evidence, such an assurance would have been unnecessary. Johnson participates no less than Hume in the extrication of philosophy and moral instruction from their medieval mooring in theology.

I concur with Nicholas Hudson that for Johnson the writer religion was itself chiefly an "ethical code," a "moral understanding" (*Samuel Johnson and Eighteenth-Century Thought* 202–3). As a moralist, Johnson inculcated

---

[11] The critic Jonathan Lamb—although rightly noting the similarities between Johnson's and Hume's attacks on the consolations of theodicy—errs in his broader suggestion that both writers seek to do away with philosophical consolation *tout court* (82–95). Lamb misrepresents "The Sceptic" as an attack on the topics of consolation by disregarding the substantial counterpoint of Hume's note.

the hope and fear of eternal rewards and punishments as a social prophylactic, a protection against the criminal excesses of worldly hopes and fears.

> The great task of him, who conducts his life by the precepts of religion, is to make the future predominate over the present, to impress upon his mind so strong a sense of the importance of obedience to the divine will, of the value of the reward promised to virtue, and the terrors of the punishment denounced against crimes, as may overbear all the temptations which temporal hope or fear can bring in his way, and enable him to bid equal defiance to joy and sorrow, to turn away at one time from the allurements of ambition, and push forward at another against the threats of calamity. (*Rambler* 3:38).

The theme is one on which Johnson the writer agrees with Johnson the hero of Boswell's biography. Upon Boswell's mentioning an acquaintance who appeared to have "not the least notion of immortality," Johnson replies, "Sir, if it were not for the notion of immortality, he would cut a throat to fill his pockets" (*Life of Johnson* 2:359). To the moralist, religion is subservient to morality—indeed, to policing the community.

The second reason that Johnson's and Hume's religious difference is not a gulf between them is that Hume, whatever his speculative views on religion, accepted, with a pragmatism as solid as Johnson's, that religious beliefs could have positive therapeutic effects within communities. Or if he did not accept this proposition, he at least entertained it seriously. In his *Dialogues concerning Natural Religion* the character Cleanthes insists on the necessity to public stability of the doctrine of divine justice (219) and speaks too of religion as "the only great comfort in life" (224). And in the dialogue "Of Providence and a Future State," Hume presents himself as the sober respondent to a sceptical, Epicurean friend who denies the practical efficacy of religious doctrine:

> There is still one circumstance, replied I, which you seem to have overlooked. . . . You conclude, that religious doctrines and reasoning *can* have no influence on life, because they *ought* to have no influence; never considering, that men reason not in the same manner you do, but draw many consequences from the belief of a divine Existence, and suppose that the Deity will inflict punishments on vice, and bestow rewards on virtue, beyond what appears in the ordinary course of nature. . . . And, those who attempt to disabuse them of such prejudices, may, for aught I know, be good reasoners, but I cannot allow them to be good citizens and politicians; since they free men from one restraint upon their passions, and make the infringement of the laws of society, in one respect, more easy and secure. (*ECHU* 147)

Hume is no more ready than Johnson to uproot religious institutions that encourage civic tranquillity.

Even if on balance Hume considered religion more a perturbation of mind than a comfort—such is the moral of *The Natural History of Religion* and perhaps part of the story of the *History of England*—he nonetheless made a serious case for the therapeutic and social virtues of the religious life. Proud of his evenhandedness, Hume boasts in his autobiographical essay "My Own Life" that the Stuart volumes of his *History* won the approval of the church primates of both England and Ireland (*Essays* xxxvii). Orthodox reviewers in France and Berlin lauded the fairness of Hume's representation of ecclesiastical history (cited in Laurence Bongie, 12–15, 41–44); French correspondents such as D'Alembert, Grimm, and Helvetius clearly mistook their man when they urged Hume to write a *Histoire Ecclésiastique* in Voltaire's vein—a "philosophical" exposé of crimes committed in the name of Christ.

What finally may be a more decisive difference between Hume and Johnson than a nuanced disagreement over the role of religion in the moral life is their dissimilarity of temperament and tone. Hume is less forgiving toward frailties of character than Johnson. In general, Hume is not as consoling as Johnson—certainly, he is not as comforting in our times of dereliction and dismay. He is far less apt than Johnson to "minister to a mind diseased," to "pluck from the memory a rooted sorrow" (*Macbeth* V.iii). His aims are no less therapeutic, but the calm elevation of his prose expects, even as it would inspire, a corresponding calm in our own souls.

Hume speaks of common life in grand generalities; Johnson, although little less generalizing—this, too, is an undeniable trait of Enlightenment prose—expects us to see our own small lives reflected and increased in the grandeur of his moral reflections. Here we find public utterance for our private problems; there writ large are the solutions that will lead to our happiness, or at least preservation. Virtue beckons by its attire in words of powerful commonality. Johnson, in Hume's terms, is primarily a "painter" of moral virtue, a "practical moralist" whose goal is to teach "the *happiness*, as well as . . . the *dignity* of virtue." Hume, by contrast, recognizes his own office chiefly to be that of an "anatomist" of human nature: "An anatomist, however, is admirably fitted to give advice to a painter; and 'tis even impracticable to excel in the latter art, without the assistance of the former" (*T* 620–21). However, Johnson and Hume each quite ably assumes both roles.

IV. The Anatomist and the Painter

Practical morality—the "painting" of happiness and virtue, misery and vice—must be grounded in a critical inspection, or "anatomy," of human nature—the latter metaphor was doubtless a vivid one for Hume and

Johnson, given the prominence of anatomical study in the Edinburgh and London of their day.[12] Hume first offers this double analogy in a letter to Francis Hutcheson, dated 7 September 1739, while book 3 of the *Treatise* ("Of Morals") was still in manuscript; we have seen its later appearance at the close of that volume, which appeared in print the following year. Hume elaborated on it further in the opening section ("Of the Different Species of Philosophy") of his *Enquiry concerning Human Understanding* (1748). Johnson offers the same double analogy in his essay for *The Adventurer* no. 95 (2 October 1753) on the need continually to keep moral writing abreast of changing mores:

> [I]t is not to be desired, that morality should be considered as interdicted to all future writers: men will always be tempted to deviate from their duty, and will, therefore, always want a monitor to recall them. . . . the anatomy of the mind, as that of the body, must perpetually exhibit the same appearances; and though by the continued industry of successive inquirers, new movements will be from time to time discovered, they can affect only the minuter parts, and are commonly of more curiosity than importance. It will now be natural to inquire, by what arts are the writers of the present and future ages to attract the notice and favour of mankind. They are to observe the alterations which time is always making with the modes of life, that they may gratify every generation with a picture of themselves. (*Adventurer* 2:426–27)

Johnson here suggests that the anatomy of human nature, having little left to discover, lacks the ongoing importance of practical morality. As Johnson himself set out chiefly to be a moral painter—to offer a new generation a picture of itself—there is perhaps a note of self-congratulation here. Still, Johnson was elsewhere more evenhanded in dividing laurels between the moral writer who discovers, and the one who adorns: "Whatever hopes for the veneration of mankind must have invention in the design or the execution. . . . Either truths hitherto unknown must be discovered, or those which are already known enforced by stronger evidence, facilitated by clearer method, or elucidated by brighter illustrations" (*Rambler* 5:59; cf. 3:14–15).

---

[12] Anatomy is used here as a metaphor drawn from that investigation of the human body which may give rise either, like William Harvey's, to medical advance, or, like Leonardo's, to more accurate and effective artistic representation. As a literary practice, the "anatomy" of a topic goes back to John Lyly's *Euphues: The Anatomy of Wit* (1578) and Robert Burton's *The Anatomy of Melancholy* (1621). Still, the "anatomy" must have seemed a particularly vivid metaphor in Johnson and Hume's Britain: in the mid-eighteenth century, Edinburgh and London succeeded Amsterdam and Leyden as the leading centers for anatomical studies (learned through the public dissection of cadavers). The practice and its occasional abuses were popular topics of the day, as evidenced in satirical prints and drawings such as William Hogarth's *The Rewards of Cruelty* (the fourth plate of the series *The Progress of Cruelty*, 1751) and Thomas Rowlandson's *The Dissecting Room* (ca. 1776).

Johnson has at times been viewed as a purely prescriptive Christian moralist, opposed on principle to the naturalistic description of the mind; in Robert Voitle's verdict from 1961, "Johnson's ideas often seem to belong to the era before Hobbes and Locke because he reacted against a novel concept of the purpose of psychology which had been gathering impetus since long before he was born, a concept which made psychology the servant of what is, rather than what ought to be" (24). This conclusion was countered several years later by Paul Alkon, who rightly demonstrated not only Johnson's interest in the naturalistic description of human nature, but also the broader framework of ethical concern in which Locke (and we might add Hobbes) situated descriptive psychology (85–108). Nonetheless, Voitle's sense of Johnson retains its interest for two reasons: first, it expresses a presumption about Johnson's "Christian humanism" that has not yet been entirely expelled; second, it formulates quite neatly what we may call the "is/ought" canard—the contention that ethical prescription (or "painting") cannot be validly inferred from naturalistic description ("anatomy"). This canard is often associated with Hume's name—although, as recent commentators have noticed, quite wrongly so.[13]

[13] Is the distinction between anatomy and painting, description and prescription, objectivity and persuasion, an unbridgeable divide? Those who have thought so have often attributed this position to Hume, going so far on occasion to call it "Hume's Law" (see, e.g., Flew 144–45; Gaarder, 279). Here is Hume the purported law-giver:

In every system of morality, which I have hitherto met with, I have always remark'd, that the author proceeds for some time in the ordinary way of reasoning, and establishes the being of a God, or makes some observations concerning human affairs; when of a sudden I am surpriz'd to find, that instead of the usual copulation of propositions, *is,* and *is not,* I meet with no proposition that is not connected with an *ought,* or an *ought not.* This change is imperceptible; but is, however, of the last consequence. For as this *ought,* or *ought not,* expresses some new relation or affirmation, 'tis necessary that it shou'd be observ'd and explain'd; and at the same time that a reason should be given, for what seems altogether inconceivable, how this new relation can be a deduction from others, which are entirely different from it. But as authors do not commonly use this precaution, I shall presume to recommend it to the readers; and am persuaded, that this small attention wou'd subvert all the vulgar systems of morality, and let us see, that the distinction of vice and virtue is not founded merely on the relations of objects, nor is perceiv'd by reason. (*T* 469–70)

Is Hume claiming here that nonmoral premises (the factual "is") can never entail a moral conclusion? In his 1959 article "Hume on 'Is' and 'Ought'," Alasdair MacIntyre persuasively argued that Hume denies only the validity of "vulgar," that is, religious, systems of morality, and that he himself establishes the facts of human need and desire as the foundation of morality. "If anyone says that we cannot make valid inferences from an 'is' to an 'ought,' I should be disposed to offer him the following counter-example: 'If I stick a knife in Smith, they will send me to jail; but I do not want to go to jail; so I ought not to (had better not) stick a knife in him'. . . . the transition from 'is' to 'ought' is made in this inference by the notion of wanting" (256–57). (MacIntyre offers a less accurate and less generous reading of Hume's "is/ought" passage in his later, apparently Thomist book of social criticism, *After Virtue* 56–61.) Annette Baier has revived and sharpened MacIntyre's argument: see *A Progress of Sentiments* 177.

Throughout this book I will show that Hume routinely moves from *is* to *ought,* and that Johnson just as routinely bases his *ought* on an *is.* In other words, Hume is an anatomist who also paints, just as Johnson is a painter who also anatomizes. Yet while the first half of this statement is now accepted by most Johnsonians, my claim about Hume may require some preliminary defense.

In the 1739 letter to Hutcheson in which Hume introduces the painter/ anatomist analogy, he is responding to a criticism Hutcheson made of the still unpublished book 3 of the *Treatise:*

> What affected me most in your Remarks is your observing, that there wants a certain Warmth in the Cause of Virtue, which, you think, all good Men wou'd relish, & cou'd not displease amidst abstract Enquirys. I must own, this has not happen'd by Chance, but is the Effect of a Reasoning either good or bad. There are different ways of examining the Mind as well as the Body. One may consider it either as an Anatomist or as a Painter. . . . I am perswaded, that a Metaphysician may be very helpful to a Moralist; tho' I cannot easily conceive these two Characters united in the same Work. . . . tho' at the same time, I intend to make a new Tryal, if it be possible to make the Moralist & Metaphysician agree a little better. (*HL* 1:32–33)

I surmise that Hume's "new Tryal" ultimately resulted in his *Enquiry concerning the Principles of Morals* (1751). Presumably it is the work's reconciliation of painting with anatomy that made it, as Hume would later say, "in my own opinion . . . of all my writings, historical, philosophical, or literary, incomparably the best" (*Essays* xxxvi).

Witness the opening pages of section 2, "Of Benevolence." "It may be esteemed, perhaps, a superfluous task to prove, that the benevolent or softer affections are estimable; and wherever they appear, engage the approbation and good-will of mankind. The epithets *sociable, good-natured, humane, merciful, grateful, friendly, generous, beneficent,* or their equivalents, are known in all languages, and universally express the highest merit, which *human nature* is capable of attaining." Hume moves from this argument from common usage to exempla and praise of benevolence drawn from Plutarch, Cicero, and Juvenal. He then affects to recall his own purpose: "But I forget, that it is not my present business to recommend generosity and benevolence, or to paint, in their true colours, all the genuine charms of the social virtues. These, indeed, sufficiently engage every heart, on the first apprehension of them; and it is difficult to abstain from some sally of panegyric, as often as they occur in discourse or reasoning" (*ECPM* 176– 77). Hume's rhetoric here recalls that of Mark Antony's elegy to Julius Caesar in Shakespeare's play—Hume, as it were, came "not to praise Caesar," but ends up doing so anyway. That he does so serves to show that the will plays no role in our response to benevolent character; the representation of social virtues automatically and ineluctably triggers panegyric.

Hume elsewhere insists that our response to benevolence is not only involuntary, but disinterested.

> Frame the model of a praiseworthy character, consisting of all the most amiable moral virtues; Give instances, in which these display themselves after an eminent and extraordinary manner: You readily engage the esteem and approbation of all your audience, who never so much as enquire in what age and country the person lived, who possessed the noble qualities: A circumstance, however, of all others, the most material to self-love, or a concern for our own individual happiness.

Hume then supplies an exemplum from the life of Demosthenes, who praises the disinterested virtue of his adversary Aeschines—and we are evidently meant to praise as well the disinterestedness of Demosthenes' tribute. In doing so, we also realize our own disinterested approbation of virtue: as all this "passed at Athens, about two thousand years ago," our moral response is independent of any expectation of personal gain or advantage (217–18).

Here we see the nexus between description and prescription: in describing what our response to Demosthenes is, Hume indicates what our response ought to be. What Hume describes as our necessary and involuntary response is also a normative response, a standard by which to judge the healthiness of a given individual's actual reaction. In this case, Hume's moral painting is simply noticeable; the normative nature of his ethics becomes still more apparent at moments in which his painting becomes mannered. Consider this rather posed moment: Hume writes that the sentiments attending benevolent action, "delightful in themselves, are necessarily communicated to the spectators, and melt them into the same fondness and delicacy. The tear naturally starts in our eye on the apprehension of a warm sentiment of this nature: our breast heaves, our heart is agitated, and every humane tender principle of our frame is set in motion, and gives us the purest and most satisfactory enjoyment" (257). The reader is apt to ask: Is this really my life Hume is describing? Is this always what happens when I am confronted with a tender spectacle, and does it always happen just like this? If not, is it my life or Hume's claim that is in error? The question vanishes only with an appreciation that what we are responding to here is not properly a claim but a representation, "moral painting." Hume is being less propositional here than pictorial; he does not so much "do philosophy," in our modern sense, as create a useful fiction. Hume's exquisitely responsive spectator looks ahead to the deliquescent heroes of later-eighteenth-century novels such as Sterne's *A Sentimental Journey* (1768) or Mackenzie's *Man of Feeling* (1771)—characters who "melt" or "burst into tears" on witnessing either the misery or the generosity of others. And yet Hume's spectator also recalls the "philosophical" advice of Hutcheson's *Essay on the Nature and Conduct of the Passions and Affections* (1728): if people know that they naturally have "generous, kind affections," then they will be encouraged to cultivate them (v–vii).

They will be further encouraged by the promise that cultivating such affections prepares one for the purest and most satisfactory enjoyment. Hume summons all his powers for a concluding tableau which, if sketched by Hogarth, might be titled "Boys Peeping at Virtue":

> But what philosophical truths can be more advantageous to society, than those here delivered, which represent virtue in all her genuine and most engaging charms, and make us approach her with ease, familiarity, and affection? The dismal dress falls off, with which many divines, and some philosophers, have covered her; and nothing appears but gentleness, humanity, beneficence, affability; nay, even at proper intervals, play, frolic, and gaiety. She talks not of useless austerities and rigours, suffering and self-denial. She declares that her sole purpose is to make her votaries and all mankind, during every instant of their existence, if possible, cheerful and happy; nor does she ever willingly part with any pleasure but in hopes of ample compensation in some other period of their lives. (279)

Hume writes here with what rhetoricians after Aristotle broadly term *energia* or "vivid illustration," personification.

Over the course of Hume's career, his style grows steadily more painterly and energetic; it is the prose of his final work, *The History of England,* that so impressed the comtesse de Boufflers, and indeed all Europe, with its "clarity, majesty, touching simplicity . . . . grace, naturalness, energy" (*HL* 2:367).[14] The comtesse declared that reading Hume's *History* "illuminates the mind, and in showing true happiness intimately tied to virtue, it discovers by the same light the one and only end of all reasonable beings. . . . You, Sir, are an admirable Painter" (*HL* 2:366–67).

Hume sought in his *Enquiries* and historical writings to "unite the boundaries of the different species of philosophy"—the easy and the abstruse, moral painting and moral anatomy—"by reconciling profound enquiry with clearness, and truth with novelty!" (*ECHU* 16). Hume recognized that anatomy by itself will never appeal widely, and he thought it would not appeal for long; Hume sought to write in such a way as to attract a "general" and durable audience, hoping both to gratify a passion for fame and to serve an enlightened age. He effectively acknowledges two

---

[14] Johnson's most provocative remark on Hume's style glances, perhaps, at the French success of his historical work: "Why, Sir, his style is not English; the structure of his sentences is French" (*Life of Johnson* 1:439). For a full explanation of Johnson's remark, see my article "'The Structure of His Sentences is French': Johnson and Hume in the History of English."

masters in the art of successfully uniting anatomy with painting, one ancient and one modern—Cicero and Addison. "The fame of Cicero flourishes at present, but that of Aristotle is utterly decayed. . . . And Addison, perhaps, will be read with pleasure, when Locke shall be entirely forgotten" (*ECHU* 7).

Johnson sought no less than Hume to reconcile "the different species of philosophy" in his periodical essays, though he would add the abstruse to the easy in a lesser proportion. Like Hume, he drew some inspiration from the periodical essays of Joseph Addison (1672–1719) and Richard Steele (1672–1729), whose *Tatler* and *Spectator* papers "brought Philosophy out of Closets and Libraries, Schools and Colleges, to dwell in Clubs and Assemblies, at Tea-Tables and Coffee-Houses" (Addison's *Spectator* no. 10, 1:44).[15] Hume announced Addisonian aspirations in his early meditation on the essay form, "Of Essay Writing" (1742): as Addison brought philosophy to tea tables and coffeehouses, Hume hopes further to improve "this League betwixt the learned and conversible Worlds, which is so happily begun." Hume pictures himself as an ambassador from the realms of learning to "the Empire of Conversation" and addresses himself with particular respect to "the Fair Sex"—an Addisonian locution—"who are . . . [its] Sovereigns" (*Essays* 535–36). One reason that Johnson considers his own age and nation as enlightened above all others is that "the gradual diffusion of knowledge" had finally extended to a broad audience of women. "Whatever might be the state of female literature in the last century, there is now no longer any danger lest the scholar should want an adequate audience at the tea-table" (*Rambler* 5:153).

The Addisonian standard of the judgment of women or "the conversible world" is a trope, finally, for the judgment of the common reader and implies a confidence in the justness of our untutored, unsophisticated responses. The central lesson that Johnson and Hume derived from Addison is that scholars ought not to neglect the world; that there is a danger both to self and others in sequestration or undue inwardness. "Of Essay Writing" is only Hume's most direct testament to this Addisonian lesson. Johnson, for his part, expounds it throughout his moral essays. A writer in the dark ages "had no further care than to retire to his closet, let loose his invention, and heat his mind with incredibilities. . . . The task of our present writers is very different; it requires, together with that learning which is to be gained from books, that experience which can never be attained by solitary diligence, but must arise from general converse, and accurate observation of the living world" (*Rambler* 3:20).[16]

---

[15] On Johnson's complicated relation to the Addisonian essay tradition, see Alkon, 178–91; on Hume's, see Nicholas Phillipson, "The Scottish Enlightenment," in *The Enlightenment in National Context*, ed. Porter and Teich, 26–35, and M. A. Box, *Suasive Art* 123–48.

[16] Cf. *Rambler* nos. 24, 89, 137, 157, 168, 177, 180; *Adventurer* nos. 85, 126, 131.

V. A Road Map

Chapter 1 attempts an accurate if brief representation of Johnson's and Hume's not unrelated lives in the world, for the benefit of readers who may not be familiar with the outlines of their professional careers. Chapter 2 elaborates, through a close analysis of parts of Johnson's *Rasselas* and the ending of book 1 of Hume's *Treatise,* the Addisonian lesson that the learned world must learn from the conversible quite as much as the converse. The reflective individual, in losing contact with certain social conventions, becomes a sadly risible figure, likely to be wrong, certain to be unhappy. For happiness, our being's end and aim, requires the approving gaze of others.

Chapter 3 seeks to establish a definition of "happiness" shared by Johnson and Hume, ultimately through unpacking the implications of Johnson's rich remark that "happiness consists in the multiplicity of agreeable consciousness." Johnson's and Hume's crucial debt to ancient eudaimonistic ethics, touched on here, is pursued more extensively in chapters 4 and 5. Chapter 4 treats Johnson's and Hume's anatomy of human nature, and the ethical questions it prompts: What ought to be the relation between motivating passions and regulative reason within the happy or flourishing individual? And why ought the individual observe the rules of justice or care about the common good? Chapter 5 elaborates on the social theory announced or implied by Hume and Johnson, connecting it back to the eclectic Stoicism of Cicero's philosophical dialogues. Cicero's social thought echoes throughout eighteenth-century philosophy and philosophical belles lettres: self-love and sociability are, if not quite the same, intimately twined. As creatures who require the esteem of others, our self-love propels us outward along widening concentric circles of family, local community, political community, and—at least for the man of letters—cosmopolis.

At the start of chapter 6, I show, however, that Johnson and Hume disapprove of the Stoic attempt to underwrite ethical obligation with the authority of a rationally discernible cosmic purpose. Both reject a physics of final causes—but both, I argue within the body of this chapter, accept some version of the "soft determinism" that the Stoics deduced from their physics. The Stoics believed in fate as an all-embracing causal network, but they nonetheless affirmed that we are free to act morally, and thus ought to be praised or blamed for our actions. In a similar vein, Hume professes—and Johnson appears to believe in—a causal "necessity" not incompatible with human "liberty" and moral responsibility.

The compatibilist argument developed in Hume's first *Enquiry* allows us, I believe, to make sense of Johnson's greatest and often misunderstood poem, *The Vanity of Human Wishes.* Without some notion of why necessity and human liberty aren't mutually exclusive, we are apt to misunderstand the therapeutic aims of Johnson's poem. We are apt as well to misunderstand the numerous *vanitas* sketches or exempla of Hume's grand *History of England*. We are apt to mischaracterize Johnson's and Hume's understandings of and tastes in tragedy. Finally, we may well make far too much of their respective references to "chance." Properly speaking, there is in their worldview no chance at all, neither on the dramatic stage nor on the stage of history. For everything that happens or ever will happen there are causes relative to some system of determination.

Chapters 7 through 9 examine Johnson's and Hume's historiographical and political writings. Chapter 7 addresses the philosophy of their historiography. Both men stressed, in ways no Roman or earlier European historians had, the motivating passions of historical actors; the several passions become, when seen through the lens of philosophical history, the causes that determine all human behavior. Primitive peoples, known or postulated, are motivated chiefly by hope and fear. Civilization progresses as the passion of self-interest comes to the fore, and flourishes once interest seeks its fulfillment not through rapine but through the conventions of justice. Yet to authors steeped in the Roman historian Velleius Paterculus, fruition savors of decay. By the 1760s, Johnson and Hume remained very cautiously optimistic about the general state of British civilization in their day, including the state of literature. Still, as I examine in chapter 8, they were apt to agree that were civilization in Britain to decline or fall, the two most likely causes would be a revived spirit of religious "enthusiasm" or fanaticism, and the economic and moral fallout from the elder Pitt's policy of imperial expansion.

In chapter 9 I address the several ways in which Johnson and Hume, in their reflections on Tudor and especially Stuart history, adapt to modern British circumstances the moderate conservatism associated with Cicero and Cato in their roles as late Republican apologists. To stake one's life for an inherited institution whose sanctity is etched on the heart, and if necessary to die for it with composure and even good humor, are for them hallmarks of magnanimity—a cardinal virtue of Cicero's *De Officiis*. But Johnson, as his career progresses, grows increasingly sceptical toward any shows of heroism or claims to individual greatness; Hume, by contrast, is increasingly drawn to the ideal of magnanimity, especially the magnanimous dying that marks the proper close to the happy life.

Chapter 10 finds a harmonious discord in Johnson's and Hume's respective views toward human endings and the belief in an immortal afterlife. What allows here for a harmony between Christian and sceptic is the generous ambiguity with which each writer presents his view of immortality—an ambiguity perfectly captured in the endings of *Rasselas* and

Hume's essay "Of the Immortality of the Soul." These endings—and the ending of my own work as well—invite the reader to choose between two possible and opposed interpretations of authorial intention. Does the work, finally, present a vision of happiness practically confined to this life, or of happiness fulfilled in a hereafter? The protocol of Enlightenment writing allows for both options, and we find Enlightenment writing, at its best, in Johnson and in Hume.

CHAPTER ONE

Authorial Lives

I. Boswell

It appears that Johnson and Hume did once dine together, in company at the chaplain's table at St. James, on August 20, 1763.[1] And if we can trust the prominent late-eighteenth-century bookseller, James Lackington, Johnson met Hume on yet another occasion, and managed to exhibit good manners:

> Dr. Johnson being one afternoon at the house of Mr. Samuel's uncle (whose name I have forgot) who lived in one of the streets that leads from the Strand to the Thames, a number of gentlemen being present, they agreed to cross the water and make a little excursion on the other side; in stepping into the boat one of the company said, Mr. Hume, give me your hand. As soon as they were seated, our Doctor asked Mr. Samuel if that was Hume the Deist. Mr. Samuel replied, that it was the great Mr. Hume, the deep metaphysician and famous historian. Had I known that (said the Doctor) I would not have put a foot in the boat with him. In the evening all agreed to sup together at a house near St. Clement's Church in the Strand, and Doctor Johnson coming in after the rest of the company had some time been met, he walked up to Mr. Hume, and taking him by the hand, said, Mr. Hume, I am very glad to see you, and seemed well pleased to find him there; and it appeared to

---

[1] See Edward Ruhe's note, "Hume and Johnson." Ruhe draws on a letter written by Dr. Thomas Birch to his friend and patron Philip Yorke.

Mr. Samuel that the Doctor had thus chose to atone for his hasty expression before related.[2]

Still, Johnson and Hume's social lives never intersected in any considerable way. Their closest biographical connection was their "mutual friend" James Boswell (1740–95). Boswell was first introduced to Hume in Edinburgh in July 1758. Boswell then thought Hume "a very proper person for a young man to cultivate an acquaintance with" (*Letters* 1:2). Four years later, shortly before he met Johnson, Boswell refers to Hume as "the greatest writer in Britain" (*Private Papers* 1:129). Hume, writing to his friend the comtesse de Boufflers in 1766, refers to Boswell, then finishing up his European Grand Tour, as "a young gentleman, very good-humoured, very agreeable, and very mad" (*HL* 2:11). Boswell settled into his role as lawyer in Edinburgh, renting Hume's James Court flat for several years (May 1771–May 1773). In the 15 August 1773 entry in his *Journal of a Tour to the Hebrides*, Boswell notes, as a rebuttal to Johnson's calling Hume a "blockhead" and a "rogue," "I always lived on good terms with Mr. Hume, though I have frankly told him I was not clear that it was right to keep company with him. 'But,' said I, 'how much better you are than your books!' He was cheerful, obliging, and instructive; he was charitable to the poor; and many an agreeable hour have I passed with him" (17). Shortly thereafter, Boswell considered writing Hume's life.

Of course, the biography with which Boswell secured his enduring fame was not that of his fellow Scotsman, but of Samuel Johnson. Johnson was the perfect subject for the biographer's art, being not only instructive and charitable but also a genuinely colorful character—opinionated, pugnacious, quirky, often slovenly, full of oversized strengths as well as fears. (Thanks to Boswell's memorial, Johnson serves to exemplify "obsessive-compulsive disorder" in Ronald Comer's widely used textbook in abnormal psychology.) Boswell's meeting with Johnson at Thomas Davies' bookshop in London on 16 May 1763 is one of the best-known stories from the *Life of Johnson*.[3] Johnson quickly warmed to the young man, and they began a friendship that would last the remaining twenty-one years of Johnson's life.

They did not, however, spend as much time together as a cursory glance at the *Life of Johnson* might suggest. After Boswell left for Europe in August 1763, he would not see Johnson again until 1766, and then only

---

[2] *Memoirs* 287–88. I am indebted to Nicholas Hudson for this anecdote.

[3] "Mr. Davies mentioned my name, and respectfully introduced me to him. I was much agitated; and recollecting his prejudice against the Scotch, of which I had heard much, I said to Davies, 'Don't tell where I come from.'—'From Scotland,' cried Davies, roguishly. 'Mr. Johnson, (said I) I do indeed come from Scotland, but I cannot help it.' . . . [Johnson replies, punning on the expression "come from Scotland,"] 'That, Sir, I find, is what a very great many of your countrymen cannot help.'" *Life of Johnson* 1:392.

briefly. With the exception of their four-month walking tour of the Scottish Highlands in 1773 (which Johnson memorialized in his *Journey to the Western Islands of Scotland*, 1775), Boswell would see Johnson only intermittently, typically during the Edinburgh law vacation, when he was able to come down to London for a few weeks. According to Hitoshi Suwabe's careful calculation, Boswell spent between 400 and 404 days in Johnson's company. Boswell did not know Johnson as extensively or as intimately as others who also wrote biographies of the great man on his death in 1784—Sir John Hawkins knew him far longer, Hester Lynch Thrale (Piozzi after 1782) knew him more deeply.

Yet Boswell's *Life of Johnson,* published in 1791, goes far beyond his personal knowledge of Johnson. It is the product of extensive research among Johnson's acquaintance, abetted by Edmond Malone's considerable editorial assistance. Most important, it is a masterpiece of literary artistry, in the ancient tradition of Plutarch and Sallust. It presents Johnson as the hero that England in the age of revolution demanded: a gruff but loveable curmudgeon who valiantly opposes encroachments of social anarchy, scepticism, and atheism.[4] As a biographical subject, Johnson's conversational habit of alternately taking both sides of an issue—he would, Boswell admits, talk often "for victory," or "talk laxly" (*Tour* 7, 350)—rendered him particularly open to interpretive shaping; Boswell superbly fashioned a Johnson after his own heart.

The popularity of Boswell's biography was such that it eclipsed not only all rival biographies, but Johnson's own writings as well. Few in the nineteenth or early twentieth centuries disagreed with William Hazlitt's verdict (1819): "The most triumphant record of the talents and character of Johnson is to be found in Boswell's Life of him. The man was superior to the author. When he threw aside his pen . . . he became not only learned and thoughtful, but acute, witty, humorous, natural, honest; hearty and determined, 'the king of good fellows and wale of old men'" (264). Along with most Johnsonians today, I do not concur with Hazlitt's preference, and mine will be first and foremost a book about Hume's and Johnson's writings, not about—what is far better known—Hume and Boswell's Johnson. Nonetheless, as the conduit for much of what Hume knew personally about Johnson, and what Johnson knew of Hume and Hume's writing, the agreeably mad Boswell shall make his due appearances throughout this study.

---

[4] See William Dowling, *The Boswellian Hero.* For a sense of where Dowling's book figures in the history of critical and scholarly views on Boswell—and for a fine introduction to the field—see Vance's introduction to his edited collection, *Boswell's Life of Johnson: New Questions, New Answers* 1–24. Clingham's more recent monograph on the *Life* argues that its portrait of Johnson is fundamentally an expression of Boswell's own rather complex psychological needs.

II. Salad Days

David Hume and Samuel Johnson were born within two years of one another, Johnson on 7 September (old style) 1709[5] in the cathedral city of Lichfield in the English Midlands, his father a bookseller; Hume on 26 April (o.s.) 1711 at his family's winter house in Edinburgh, his father a lawyer and proprietor of the Ninewells estate in Berwickshire near the English border. Both were thus born into what was broadly recognized in eighteenth-century society as the "middling ranks" of society, or the "middling sort" of people. Both were also born and brought up in the established churches of their respective countries—an important fact in eighteenth-century life, when so many of the avenues to preferment, from university education to public office, were connected to church conformity. Johnson's family was Church of England, a communion in which Johnson remained all his life; Hume's was Church of Scotland, an affiliation he never abandoned, whatever his private views. The "Scottish Sabbath" of Hume's boyhood days—a full day of family prayer in the morning, two long services and sermons at the Kirk, devotional reading and psalm-singing at home—evidently made a considerable impression on the mature philosopher, who as late as 1748 still spoke, in illness, "of the Devil, of Hell, and of Damnation" (*Life of Hume* 217). Hume's manner of keeping Sabbath in his maturity was no doubt a more relaxed affair, but he did presumably maintain a pew either in St. Giles Cathedral or the Cannongate Church once he and his sister Katherine set up house in Edinburgh in 1762. Samuel Johnson seldom went to church.

Neither Hume nor Johnson inherited political commitments that could stand in the way of their careers. Although Johnson and Hume were both raised in neighborhoods rife with support for the Stuart cause—several of Hume's Ninewells neighbors supported the abortive Jacobite uprising of 1715 (*Life of Hume* 32), and the large electorate of Lichfield had "a strong and aggressive Jacobite element" (Cannon 42)—their own families were loyal to the Revolution of 1688 and, after the English-Scottish Union, the accession of the House of Hanover in 1714. The Humes of Ninewells were solid Whigs. The political sympathies of Johnson's own family are only somewhat less certain: Boswell, not particularly reliable in this regard, claims that Michael Johnson, Samuel's father, "retained his attachment to the unfortunate house of Stuart" (*Life of Johnson* 1:37), but the fact remains that he held public office in Lichfield, having taken the required oath of loyalty to George I.

---

[5] "Old style," or o.s., means according to the Julian calendar, which in Britain was not replaced by the Gregorian calendar until 1752. According to this "new style," Johnson's birthday falls on September 18. In general, I will provide new style dating throughout this book.

Hume was born to greater financial security than Johnson, but as a younger brother it was clear that he would eventually, like Johnson, have to work for his money. The clergy or the law were eminently respectable professions either for the younger son of Scottish gentry or the elder son of a respectable provincial bookseller. The clerical life never appealed to either man. Hume's family intended him from his youth to become a lawyer, and although he was to abandon his legal studies before his admittance to the bar, his training was sufficient to gain him the commission of judge advocate to a military campaign in 1746.[6] Throughout his life, Johnson often expressed regret that he had never entered the legal profession; however, his mastery of theoretical jurisprudence was such that in the late 1760s he ghostwrote law lectures for his friend Robert Chambers, Vinerian Professor of English Law at Oxford.

The two men's formal education was comparable in its brevity, although Hume's was no doubt a more pleasant affair. The collegiate education offered in early-eighteenth-century Scottish universities was closer to that of a classical high school than a modern college; Hume accordingly went to Edinburgh University in February 1723, not yet twelve years old, and finished his course of study, without a degree, by 1725. Johnson, at what seems to us the more likely age of seventeen, entered Pembroke College, Oxford, in October 1728. He counted on financial support promised by a friend of his family; the funds, however, never materialized, and, dogged by poverty, he left after thirteen months. This experience of want, along with his precarious finances during his early years in London, gave Johnson a greater sympathy with the poor than was usual among eighteenth-century authors; Johnson was well able to perceive "how much evil is produced, and how much good is impeded by embarrassment and distress, and how little room the expedients of poverty leave for the exercise of virtue" (quoted in Chapin, *Religious Thought* 139; cf. *Rambler* no. 166). Hume, in his writing if not in his charitable giving, was less sympathetic to the poor, typically treating poverty, in the abstract, as simply a source of shame (*T* 307).[7]

III. Spiritual Crisis and Its Aftermath

The most significant parallel in the lives of Johnson and Hume is that they simultaneously suffered a grave depression, and a loss of religious

[6] Hume was made judge advocate by Lieutenant General James St. Clair, under whom he served as secretary from 1746 to 1748. Hume attended St. Clair first during a comically ill-fated military campaign against the coast of Brittany, and next during an inconsequential but decidedly more pleasant embassy to the courts of Vienna and Turin.

[7] Harvey Chisick offers a comprehensive analysis of Hume's attitude toward the laboring poor, and "the people" more generally.

faith. These crises marked a turning point in each man's life, after which their views toward things unseen would diverge. Johnson, a twenty-year-old in Lichfield, and Hume, an eighteen-year-old at Ninewells, both fell into the slough of despond in 1729; neither fully emerged until 1734. Walter Jackson Bate summarizes the nature of Johnson's breakdown: "[H]e now fell into an appalling state of mind, in which feelings of intense anxiety alternated with feelings of utter hopelessness and a lassitude so complete that, as he later confided to his friend Dr. John Paradise, he could stare at the town clock without being able to tell the hour" (*Samuel Johnson* 115). Johnson wrote a full description of his case to Dr. Samuel Swynfen, a physician in Birmingham and his godfather; unfortunately the letter has not survived. Hume described his own case in a letter, probably not dispatched, to an unnamed physician—probably either Dr. John Arbuthnot or Dr. George Cheyne.[8] Fortunately, this letter does survive.

Hume's disease—diagnosed by a local physician as "the Disease of the Learned"—consisted at first of a "Coldness" or "Laziness of Temper," soon accompanied by "Scurvy Spots" and "a Ptyalism or Watryness in the mouth". (This "disease of the learned" was analyzed by Cheyne in *The English Malady: or, a Treatise of Nervous Diseases of all Kinds,* a work that Johnson purchased on its publication in 1733.[9]) While Hume recognized his cold melancholy as a physiological disorder, he also situated his aliment within a psycho-religious tradition. By "French mysticks," Hume probably has in mind Quietists of the later seventeenth century such as Madame Guyon (d. 1717):

> I have notic'd in the Writings of the French Mysticks, & in those of our Fanatics here, that, when they give a History of the Situation of their Souls, they mention a Coldness & Desertion of the Spirit, which frequently returns, & some of them, at the beginning, have been tormented with it many Years. As this kind of Devotion depends entirely on the Force of Passion, & consequently of the Animal Spirits, I have often thought that their Case & mine were pretty parralel, & that their rapturous Admirations might discompose the fabric of the Nerves & Brain, as much as profound Reflections, & that warmth of Enthusiasm which is inseperable from them.

Hume here compares his own "Desertion of Spirit," resulting from prolonged solitary study, to the dark night of the soul experienced by mystics and enthusiasts—a dejection he attributes to their intense solitary devotions. He thus admits a secret kinship between the lonely and passionate

---

[8] Burton argued for Cheyne, while Mossner argued for Arbuthnot (*Life of Hume* 84–85); David Fate Norton, who reproduces the letter in *The Cambridge Companion to Hume* (345–50), remains undecided, but favors Arbuthnot. The letter appears in *HL* 1:12–18, dated "March or April 1734"; it is astutely analyzed by Passmore, "Enthusiasm, Fanaticism and David Hume."

[9] Johnson's debt to Cheyne is assessed by Sachs, 14 n.59.

labors of the enlightened scholar and those of the enthusiasts he, like Johnson, will relentlessly satirize. More generally, he evidences a sympathetic interest in religious experience that his scepticism will distance him from, but never efface. In 1751, Hume would write to his friend Gilbert Elliot of Minto that in his *Dialogues concerning Natural Religion,* then in manuscript, his sympathy was with the philosophical theist, Cleanthes;

> Any propensity you imagine I have to the other Side [i.e., that of the religious sceptic Philo], crept in upon me against my Will; And tis not long ago that I burn'd an old Manuscript Book, wrote before I was twenty; which contain'd, Page after Page, the gradual Progress of my Thoughts on that head. It begun with an anxious Search after Arguments, to confirm the common Opinion: Doubts stole in, dissipated, return'd, were again dissipated, return'd again; and it was a perpetual Struggle of a restless Imagination against Inclination, perhaps against Reason. (*HL* 1:154)

Johnson's own crisis of his early twenties turned, in part, on his struggle against religious doubts.[10] Johnson later remarked to Boswell, "Every thing which Hume has advanced against Christianity had passed through my mind long before he wrote" (*Life of Johnson* 1:444)—referring back, in all likelihood, to his dark days of the early 1730s. In the October before he died, Johnson sketched an outline for a book on the nature of religious scepticism; the topic was, it seems, never far from his thoughts. Yet Johnson continued, long after Hume had evidently ceased, his "anxious Search after Arguments, to confirm the common Opinion"—or as Boswell expressed it, "his elevated wish for more and more evidence for spirit" (2:150).

Johnson retained a sceptical edge throughout his life. His requirements for assigning any degree of probability to a variety of historical claims about matters of fact were little less strict than Hume's. "No man," wrote Boswell, "was more incredulous as to particular facts, which were at all extraordinary" (2:247). In 1762, Johnson helped to debunk the news that a ghost was communicating with a young girl in Cock Lane, Smithfield. Eleven years later, during his journey to Scotland, he sceptically examined the reasons for and against believing in the "second sight," "by which things distant or future are perceived, and seen as if they were present"; his conclusion is to some degree emblematic of his entire religious life: "I never could advance my curiosity to conviction; but came away at last only willing to believe" (*Journey* 107–10).

It was also during his journey to Scotland that Johnson expressed strongest reservations about accepting the then popular epic poems of Os-

---

[10] The religious sides of both Johnson's and Hume's early crises is sensitively treated by Chapin, *Religious Thought* 16–23.

sian as the genuine and complete productions of a third-century Highland bard, conveniently discovered by the Erse speaker James Macpherson. (We know now that Macpherson actually wrote the bulk of the poems himself.) [11] Hume expressed to Edward Gibbon his doubts concerning the authenticity of the poems (*HL* 2:310–11) and wrote a manuscript essay "On the Poems of Ossian," in which he elaborates on those doubts; however, he never published his reflections on the affair—probably to avoid embarrassing Edinburgh friends such as Hugh Blair who praised Ossian as a national treasure. Johnson had no such qualms about promulgating his own doubts. In the *Journey*, he writes, "The editor, or author [i.e., Macpherson], never could shew the original; nor can it be shewn by any other; to revenge reasonable incredulity, by refusing evidence, is a degree of insolence, with which the world is not yet acquainted; and stubborn audacity is the last refuge of guilt" (118).

His private reasoning on the matter is, however, still more sceptical. In talks with Boswell, he claims not simply that the authentication of Ossian's authorship would require further evidence (i.e, manuscript originals or proof of oral transmission among Highlanders). Rather, he is prepared to reject one whole class of evidence, to wit, testimony to having heard the recital of a poem in cases in which (a.) that testimony is offered by people who may be assumed to have some familiarity with the characters or basic plot of the poem; and (b.) the poem in question in any way flatters regional or national pride. Boswell reports: "He would undertake, he said, to write an epic poem on the story of Robin Hood, and half England, to whom the names and places he should mention in it are familiar, would believe and declare they had heard it from their earliest years" (*Tour* 380). Johnson no less than Hume understands the will to believe as a natural psychological phenomenon, and one that may taint certain classes of testimony.

This, of course, is also a premise of Hume's essay "Of Miracles," first appearing in 1748. "With what greediness are the miraculous accounts of travellers received, their descriptions of sea and land monsters, their relations of wonderful adventures, strange men, and uncouth manners? But if the spirit of religion join itself to the love of wonder, there is an end of common sense; and human testimony, in these circumstances, loses all pretensions to authority" (*ECHU* 117). Yet Hume goes further in his critique of reported miracles, rejecting all testimony for them as an untenable class of evidence. Hume argues not only that there neither is not, but that there could not be testimony sufficient to warrant a belief in the suspension of the regular laws of nature: "[N]o testimony is sufficient to es-

[11] For an overview of the poems' history and a critical analysis, see my *Fate of Eloquence* 189–225.

tablish a miracle, unless the testimony be of such a kind, that its falsehood would be more miraculous, than the fact, which it endeavours to establish; and even in that case there is a mutual destruction of arguments, and the superior only gives us an assurance suitable to that degree of force, which remains, after deducting the inferior" (*ECHU* 115–16). Such a maxim sits uneasily with a doctrinal commitment to believing in gospel miracles, especially the central Christian miracle of the resurrection. Hume, for his part, espoused a strong fideism at the end of "Of Miracles": normal rules of evidence do not matter to religious belief, because "our most holy religion is founded on *Faith,* not reason" (130).

To orthodox Anglicans, by contrast, the reasonable belief in miracles buttressed the divine authority of Scripture; the credibility of witnesses to the central miracles related in the Old and New Testaments is thus carefully to be established (Reedy 46–59). In responding to Hume's argument in "Of Miracles," Johnson tempers his scepticism with orthodoxy, offering Boswell a short disquisition that might have been penned by any number of late-seventeenth-century Anglican divines:

> Why, Sir, the great difficulty of proving miracles should make us very cautious in believing them. But let us consider; although GOD has made Nature to operate by certain fixed laws, yet it is not unreasonable to think that he may suspend those laws, in order to establish a system highly advantageous to mankind. Now the Christian religion is a most beneficial system, as it gives us light and certainty where we were before in darkness and doubt. The miracles which prove it are attested by men who had no interest in deceiving us; but who, on the contrary, were told that they should suffer persecution, and did actually lay down their lives in confirmation of the truth of the facts which they asserted. . . . Then, Sir, when we take the proofs derived from the prophecies which have been so exactly fulfilled, we have most satisfactory evidence. Supposing a miracle possible, as to which, in my opinion, there can be no doubt, we have as strong evidence for the miracles in support of Christianity, as the nature of the thing admits. (*Life of Johnson* 1:444–45) [12]

The fine qualification of Johnson's closing remark—"as strong . . . as the nature of the thing admits"—counterbalances the assurance of the Christian premises announced earlier. Reason will only go so far in these matters. Hence the need for church authority.

Johnson's commitment to the Church of England was well-known to his contemporaries. Hume heard tell of Johnson's claim—or actually heard

---

[12] Cf. *Life of Johnson* 3:188. Donald Siebert addresses Johnson's deft, if mischievous, handling of the species of probable reasoning found in Hume's "Of Miracles" ("Johnson and Hume on Miracles"); James Force persuasively contends, however, that Johnson was only acquainted with Hume's essay indirectly, presumably through Boswell's comments on it—had he read the essay he would have noted that Hume also discounts the argument from prophecy.

from Johnson?—that he would "stand before a battery of cannon, to re-store the Convocation to its full powers" (*Life of Johnson* 1:464).[13] Boswell related this quip to Johnson, thinking it a joke; "Little did I apprehend that he had actually said this: but I was soon convinced of my error; for, with a determined look, he thundered out 'And would I not, Sir?'" John-son firmly believed that while the state should give its entire, undivided support to the enforcement of the church's creed and articles, it ought not to meddle in the church's internal affairs (Reddick, "Johnson beyond Jacobitism" 1001–3). Hume, by contrast, had no such scruples about the state's interference in church government; indeed, he thought the church ought to be wholly subservient to the civil ends of metropolitan authority.

Hume did not, however, discount the civil benefits of an established church—and, as he maintained throughout *The History of England,* he thought the Church of England quite the best one. The proper role of the church, in his view, was to regulate the morals of the people, or that vast majority that Hume doubted would ever become philosophical. In his def-erence for church establishments Hume followed in the footsteps of his beloved Cicero, of whom he notes, "[I]t appears, that, whatever sceptical liberties that great man might take, in his writings or in philosophical con-versation; he yet avoided, in the common conduct of life, the imputation of deism and profaneness" (*NHR* 59). Shaftesbury—whom Hume had read by the time he was fifteen years old—commented with approval that "some provision for the performance of seemly religious rites was a part of ancient policy" (*Characteristics* 1:13–14). Hume, writing from Paris in 1764 to offer advice concerning a young man reluctantly entering the ecclesiastical profession, concludes: "I should tell him, that the Pythian or-acle, with the approbation of Xenophon, advised every one to worship the gods—*nomo poleos* [for the law, or good, of the state]" (*HL* 1:439).

Hume was prepared, well into middle age, to perform seemly rites. Dur-ing his second residence in France, 1763–1766, he attended English chapel services; back in Scotland, he went to church at the invitation of friends, if not more regularly (*Life of Hume* 328–29, 491, 575). Roger Emerson argues that Hume's failure to attain a university position at Edin-burgh in 1744–45 or at Glasgow in 1751–52 was not primarily due to a reputation for heterodoxy: indeed, his advocates thought him qualified to sign the Westminster Confession (the Presbyterian articles of faith) and to lead his students in prayer (16). However, the cabal that opposed him at Edinburgh 1745 was not so sure about his religious qualifications. A pam-phlet or pamphlets attributed to William Wishart, principal of the univer-

---

[13] The Convocation of Canterbury had been the principal mouthpiece of high-church clergy after 1688; it was silenced after 1717 by the successive prorogations of a Whig-dominated Parliament. Paul Langford assesses both the Whig motives for suspending the convocation, and Tory motives for nonetheless holding convocation elections.

sity, argued that the author of the *Treatise of Human Nature* (widely known to be Hume, although he published the work anonymously) was unfit for a chair that included among its duties lecturing each Monday on the truth of the Christian religion.

Hume responded in the anonymous pamphlet, *Letter from a Gentleman to his Friend in Edinburgh: Containing Some Observations on a Specimen of the Principles concerning Religion and Morality, said to be Maintained in . . . A Treatise of Human Nature.* In it, Hume defends the *Treatise*'s compatibility with Christian orthodoxy. Its scepticism, intended only to "abate the pride of *mere human Reasoners*" (19), harkens back to Socrates, Cicero, and "all the ancient Fathers, as well as our first Reformers. . . . In reality, whence come all the various Tribes of Hereticks, the *Arians, Socinians* and *Deists,* but from too great a Confidence in mere human Reason, which they regard as the *Standard* of every Thing, and which they will not submit to the superior Light of Revelation?" (21). Could Swift or Johnson have said this any better?

IV. Living in the Material World

In the London that the young Johnson and Hume both entered upon in 1737, much ink was spilled over religious controversies, philosophical and sectarian. Matthew Tindal's *Christianity as Old as the Creation* (1730), soon known as "the Deist's Bible," caused quite the greatest stir, prompting well over a hundred pamphlet responses; Joseph Butler's *Analogy of Religion, Natural and Revealed, to the Constitution and Course of Nature* (1736) proved a formidable response to the Deist challenge. (Hume's respect for Butler's judgment was such that in 1737 he excised the section "Of Miracles" from his still unpublished *Treatise* in the hope, never realized, that Butler would read and approve the piece. "Of Miracles" first appeared in print as part of Hume's *Enquiry [orig., Philosophical Essays] concerning Human Understanding,* 1748.) In the same year, William Warburton's *The Alliance of Church and State* defended the Anglican establishment against dissenters who would repeal the Test and Corporation Acts. (Johnson, according to Boswell, "had always a high opinion of Warburton" [*Life of Johnson* 1:263].) Yet all was far from quiet within the Church of England: by the time that Butler was made bishop of Bristol in 1738, his brand of reasonable (and somewhat "Pelagian") Christianity came under attack from a new quarter, the rising Methodist movement led by Wesley and Whitefield.

As heated as religious controversy became, it nonetheless paled next to the passion of Londoners, and to some degree the nation at large, for parliamentary politics. Political debate was all the rage. Johnson and Hume properly began their lives of writing—Johnson having already failed as a provincial schoolmaster, Hume having failed at a still less likely stint as a merchant's clerk in Bristol—at a time when the "literary world," in its broadest sense, was animated by the polemics of the opposition to Sir Robert Walpole, George II's "prime minister" (the term began as a piece of opposition sarcasm, and did not become an official title until 1905). Much has been written in recent years about the political ideology or ideologies of the so-called "Country party," those Tory back-benchers and disaffected Whigs who opposed the "court" policies of Walpole and his Whig majority in Commons. J. G. A. Pocock has written influentially, if rather sweepingly, on Country ideology as a "classical republican" ideology, one that invokes agrarian and constitutional ideals derived from Aristotle, Polybius, Machiavelli, and Harrington to oppose a burgeoning commercial modernity and the plutocratic "corruption" of a free people (*The Machiavellian Moment* chaps. 13–14). The "Country party" may not have been as ideologically consolidated as either Pocock would now like, or Lord Bolingbroke would have then liked, it to be. In any event, opposition to Walpole, unified or not, inspired a great deal of literature, both high and low.[14]

Among that literature of opposition we find the early publications of Samuel Johnson. On moving to London in 1737 with limited funds in pocket, Johnson quickly joined the scribbling tribe. And much of what he scribbled, in his first few years, is clearly in the swim of opposition writing, including the unsigned poem *London* (1738)—the first of Johnson's two great "imitations" of satires by the Roman poet Juvenal—and the pamphlet *Marmor Norfolciense* (1739). These works, especially the latter, contain staple themes of the Country party: attacks on standing armies as instruments of ministerial tyranny; on excise laws and commissioners; on the ministerial "corruption" of MPs through bribes and "places"; on ministerial extravagance and the government's consequent debt.

The added spice of *Marmor Norfolciense* comes from its anti-Hanoverian sentiment—its satire on King George as a foreigner who is heedless of England's present and future good. We may label this sentiment "Jacobitical," though how deep or how far Johnson's sympathy for the House of Stuart ran is at present a topic of much academic controversy.[15] By 1762 Hume

[14] Literature inspired by the Bolingbrokean opposition to Walpole has been surveyed by Kramnick, *Bolingbroke and His Circle,* as well as Goldgar and Gerard. Bolingbroke's vision of an ideologically coherent opposition has, however, been effectively questioned in Alexander Pettit's recent study of lesser-known writers opposed to both Walpole *and* Bolingbroke.

[15] In a recent book, the historian J. C. D. Clark argues (largely from circumstantial evidence) that Johnson was throughout his life a Jacobite Nonjuror, loyal to the Stuart dynasty; see also Erskine-Hill, *Poetry of Opposition and Revolution,* chaps. 4 and 5 ("Johnson: Poems on Affairs of State"). Howard Weinbrot offers a systematic refutation of Clark's premises and conclusions ("Johnson, Jacobitism, and the Historiography of Nostalgia"); one must beware, however, of Weinbrot's own mistaken insistence, against Clark's situation of Johnson within an "Anglo-Latin" Tory culture, that Johnson was "at war" with the Greco-Latin literary tradition. For a balanced view of Johnson's limited sympathy for the Stuarts, see Cannon, 36–67.

apparently considered Johnson "a keen Jacobite, yet [he] hates the Scotch" (Boswell, *Private Papers* 1 : 128). It is unclear, however, from what sources Hume derived his opinion about Johnson's politics: gossip or hearsay seem likelier than Johnson's own writings, especially those after 1742. (A few months before Hume's remark, Johnson had been tarred with the brush of "Jacobitism" by both John Wilkes in *The North Briton* nos. 11 and 12, and Charles Churchill in book 3 of *The Ghost*). It also appears that "Jacobite" was used rather loosely by the 1750s and 1760s to refer to anyone at all sympathetic to the historical claims and the ultimate fate of the Stuarts; few by that date could expect the restoration of a Stuart king in Hanoverian England (although Hume's good friend Lord Elibank appears to have been one of them). Thus in 1754 the bishop of Gloucester called Hume himself—never in the least anti-Hanoverian—"an atheistical Jacobite" for having written sympathetically of Charles I in the first volume of his *History of England* (*History* 1 : xiv).

Like Johnson, Hume arrived in London in 1737; unlike Johnson, he had the good fortune to have a patrimony that, according to Mossner's calculation, afforded him a little under fifty pounds a year (*Life of Hume* 25). This frugal independency had enabled him to spend the years 1734 to early 1737 in rural France, writing what would become his first book, *A Treatise of Human Nature* (2 vols., 1739–40).[16] It was composed largely in the small country town of La Fleche, on the Loire River in Anjou, the site of the Jesuit college that had educated Descartes, and that remained a Cartesian center.

Appropriately, the *Treatise* is more of an exchange with Descartes than with British politics or political theory. Book 1, "Of the Understanding," is a sustained argument against rationalist faculty psychology from Plato to Descartes; it contains Hume's well-known explanation of causation as a psychological rather than a logical phenomenon, a species of sensation based on experience rather than an operation of reason. Having debunked the rationalists' inordinate claims of behalf of reason, Hume of-

---

[16] That Hume had the wherewithal to compose his works without patronage, subscription, or publisher's contract while Johnson had to work to order for booksellers redounded to Hume's credit in a society in which *otium* was still, as in Athens, equated with disinterestedness. Years later, in an early memoir of Johnson, William Shaw would recall the 1750s as a time when

> the literary character of *David Hume* broke forth in its strongest lustre. He was the fashionable writer of the day. He had always kept himself independant of Booksellers. This was a circumstance that considerably increased it [his literary character?] with some people, as they are pleased to distinguish between an author who writes for subsistence; and one, who though able to live without writing, yet sells what he writes with as much anxiety, as if he wrote for a livelihood. This . . . they call a gentleman-author, and, without much regard to the comparative merit of the two, very often, and very absurdly, give him the preference. (*Early Biographies* 163)

fers in book 2, "Of the Passions," an elaborate etiology of the passions that motivate us. Hume's naturalistic account of the passions may be an attempt to supersede Descartes's own mechanistic (physiochemical) story, in *Les passions de l'âme* (1649), of how passions submit to the will even while soul and body rest inviolably dual.

When Hume left his Cartesian retreat, coming to London in 1737 seeking a publisher for his *Treatise,* he quickly became acclimated to the political ether of the metropolis. With the professed intention of being an impartial judge between court and Country partisans, Hume entered the political arena, publishing *Essays: Moral and Political* in two volumes between late 1741 and early 1742. His essay "That Politics May be Reduced to a Science" exemplifies the approach that would characterize all his further political and historical endeavors—the attempt to mediate between extremes, to turn opposed fanaticisms into constructive dialogue:

> Would men be moderate and consistent, their claims might be admitted; at least might be examined. The *country-party* might still assert, that our constitution, though excellent, will admit of mal-administration to a certain degree; and therefore, if the minister be bad, it is proper to oppose him with a *suitable* degree of zeal. And, on the other hand, the *court-party* may be allowed, upon the supposition that the minister were good, to defend, and with *some* zeal too, his administration. I would only persuade men not to contend, as if they were fighting *pro aris & focis,* and change a good constitution into a bad one, by the violence of their factions. (*Essays* 30–31) [17]

In the early 1740s, at the same time that Hume sought to pioneer "scientific" impartiality in political debate, Johnson veered away from his earlier opposition virulence and toward an ideal quite similar to Hume's. Between 1741 and 1744 Johnson wrote for the *Gentleman's Magazine* a series of *Debates in the Senate of Magna Lilliput,* a transparently veiled account, taken for years as an authentic one, of speeches delivered in the two houses of Parliament. The House of Commons had closed parliamentary proceedings to the press in 1738, so that Johnson—who himself visited the gallery of Commons just once—had to invent the speeches he attributed to MPs, working from the slightest notes supplied from sources paid to leak information to the magazine. In these speeches, Johnson often

---

[17] If Hume himself leaned in the direction of either "faction" in 1741, it is toward sounding at moments like something of an opposition rhetor. In his essay "Of Eloquence" Hume echoes, with at least half a heart, the Opposition's call for a great and virtuous orator after the model of Demosthenes and Cicero to fire the civic virtue that had waned in Walpole's Britain. Walpole's "corruption" of Parliament is, moreover, suggested in "Of the Independency of Parliament" and "A Character of Sir Robert Walpole"—the latter reprinted by Edward Cave in his *Gentleman's Magazine,* March 1742, during Johnson's tenure as contributor. See my *Fate of Eloquence* 24–45, and "Theorizing Civic Eloquence in the Early Republic."

gave to MPs the Demosthenic eloquence the absence of which the opposition lamented; more significantly, he distributed his eloquence among members of opposing factions with balanced impartiality. Indeed, one of his finest speeches is given to his former nemesis, Sir Robert Walpole (called Sir Retrob Walelop in the *Debates*' less than subtle "Lilliputian" code), defending his record against the opposition's concerted effort to cashier him in 1741—an effort that ultimately forced his resignation the following year.[18] Walpole here speaks with the dignity and sense of Demosthenes in his then much admired apologia, "On the Crown."

Johnson later wrote, in the preface to the *General Index to the First Twenty Volumes of the Gentleman's Magazine* (1753), that the parliamentary debates he composed during and after Walpole's ministry include "such a Series of Argumentation as has comprised all Political Science"; the debates "ascertained the Right of the Crown and the Privileges of the People, so as for ever to prevent their being confounded in the cause either of Tyranny or of Faction" (quoted in DeMaria, *Life* 52–53). Johnson also wrote miscellaneous pieces for the *Gentleman's Magazine* during the 1740s—abridgements, advertisements, as well as more short biographical essays of figures including Admiral Blake and Sir Francis Drake. His major biographical work of this period, the *Life of Savage* (1744)—an account of the literary life and shady doings of his late London friend, Richard Savage (1698–1743), improvident poet, soi-disant abandoned bastard of noble parentage, and murder-suspect—is arguably, like his parliamentary *Debates*, a masterpiece of judiciousness.[19]

V. The Sweet Smell of Success

For both Johnson and Hume, the period from the late 1740s through the mid-1760s was a "miraculous epoch," a period of great labor and glad recognition. It is when both men acquired, in overlapping circles, the literary fame that each of them sought, and that each of them would come to moralize.

In the years following the first two volumes of his *Essays,* Hume wrote further essays and "dissertations"—including "Of the Standard of Taste"

---

[18] Johnson's account of the debate in Commons over the 1741 motion to remove Walpole is printed with useful notes by Donald Greene in *Major Works,* 103–112. See also Robert Giddings on the artistry of Johnson's presentation of Walpole's final speech.

[19] William Vesterman notes that Johnson's careful balancing of praise and blame in the *Life of Savage* contrasts both with "the ponderosity of the early [opposition] satires" (48) and with the melodramatic benevolence or malice of the characters in Savage's own life. More recently, Richard Holmes has written an engaging though melodramatic account of Johnson's *Life of Savage* that discounts Johnson's efforts at judiciousness to play up his identification with Savage as a dark double, Johnson's "Mr. Hyde."

and *The Natural History of Religion*—and continually revised, often sub-stantially, pieces already in print. On a larger scale, he recast his early *Treatise* into two shorter and more readily palatable works, *An Enquiry concerning Human Understanding* (1748), and *An Enquiry concerning the Principles of Morals* (1752). The first *Enquiry* is a reworking of book 1 of the *Treatise*, in which the earlier work's exuberant metaphysics are much abbreviated, and new sections are added—including the hitherto suppressed "Of Miracles"—that evince themes Hume will develop throughout the rest of his career: testing and restricting the claims of philosophical theology (especially the popular argument from design, and what may or may not validly be inferred from it); and formulating rules for the evaluation of historical testimony. The first of these themes would reach its maturity with Hume's posthumously published *Two Essays*, "Of Suicide" and "Of the Immortality of the Soul" (1777), and *Dialogues concerning Natural Religion* (1779). The second theme appears like a *basso continuo* throughout his *History of England*.

Hume's grand *History of England* appeared in six volumes between 1754 and 1762, during which time he held the position of librarian of the Faculty of Advocates at Edinburgh, and so had command of an extensive collection—roughly thirty thousand volumes.[20] Frederick Whelan aptly assesses Hume's aim in writing his *History:* "Although Hume's turn to the writing of history . . . is sometimes deplored by modern specialists as a de-sertion of philosophy, there was no such disjuncture in Hume's own view of his project . . . the study of history provided an opportunity to confirm the account of human nature put forward in the *Treatise;* to record in a concrete fashion the development of a government, of which the origins are analyzed abstractly in the *Treatise;* and to observe in practice the dan-gers of the 'fanaticism' that can result from . . . nonskeptical claims of insight and assurance" (5). Hume spent the years from late 1763 to early 1766 in Paris, first as secretary to Lord Hertford's embassy to the court of France, and then, in Hertford's absence, as chargé d'affaires. Lionized in the salons and among the *philosophes* of Paris, Hume also had an affair, which may or may not have been only of the heart, with Marie-Charlotte-Hippolyte de Campet de Saujeon, the comtesse de Boufflers (1724–c.1800), *salonnière* and mistress of the Prince de Conti, second in line to the throne of France. Hume spent 1767–69 in London, and for the first eleven months of that time served as undersecretary of state for the North-ern Department, dealing in diplomacy with countries north of France, chiefly Russia. It was during this time that he witnessed the "Wilkes and Liberty" riots of 1768, grew increasingly critical of both British policy and

---

[20] Hume resigned his post as librarian in 1757, but thereafter retained liberty of the li-brary. The Advocates' Library became the National Library of Scotland in the 1920s.

extraparliamentary political agitation, and began on his life's last work, a series of eloquent letters on affairs of state.

Intriguingly, during the period of Hume's closest association with the comtesse de Boufflers, she and Johnson also commenced an acquaintance, one that would last many years. Without going so far as to suggest a bizarre love triangle, I would note these curious and tantalizingly incomplete pieces of a puzzle. In the summer of 1763 the comtesse honored Johnson with a visit to his house in London: the story of the visit, as colorfully related to Boswell by Topham Beauclerk (*Life of Johnson* 2:405–6), inspired an oil painting by W. P. Frith in 1886 (reproduced in Brownell, pl. 20). Johnson appears to have maintained a correspondence with her— the only letter that survives is reprinted by Boswell, and dated in successive editions either July 1771 or July 1775 (2:405). The casual intimacy of this letter suggests a far more extensive correspondence. And yet consider the well-known social status of the comtesse: she was a married woman who lived apart from her husband up through the time of his death in 1764, and who lived as a prince's mistress. That this arrangement, à la mode in polite French circles, did not raise Hume's eyebrows we need not wonder; it may, however, come as a surprise to Johnsonians of a certain stripe that their hero paid the comtesse the highest respect over an indefinite period of time.

It was, of course, flattering to be sought out by a comtesse, and still more gratifying to be sought after for one's literary accomplishments. In 1763, Johnson and Hume were the most famous men of letters in the English-speaking world. By 1762, Johnson was granted a pension of three hundred pounds per annum, in honor of his literary achievements, at the behest of Lord Bute.[21] (Hume was granted a pension of four hundred pounds per annum in 1766, on the less glamorous grounds of retiring from service as Lord Hertford's secretary.) In the 1770s, Johnson was called on to write several political pamphlets in defense of Lord North's ministry. His reply to rebellious American colonists, *Taxation No Tyranny* (1775), earned Johnson a fair share of resentment among friends of America such as the Reverend W. Johnstone Temple, who wrote Boswell, "How can your great, I will not say your *pious,* but your *moral* friend, support the barbarous measures of administration, which they have not the face to ask even their infidel pensioner Hume to defend" (*Life of Johnson* 2:316–17). *Taxation No Tyranny* is also, in all likelihood, what earned Johnson an honorary doctorate from Oxford University, of which Lord North was the Chancellor,

---

[21] Donald Greene writes: "Why Bute in 1762 offered, and Johnson accepted, the famous pension of three hundred pounds a year remains something of a mystery, but it seems safe to assume that Bute did so primarily because he wanted to enhance the 'image' of the new administration as a patron of the arts, and Johnson because he was willing for it to be enhanced" (*PW* 314).

in March 1775. (In 1765, Johnson had been awarded an honorary LL. D. from Trinity College, Dublin.) Boswell, always eager to stress Johnson's authority, popularized the now ubiquitous title "Dr. Johnson"; we do well to remember that Johnson was, during most all his years of writing, Mr. Johnson.

During roughly the same time that Hume produced the bulk of his writings—from 1748 to the early 1760s—Johnson produced a body of writing that is, in its variety, cogency, and sheer size, little short of amazing. He published his finest poem, the second of his Juvenalian imitations, *The Vanity of Human Wishes,* in 1749. It was the first work on the title page of which Johnson put his own name, a sign of his new self-confidence. By this time Johnson was well at work on his *Dictionary of the English Language,* assisted by six amanuenses who copied out the quotations, marked by Johnson in his books, which were used to illustrate each word. These quotations, so liberally included in Johnson's *Dictionary,* distinguished it from its English-language predecessors.[22] The *Dictionary* appeared in two volumes in 1755. During the years leading up to its appearance and until 1759 Johnson lived at Gough Square, in the house that is still on every literary tour of London; his wife, Elizabeth ("Tetty") lived most of these years in a small house in rural Hampstead until her death in March 1752. Johnson never remarried.

While working on his *Dictionary,* Johnson produced with off-handed brilliance two series of periodical essays, *The Rambler* (published twice weekly, March 1750–March 1752), and *The Adventurer* (to which Johnson contributed intermittently from March 1753 to March 1754). He later put out a periodical not unironically titled *The Idler* (published weekly, April 1758 to April 1760). The bulk of Johnson's essays are concerned with topics of moral philosophy—centrally with the psychology of the passions and the morality of everyday life.

Johnson's most widely read work is his *Rasselas, Prince of Abyssinia* (1759), a philosophical tale cast as an Oriental adventure; Voltaire's *Candide,* published in the same year, has ever been recognized as its closest literary analogue. Johnson's major undertaking of the late 1750s and early 1760s was his edition, with notes and a justly famous preface, of *The Plays of William Shakespeare;* it was published in eight volumes in 1765. Johnson admired Shakespeare's plays as "the mirrour of life"; from reading Shakespeare, he marveled, "a hermit may estimate the transactions of the world, and a con-

---

[22] The writers enshrined by Johnson are above all Shakespeare, Milton, and Pope; John Locke; and sermon and devotional writers (e.g., Tillotson, Atterbury, Jeremy Taylor). Robert DeMaria offers an incisive introduction to the art of the *Dictionary* in *Life of Samuel Johnson* 110–28. For a more in-depth view of Johnson's labors, see Reddick, *The Making of Johnson's Dictionary, 1746–1773.* The fourth edition of the *Dictionary,* revised and expanded, was published in 1773. Unless otherwise noted, my quotations are drawn from the 1755 edition.

fessor predict the progress of the passions." Finally, it is during this period that Johnson apparently began ghostwriting sermons "for sundry bene-ficed clergymen that requested them" (*Sermons* xxi); twenty-eight in total are attributed to him by the editors of the Yale edition of Johnson's *Sermons,* most of them written for his friend John Taylor, a clergyman in West-minster. Johnson may have written far more.

Johnson's last great undertaking, late in life, consisted of writing bio-graphical and critical prefaces for each of the fifty-two poets, from Abra-ham Cowley (d. 1667) to George Lyttelton (d. 1773), contained in the sixty-eight volume set *Works of the English Poets* (1779–81). In 1781, John-son's prefaces were first published separately as a four-volume set, *The Lives of the Most Eminent English Poets.*

VI. Sociable Writing

However voluminous and variegated their respective bodies of writing, Johnson and Hume do clearly and in common pursue a limited number of humanist themes. Their most basic theme is our sociability: sociability subsumes not only our individual interests, but ought in some fashion to delimit an individual's very inquiries. Accordingly, both Hume and John-son judged their own chosen life—the life of critical reflection and of writing—by a standard of social utility, and reserved some of their harsh-est comments for writings that appeared to them useless. Each applied as a criterion the usefulness or sheer viability of any moral knowledge to or in society. All that turns to dust outside academic cells deserves to be forgotten. Johnson and Hume intended their writings, along with those of other enlightened authors, to occupy the shelves left bare when all useless books were suitably disposed of—especially all purely specula-tive metaphysics, from the Scholastics to Soame Jenyns, from Anselm to Malebranche.

How will this book help me "better to enjoy life, or better to endure it"? The phrase is from a book review Johnson wrote in the 1750s of a book by a writer, now otherwise forgotten, named Soame Jenyns. In his *Free Inquiry into the Nature and Origin of Evil,* Jenyns addresses that perennially favorite philosophical problem, the so-called "problem of evil." If there's a good God in the heavens, then why is there so much natural and moral evil here on earth? Jenyns offers a number of speculative answers, including the the-ory that there are species of beings in the universe, intermediate between ourselves and God, whose enjoyment of our personal woes explains the purpose of apparently senseless suffering in the great scheme of things. Johnson, not surprisingly, finds this an unreal solution to the problem of human suffering. After tartly attributing Jenyns' own career as an author to the malicious sport of the superior beings he postulates, Johnson concludes his review with a direct statement of the Enlightenment's utilitarian test of writing: "Many of the books which now crowd the world, may be justly suspected to be written for the sake of some invisible order of beings, for surely they are of no use to any of the corporeal inhabitants of the world. Of the productions of the last bounteous year, how many can be said to serve any purpose of use or pleasure? The only end of writing is to enable the readers better to enjoy life, or better to endure it" (*MW* 536).

Not to be outdone in sentiments of this type, Hume concludes his *Enquiry concerning Human Understanding* with this challenge: "When we run over libraries, persuaded of these principles, what havoc must we make? If we take into our hand any volume; of divinity or school metaphysics, for instance; let us ask, *Does it contain any abstract reasoning concerning quantity or number?* No. *Does it contain any experimental reasoning concerning matter of fact and existence?* No. Commit it then to the flames: for it can contain nothing but sophistry and illusion" (165).

The mature Hume thought that even his youthful *Treatise* smelled too strongly of the library—its metaphysics were too speculative at points, its style not sociable enough. It appeared to him not to have been written for the corporeal inhabitants of the world—or, at least, of London, Edinburgh, or Paris. Hume wrote of the *Treatise* in 1751, "I was carried away by the Heat of Youth & Invention to publish too precipitately. . . . I have repented my Haste a hundred, & a hundred times" (*HL* 1:158).[23] That the *Treatise* appeared pedantic to Hume may at first seem incredible to us who have lived to see philosophical prose as it has been professionally mangled by German university professors from the late eighteenth century onward, and more recently by French intellectuals and their American and British acolytes.

The love of difficulty is certainly one of the things that keep professional philosophers returning to the *Treatise,* especially its first book, "Of the Understanding." Let us turn to examine it once again, alongside Johnson's justly admired philosophical tale, *Rasselas.* Both works tender sociable solutions to speculative quandaries; the way in which one text does so may help illuminate the way of the other.

[23] Cf. Hume's preface to his abstract of the *Treatise* (*T* 643–44); *LG* 33; and "My Own Life," *Essays* xxxv.

CHAPTER TWO

Experimental Reasoning
in the Shadow of Descartes

Hume and Johnson both offer what are in effect parables about taking up the enlightened life of letters—stories about leaving behind a sequestered place and entering a social world of experience and exchange. The closing movement of book 1 of Hume's *Treatise* and all but the close of Johnson's *Rasselas* tell a similar tale—a cautionary one about the related ills of rationalist reason, the inward turn, philosophical solitude, and the snares of superstition; a celebratory one about the mutual reinforcements of experimental knowledge, social converse, and the wisdom of the heart. Inasmuch as the metaphysical ills that Johnson and Hume would overcome may be rolled into one, that one may be conveniently referred to as "Descartes."

Both Hume and Johnson were well aware of Descartes's inward-turning rationalism and his reliance on a priori truths. Hume wrote the bulk of his *Treatise* in the small French town of La Fleche, whose Jesuit college was the alma mater of Descartes and a center of Cartesianism through the eighteenth century. Johnson had in his personal library both Descartes's *Opera Philosophica* and a separate copy of the *Meditations;*[1] he refers in *Rambler* no. 43 to Descartes as the philosopher who could prove his being through his doubt of it. A few years later, in 1755, Johnson wrote to his friend Hill Boothby: "You know Des Cartes's argument, 'I think therefore I am.' It is as good a consequence 'I write therefore I am alive'" (*JL* 1 : 118). Johnson wrote Hill Boothby on this occasion ostensibly to disprove a rumor that he had died, and implicitly to interest her all the more in his life. While we

---

[1] Items no. 77 and 451 in Fleeman's *Sale Catalogue of Samuel Johnson's Library.*

47

wouldn't want to press Johnson's delicate wit here into too strict a philosophical service, it does seem fair to say that Johnson's manner of distinguishing himself from Descartes is telling: one speaks of an inward turn, one of an outward. For Descartes, of prime importance is to determine one's being and corollary truths independent of sense experience; for Johnson, to do, in this world, is to be.

I. Rasselas's Escape from the Valley

The salient features of Descartes's neo-Augustinian method are neatly listed by Charles Taylor as an "emphasis on radical reflexivity, the importance of the cogito, the central role of a proof of God's existence [Anselm's ontological proof] which starts from within, from features of my own ideas." (143). Johnson was inclined to this inward turn in his private life, yet fought against it on principle and in public. Walter Jackson Bate remarks, "Johnson is probably the most extraordinary example in modern times of a man who in his own character concretely and dramatically exemplifies the Augustinian tradition of individualism and 'interiority' . . . and yet, far from welcoming it or turning to it with conscious choice, distrusted and in many ways tried to resist it" (*Samuel Johnson* 455). We may see that distrust and resistance in the pages of his popular philosophical tale, *Rasselas*. In the work's penultimate chapter, Johnson adduces a familiar argument for the soul's immortality that relies on the inward turn; I will address the ending of *Rasselas* in my final chapter, and suggest the ways in which this appeal to the a priori is, in context, not altogether unironic.

Here I would like to focus on the first third of Johnson's tale, which I see as a philosophical fable on the value of experimental over a priori reasoning—of empirical knowing over Cartesian inwardness. Johnson observed the tension between these two ways of knowing early in his career, in his "Life of Dr. Herman Boerhaave, Late Professor of Physic in the University of Leyden" (1739). Boerhaave delivered an oration at Leyden in 1715 "in which he declares himself in the strongest terms, a favourer of experimental knowledge"; his declaration elicited a heated rejoinder from "a professor of Franeker, who having long entertained a high esteem for Descartes, considered his principles as the bulwark of orthodoxy" (*MW* 62).[2]

---

[2] Johnson concludes with praise of Boerhaave: "[H]e examined systems by experiments, and formed experiments into systems. He neither neglected the observations of others, nor blindly submitted to celebrated names" (*MW* 68). Forty years later, Johnson wrote in defense of the Royal Society: "[T]he most zealous enemy of innovation must admit the gradual progress of experience, however he may oppose hypothetical temerity"—echoing Newton's oft-quoted phrase, *Hypotheses non fingo* (*Lives* 1:209). The full significance of the term *experience* in Johnson's usage is addressed by Jean Hagstrum, 8–14.

Johnson returns to this clash between ways of knowing, and champions experimental reasoning, in the first panel of the triptych of *Rasselas*.[3]

Rasselas begins as the story of a young Abyssinian prince who, as he awaits his succession to the throne in the sequestered "Happy Valley," grows bored with the sensual satisfactions of the palace and enclosed grounds, and feels the valley to be more a prison than an Eden. Thus, "Rasselas . . . in the twenty-sixth year of his age, began to withdraw himself from . . . pastimes and assemblies, and to delight in solitary walks and silent meditation" (12). Rasselas complains to his elderly instructor: "That I want nothing . . . or that I know not what I want, is the cause of my complaint . . . When I see the lambs chasing one another, I fancy that I should be happy if I had something to persue" (15–16). Now, empirically speaking, the lambs merely chase one another in circles—just as in Ecclesiastes, a book to which *Rasselas* is often compared, all nonhuman nature revolves in circles: "The sun also ariseth, and the sun goeth down, and hasteth to the place where he arose" (1:5). Rasselas is unhappy because, like Ecclesiastes, he desires a goal, a *telos:* "the eye is not satisfied with seeing, nor the ear filled with hearing" the cycles of nature (1:8). But this insight is not available to Rasselas, as he has not yet learned to see the animals properly and to learn from observation. Here, he simply projects his own categories—the pursuit of a future goal—onto the animals' chasing one another in the present; he erroneously conflates their pursuit of one another with his own "fancy that I should be happy if I had something to persue." Such is the risk of silent meditation.

Along with Rasselas's first desire—something to desire—comes his first challenge: how to escape from the Happy Valley. Yet Rasselas's first response is an inward turn that, ironically, encloses him in a kind of valley inside the Valley:

> The first beam of hope, that had ever darted into his mind, rekindled youth in his cheeks, and doubled the lustre of his eyes. He was fired with the desire of doing something, though he knew not yet with distinctness, either end or means. . . . His chief amusement was to picture to himself that world which he had never seen; to place himself in various conditions; to be entangled in imaginary difficulties, and to be engaged in wild adventures; but his benevolence always terminated his projects in the relief of distress, the detection of fraud, the defeat of oppression, and the diffusion of happiness.
>
> Thus passed twenty months of the life of Rasselas. He busied himself so intensely in visionary bustle, that he forgot his real solitude; and, amidst hourly

---

[3] Following Frederick Hilles, Emrys Jones, and Nicholas Hudson ("Three Steps to Perfection"), I find in *Rasselas* three distinct parts or movements: life in the Happy Valley (chaps. 1–16), travels in Egypt (chaps. 17–32), and a final mixture of episodes on the theme of insufficiency, or the hunger of the imagination (chaps. 33–49).

preparations for the various incidents of human affairs, neglected to consider by what means he should mingle with mankind. (chap. 4, 17–18)

The inward turn certainly won't get him out of the Valley. After ten more months of fruitless meditation, Rasselas meets up with an engineer and would-be aeronaut (chap. 6), who plans to fashion wings, based on those of bats, that might enable humans to fly over the encircling mountains and escape the Valley. This engineer fancies himself a man of the new science: as Gwin Kolb points out in his learned notes to the tale, Johnson drew much of the engineer's speeches from *Mathematical Magick: or the Wonders that May Be Perform'd by Mechanical Geometry* (1648), by Bishop John Wilkins, "distinguished Fellow of the Royal Society and perhaps the foremost aerial enthusiast of his age" (22, n.1). But here are the engineer's mechanical assumptions:

[F]ishes have the water, in which yet beasts can swim by nature, and men by art. He that can swim needs not despair to fly: to swim is to fly in a grosser fluid, and to fly is to swim in a subtler. We are only to proportion our power of resistance to the different density of the matter through which we are to pass. You will be necessarily upborn by the air, if you can renew any impulse upon it, faster than the air can recede from the pressure. (24–25)

A few paragraphs later we see the result of his labors, the flight of the bat-man:

In a year the wings were finished, and, on a morning appointed, the maker appeared furnished for flight on a little promontory: he waved his pinions a while to gather air, then leaped from his stand, and in an instant dropped into the lake. His wings, which were of no use in the air, sustained him in the water, and the prince drew him to land, half dead with terrour and vexation. (28)

The engineer fails because for all his professions he too neglects to observe the animals carefully—that is, to observe nature and to learn, experimentally, from it. The analogy between the bat's aerodynamic makeup and our own is preposterous; the analogy between the elements of water and air is speculative at best. Johnson's gentle satire of the engineer is in effect a satire against, in Bernard Mandeville's words from a generation earlier, "that lofty self-sufficient Reason that boldly trusts to its own Wings, and leaving *Experience* far behind mounts upon Air" (*Treatise on the Hypochondriack . . . Diseases* 130).[4]

---

[4] Mandeville's *Treatise* was, according to John Hawkins, a work Johnson admired (*Miscellanies* 2:20); Hume's debts to the work are assessed by John Wright, 190–91.

Rasselas makes his escape only when he and his newfound advisor, the sage Imlac, learn from the rabbits how to burrow obliquely into, and through, the mountain:

> As they were walking on the side of the mountain, they observed that the conies, which the rain had driven from their burrows, had taken shelter among the bushes, and formed holes behind them, tending upwards in an oblique line. "It has been the opinion of antiquity," said Imlac, "that human reason borrowed many of its arts from the instinct of animals; let us, therefore, not think ourselves degraded by learning from the coney. We may escape by piercing the mountain in the same direction." (chap. 13, 57–58)

People do and ought to learn experimentally; it is indeed what distinguishes our achievements from those of the animals, whose performances, Johnson maintains, are chiefly instinctive. As he writes in the *Rambler*: "Surely he that contemplates a ship and a bird's nest, will not be long without finding out, that the idea of one was impressed at once, and continued through all the progressive descents of the species, without variation or improvement; and that the other is the result of experiments compared with experiments, has grown, by accumulated observation, from less to greater excellence, and exhibits the collective knowledge of different ages, and various professions" (3:223). (Hume, for anti-Cartesian reasons, tended to stress the ways in which the intelligence of animals differs in degree rather than in kind from our own, noting for example that animals share our basic appetites, passions, and capacity for experimental reasoning.[5] Although Johnson was concerned to distinguish animals' ways of knowing from our own, he nonetheless disapproved of Descartes's extreme mind/body dualism, and its corollary assumption that animals, lacking mind, are simple automatons.) [6]

Experimental knowledge is social, collective, historical, progressive. Experiment, for us, leads to success; it forms a counterpoint to the ineffectualness or even delirium of those who start out from a consideration of their own ideas. Rasselas and Imlac manage their own escape from a Valley without experience, but not before Rasselas learned one more lesson, in a short exhortation by Imlac against "superstition" as a nonempirical shackle of the mind:

[5] See *T* 397–98, *ECHU* 104–8, *ECPM* 300. Despite Hume's provocative parallels of human and animal understanding and emotions, Antony Pitson points out that for Hume animals finally are *not* like us as they lack moral agency, which is founded on the ability to assume a general point of view ("The Nature of Humean Animals").

[6] Johnson opposed the Cartesian theory of animals as an a priori argument divorced from common experience, and also, I suspect, on the pragmatic grounds that it sanctions cruelty to animals (*Idler* 2:33, cf. 2:319–20). Johnson also sided with Locke against Descartes's complete identification of us with our thinking: *Idler* no. 24, surveying the philosophical debate, concludes, "[T]here must necessarily be minds that do not always think" (2:77).

They returned to work day after day, and, in a short time, found a fissure in the rock, which enabled them to pass far with very little obstruction. This Rasselas considered as a good omen. "Do not disturb your mind," said Imlac, "with other hopes or fears than reason may suggest: if you are pleased with prognosticks of good, you will be terrified likewise with tokens of evil, and your whole life will be a prey to superstition. Whatever facilitates our work is more than an omen, it is a cause of success." (59)

In the next part of the tale, Rasselas and Imlac, accompanied by the Princess Nekayah and her maid Pekuah, flee to Cairo (the big city), and converse with a wide variety of different men and women in a series of "experiments upon life." As Rasselas exclaims, "Whatever be the consequence of my experiment, I am resolved to judge with my own eyes of the various conditions of men, and then to make deliberately my *choice of life*" (68, 56).[7] The experiments that lead to knowledge of human nature and society are properly conducted sociably, through converse with others.[8] As Rasselas will discover, however, knowledge does not carry with it motivating force[9]—hence his *choice* of a specific career or occupation or place to live is not facilitated by knowing a wide range of "walks of life." Rasselas and his companions are still adrift by the end of the tale—but not for want of knowing.

II. Hume's Escape from the Cartesian Self

In the closing sections of book 1 of his *Treatise*—"Of Personal Identity" and "Conclusion of this Book" (T 1.4.6–7)—Hume opposes the inward turn on grounds little less practical than Johnson's. He too would demonstrate that the inward turn of mind leads to states of solitude that are insupportable; he would demonstrate as well, however, that to think of our-

---

[7] One ought, perhaps, to qualify Johnson's professed commitment to "experiment" in a number of ways: as Oscar Kenshur observes, there is something paradoxical in the "experience" that the reader of *Rasselas,* and sometimes Prince Rasselas himself, derives from precepts; Kenshur calls this "the paradox of mediated inductivism" (196–209). In a related vein, Joel Weinsheimer stresses the degree to which Johnson was committed, in an empiricist age, to an earlier—and contemporary—idea of literature as primarily an imitation of other literature (*Imitation,* esp. 9–16); cf. Neil Hertz's provocative essay, "Dr Johnson's Forgetfulness, Descartes' Piece of Wax."

[8] Such is also the moral of Henry Fielding's masterpiece, *Tom Jones* (1749), a work Johnson unfairly disparaged. Fielding comments in his own essayistic voice on the character of "the Man of the Hill," a misanthropic recluse whose erroneous opinions derive from his bookish abstraction and limited converse with the world: "[T]here is another Sort of Knowledge beyond the power of Learning to bestow, and this is to be had by Conversation. . . . For however exquisitely Human Nature may have been described by Writers, the true practical System can be learnt only in the World" (IX.i, 492).

[9] On Johnson's motivational psychology, see below, chapter 4.

selves as inward beings leads to positions that are logically untenable. The first of these goals calls for moral painting; the latter requires careful anatomy.

Hume's anatomical efforts in "Of Personal Identity" have, unfortunately, been misunderstood by many literary and cultural historians. Here are the sentences of Hume's often taken out of context:

> For my part, when I enter most intimately into what I call *myself,* I always stumble on some particular perception or other, of heat or cold, light or shade, love or hatred, pain or pleasure. I never can catch *myself* at any time without a perception, and never can observe anything but the perception. When my perceptions are remov'd for any time, as by sound sleep; so long am I insensible of *myself,* and may truly be said not to exist. . . . If any one upon serious and unprejudic'd reflexion, thinks he has a different notion of *himself,* I must confess I can no longer reason with him . . . But setting aside some metaphysicians of this kind, I may venture to affirm of the rest of mankind, that they are nothing but a bundle or collection of different perceptions, which succeed each other with an inconceivable rapidity, and are in a perpetual flux and movement. Our eyes cannot turn in their sockets without varying our perceptions. Our thought is still more variable than our sight; and all our other senses and faculties contribute to this change; nor is there any single power of the soul, which remains unalterably the same, perhaps for one moment. The mind is a kind of theatre, where several perceptions successively make their appearance; pass, re-pass, glide away, and mingle in an infinite variety of postures and situations. There is properly no *simplicity* in it at one time, nor *identity* in different; whatever natural propension we have to imagine that simplicity and identity. (*T* 252–53)

The key mistake many critics and historians tend to make about Hume is, in light of this passage, to see him as a "deconstructor of self." Such readers willy-nilly follow earlier commentators from Thomas Reid and James Beattie through Leslie Stephen in wrongly assuming the centrality in Hume's writings of "perceptualism"—the idea that we can only know the impressions and ideas that pass through our own minds—and deducing as Hume's intended consequence a conviction of our perceptual isolation and of the insubstantiality of the external and social world. According to this reading, we are opaque even to ourselves, since the individual cannot be said to exist as a subsistent self but only as a succession of disjointed perceptions. Still more fabulously, many latter-day scholars who read Hume on identity in this manner take their reading to be a more or less accurate representation of the eighteenth-century worldview—which is then often assumed to be more or less continuous with our own. W. K. Wimsatt stated categorically that "the world . . . had been fragmented into atoms or moments of discrete experience by the Humean dissociation" (*Literary Criticism* 304); similar hyperboles, often from otherwise very responsible scholars, have been common in the past twenty-five years.[10] A subset of these scholars claim to discover the missing link between Hume and Johnson in their comparable responses to a perception, generally available by the mid-eighteenth century, of the insubstantiality of the self and the consequent fictiveness of the characters we proceed to be.[11]

Hume, for all his good humor, would probably be appalled by this gross misconstruction of his motives and intentions. Most fundamentally, Hume does not, and with any consistency cannot, think of experiences as logically private; his central doctrine of sympathy, as we shall see, is built on the contrary assumption that our perceptions are almost transparently available to one another.[12] Hume would not say that all we can know is our own perceptions; consequently, he does not hold that the self is no more than the disjointed perceptions we may observe in the course of a contrived thought experiment. The section "Of Personal Identity" has limited polemical significance, largely as a salvo against Descartes.

Annette Baier calls all of book 1, part 4, of the *Treatise* a "*reductio ad absurdem* of the Cartesian intellect" (*A Progress of Sentiments* 21).[13] It is a set piece designed to show the problems we set for ourselves when we attempt

[10] A representative sampling might begin with A. D. Nuttall, especially [11]–23, 93–97. Nuttall offers nuggets such as "in Hume the shadow of solipsism lengthens"; Hume "ascribed a fictitious status to the self and public objects," and his influence extends to T. S. Eliot. Nuttall is sometimes cited as a serious authority—see, for instance, Chester Chapin, "Samuel Johnson and the Scottish Common Sense School," 64. Numerous critics have since claimed that Hume is a barometer of, or somehow responsible for, an intellectual climate in which the self was widely regarded as something to be shaped, a mere succession of perceptions from which identity must be fictionally extrapolated: see Braudy, "Penetration and Inpenetrability in *Clarissa*" (180–85); Spacks (1–15); Bender (35–38); Wolff (379–85). Christopher Fox (7–19) and Felicity Nussbaum (40–44) correctly note that inasmuch as personal identity was a philosophical puzzle or spiritual problem in eighteenth-century England, the terms of its debate were largely drawn not from Hume but from Locke's *Essay*.

[11] Fredric Bogel treats Johnson and Hume as responding to a similar existential crisis (*Literature and Insubstantiality* 28–31, 50–56)—as does my early *SEL* article and an essay by Toni O'Shaughnessy, "Fiction as Truth: Personal Identity in Johnson's *Life of Savage*." For Susan Manning (38–46), and subsequently for Greg Clingham (*James Boswell* 97–103), this crisis is the precipitate of Calvinist anxieties about inhabiting an inscrutable universe.

[12] Donald Livingston explains: in saying "'The mind can never exert itself in any action, which we may not comprehend under the term of *perception*' (*T* 456) . . . Hume is not saying that the actions are perceptions (in the sense of logically private mental images); he is saying, rather, that we are to understand perceptions to include actions conceived of in the common way. And because perceptions can be thought of in a physicalist context, the actions of one mind can be public to another. Hume is quite clear on this: 'So close and intimate is the correspondence of human souls that no sooner any person approaches me, then he diffuses on me all his opinions, and draws along my judgment in a greater or lesser degree' (*T* 592)" (*Hume's Philosophy of Common Life* 64).

[13] Similar points are made by Capaldi, "Hume's Theory of the Passions" 181; Livingston, *Hume's Philosophy of Common Life* 22–25; Gaarder, 272–74; Damrosch, *Fictions of Reality* 36–37. Baier later accounts for Hume's famous analysis of causation in book 1, part 3 (and later in secs. 4–5 of *ECHU*), as yet another blow against Cartesianism, arguing that Hume did not intend to deny the principle of induction but only to ground valid causal inferences in experience and not in "rationalist reason" (*A Program of Sentiments* 59).

to adduce either empirical or a priori truths from the isolated self's reflection on itself. And it sets the untenable empirical conclusions derived by the inward turn against the untenable a priori conclusions reached by Descartes. Norman Kemp Smith noted something of this fifty years ago: "In describing the self as only a 'bundle or collection' of perceptions, he is overstating his position in opposition to the equally one-sided insistence upon its supposedly simple, self-sufficing nature" (98). Who are the spokesmen for the self-presence of self, the unalterable ego, but Descartes and his followers? Hume nods in their direction at the opening of "Of Personal Identity," in a sentence that ought to cue us as to the section's polemical intentions: "There are some philosophers, who imagine we are every moment intimately conscious of what we call our SELF; that we feel its existence and its continuance in existence; and are certain, beyond the evidence of a demonstration, both of its perfect identity and simplicity" (*T* 251). In case we fail to recognize these philosophers as Cartesians, Hume spells it out in his helpful *Abstract of a Book lately Published, Entitled A Treatise of Human Nature* (1740): the author "asserts, that the soul, as far as we can conceive it, is nothing but a system or train of different perceptions"; by contrast, "*Des Cartes* maintained that thought was the essence of the mind; not this thought or that thought, but thought in general" (*T* 657).

Hume's meditations on personal identity toward the end of book 1 have no consequences in the following books of the *Treatise,* in which Hume insists that a sense of self is always intensely present to our consciousness (see, e.g., *T* 317, 318, 488). Hume focuses in these later books, and throughout his later writings, on the self in its passional, social, and ethical dimensions. Indeed, book 1 of the *Treatise* is something of a self-consuming artifact within Hume's larger system; its well-known final section, "Conclusion of this Book," gives us reason to believe that Hume's epistemological inquiry as a whole has been a philosophical comedy of errors. Ultimately, the significance of the section "Of Personal Identity" may lie in its contribution to Hume's moral painting of the dangers of solitude.

At the start of his "Conclusion," Hume pictures himself as one who has been driven on, unreflectively, by the calm passion of curiosity—but then, his solitary, inward reasonings on the nature of understanding usher in melancholy and despair, above all feelings of social isolation: "I am first affrighted and confounded with that forelorn solitude, in which I am plac'd in my philosophy, and fancy myself some strange uncouth monster, who not being able to mingle and unite in society, has been expell'd from all human commerce, and left utterly abandon'd and disconsolate" (*T* 264).[14] Such is the result of the inward turn in philosophy: "When I

[14] Sensitive to the tone of the opening passage of the "Conclusion," John Richetti writes of its "persona who begins in clowning mock terror and isolation and passes gradually to a par-

turn my eye inward, I find nothing but doubt and ignorance." Rather than finding in this doubt a Cartesian proof for one's transcendent ego, Hume finds only the possibility of limitless error:

> For with what confidence can I venture upon such bold enterprizes, when be-side those numberless infirmities peculiar to myself, I find so many which are common to human nature? Can I be sure, that in leaving all established opin-ions I am following truth; and by what criterion shall I distinguish her, even if fortune shou'd at last guide me on her foot-steps? After the most accurate and exact of my reasonings, I can give no reason why I shou'd assent to it; and feel nothing but a *strong* propensity to consider objects *strongly* in that view, under which they appear to me. (265)

At the impasse of abstract reasoning lies the assurance of feeling, pro-pensity, nature. And the heart is fortified through social intercourse:

> Most fortunately it happens, that since reason is incapable of dispelling these clouds, nature herself suffices to that purpose, and cures me of this philo-sophical melancholy and delirium, either by relaxing this bent of mind, or by some avocation, and lively impression of my senses, which obliterate all these chimeras. I dine, I play a game of back-gammon, I converse, am merry with my friends; and when after three or four hour's amusement, I wou'd return to these speculations, they appear so cold, and strain'd, and ridiculous, that I cannot find in my heart to enter them any farther.

The social instincts prove salvational. The narrator here—it feels odd by now to identify the speaker with Hume in any simple way—is saved by "my natural propensity, and the course of my animal spirits and passions" (269).

Salvation, moreover, brings with it new knowledge: the speaker comes to recognize the motivating force of the passions. Thus, when Hume's speaker returns to his study, he is now intensely aware that "curiosity," "concern . . . for the condition of the learned world," and "ambition . . . of acquiring a name" propel him to do so (270–71). What these passions specifically propel him to do is to theorize his salvational experience by writing about humans as natural and social beings in books 2 and 3 of the *Treatise,* and most all of his subsequent work. His task is now to discover and delineate "those several passions and inclinations, which actuate and govern me" (271), and in doing so, to replace "superstition," which can

---

alyzing crisis. . . . But this paralysis is resolved abruptly by the 'natural' cycle that returns him to social distraction. . . . The 'Conclusion' rehearses in its modulation from melodrama to comedy the plot of Hume's thought: the displacement of philosophy by philosophical writ-ing, which is not truly skeptical as such but is a literary deployment of skepticism to place thought in psychological and moral reality" (227–28).

"disturb" society, with mild and calm philosophy (271–72). No less important, Hume here and hereafter emphasizes—once again, against Descartes—that doing philosophy involves *writing* as more than just a transparent medium of thought; alone in a study, writing is something an embodied self does, a time-bound activity inseparable not only from thinking, but from the broader story of one's own life.[15]

Hume would probably not be surprised by the idealist misreading of the *Treatise* that has flourished among literary circles in recent years; he lived to see its roots first in the cabal at Edinburgh that opposed his appointment to a chair of moral philosophy in 1745, and later in James Beattie's very purple *An Essay on the Nature and Immutability of Truth; In Opposition to Sophistry and Scepticism* (1770). Beattie contends that Hume's metaphysics promote universal scepticism, atheism, and through sapping the foundations of natural law, anarchy. Johnson was well disposed to Beattie's Christian principles, if not necessarily his philosophy: "Beattie's book is, I believe, every day more liked; at least, I like it more, as I look more upon it" (letter to Boswell, August 1772, *Life of Johnson* 2:201–02).[16] In 1773, Joshua Reynolds painted a heroic portrait of Beattie that shows him serenely holding [*An Essay on*] *Truth* in his hands; in the left portion of the canvas, three shadowy figures, typically thought to include a thin Voltaire and a broad-backed Hume, are being expelled by a winged Genius, presumably the Spirit of Truth.[17]

Largely because of Beattie's popular caricature of the *Treatise*, Hume formally disowned the work toward the end of his life. In a letter of October 1775 to his London printer, William Strahan, Hume gave instructions to have published an advertisement disowning the *Treatise*, remarking, "It is a compleat Answer to Dr. Reid and to that bigotted silly Fellow, Beattie"

[15] As Hassan Melehy argues, Descartes sought to obviate not only the experiential foundation of knowledge but also the foundation of knowledge in writing; Descartes sought to define his work as philosophy and *not* as literature.

[16] Boswell reports Johnson's even grander claims for Beattie's refutation of Hume's metaphysics: see *Life of Johnson*, 2:497; 5:273–74 (on Beattie having successfully "confuted" Hume). Be this as it may, Chester Chapin's attempt to link Johnson via Beattie to the so-called "Scottish Common Sense School" is problematic at best. According to Chapin, when in 1763 Johnson "refutes" Berkeley by kicking a stone (*Life of Johnson* 1:471) his implicit argument is congruent with Beattie's formulation of "common sense": that "power of mind which perceives truth . . . by an instantaneous, instinctive, and irresistible impulse" ("Samuel Johnson and the Scottish Common Sense School" 56). The central flaw of Chapin's argument is its assumption that there *is* a "Scottish common sense school" in Johnson's lifetime. Historically, this "school" only begins in the early nineteenth century, with Dugald Stewart's serious philosophical development of Reid's critique of the eighteenth-century way of ideas (James Somerville, 63, 145–49, 333–36). Since Johnson kicked the stone seven years before even Beattie published, Douglas Lane Patey makes a plausible case for Johnson's having in mind David Hartley's *Observations on Man* (1749), a work that emphasizes the importance of touch and muscular effort in our knowledge of the external world.

[17] Reynold's *The Triumph of Truth* is discussed by Edgar Wind, 29–30.

(*HL* 2 : 301).[18] The advertisement, prefixed to editions of Hume's *Enquiries* through the Green and Grose edition of 1874–75, reads:

> Most of the principles, and reasonings, contained in this volume, were pub-
> lished in a work of three volumes, called *A Treatise of Human Nature:* A work
> which the Author had projected before he left College, and which he wrote
> and published not long after. But not finding it successful, he was sensible of
> his error in going to the press too early, and he cast the whole anew in the fol-
> lowing pieces, where some negligences in his former reasoning and more
> in the expression are, he hopes, corrected. Yet several writers, who have
> honoured the Author's Philosophy with answers, have taken care to direct all
> their batteries against that juvenile work, which the Author never acknowl-
> edged, and have affected to triumph in any advantages, which, they imag-
> ined, they had obtained over it . . . Henceforth, the Author desires, that the
> following Pieces may alone be regarded as containing his philosophical sen-
> timents and principles. (*Life of Hume* 582)

But careful readers did not need to wait until Hume's advertisement of 1775 to know Hume's opinion of the section "Of Personal Identity." Hume sought in the *Treatise* itself to disabuse readers of the notion that he *en-dorsed* the Heraclitan account of identity he there sketches. In an appen-dix note to this section, originally attached to the separately published book 3 of the *Treatise* (1740), Hume avers that his account of mind as a succession of distinct but causally related perceptions is "very defective." (Philosophers indeed continue to elaborate on its defects.) [19] "For my part, I must plead the privilege of a sceptic, and confess, that this difficulty is too hard for my understanding" (*T* 635–36). But Hume knew that not all readers of the *Treatise* would have access to an appendix added to its sec-ond volume, which sold still worse than the first. Hume thus reiterates its point in his *Letter from a Gentleman to his Friend in Edinburgh* (1745), where he emphasizes that the "identity crisis" of the sceptical self as expressed in book 1 of the *Treatise* and quoted out of context by detractors at the Uni-versity of Edinburgh (4–8) is the effect of "*Philosophical Melancholy and Delusion*" (20).

---

[18] James Somerville offers a detailed investigation into the circumstances surrounding Hume's letter to Strahan—and a powerful reminder that Hume did not fail to distinguish between Reid, whom he respected (without fully understanding the nature of his critique), and Beattie, to whom no philosophical respect is due.

[19] Wittgenstein and ordinary language philosophy have inspired many a critique of Hume's section on personal identity: see my bibliography for Godfrey Vesey; Terence Penelhum ("Hume on Personal Identity"); R. T. Herbert. Annette Baier, by contrast, strives to give a fa-vorable account of Hume's section on personal identity, arguing that Hume implicitly antic-ipates the solutions of later philosophers, including Penelhum, to the problems he poses (*A Progress of Sentiments* 101–28, 136–38).

III. Toward Final Ends

Rasselas and Hume's *Treatise* are built in crucial ways on consonant themes, perhaps *the* characteristic themes of their historical moment: trust in observation and common sense, in tempered passions and equable converse, in an understanding based more on narrative than on intuition or deduction. Johnson bequeathed these themes to novelists—themselves properly "moral writers," in Johnson's estimation—from Charlotte Lennox's *The Female Quixote* (1752), the climactic chapters of which may have been penned by Johnson, to Jane Austen's *Sense and Sensibility* (1811) and Walter Scott's *Waverley* (1814). In all these stories, the protagonist is led by a passionate imagination into quixotic or "romantic" gulfs and is shocked by crisis back to a shared sense of social reality and moral duty.

What we ought not miss is that each tale equates the proper way of knowing not only with truth (or a reasonable approximation of it), but more important still, with the true end of human life—*happiness*. In *Rasselas,* we find this most clearly illustrated in the episode in which Imlac and company meet a very deluded and very unhappy Egyptian astronomer. When first we encounter him, he fully believes that he has possessed for five years "the regulation of weather, and the distribution of the seasons: the sun has listened to my dictates, and passed from tropick to tropick by my direction." He has, however, been miserable—"far less happy than before"—because he has not had one person to share the secret of his powers, or to succeed to those powers in his absence; hence he is relieved to make the acquaintance of the learned and benevolent Imlac, whose friendship he considers "the greatest blessing of my life" (*Rasselas* 144–46).

This poor soul has considered himself the regulator of the weather ever since the moment when he thought of rain and rain came (a simple *post hoc ergo propter hoc* fallacy). He persists in his conviction, however, only as long as he remains sequestered from society. Consequently, he is brought about to commonsense views about the weather—and his place in the cosmos, generally—by talking with other people. Imlac first befriends the astronomer, but it is, significantly, Rasselas's sister, the princess Nekayah, and her servant Pekuah who succeed in reintegrating him into society. On their first meeting, the "ease and elegance" of Pekuah's conversation "took possession of his heart"; the women thereafter receive him at Imlac's house, where "he began gradually to delight in sublunary pleasures . . . [and] laboured to recommend himself by assiduity and compliance." Nature, the heart, and an Addisonian ideal of society all prove salvational. Cured by these, the astronomer attributes his former melancholy delusion to having "passed my time in study without experience" (158–61).

The episode of the astronomer reads like a gloss on an exemplum, itself borrowed from Latin Stoic literature,[20] that Hume offers in his *Treatise:* "A perfect solitude is, perhaps, the greatest punishment we can suffer. . . . Let all the powers and elements of nature conspire to serve and obey one man: Let the sun rise and set at his command: The seas and rivers roll at he pleases . . . He will still be miserable, till you give him some one person at least, with whom he may share his happiness, and whose esteem and friendship he may enjoy" (363). The only happiness is a shared happiness. But of what other than mutuality does happiness consist?

[20] Hume's and Johnson's ultimate source for the notion of the native sociability of man lies in ancient Stoic doctrine, probably as filtered through Cicero's dialogues. The interlocutor Cato elaborates on the Stoic position in Cicero's *De Finibus* III.xx: "And the fact that no one would care to pass his life alone in a desert, even though supplied with pleasures in unbounded profusion, readily shows that we are born for society and intercourse." Hugo Grotius revived this Stoic doctrine in his *De Iure Belli ac Pacis* (1625), a work that was translated into English by Basil Kennet during the time that Hume was completing his *Treatise* (1738). See also Pope's *An Essay on Man* (1734): "Abstract what others feel, what others think, / All pleasures sicken, and all glories sink" (4:45–46).

CHAPTER THREE

Happiness

In the *Life of Johnson*, Boswell confronts his excitable mentor with an opinion about happiness imputed to Hume. Boswell (wrongly) maintains that for Hume "all who are happy are equally happy"—and Johnson duly criticizes this philosophical position. It is odd that this exchange should be slighted in modern commentary—as far as I know, it has never received critical attention—as we tend in general to acknowledge the centrality of happiness to eighteenth-century philosophical and political thought.[1] As I hope to show in this chapter, Johnson's and Hume's respective ideas concerning the nature of *secular* happiness, when set in the context of their own writings and not of Boswell's biography, are largely the same.[2] Boswell introduces Hume's alleged opinions on happiness in order to provide an occasion for Johnson to refute not only the scepticism and irreligion, but also the supposed leveling effect, of modern Whiggish philosophy.[3] Yet Hume was no more a leveler than Johnson—or a Greek philosopher.

[1] In *L'Idée du Bonheur . . . au XVIIIe Siècle,* Robert Mauzi amply proves his claim that "Until the Kantian revolution, all reflections on the nature of man and the legitimate ends of his action reposed on this postulate: *man is made to be happy.* Christians, men of fashion and philosophers of the seventeenth and eighteenth centuries agreed on this, even if the word *happiness* appears in very different contexts" (80).

[2] In *The Pursuit of Happiness* Peter Quennell addresses both Johnson and Hume as men who similarly maintain that happiness, despite its elusiveness, is the wise man's duty (15, 24 [Johnson], 46 [Hume]). Quennell's delightful book, however, properly belongs more to the "conversible" than to the "learned" world.

[3] Boswell records for 21 July 1763, Johnson's disdain for "the levelling doctrine": "Sir, your levellers wish to level *down* as far as themselves; but they cannot bear levelling *up* to themselves" (*Life of Johnson* 1:448). Johnson's particular target here is Catherine Macaulay, later dubbed by Burke "our republican virago," who began publishing her anti-Humean *History of England* in 1763.

The Passion for Happiness

I. Happiness Is in the Eye of the Beheld

Boswell records this conversation from February 1766:

> I mentioned Hume's notion, that all who are happy are equally happy; a little miss with a new gown at a dancing school ball, a general at the head of a victorious army, and an orator, after having made an eloquent speech in a great assembly. JOHNSON. 'Sir, that all who are happy, are equally happy, is not true. A peasant and a philosopher may be equally *satisfied*, but not equally *happy*. Happiness consists in the multiplicity of agreeable consciousness. A peasant has not capacity for having equal happiness with a philosopher.' (*Life of Johnson* 2:9)

The exchange between Hume and Johnson that Boswell here stages raises a number of crucial questions that, when answered, will allow us to see that the two men's opposition on the question of happiness is far less thorough than it may at first appear to be.

The first question is, Where does "Hume's notion, that all who are happy are equally happy," come from? The probable answer is that Boswell is recalling a passage from Hume's 1742 essay, "The Sceptic." This piece is interesting, among other reasons, for not being in Hume's own voice—it is, rather, an extended prosopopoeia in which an exemplary Sceptic speaks his opinions. It is the concluding movement of a quartet in which Hume renders, in the voices of four separate speakers, the respective sentiments of the four main schools of Hellenistic philosophy: "The Epicurean," "The Stoic," "The Platonist," "The Sceptic." Hume offers in a footnote to the four essays that his intention is "to deliver the sentiments of sects, that naturally form themselves in the world, and entertain different ideas of human life and of happiness" (*Essays* 138n.). Those differing ideas are orchestrated contrapuntally: the Epicurean professes a life of successive pleasures, while the Stoic dedicates himself to contrastive principles (industry vs. indolence, virtue vs. fortune, fame vs. death); the Platonist directs his own life toward the One, while the Sceptic wryly observes the heterogeneous lives of others. Here, then, is the Sceptic delivering his sceptical reflections on the pursuit of happiness:

> [I]t is not from the value or worth of the object, which any person pursues, that we can determine his enjoyment, but merely from the passion with which he pursues it, and the success which he meets with in his pursuit. Objects have absolutely no worth or value in themselves. They derive their worth merely from the passion. If that be strong, and steady, and successful, the person is happy. It cannot reasonably be doubted, but a little miss, dressed in a new gown for a dancing-school ball, receives as compleat enjoyment as the greatest orator, who triumphs in the splendor of his eloquence, while he governs the passions and resolutions of a numerous assembly. (*Essays* 166)

Note that in evoking this passage Boswell has made three mistakes—or has thrice misled Johnson. First, he uncritically identifies its speaker with Hume. Boswell is certainly not the last to do so;[4] however, I believe the identification to be mistaken. I will suggest below that Hume's ethical position, taken all in all, more closely approximates that of his Stoic—as does Johnson's. (Indeed, even Hume's Sceptic admits that the Stoic eudaimonia is best; he doubts only that we can—all of us, all of the time—steadily pursue it.)

Second, Boswell adds to the Sceptic's antithetically balanced examples of the little miss's happiness and that of the greatest orator a tertium quid: the glee of "a general at the head of a victorious army." While this detail could conceivably be attributed to mistaken recollection, it is more likely that Boswell, knowing Johnson's tendency to satirize both martial heroism (see, for example, the original *Idler* no. 22) and the unreasonable praise bestowed upon victorious "projectors" such as Alexander and Caesar (*The Adventurer* no. 99), injects it deliberately, to goad Johnson to a brilliant conversational victory over "Hume"—properly, the Sceptic.

Finally, Boswell misrepresents the Sceptic's argument. The Sceptic does not hold that "all who are happy are equally happy"—for happiness, in the Sceptic's model, presumably admits of degree in proportion to the strength, steadiness, and success of the passion that pursues its object. The little miss at a dancing-school ball and the great orator in an assembly will be equally happy only assuming that the two possess roughly the same sensibility or, as Hume elsewhere describes it, "delicacy of passion" (*Essays* 3–8).

The Sceptic apparently assumes this equality of sensibility between the little miss and the orator. Both, presumably, have pursued their respective objects of desire—the admiration of the dancing school, the applause of the assembly—with equivalent strength and steadiness. Their passions have, moreover, both been *appropriate* ones: for as the Sceptic proceeds to explain, happiness will crown only passions that are "neither . . . too violent nor too remiss"; that are "benign and social, not rough and fierce" (*Essays* 167). Finally, both the little miss and the orator have, in the instant the Sceptic imagines, attained their objects with suitable éclat. Yet we need observe that happiness is here represented as a process as well as an attainment, an arc as well as an apogee. The person who pursues his or her object with the appropriate passion is happy in, or enjoys, the pursuit; but when the object pursued is attained, the person feels for a moment—before pursuit begins anew—a more concentrated or a "complete" enjoyment that appears, in both the case of the little miss and the great orator, as a surge of self-approval.

[4] The identification is assumed by Mossner, *Life of Hume* 141; Mauzi, 539–42; Box, *Suasive Art of David Hume* 136–37.

The object of both the little miss's and the great orator's pursuit is basically the same: it is a flush of joy in being seen approvingly *by others*. In a mirror version of the famously bleak pronouncement of Sartre's *Huis Clos*—"L'enfer, c'est les autres"—the Sceptic maintains that a necessary condition of our happiness is that it is reflected back to us in the agreeable eyes of others. In this, at least, the Sceptic and Hume are one. Hume bases his entire moral theory on the presence of a more or less disinterested spectator; in Charlotte Brown's formulation, it is "a theory that takes the central moral concepts to be those used by spectators in the assessment of character traits and motives—the concepts of praise and blame, approbation and condemnation, respect and contempt" (20–21). Brown proceeds to explain how Hume's spectator theory accommodates an account of virtuous agency: "[W]e will be loveable in our own eyes only if we are or would be morally loveable in the eyes of others. . . . According to Hume, being morally loveable in our own eyes is an important ingredient of happiness" (30).[5]

The intrinsically social nature of happiness—specifically, the notion that we will be estimable in our own eyes only if we are so in those of others— is also a central theme of Johnson's. Consider again Johnson's episode of the learned astronomer in *Rasselas* (chaps. 40–46): once cured of the delusions he nursed in solitude, he regrets having hitherto "missed the endearing elegance of female friendship, and the happy commerce of domestick tenderness" (161). "No man is so much abstracted from common life," Johnson elsewhere avers, "as not to feel a particular pleasure from the regard of the female world" (*Rambler* 3:52). Hume, in his deathbed autobiography, lays claim to precisely the "female friendship" that the astronomer lacked in order to prove that his life was a happy one: "My company was not unacceptable to the young and careless, as well as to the studious and literary; and as I took a particular pleasure in the company of modest women, I had no reason to be displeased with the reception I met with from them" ("My Own Life," *Essays* xl–xli). One hears much these days, in cinema studies and elsewhere, about "the male gaze," but for the eighteenth-century man of letters, true excitement was not to be found in watching, but in being beheld.

The eighteenth-century man of letters generalized his experience into a rule: all seek the particular pleasure of social love and approval, and all do so within the broader pursuit of happiness. The aim of human happi-

---

[5] Cf. Terence Penelhum: for Hume, others are "the co-creators of my self-image, and to understand the character of my self-concern it is necessary to take the measure of the society of which I am a member"; the self is a "social construction" ("Hume's Moral Psychology" 143). Hume's successor in a spectatorial theory of morals was Adam Smith; for a perceptive reading of Smith's negotiations with the anxieties entailed by the quest for public approval, see Marshall, *The Figure of Theater* 185–92.

ness is of course central to Hume's moral enterprise; it bears remarking that the topic is no less central to Johnson. In his 1739 annotations to Crousaz's *Commentary* on Pope's *Essay on Man,* Johnson writes on the notion of "a Ruling Passion": "I am conscious of none but the general desire of happiness" (*Major Works* 92). In a work published eighteen years later, his review of Soame Jenyns's *A Free Inquiry into the Nature and Origin of Evil* published in the *Literary Magazine* (1757), Johnson approves of little else in Jenyns save for his "opinion of the value and importance of happiness," which he then quotes: "Happiness is the only thing of real value in existence" (*Major Works* 530). Johnson's general claim in his periodical essays is that although there is only in an afterlife with God "total happiness" (*Rambler* 3:151)[6]—and hence only religious hope can appease "decaying man" (3:367)—a "reasonable being" this side of the deathbed nonetheless has in his power "a great part . . . of his present happiness" (3:159).

II. The Dialectic of Happiness

As well as agreeing on the social nature of happiness, Johnson, the Sceptic, and Hume could agree on the *dialectical* nature of happiness, or the notion that happiness is alternately kinetic and static. Happiness may be realized in signal moments (such as the "complete enjoyment" of the orator in his triumph), but it requires and indeed, in what may appear a paradox, also consists of a life that pursues happiness or objects with which happiness may be associated (approbation, fame, tranquillity, riches, a fine suit of clothes, or the tankards so readily tilted in Hogarth's "Beer Street").

This dialectical understanding of happiness was first elaborated in the modern era by Hobbes, who writes in part 1 of *Leviathan,* "Felicity is a continual progress of the desire from one object to another; the attaining of the former being still but the way to the latter. The cause whereof is that the object of man's desire is not to enjoy once only and for one instant of time, but to assure forever the way of his future desire" (1.11). In Hobbes's definition, happiness *is* a pursuit, or "progress," and attainment simply the punctuation that relieves a life of flow. Hobbes sets up his model of happiness in opposition to all classical models, which present the happy life as

---

[6] Johnson resists the evangelical definition of "happiness" *in this life* as a consciousness of one's personal salvation through God's grace, an effect of the type of "conscious" conversion Johnson never had. Johnson was encouraged to pursue this happiness by his evangelical friend Ms. Hill Boothby in the early 1750s. "We are all alike bad, my dear friend," Boothby wrote to Johnson, "till a change is wrought upon us, not by our own reasoning, but by the same Divine Power, who first created, and pronounced all he had made, *very good.* . . . Is this enthusiasm? Indeed it is truth: and, I trust, you will some time be sure it is so; and then, and not till then, will you be happy, as I ardently wish you" (quoted with valuable commentary by Chester Chapin, *Religious Thought* 61–62).

a more or less stable *attainment,* and one that would be substantively the same for every happy person. Hobbes dismisses such a simple teleology: "But for an utmost end, in which the ancient philosophers have placed felicity, and have disputed much concerning the way thereto, there is no such thing in this world, nor way to it, more than to Utopia: for while we live, we have desires, and desire presupposeth a farther end" (*Human Nature,* chap. 7, para. 6).

Locke basically concurs with Hobbes that happiness is a continuous course of pursuit and pause; Locke, however, stresses the stops. He writes, "For who is content is happy. But as soon as any new uneasiness [which, for Locke, is coextensive with "desire"] comes in, this Happiness is disturb'd, and we are set afresh on work in the pursuit of Happiness." This pursuit does not, for Locke as for Hobbes, negate the possibility of a basal or cumulative happiness—as Locke writes, in pursuit we seek "the making *or increase* of our Happiness" (*An Essay concerning Human Understanding* 273, emphasis mine).[7]

Johnson's own writings includes echoes of both Hobbes and Locke on happiness. Johnson is at his most Hobbesian in his comment to Boswell, "Life is a progress from want to want, not from enjoyment to enjoyment" (*Life of Johnson* 3:53). With Hobbes, Johnson sometimes thinks of happiness as a phenomenological rather than an ethical category. He then treats happiness as precisely that which eludes present consciousness. Does anyone feel happy in the moment? "Never," quoth Johnson, "but when he is drunk" (*Life of Johnson* 2:351). Unless incapacitated by drink, humans feel the ceaseless propulsion of desire and aversion. Boswell thought the point worth pursuing:

'Sir, you observed one day at General Oglethorpe's, that a man is never happy for the present, but when he is drunk. Will you not add,—or, when driving rapidly in a post-chaise?' JOHNSON. 'No, Sir, you are driving rapidly *from* something, or *to* something.' (*Life of Johnson* 3:5)

At moments, Johnson figures happiness as an ever-receding point, a horizon always out of reach. His most forceful expression of this comes in *Adventurer* no. 69: "I am afraid, every man that recollects his hopes, must confess his disappointment, and own, that day has glided unprofitably after day, and that he is still at the same distance from the point of happiness" (2:391).

Johnson tended, however, to keep his Hobbesian phenomenology in the closet. He considered Hobbes too morally dangerous a source when

---

[7] Locke equates "uneasiness" with "desire" on p. 251, and passim.

it came to compiling quotations for his *Dictionary;*[8] the more respectable Locke is preeminently the philosopher of Johnson's illustrative quotations. Accordingly, one of his illustrations of "happiness" comes from Locke's extended discussion of it, conflating some of the language (or working with a different edition) of the following passage: "[T]he various and contrary choices, that Men make in the World, do not argue, that they do not all pursue Good; but that the same thing is not good to every Man alike. This variety of pursuits shews, that every one does not place his happiness in the same thing, or chuse the same way to it" (268).

Locke may sound like an ethical relativist here, but the impression is misleading. With all other late-seventeenth- and eighteenth-century moralists, he assumed that there are uniform and necessary conditions for happiness—appropriate passions, virtue, health, belonging, a moderately commodious life ("competence," as Pope calls it in epistle 4 of *An Essay on Man*). Locke differs from Aristotle only in allowing for a wider range of pursuits within the happy life, of a broader variety of experiential goods (pleasure, ease, activity, thrills) as well as material goods. Locke also emphasizes, as a necessary condition of happiness, the intention to pursue.

In either Locke's or Hobbes's notion of happiness as varied pursuit, attainment, and pursuit, readers of a materialist bent may be apt to see the effect of a burgeoning marketplace of objects and services, all of them needing homes and clients. Such readers might adduce for support Johnson's anatomy of happiness and urban economic activity, *The Adventurer* no. 67. Here, Johnson suggests the myriad of different activities and commodities that London—or any "great city"—makes available to ready money, and maintains that however superfluous or useless any good may at first seem, its manufacture, sale, purchase, and potential enjoyment all contribute to "the happiness of life":

> But that the happiness of man may still remain imperfect, as wants in this place are easily supplied, new wants likewise are easily created: every man, in surveying the shops of London, sees numberless instruments and conveniences, of which, while he did not know them, he never felt the need; and yet, when use has made them familiar, wonders how life could be supported without them. Thus it comes to pass, that our desires always increase with our

---

[8] Thomas Tyers (1726–87) reports Johnson as saying: "When I published my Dictionary, I might have quoted *Hobbes* as an authority in language, as well as many other writers of his time: but I scorned, sir, to quote him at all; because I did not like his principles" (*Early Biographies* 82). According to both Tyers and Boswell (*Tour* 238–39), Johnson was apt to lump Hobbes and Hume together—ironically, as Hume entirely disapproved of Hobbes: "Hobbes's politics are fitted only to promote tyranny, and his ethics to encourage licentiousness. Though an enemy to religion, he partakes nothing of the spirit of scepticism; but is as positive and dogmatical as if human reason, and his reason in particular, could attain a thorough conviction in these subjects" (*History* 6:153).

possessions; the knowledge that something remains yet unenjoyed, impairs our enjoyment of the good before us.

Johnson's passage is, in effect, a materialist gloss on Hobbes's and Locke's definitions of happiness, rooting their metaphysics in the realities of the market. That happiness is a progress of desire from one object to another reflects and is finally founded on an ever-increasing number of manufactures and services in the world. Happiness needs to be "imperfect"—to oscillate between pursuit and attainment—in order to accommodate ever new objects and thereby allow all who "will diligently labour, in whatever occupation," to "lie down every night with the pleasing consciousness, of having contributed something to the happiness of life" (384–87).

"In a capitalist society, or as Hume would have said a 'commercial society,' economic growth constantly expands the frontier of necessity. The luxuries of the few gradually become the necessities of all." These lines are from Michael Ignatieff's fine essay on the history of changing Western attitudes toward, and conceptions of what qualify as, human needs (93). Ignatieff finds Hume and Adam Smith singularly important in announcing a modern ideology that could vindicate "this blind upward spiral of needs" (110)—he might have added, as a precursor in all but tone, Bernard Mandeville.[9] Yet we have seen that Johnson was scarcely less complicit in the Enlightenment project of political economy. For Johnson, commodities comprise a real good—if not an unmixed one.

Johnson, unlike Hume, partially sympathizes with the man of few needs, be he ancient sage or Christian saint. Thus, as a counterpoint within the commercial celebration of *Adventurer* no. 67 Johnson culls from Diogenes Laertius's *Lives of Eminent Philosophers* the quip from Socrates as he passed through a fair at Athens: "[H]ow many things are here that I do not want!" However, although Johnson intermittently seeks to moderate our desire for material things, he nonetheless accepts that desire as a primary motive in life. He does so even in his ghostwritten sermons:

The desire of happiness is inseparable from a rational being. . . . He that desires happiness must necessarily desire the means of happiness, must wish to appropriate, and accumulate, whatever may satisfy his desires. It is not sufficient to be without want. He will try to place himself beyond the fear of want; and endeavour to provide future gratifications for future wishes, and lay up in store future provisions for future necessities. (*Sermons* 194)

Pursuing the means of happiness becomes an end in itself: it, if anything, substitutes for the utmost end in which the ancient philosophers

[9] E. J. Hundert aptly characterizes Mandeville's vision of man as one of "a consuming and displaying animal, a creature whose boundless appetites are systematically directed by the desire for esteem to an expanding world of available goods" (151–52).

placed felicity. Our happiness is such that our endeavors toward it largely compose it. As Johnson writes in *Adventurer* no. 111, closely paraphrasing Locke: "[L]ife affords no higher pleasure, than that of surmounting difficulties, passing from one step of success to another, forming new wishes and seeing them gratified. He that labours in any great or laudable undertaking . . . is always moving to a certain end, and when he has attained it, an end more distant invites him to a new persuit" (454–55). In the pursuit and occasional satisfaction of suitable desires lies happiness.

Hume makes precisely the same point in his essay "Of Refinement in the Arts" (originally titled "Of Luxury"): "In times when industry and the arts flourish, men are kept in perpetual occupation, and enjoy, as their reward, the occupation itself, as well as those pleasures which are the fruit of their labour" (*Essays* 270). However, in his *Enquiry concerning the Principles of Morals* Hume speaks at one point as though, in the progress of desire (or "need"), satisfaction or pleasure was an *ever*-receding horizon:

> All men, it is allowed, are equally desirous of happiness; but few are successful in the pursuit: One considerable cause is the want of strength of mind, which might enable them to resist the temptation of present ease or pleasure, and carry them forward in the search of more distant profit and enjoyment. . . . A man of strong and determined temper adheres tenaciously to his general resolutions, and is neither seduced by the allurements of pleasure, nor terrified by the menaces of pain, but keeps still in view those distant pursuits, by which he, at once, ensures his happiness and his honour. (239–40)

"Keeps *still* in view those distant pursuits": simple logic requires that an ever-distant prospect can never be attained. One insures one's happiness, paradoxically, by persistently locating one's happiness in the offing.[10] This language of pursuit is more rigorous than that earlier expressed through the persona of "The Sceptic"—indeed, speaking here in his own voice, Hume echoes his characterization of "The Stoic," who pursues the "GLORY" or "immortal fame" afforded a life of virtue: "Elevated by so sublime a prize, the man of virtue looks down with contempt on all the allurements of pleasure, and all the menaces of danger" (*Essays* 153–54).

The prize of Hume's Stoic is to be regarded by others beyond his death with the same esteem he regarded himself in life, when imagining himself as seen through the eyes of others. Hume's Stoic—and Hume's own moral theory—subscribes to a fundamental tenet of Cicero's "decorum": the importance of seeing ourselves as others would (*De Officiis* 1.147). If there is a tension or contradiction in Hume's essay between basing the Stoic's

---

[10] Hume's happy man here embodies a secularized version of the Protestant asceticism and "rational bourgeois economic life" analyzed by Max Weber in *The Protestant Ethic and the Spirit of Capitalism* (170–74).

happiness on a bedrock of inner conviction and, in the glance toward fame, basing it upon the winds of external reputation, this tension simply reproduces an ambivalence found in Cicero's own portrait of the Roman Stoic.[11]

A second complication of Hume's essay lies in its portrayal of the Stoic as a man of exquisite feeling. The Stoic's quest for fame may require endlessly deferring (some) pleasures, but it turns out that far better pleasures remain: notwithstanding his elevated ambition, the Stoic is by no means austere. "He feels too strongly the charm of the social affections ever to counteract so sweet, so natural, so virtuous a propensity. Even when, bathed in tears, he laments the miseries of human race, of his country, of his friends, and unable to give succour, can only relieve them by compassion; he yet rejoices in the generous disposition, and feels a satisfaction superior to that of the most indulged sense" (151). The arduous pursuit of happiness is attended with a similar pleasure in Hume's *Enquiry,* where an "agreeable" state of mind accompanies "the enlarged virtues of humanity, generosity, [and] beneficence":

> [T]he immediate feeling of benevolence and friendship, humanity and kindness, is sweet, smooth, and agreeable, independent of all fortune and accidents. These virtues are besides attended with a pleasing consciousness or remembrance, and keep us in humour with ourselves as well as others; while we retain the agreeable reflection of having done our part towards mankind and society. . . . What other passion is there where we shall find so many advantages united; an agreeable sentiment, a pleasing consciousness, a good reputation? . . . Inward peace of mind, consciousness of integrity, a satisfactory review of our own conduct; these are circumstances, very requisite to happiness, and will be cherished and cultivated by every honest man, who feels the importance of them. (282–83)

Hume, in his most Shaftesburian mood, presents virtue as its own reward; indeed, the virtuous life alone affords pleasures that are "very requisite to happiness." Virtue demands no real self-denial, but offers instead present satisfaction, pleasing recollection, and distant pursuits. Virtue offers—to use Johnson's phrase—"a multiplicity of agreeable consciousness."

III. The Multiplicity of Agreeable Consciousness

Johnson's phrase is like a bell to toll us back to the anecdote from which we began. As we have seen, Johnson rebuts Boswell's proposal that "all who

---

[11] Geoffrey Miles expertly examines Cicero's writings—and Shakespeare's Roman characters—in light of this ambivalence: see esp. pp. 23–37.

are happy are equally happy"—an opinion erroneously attributed to Hume and based on a misreading of the Sceptic's own position. Johnson avers, to the contrary: "A peasant and a philosopher may be equally *satisfied,* but not equally *happy.*" Here, Johnson is concerned to distinguish "satisfaction" from "happiness"—in a way that the Sceptic, at least, does not distinguish "enjoyment" from "happiness." In making this distinction, Johnson harkens back in a general way to classical notions of the happy or flourishing life as the one form of life that is best for everyone, although it is not in everyone's power to attain. More specifically, Johnson appears to allude to Aristotle's argument against identifying pleasure with happiness. Aristotle notes that one can be entirely satisfied with one's life and still fail to achieve what others would recognize as "happiness," adducing the case of the mentally retarded adult—"No one would choose to live his entire life with the mentality of a child, even if he were to enjoy to the fullest possible extent what children enjoy" (*Nicomachean Ethics* 1174a 1–2).

We might say that the childish adult—or Johnson's peasant—has not the same capacity for happiness as the philosopher because happiness involves a certain caliber of rational activity. Johnson clarifies this point in a conversation from April 1778, during one of the periodic intervals in which he abstained from wine: "BOSWELL. 'I think, sir, you once said to me, that not to drink wine was a great deduction from life.' JOHNSON. 'It is a diminution of pleasure, to be sure; but I do not say a diminution of happiness. There is more happiness in being rational'" (*Life* 3:245–46). For Aristotle, of course, the objective good for a human being is a virtuous life guided by reason and graced by good fortune—this is human flourishing, and also, secondarily, subjective happiness.[12] Johnson evoked Aristotle's theory of happiness in one of his *Dictionary* illustrations of "felicity" (a word that Johnson cross-defines with "happiness"): in the following quotation from Milton's *Paradise Regained,* book 4, Christ speaks, disapprovingly, of Aristotle's ethics:

> Others in virtue plac'd *felicity;*
> But virtues join'd with riches and long life . . .
> [ll. 297–98]

We may assume that Johnson would have been less disdainful than Milton's Christ of including material prosperity and good fortune as necessary conditions for happiness in this world.

Yet the definition of "happiness" that Johnson coins in his exchange with Boswell—and Boswell's Hume—is still not quite Aristotelian. It does

---

[12] Deal Hudson stresses that the eudaimonistic view of happiness—according to which the claim to happiness is subject to third-personal appraisal—is not incompatible with a subjective view of happiness as a desirable mental state (61–64).

not quite accord with Aristotle's stress on the objective conditions of happiness. For Aristotle, happiness is chiefly if not wholly a way of life; for Johnson it is largely—although, given its link to virtue, not wholly—a reaction to a way of life, a subjective attitude toward one's life. As Johnson points out in *The Rambler* no. 150, "[N]o man can enjoy happiness without thinking that he enjoys it" (5:35), thereby assuming that a requisite condition of happiness is a certain state of consciousness. The assumption is not incontestable: an Aristotelian might counter with the example of a person who, though not given to thinking about it from day to day, wakes up one morning to say, "I suppose I do have a happy life." But Johnson, ever the psychologist, would inquire into what this person was thinking about during those long stretches in which happiness was not on his or her mind.

As Johnson puts it, "Happiness consists in *the multiplicity of agreeable consciousness.*" What precisely does Johnson mean by this pithy phrase? The term "agreeable" is usefully bivalent, denoting either states of consciousness that are pleasing or "agreeable" to the subsistent self, or states of consciousness that "agree" or harmonize with one another. But the "multiplicity" of which Johnson speaks appears more problematic. In light of Johnson's larger body of writings, the phrase allows for two possible interpretations: it might refer either to a *temporal* multiplicity of agreeable consciousness, or to a *spatial* or *interpersonal* multiplicity of agreeable consciousness.

In a further complication, temporal multiplicity may itself mean one of two things. It could refer to a varied succession of agreeable states, of the type exemplified in the life of Hume's "Epicurean," whose day passes from bacchic delights to the pleasures of virtue and conversation, from the delights of social company to seizing the night with his mistress Caelia (*Essays* 141–45). Johnson indeed recognizes the therapeutic value of varying one's day in the learned astronomer episode of *Rasselas:* "The sage confessed to Imlac that since he had mingled in the gay tumults of life, and divided his hours by a *succession* of amusements, he found the conviction of his authority over the skies fade gradually from his mind." (161–62, emphasis mine).

Yet Johnson's writings, as a whole, lend still more authority to a second possible meaning of a temporal "multiplicity of agreeable consciousness": the pleasurable contemplation of past, present, and future prospects. Happiness, then, would be a mental state in which all are of a piece ("agreeable") and all please. This is largely the happiness of the industrious and virtuous man Hume limns in his *Enquiry concerning the Principles of Morals,* whose present consciousness incorporates both pleasing recollections and still distant pursuits. But the prospect of a happy futurity implies for Johnson not only the happiness of pursuit, but also the otherworldly

expectations of Christian faith. Sometimes Johnson's remarks are ambigu-
ously poised between these two possible referents, as when he writes to
Boswell in July 1778, "Without asserting Stoicism, it may be said, that it
is our business to exempt ourselves as much as we can from the power of
external things. There is but one solid basis of happiness; and that is, the
reasonable hope of a happy futurity" (*Life* 3:363). At other times, Johnson recognizes—though rarely partakes in—the pure anticipation of
otherworldliness, as when Imlac observes of the monks of St. Anthony's:
"[T]heir toils are cheerful, because they consider them as acts of piety, by
which they are always advancing towards endless felicity" (*Rasselas* 165). As
a Christian, Johnson's eudaimonism is, like Augustine's, always centered
on a telos, the love of God, that is not of this world; and Boswell can occasionally entice him into speculating on what endless felicity might be like:
"Why, sir, the happiness of an unembodied spirit will consist in a consciousness of the favour of GOD, in the contemplation of truth, and in the
possession of felicitating ideas" (*Life* 2:162).[13]

But Johnson did not wholly relegate the hope of happiness to a world
elsewhere. In certain contexts, Johnson might invoke "celestial Wisdom,"
paradoxically, to "make the Happiness she does not find" (*The Vanity of
Human Wishes,* lines 367–68); in others, such as in the lines he annexed
to Goldsmith's "The Traveller," he maintains, "Our own felicity we make
or find," here and now, and we are most apt to do either in "the smooth
current of domestic joy" (lines 432–34). What else, then, might the "multiplicity of agreeable consciousness" mean for us here?

The multiplicity in question may be not (only) temporal, but spatial or
interpersonal: that is, to be happy we must see our happiness reflected in
the agreeable consciousness of others. This is the lesson, we have seen, of
both the master of the universe exemplum in Hume's *Treatise* (363), and
the mad astronomer episode in *Rasselas*. The urbane, sociable philosopher—in other words, the Enlightenment philosopher—has this lesson

[13] Nicholas Hudson associates Johnson with what he terms "Christian Epicureanism," arguing that Johnson grounds moral obligation on the principle of ultimate self-interest or
pleasure—the prospect of future private happiness (*Samuel Johnson and Eighteenth-Century
Thought* 66–72). However, it was not Epicureanism alone, but Aristotelianism and all of the
Hellenistic schools (with the possible exception of the more severe strains of Stoicism) that
counted a pleasurable mental state as a criterion, quality, or concomitant of happiness. Moreover, as Johnson observes, Epicurean pleasure is peculiar in "consist[ing] in the absence of
pain" (*The Idler* 30); the heaven of "felicitating ideas" that Johnson imagines in his exchange
with Boswell appears far removed from the idling, thoughtless life of the modern Epicurean
portrayed in *The Idler* no. 9. Epicureanism was a school of which Johnson consistently disapproved, associating it with self-indulgent, sensual indolence: see *Sermon* no. 27 (289)
and *Idler* no. 19 (59–60). Inasmuch as Hudson's notion of Christian Epicureanism simply re-
vives the hoary charge against, in C. S. Lewis's phrase, the "theological hedonism" of the
eighteenth century, it is effectively qualified by Paul Alkon's sensitive appeal to Lockean
and eighteenth-century assumptions concerning our religious *obligation* to pursue rational
happiness (54–61).

by heart. Part of the reason for Johnson's choice of a peasant as one who, as opposed to the philosopher, can never be deemed truly happy, is that the peasant, who by definition inhabits a sparsely populated rural world, cannot meet the social conditions for happiness. Johnson is elsewhere quite adamant on this point. The Indian alone in his tent may be "content," but not, relative to the urban dweller, sociable and "happy."[14] When told of an officer who had lived in "the wilds of America" and expressed his happiness "amidst the rude magnificence of Nature, with this Indian woman by my side, and this gun with which I can procure food when I want it," Johnson animadverted, "If a bull could speak, he might as well exclaim,—Here I am with this cow and this grass; what being can enjoy greater felicity?" (*Life* 2:228). As Johnson (may have) remarked to Boswell, "Why, Sir, you find no man, at all intellectual, who is willing to leave London. No, Sir, when a man is tired of London, he is tired of life; for there is in London all that life can afford" (3:178).[15] Hume, although preferring Edinburgh or Paris, concurs with Johnson's general point; he notes that it is impossible "that, when enriched with science, and possessed of a fund of conversation, [men] should be contented to remain in solitude, or live with their fellow-citizens in that distant manner, which is peculiar to ignorant and barbarous nations. They flock into cities; love to receive and communicate knowledge; to show their wit or their breeding; their taste in conversation or living, in clothes or furniture" ("Of Refinement in the Arts," *Essays* 271).

---

[14] *The Adventurer* no. 67 (388–89). Johnson published this essay in 1753; the very next year saw the publication of Rousseau's *Discourse on Inequality,* a work that turns Enlightenment orthodoxy on its head. "If these savages are as unhappy as it is claimed, by what conceivable depravity of judgement do they refuse steadfastly to civilize themselves in imitation of us and to live happily among us, whereas one reads in a thousand places that Frenchmen and other Europeans have voluntarily found refuge among these peoples, spent their whole lives there without being able to leave such a strange way of life . . . If one suggests that savages have not enlightenment enough to judge their own condition or ours, I shall reply that the judgement of happiness is less an affair of reason than of feeling" (168 [note P]).

[15] Donald Greene, in "The *Logia* of Samuel Johnson and the Quest for the Historical Johnson," argues from its absence from Boswell's journals that Johnson never spoke any version of the second and most famous of these lines on London life. Be that as it may, the comment here attributed to Johnson agrees with the general tenor of his writings on London—"after he got over the country boy's normal repulsion by the confusion of the 'big city' as recorded in *London*" (Greene, 3). As evidence, I would adduce three themes from his periodical essays: 1.) with all its tribulations—it is the peculiar site of gaming, street-fighting, seduction and betrayal, prostitution, and the incidental perversity of polite masters towards their servants— London affords the true test of virtue, and, like Milton, Johnson would not have virtue go untested (*Idler* no. 80); 2.) London is, despite those fops who wear only the "tinsel" of politeness (*Rambler* no. 147), home to "the arts of civility" and enlightened sociability (*Rambler* no. 149, par. 6, and no. 157); country conversation, by contrast, is often marred by inveterate, petty malice (*Rambler* no. 46), just as life in remote situations is marred by the violence of feuds (*Journey* 45); 3.) tellingly, while many of Johnson's country characters long, reasonably or unreasonably, for life in the city, none of his city characters find happiness in country retirement (*Rambler* no. 6 and no. 135; *Idler* no. 71; *Adventurer* no. 102).

"Multiplicity of agreeable consciousness," in all its multiple meanings, may thus afford an apt definition of "happiness" for both Johnson and Hume. By 1766—the year that Boswell brought up the topic with Johnson—Johnson and Hume basically agree on three interrelated points. First, happiness is primarily—though given its essential link to virtue, by no means wholly—an agreeable mental state. Second, happiness is not the same thing as present contentment; it can only be had by rational agents who act *in time,* steadily pursuing the goals dictated by appropriate (i.e., moderate, benign) passions, and recollecting the past effects of these passions. Third, happiness, here on earth (which is for Hume and is not for Johnson the only site of happiness), is necessarily social and is therefore facilitated by city living. It would seem preferable to live in great cities that are commercial hubs, as well as the seats of assemblies and dancing schools.

Although Hume is introduced to Johnson in the pages of Boswell's text, we need not limit to its Boswellian compass the intellectual give-and-take of two men who have both left us so many texts of their own. We must ever recall that the dialogue that Boswell staged between Johnson and Hume was motivated by his own literary-biographical aims, one of which was to present Johnson as a Hercules of Tory Anglicanism; Hume is little more, in the chiaroscuro of the *Life,* than a shade to set off the radiance of his hero. I have aimed here toward a more just representation of their respective views, and of "happiness" as part of an eighteenth-century philosophical lexicon—which is itself a continuation and transformation of an ancient Greek way of talking about life.[16]

[16] The eighteenth-century obsession with "happiness" would be eclipsed in the Romantic era by the praise of "joy," which denotes an exaltation of spirit, less a conscious way of life than a surge of emotion in the moment. "Joy" is a blessing not limited to the urbane philosopher or poet, but available—perhaps more readily—to the rural peasant. This is the "joy" constantly evoked in the poems of Blake, Wordsworth, and (less confidently) Coleridge; this is the *Freude* of Schiller and Beethoven.

CHAPTER FOUR

Reasoning with the Passions

What is the proper relationship between reason and passion within the happy or flourishing person? This is the central question of all the schools of Hellenistic philosophy, and each of Hume's "four philosophers" has his own answer. His Epicurean is a complete naturalist: "When by my will alone I can stop the blood, as it runs with impetuosity along its canals, then may I hope to change the course of my sentiments and passions" (*Essays* 140). His Stoic "proceeds in the pursuit of happiness" through the "agreeable occupation" of "the cultivating of our mind, the moderating of our passions, the enlightening of our reason" (148–49). His Platonist admires nothing but reason, as a tributary of divine reason: "it is MIND alone, which we admire" (157). Finally, his Sceptic, as we saw in the last chapter, locates happiness in the calm, social, and steady "passions and inclinations . . . *enjoy*[*ing*] their objects" (167), although unlike the other philosophers the detached Sceptic does not himself claim to pursue happiness. Indeed, the Sceptic ends on a note of bitterness we hear but occasionally in Hume's oeuvre: "In a word, human life is more governed by fortune than reason; is to be regarded more as a dull pastime than a serious occupation; and is more influenced by particular humour, than by general principles. . . . While we are reasoning concerning life, life is gone; and death, though *perhaps* they receive him differently, yet treats alike the fool and the philosopher" (180). In the words of the preacher: "And how dieth the wise man? as the fool" (Ecclesiastes 2:16).

The careful reader will find traces of the Epicurean, the Stoic, and the Sceptic throughout Hume's writings—all but the Platonist, for whom

Hume evidently has little sympathy.[1] But the chief ethic that one finds in Hume's writings—and, I will argue, in Johnson's—is the eclectic, Ciceronian brand of Stoicism Hume delineates in "The Stoic": a sociable Stoicism whose end is "the moderating of our passions, the enlightening of our reason." Duly enlightened, reason will judiciously serve the sovereign passions, to the benefit of oneself, one's community, one's nation, and perhaps still further afield.

In asserting that passions not only do but ought to impel us, both Johnson and Hume pit their classicism against a lingering Augustinian suspicion of *cupiditas* or *concupiscentia;* in their moral writings, pride, avidity, even avarice contribute to the pageant of human flourishing. Indeed, we will see that for them *caritas,* or benevolence, is no less necessary to restrain than acquisitiveness in the moral sphere in which the passions are most in need of regulation—that of justice.

I. Ciceronian Stoicism

In their theories of motivation and, as we shall see later, their notions of justice and community, Johnson and Hume draw upon topoi from Roman Stoicism—the peculiar dilution of earlier and more systematic Stoic doctrine introduced into Rome by Panaetius of Rhodes (c. 189–109 B.C.E.) during the time of Scipio Africanus the Younger. Although professedly a Stoic, Panaetius followed the school of Aristotle in denying the doctrine of Zeno of Citium (the fourth-century founder of Stoicism) that virtue is sufficient for happiness, and admitting as goods those external things— status, wealth, health—requisite to the active exercise of virtue. In fitting Stoicism to the needs of actual Roman citizens, Panaetius modeled his ethics not on the perfectly virtuous sage such as Socrates or Zeno, but rather on the *kathekon,* or "appropriate action," of the less-than-perfect person going about his or her daily business.[2]

---

[1] Hume respected Plato as a belle-lettrist rather than as a philosopher. In his *History of England,* we first meet Lady Jane Gray, whom Hume admires, "reading Plato, while the rest of the family were engaged in a party of hunting in the park"; for Hume, Plato is a laudable part of a "passion for literature and the elegant arts," especially suitable, it seems, for women readers (3:402). Hume retells Aristophanes' fable of the original androgyne from Plato's *Symposium* 189c–193d in "Of Love and Marriage," an essay very much for "the female world." Pat Rogers addresses the general neglect of Plato's philosophy in eighteenth-century Britain (Shaftesbury's *The Moralists* and the works of James "Hermes" Harris notwithstanding) in his contribution to Baldwin and Hutton's *Platonism and the English Imagination* (181–85); Michael Prince makes a strong case, however, for seeing a "Platonic revival" in the field of aesthetics, 1730–1770 (163–89). Misunderstandings of Socrates during this period are canvased in the articles of Kevin Berland.

[2] E. Vernon Arnold notes, "Thus the triumph won by Panaetius for the name of Stoicism was purchased by the sacrifice not only of its physics, but very largely of its ethics also; and

Panaetius was deemed by Cicero "almost the chief of the Stoics" (*Academica* 2.108); it was from him that Cicero adapted much of his own ethical writing, in particular *De Officiis* (*officium* being Cicero's Latin rendering of the Stoic *kathekon*). In that work and also in *De Finibus,* Cicero followed Panaetius in seeking only to temper or moderate the passions that were necessary to the Roman citizen, passions including ambition and military courage, love of *patria,* and love of fame.[3] Cicero's is not the stern *apatheia* of Epictetus in his primer, nor the disinterested cosmopolitanism of Diogenes or Christ. Neither is it the intensely individualistic *constantia sapientis* of Seneca.[4]

According to the old saw, all of Western philosophy consists of footnotes to Plato; in the eighteenth century, however, philosophy was more immediately an appendix to Cicero.[5] Hume's "The Stoic" condenses Cicero's borrowings from Panaetius, with an added dash of Hutchesonian benevolism.[6] One might call Hume's a "soft" or moderated Stoicism: rather than

---

the success of the new system might not unfairly be described as a victory of literature over logic, of reasonableness over reason, and of compromise over consistency. However this may be, Panaetius undoubtedly succeeded in presenting Greek philosophy to his Roman friends in a form in which it recommended itself alike to their reasoning powers and to their moral sense" (103).

[3] Cicero invokes Panaetius as an authority in *De Finibus* 4.23, 78–79. From the three philosophical debates presented in that work, the ethics that emerges victorious is clearly the Stoic/Peripatetic synthesis that Cicero associates in book 4 with Panaetius and in book 5 with Antiochus (d. 68 B.C.E.) of the fifth, or "Old," Academy. In *Tusculan Disputations* 4–5, Cicero embraces a purer form of Stoic doctrine, attacking the Peripatetic view that the passions need only be moderated, not expunged; however, Cicero acknowledges the inconsistency of this position with his earlier ethics and attempts to dismiss it with a nod to the pragmatic—and dialogic—nature of his writing: "I live from day to day; I say anything that strikes my mind as probable: and so I alone am free" (4.33). This appeal to probability rather than certainty (the latter rather cavalierly equated here with consistency) characterizes Cicero's moderate scepticism in matters of logic or epistemology, a scepticism Johnson and Hume would both adopt.

[4] Geoffrey Miles cogently distinguishes between Cicero's "Roman Stoicism: moderate, public-spirited, placing all its emphasis on the social virtues" and Seneca's celebration of "a more heroic ideal of the constancy of the wise man . . . unmoved by passion, unshaken by disaster," combining "the imperviousness of a rock with the serene detachment of a god" (11–14, 26–27). Miles notes that it is invariably the Senecan strain of Stoic thought that Christian writers attack as arrogant and inhuman.

[5] Of Cicero's works, *De Officiis* and *De Natura Deorum* are probably of most importance to Enlightenment thought in Britain. They are of Cicero's corpus the two most frequently cited works in both *The Spectator* and Johnson's *Rambler.* Johnson planned at one point to translate both *De Natura Deorum* and *Tusculan Disputations* (*Life of Johnson* 4:381); Hume, of course, imitates the former in his own *Dialogues concerning Natural Religion.* A dissertation could be written on verbal echoes of *De Officiis* in the periodical essays of Addison, Johnson, Mackenzie, et al. Hume begins his literary career by announcing to Hutcheson in 1739, "Upon the whole, I desire to take my Catalogue of Virtues from *Cicero's Offices,* not from the *Whole Duty of Man.* I had, indeed, the former Book in my Eye in all my Reasonings" (*Letters* 1:34). Cf. *ECPM* 319n. Peter Jones broaches the topic of Hume's debt to Cicero (29–43); I know of no comparable treatment of Johnson and Cicero.

[6] Hume emphasizes extensive benevolence or charity in a way that Cicero does not: when Hume's Stoic praises relieving the distressed and comforting the afflicted, he closely echoes not Cicero but passages of Hume's own ethical writing. Marie Martin catalogs these echoes,

extirpating the passions, or redefining them as a subset of reason, as the earliest Greek Stoics sought to do, it strives instead to *reason with the passions*. I hope that this phrase will bear two meanings: first, the prescriptive sense in which the ethical person ought to make his passions reasonable ones—to "bring them to reason," as we say of an obstreperous child; but also, the purely descriptive sense in which all we have to reason with are our passions—they are the primal stuff, the spark, the engine of all our instrumental reasonings.

This latter sense lies at the heart of eighteenth-century motivational psychology. Alexander Pope did no more than elegantly express what oft was thought in his couplet, "On life's grand ocean diversely we sail, / Reason the card [mariner's chart], but Passion is the gale" (*Essay on Man* 2: 107–8). The sentiment was indeed so common that Johnson could object to Pope's philosophical poem on the grounds that "a man of no very comprehensive search may venture to say that he has heard all this before" (*Lives* 3:244). One place where both Johnson and Hume would have heard this before is *The Spectator* no. 408, in which a (real or fictive) correspondent elaborates on a motto attributed to Cicero—"The affections of the heart ought not to be too much indulged, nor servilely depressed": [7]

> We shall no more admire at the proceedings of *Catiline* or *Tiberius,* when we know the one was actuated by a cruel Jealousy, the other by a furious Ambition; for the Actions of Men follow their Passions as naturally as Light does Heat, or as any other Effect flows from its Cause; Reason must be employed in adjusting the Passions, but they must ever remain the Principles of Action. . . . the Passions . . . are to the Mind as the Winds to a Ship, they can only move it, and they too often destroy it; if fair and gentle, they guide it into the Harbour, if contrary and furious, they overset it in the Waves. (3:524) [8]

Accordingly, both Johnson and Hume insist that the passions must be restrained or regulated in order that human life may flourish in our necessarily social world. The passions may be regulated by, singly or together, the faculty of reason (which for Johnson is sometimes assisted by revelation); a self-reflexive avidity for possessions; and a balance of countervailing passions—for instance, envy restrained by pride. Describing and prescribing the regulation of the passions is the proper office of moral philosophy, which aims to secure as much human happiness as possible.

---

concluding that charitable benevolence "is a conception taken from . . . the *Whole Duty of Man,* not Cicero's *Offices*" (390).

[7] The quotation is attributed to *De Finibus* but, as Donald Bond notes in his edition of *The Spectator,* it seems rather to be a reminiscence of *De Officiis* 1.34.124.

[8] Cf. Fontenelle: "Les passions sont chez les hommes des vents qui sont nécessaires pour mettre tout en mouvement" (quoted in F. B. Kaye, Introduction to Mandeville, *Fable of the Bees* 1:lxxxii).

II. The Combat of Passion and Reason?

In book 2 of his *Treatise,* Hume, playing the enfant terrible, attributes to his fellow philosophers what he will later reveal to be an untenable position:

> Nothing is more usual in philosophy, and even in common life, than to talk of the combat of passion and reason, to give the preference to reason, and to assert that men are only so far virtuous as they conform themselves to its dictates. Every rational creature, 'tis said, is oblig'd to regulate his actions by reason; and if any other motive or principle challenged the direction of his conduct, he ought to oppose it, 'till it be entirely subdu'd, or at least brought to a conformity with that superior principle. On this method of thinking the greatest part of moral philosophy, antient and modern, seems to be founded. (413)

To most students of English literature today, this "usual" moral philosopher would seem to describe Johnson quite well. In an otherwise sterling book on Johnson, Paul Alkon attributes to Johnson the "method of thinking" sketched by Hume: "Because he viewed reason as our most celestial faculty, Johnson vigorously reaffirmed the classical doctrine that reason ought to predominate over imagination at all times and, with the possible exception of the divinely irrational impulse towards compassion, over the passions as well" (65).[9] And indeed, Johnson *sometimes* speaks in the usual way of the combat of a worthy reason and the craven passions. Hence, "By every victory over appetite or passion, new strength [is] added to the mind" (*Rambler* 3:308). "Nothing is more unjust, however common, than to charge with hypocrisy him that expresses zeal for those virtues, which he neglects to practise; since he may be sincerely convinced of the advantages of conquering his passions, without having yet obtained the victory" (3:76). Johnson seems here to imply the ethical position that no conduct can be virtuous unless the will to perform it is undetermined by passion.

But the rhetorical or "dialogic" nature of Johnson's writing ought to make us suspect short excerpts. A more comprehensive consideration of Johnson's essays indeed shows these quotations to be misleading. Although Johnson sometimes invokes, for propaedeutic clarity, the binary opposition of reason and passion, the *perturbatio delenda est* theme is not characteristic of his overall writings on the passions and their relation to the fac-

---

[9] Alkon here contradicts an earlier part of his own monograph in which he acknowledges that for Johnson the "primary passions" and appetites "somewhat mechanically" determine our behavior, though they are subject to regulation by reason (13–14). Cf. also Alkon's recognition that Johnson, with Locke, considered the will to be "always determined" by the promptings of "desire" (82).

ulty called "reason" (a term whose meaning, we will shortly see, was much disputed in the eighteenth century). Johnson is, in general, a far more subtle thinker about the relation of the passions to reason, to human life, and to human happiness.

Several commentators on Johnson have recognized, in a general way, that the passions play a large and important role in Johnson's system of life, but they have all been more or less inconclusive as to what precisely that part is.[10] I will contend that Johnson concurs, up to a point, with the analysis of the motivating passions adopted by Hume—who endeavored to prove, against "the fallacy" that reason combats the passions, "*first,* that reason alone can never be a motive to any action of the will; and *secondly,* that it can never oppose passion in the direction of the will" (*T* 413).

It is first important to note that, although Hume actually *uses* "reason" in a variety of ways,[11] he carefully *defines* the term in a delimited manner as meaning either "demonstrative reasoning"—which is limited to what we do when we do arithmetic or algebra—or "probable reasoning," which is the kind of cause and effect calculation that we make in the real world (*T* 1.3.1–2).[12] The latter is the only type of reasoning that applies to "matters of fact." Hume thus unseats reason from its earlier Platonic and Christian throne, whence it presided as an organ of morality, and gives it a role of pure instrumentality, the calculation of logical propositions.[13] So de-

[10] In order from less to more conclusive: Arieh Sachs announces, quite stirringly, that "Johnson always satirizes the human ideal of a *purely* rational state" and advocates instead "passionate intelligence" (xiv), but reason and passion remain firmly opposed throughout most of Sach's study. Alan McKenzie carefully dissects the psychological and physiological workings of the passions in *The Rambler* (171–93), but his conclusion appears perfunctory, as well as unwarranted: "[T]he principal effect of the passions in *The Rambler* is to turn men and women aside from 'the path' . . . of virtue and truth" (181). J. S. Cunningham convincingly argues that "Johnson regards the passions as the major sources of our energetic engagement with the temporal world" (152), but in conclusion portrays Johnson as more ambivalent about the passions than I believe Johnson to be (155–56).

[11] David Fate Norton distinguishes seven principal senses of "reason" in Hume's philosophical writing, including "reason as probable reasoning, factual reasoning, or probability"; "Reason as instinct" (with reference to the psychological as opposed to logical features of inferential thought); and "Reason as a calm, reflective passion" (*David Hume* 96–98, n. 4).

[12] In light of Hume's deflation of reasoning's role in our judgments concerning cause and effect in the first book of the *Treatise,* critics have often felt Hume's subsequent insistence on the causal principle to be contradictory. Basil Willey, for example, found it paradoxical that "the very man who showed that, for all we can tell by ratiocination, anything may be the cause of anything, or there may be no such thing as 'cause' at all, was also the man who disproved miracles because they violated the inviolable laws of nature" (251). Against such detractors, James Noxon argues that Hume's "psychogenetic explanation" of causation in the *Treatise* is logically separable from his philosophical analysis of it (*Hume's Philosophical Development* 135–37, 157–65); and that after the *Treatise,* Hume's interests lie in critical analysis, "formulating criteria by which to distinguish rationally justified beliefs from groundless opinions, from superstition and prejudice"—"tests of significance, rules of evidence, principles of inference, standards of testimony, and the like" (163–64).

[13] Cf. Charles Taylor: "We could say that rationality is no longer defined substantively, in terms of the order of being, but rather procedurally, in terms of the standards by which we construct orders in science and life. For Plato, to be rational we have to be right about the

fined, reason no longer provides a possible motive to any act of the will. Martha Nussbaum aptly describes cognition according to Hume's model as "motionless, performing calculations without commitment"; the passions, by contrast, possess motion—they "reach out" (374–75). Volition itself, for Hume, is simply a direct passion, a response to some present or anticipated "good or evil" (*T* 438–39).

Similarly, despite those passages from the *Rambler* in which Johnson seems to reject passion as a determinant of the virtuous will, he too defines volition, in his *Dictionary,* as itself a passion. "Volition" is "the act of willing," and "to will" is "to desire that anything should be, or be done." "Desire," in turn, is cognitive, but not necessarily rational: Johnson illustrates his definition of the term ("wish; eagerness to obtain and enjoy") with a quotation from Locke: "*Desire* is the uneasiness a man finds in himself upon the absence of any thing, whose present enjoyment carries the idea of delight with it." Desire, then, is what must move us if we are to move at all.[14] Correspondingly, Johnson defines "reason" in a purely instrumental way: "the power by which man deduces one proposition from another, or proceeds from premises to consequences; the rational faculty."

However, when Johnson writes as a moral essayist rather than as a lexicographer, using one's reason most often means "being reasonable," that is, acting not in accord with certain deductive knowledge, but determining proper behavior according to probable knowledge of causes and effects, based on experience and an all-things-considered quality. Johnson the practical moralist determines what "it is reasonable to suppose," or "it seems to me reasonable to enjoy" (*Rambler* 3:168, 179).[15] Moreover, in *Rasselas* Johnson relentlessly satirizes the notion that "right reason" could have motive force. The rationalist philosopher that Prince Rasselas meets in chapter 18 discourses "with great energy on the government of the passions," comparing "reason to the sun, of which the light is constant, uniform, and lasting"; reason, he concludes, must wholly govern the will. Later, when his only daughter dies of a fever, he reveals himself to be, as we all are, a creature of the passions. Disconsolate, he exclaims, "What comfort can truth and reason afford me? of what effect are they now, but to tell me, that my daughter will not be restored?" (70–76).

---

order of things. For Descartes [and Locke, and most subsequent philosophers] rationality means thinking according to certain canons" (156).

[14] "A concept of love or desire has been put forward time and again as the single root of all emotions. Examples are: the *amor* or *dilectio* of Augustine, Spinoza's *cupiditas,* Freud's libido, as well as the notion of *Maya* in Hindu thought" (James Hillman, 160). Of desire in Hobbes, David Fate Norton writes, "*Desire* is not the name for a distinctive psychological activity; rather, it is the name we apply to entirely physical activity (bodies in motion) at the macrocosmic or submacrocosmic level. *Desire* is a term entirely analogous to *impetus* or *pressure* as these are applied to solids or fluids" (*David Hume* 23–24).

[15] Geoffrey Harpham offers an illuminating analysis of the differences between "reason" and "reasonableness."

In chapter 22, Johnson directly attacks the moral rationalism of Samuel Clarke's *Discourse concerning the Unchangeable Obligations of Natural Religion* (6th ed., 1724).[16] Clarke believed the basic principles of morality to be rationally available to, and morally binding on, man and God alike. In determining the basis of moral motive and obligation, Clarke had a habit of resorting to vague phrases such as "the reason of things" and the "'fitness or unfitness' of the application of different things or different relations one to another"—a habit dryly parodied in Johnson's portrait of another philosopher who would enlighten young Rasselas:

> "When I find young men so humble and so docile," said the philosopher, "I can deny them no information which my studies have enabled me to afford. To live according to nature, is to act always with due regard to the fitness arising from the relations and qualities of causes and effects; to concur with the great and unchangeable scheme of universal felicity; to co-operate with the general disposition and tendency of the present system of things."
>
> The prince soon found that this was one of the sages whom he should understand less as he heard him longer. He therefore bowed and was silent, and the philosopher, supposing him satisfied, and the rest vanquished, rose up and departed with the air of a man that had co-operated with the present system. (88–89)

Besides parodying Clarke, Johnson also satirizes here a certain strain of Stoic philosophy: "a life led according to nature" is a tag from Zeno of Citium, meant to encapsulate the strict determinism and providentialism of Stoic physics. Significantly, the two aspects of Stoic doctrine Johnson sees fit to satirize are its claim to uproot the passions, and its cosmological rationalism—the doctrine of the Logos.[17] Significant too is that both these aspects of Stoic doctrine were abandoned by Panaetius and played little role in the eclectic Stoicism of Cicero.[18]

[16] For a good synopsis of Clarke's philosophy, see Schneewind, 310–23. Johnson's echoes of Clarke are identified by Gwin Kolb in his notes to the Yale edition of *Rasselas*.

[17] On Stoic cosmology, see Cicero, *De Natura Deorum*, book 2, and Rackham's introduction to the Loeb edition, viii–ix.

[18] Blindness to the varieties of Stoicism has misled some eminent Johnsonians into the clearly untenable position that Johnson opposed Stoicism, *tout court*. Thus Donald Greene rejects the idea, current since George Saintsbury (d. 1933), that Johnson's moral writing was influenced by Stoicism and declares instead that Johnson "reject[ed] Stoicism . . . vehemently," associating it "with the original sin of pride" ("Johnson, Stoicism, and the Good Life" 23). Howard Weinbrot makes still more extravagant claims about the irrelevance or negative relevance of *all* the ancient philosophical schools to eighteenth-century literature (*Britannia's Issue* 55–66). But if, as Greene claims, Johnson had nothing but contempt for Stoic doctrine—or, a fortiori, if, as Weinbrot claims, all the ancient schools were passé—then why does Johnson bother to bring up Stoicism at all? Why flog a dead horse? And why does his friend Elizabeth Carter—whom Greene also depicts as a vehement anti-Stoic—bother to translate the Stoic manual writer Epictetus? Johnson's fundamental, although nuanced, commitment to Stoicism is addressed by Lawrence Lipking's "Learning to Read Johnson," which locates the chief inspiration for his instructional writings in the first century Stoic allegory of virtue, *The Table [or Picture] of Cebes*.

Hume and Johnson basically agreed to limit reason to an instrumental role in daily life, and to limit one's philosophical scope to daily life—following Pope's injunction, "Know then thyself, presume not God to scan, / The proper study of Mankind is Man" (*Essay on Man* 2.1–2). Let us proceed, then, to look step by step at Hume's elaboration of the motivational psychology we find in Pope's poem—and ask to what extent Johnson, too, subscribes to this theory of motivation.

First, Hume maintains: "Since reason alone can never produce any action, or give rise to volition, I infer, that the same faculty is as incapable of preventing volition, or of disputing the preference with any passion or emotion. . . . Nothing can oppose or retard the impulse of passion, but a contrary impulse" (*T* 414–15). Johnson concurs with Hume's premise that "reason alone can never produce any action." He recognizes, in a morally neutral way, that the passions are the sole motivating force in life, the elements whose constant recombinations are responsible for all the variety of human affairs:

> It has been discovered by Sir Isaac Newton, that the distinct and primogenial colours are only seven; but every eye can witness, that from various mixtures in various proportions, infinite diversifications of tints may be produced. In like manner, the passions of the mind, which put the world in motion, and produce all the bustle and eagerness of the busy crouds that swarm upon the earth; the passions, from whence arise all the pleasures and pains that we see and hear of, if we analize the mind of man, are very few; but those few agitated and combined, as external causes shall happen to operate, and modified by prevailing opinions and accidental caprices, make such frequent alterations on the surface of life, that the show while we are busied in delineating it, vanishes from the view, and a new set of objects succeeds. (*Adventurer* no. 95, 2:428–29)

Johnson's analogy with Newtonian optics gives a perfectly naturalistic, even mechanistic cast to his survey of passional motivation. Johnson is so far in accord with Hume's attempt—to quote the subtitle of the *Treatise*—"to introduce the experimental Method of Reasoning into Moral Subjects."

But does Johnson accept Hume's inference from the inertness of reason that "nothing can oppose or retard the impulse of passion, but a contrary impulse"? Johnson is loath to accept this mechanistic principle as axiomatic—but he does, in practice, recognize its usefulness. Johnson would be apt to rephrase Hume's law in a more pragmatic fashion: in daily life, what typically opposes or retards the impulse of passion is a contrary impulse. And so, with Hume, Johnson contributes to the psychology of countervailing passions found earlier in Mandeville[19] and finessed in Fielding's

---

[19] Mandeville introduced his two-part *Fable of the Bees* (1714–1728) with the credo, "I believe Man . . . to be a compound of various Passions, that all of them, as they are provoked and come uppermost, govern him by turns, whether he will or no" (1:34). In Mandeville's analysis, our pride or "love of glory"—our desire for others to love us as much as we love

Tom Jones.[20] In what seems a grudging nod to Mandeville's "selfish" system of morals, Johnson acknowledges that the passion of envy may be cured by an appeal to pride:

> I have hitherto avoided that dangerous and empirical morality, which cures one vice by means of another. But envy is so base and detestable, so vile in its original, and so pernicious in its effects, that the predominance of almost any other quality is to be preferred. . . . Let it, therefore, be constantly remembered, that whoever envies another, confesses his superiority, and let those be reformed by pride who have lost their virtue. (*Rambler* 5:200)

Johnson's appeals to the "empirical morality" of countervailing passions are more common than he cares here admit. For example, we would all be licentious, Johnson writes, if pleasures had no price-tags: "Appetites, though too powerful for reason, are kept under restraint by avarice" (5:305). Civic life itself is made possible by a criminal law through which hope of gain is outweighed by fear of punishment:

> While mankind continued in the state of gross barbarity in which all were eager to do wrong and all unwilling to suffer, it is apparent that every man's fear would be greater than his hope, for an individual, thinking himself at liberty to act merely for his own interest, would consider every other individual as his enemy who acted only by the same principle. When they came to deliberate how they should escape what many had felt and all dreaded, they would soon find that safety was only to be obtained by setting interest on the side of innocence, by such a scheme of regulation . . . which should repress the pas-

---

ourselves—will, if properly groomed by cunning "politicians," outweigh all other passions, including lust, love of progeny, avarice, and even our most basic impulses toward self-preservation (1:54–55, 68–75, 222). All the statesman's civilizing art lies in "playing our Passions against one another" (1:145). In times of peace, our fear of criminal punishment must be elevated over our natural propensity to anger; in times of war, our natural anger must be incited and supplemented by the artificial notion of valor—which is itself a compliment to our pride (1:202–10, 333–34). Hume, despite his disagreements with Mandeville's "selfish" system of morals, listed him among the "late philosophers in *England,* who have begun to put the science of man on a new footing" (*T* xvii). With similar reservations, Johnson praised Mandeville as a writer who "opened my views into real life very much" (*Life of Johnson* 3:292). Hume and Johnson's debts to Mandeville are assessed by E. J. Hundert, 59–61, 75–86, 204–5.

[20] A model instance of Fielding's psychology of the passions is found in his detailed account, in *Tom Jones* 6.13, of why the poacher and ne'er-do-well George Seagrim decides to deliver Sophia's purse to Tom Jones rather than keep it for himself. The scene involves a complex dialogue between avarice, fear, and conscience (a faculty dismissed by the Scots philosophers following Hutcheson), which concludes: "By this friendly aid of fear, conscience obtained a compleat victory in the mind of Black George, and after making him a few compliments on his honesty, forced him to deliver the money to Jones." Cf. 1.13, Fielding's analysis of the passions and the interests that motivate Captain Blifil to spurn his brother, Dr. Blifil; and see my *The Fate of Eloquence in the Age of Hume,* 178–79, for further references to the psychology of the passions in Fielding's novels. Bernard Harrison ably defends Fielding from the charges of philosophical naiveté leveled against him by Johnson and Sir John Hawkins (10–27, 89–112).

sions of anger and revenge by making their gratification the cause of immediate misery. . . . If the evil of penalty could not exceed the advantage of
wickedness the mind . . . could never pass beyond an equipoise of passion,
and the nearer good would generally outweigh the remoter evil. But such is
the frame of man, that the dread of evil may be always made more powerful
than the appetite of good. (*English Law* 1:308–9)

Similarly, the religious life aims at counterbalancing temporal hopes and
fears with eternal hopes and fears: "The great task of him, who conducts
his life by the precepts of religion, is to make the future predominate over
the present, to impress upon his mind so strong a sense of . . . the value
of the reward promised to virtue, and the terrors of the punishment denounced against crimes, as may overbear all the temptations which temporal hope or fear can bring in his way" (*Rambler* 1:38). Johnson's views
into real life were evidently quite influenced by Mandeville—and thereby
approach Hume's.

III. Reason Enslaved?

We need now contend with Hume's most memorable pronouncement:
"We speak not strictly and philosophically when we talk of the combat of
passion and of reason. Reason is, and ought only to be the slave of the passions, and can never pretend to any other office than to serve and obey
them" (*T* 415). Johnson would not endorse a strong version of this claim.
The question, however, is—did Hume?

With a boldness typical of his early style—a style he disowned later in
life, along with the *Treatise* itself—Hume turns the traditional Platonic on-
tology, enshrined in Cartesianism, on its head. As Norman Kemp Smith
noted with some embarrassment, "Hume occasionally, in what may be
called 'excess statements,' presses his arguments to the point of sheer
paradox" (230–31). While paradoxical to the philosopher, the claim that
reason *is* the slave of the passions accords with mainstream Protestant
theology. Puritans, Huguenots, and Jansenist Catholics could all agree that
reason is, among fallen mankind, "the slave of the passions."[21] Hume's
devilish innovation is to assert that reason not only is but *ought to be* a slave.

---

[21] The French Protestant Pierre Bayle, in his massively learned *Dictionnaire Historique et Critique* (1697), quotes a fragment of Cicero's *De Republica* to prove that the lamentable
"esclavage de la raison"—"la servitude de l'âme sous l'empire des passions"—was also felt and
acknowledged among the pagan philosophers; Cicero is adduced to silence Jacques Esprit's
contention that the ancient philosophers were ignorant "que le puissance de la Raison s'est
perdue" (Bayle, 2:560–61, article "Ovide," note H). Peter Jones has suggested that Bayle
provided a source for Hume's phrase "the slave of the passions" (5); reason's servitude to the
passions is, however, a commonplace among seventeenth-century French writers, including
La Rochefoucauld, Pascal, and Fontenelle. See F. B. Kaye's Introduction to Mandeville's
Fable, 1:lxxix–lxxxvii.

This if anything would be the sort of paradox that Boswell's Johnson famously deplored—the type that would mark Hume as a "vain man . . . gone to milk the bull." Yet we need to consider two things about Hume's claim. First, it is clear from the context of the *Treatise* as a whole—and, a fortiori, from Hume's later writings—that Hume does not subscribe to a strong version of this claim; rather, his youthful desire to surprise leads him here to mislead. Second, Johnson himself subscribes to a soft version of this statement. Accepting the Protestant orthodoxy that reason *is,* more or less, the slave of the passions, he makes it his goal as a practical moralist to enlighten the passions. The possibility of doing so hinges on recognizing that passions are fundamentally connected to judgments about what is good or desirable and what is not; Johnson would regulate our passions by correcting or tempering those judgments. Johnson would, in short, make our passions more reasonable, that is, better suited to the requirements of moral and civic life. Hume's practical goal, as we shall see, is quite the same, although he is tethered in the *Treatise* by the dubious psychological assumption that passions are wholly noncognitive—attended by, but not involving, judgments about the world.

As we shall see in section iv of this chapter, Johnson in his moral writing often distinguishes "reasonable" from "unreasonable" passions, thereby implicitly acknowledging passions to be cognitive claims or based on cognitive claims, and thus capable of moral discipline and correction. A passion is an "opinion" about a state of affairs, and as such, if it "is discovered to be groundless, it is to be eradicated like other false opinions" (*Rambler* 4:309). Johnson follows in the footsteps, ultimately, of the Stoic analysis of the passions he found in Cicero; more immediately, he follows Locke and, although he may not have read him, Hutcheson.[22] Locke defined the passions, in passing, as "so many instances of Modes of Pleasure and Pain resulting in our Minds, from various Considerations of Good and Evil" (232–33); the *Essay,* however, has little to say about the passions. Francis Hutcheson, who had much to say about them, elaborated on Locke's definition: the passions are "Modifications, or Actions of the Mind consequent upon the Apprehension of certain Objects or Events, in which the Mind generally conceives Good or Evil" (1). For both Locke and Hutcheson, passions are called into action by some thought or judgment about the desirability or undesirability of something.

---

[22] On the Stoic reduction of passions to propositions to which we can assent or not assent, see Cicero, *Tusculan Disputations* 3.24–25; Martha Nussbaum, 373–86. In the language of *Tusculan Disputations* 4, the Stoics admit four basic *perturbationes* (Cicero's rendering of the Greek *pathe*)—disorders of the soul. In summarizing Cicero, Hutcheson—ever a man of his times—presents the passions of the soul shorn of pathology. "Cicero . . . gives from the Stoicks, this general Division of the *Passions:* First, into *Love* and *Hatred,* according as the Object is good or evil; and then subdivides each, according as the Object is *present* or *expected.* About Good we have these two, *Libido & Leatitia, Desire* and *Joy:* About Evil we have likewise two, *Metus & Aegritudo, Fear* and *Sorrow*" (59).

Hume's definition of passion, while evidently drawing on Locke, is more problematic than Hutcheson's. Although Hume distinguishes, rather tentatively, between "calm" and "violent" passions (*T* 276), he chooses to address only the latter in defining passion as "a violent and sensible emotion of the mind, when any good or evil is presented, or any object, which, by the original formation of our faculties, is fitted to excite an appetite" (437).[23] This philosophical definition presents two difficulties for the practical moralist. By first attributing all motive force to the passions, and then dissociating passions from judgments, and making them instead the immediate responses to good and evil—indeed, by making them constitutive of what we call good and evil—Hume commits himself to the conclusion that human motivation or behavior can never be questioned or corrected. Hume's naturalism here is at odds with any prescriptive ethics. The problem is exacerbated by another feature of Hume's definition of passion, its conflation of passion and appetite. Hume presumably blends the two in order to account for things such as our sexual desire or "love of food" without recourse to the terms of Christian vices, "lust" or "gluttony";[24] the effect, however, is to nullify the cognitive and evaluative elements of the passions, to the detriment of his own ethical and therapeutic aims.

The *Treatise* as a whole, however, contains elements that offer possible solutions to the problems presented by Hume's notion of the passions. Hume in practice if not in theory concedes that passions may themselves be reasonable or unreasonable. Let us provisionally grant Hume his stated view of passion as an impulse that may not be gainsaid—what is it that passion would have reason, as its slave, *do*? The answer, it turns out, is—quite a lot. In the paragraph that precedes his salient paradox, Hume concedes,

'Tis obvious, that when we have the prospect of pain or pleasure from any object, we feel a consequent emotion of aversion or propensity, and are carry'd to avoid or embrace what will give us this uneasiness or satisfaction. 'Tis also obvious, that this emotion rests not here, but making us cast our view on every side, comprehends whatever objects are connected with its original one by the relation of cause and effect. Here then reasoning takes place to discover this relation; and according as our reasoning varies, our actions receive a subsequent variation. But 'tis evident in this case, that the impulse arises not from reason, but is only directed by it. (*T* 414)

[23] Cf. the *Treatise*, 2.3.3—"A passion is an original existence.... When I am angry, I am actually possest with the passion" (415).

[24] Thus Hume writes of "that love, which arises betwixt the sexes," as a "compound passion," "deriv'd from the conjunction of three different impressions or passions, *viz.* The pleasing sensation arising from beauty; the bodily appetite for generation; and a generous kindness or good-will" (*T* 394).

Instrumental reason, it turns out, is the type of slave that "guides" impulse after due consideration of "cause and effect." It attempts to determine the consequences or ramifications, the if/then relations, of the action or actions to which a passion prompts us. Through reasoning—and, by extension, through the effects upon us of the moralist's reasoning—we may "vary" our volition and action. Thus judgment, although extricated from the fabric of passion, still invariably "accompanies" passion (416); past judgments can, presumably, modify future impulses.

Reason, as one Humean has remarked, is like the educated and educating Greek slave of a Roman master.[25] A Johnsonian analogy might be: reason is to passion as a potentially less fallible Imlac is to Rasselas and company—an enlightened guide to a princely train.

IV. Reasonable and Reasoning Passions

An "enlightened guide to the passions" also describes the office of the practical moralist, as it is understood by both Johnson and Hume. Both would reason with the passions, that is, modify their motivational force through inductive reasoning. The only modification most passions require, in practice, is simple moderation, according to the Aristotelian rule (*Nicomachean Ethics* 1106a–b). The Aristotelian doctrine that virtue is a mean between two excessive passions—for instance, true courage lies between cowardice and foolhardiness—was accepted by Panaetius, and hence disseminated by Cicero (Arnold 103); what is perhaps antiquity's most famous tag is familiar to us in Cicero's Latin: *Mediocritas optima est* (*De Officiis* 1.36.130). Hume writes: "No quality, it is allowed, is absolutely either blameable or praise-worthy. . . . A due medium, says the Peripatetics, is the characteristic of virtue" (*ECPM* 233).

Horace's corresponding lines on valuing *auream mediocritatem* (*Odes* 2.10.5–8) supply the epigraph to *Rambler* no. 38—and lie behind much

---

[25] David Fate Norton's analogy is crisp: "These Greeks were, no doubt, restricted in their activites and rights, and they were subordinate to their Roman masters. However, given that they educated those very masters and influenced not only their ideas of what was true and false, but also their ideas of good and evil, it seems scarcely credible to claim that their subordination was thorough or complete. Similarly, although Hume says that reason is subordinate to the passions . . . there is little evidence that the thorough subordination of reason to feeling is the central teaching of his philosophy, and much evidence to the contrary" (*David Hume* 126). Cf. Peter Jones: "Hume's own elaboration of the claim that man is governed not by reason but by his passions, considerably weakened its first dramatic impact: man is influenced primarily by inductive reasoning, which is more like feeling than it is like *a priori* thought, by his passions, which can be modified by inductive reasoning, and by certain basic responses which seem to be independent of any thought; the domain and practical influence of *a priori* thought and deductive reasoning from necessary premises are very slight" (187–88).

of Johnson's moral exhortation. "Happiness, as well as virtue, consists in mediocrity" (*Rambler* 1:206). "What passion in excess will not become vicious?" (*Idler* 2:177). Yet Johnson also notes, "It may be laid down as an axiom, that it is more easy to take away superfluities than to supply defects; and, therefore, he that is culpable, because he has passed the middle point of virtue, is always accounted a fairer object of hope, than he who fails by falling short" (*Rambler* 3:136).[26]

For Johnson, the passions need to be "sufficiently regulated" (3:35)— and that regulation can come from several sources. Moral philosophy is, of course, a chief source; yet some "instructors of mankind have not contented themselves with checking the overflows of passion, and lopping the exuberance of desire, but have attempted to destroy the root as well as the branches; and not only to confine the mind within bounds, but to smooth it for ever by a dead calm" (3:349).[27] Who are these moralists who would bottle up the wind? Technically, no Stoic sought to do so—Stoic doctrine consistently approves at least the reasonable passions. Cicero notes that even the earliest Stoics approved three passions, the reasonable versions of hope, joy, and fear: rational wishing, rational uplift, and prudent caution (*Tusculans* 4:12–14).[28] One might, however, read Epictetus's *Encheiridion* as prescribing a rather barren apathy; consider, for example, this piece of Stoic advice, no less startling for being well known: "If you are fond of a jug, say 'I am fond of a jug'; for when it is broken you will not be disturbed. If you kiss your own child or wife, say to yourself that you are kissing a human being; for when it dies you will not be disturbed" (sec. 3). The impracticality of this sage advice becomes a familiar object of satire in eighteenth-century literature; from Fielding's *Joseph Andrews* 4.8 to chapter 18 of Johnson's *Rasselas,* we find professed sages crumble on receiving news of a child's death.

Even Epictetus, however, was not rejected by Johnson: "It is the sage advice of Epictetus," he writes, "that a man should accustom himself often to think of what is most shocking and terrible, that by such reflexions he may be preserved from too ardent wishes for seeming good, and from too much dejection in real evil" (*Rambler* 3:13). Again, we can learn from Epictetus to moderate the passions we ought not to expunge, "If we remember, that whatever we possess is to be in our hands but a very little time, and that the little, which our most lively hopes can promise us, may be made less, by ten thousand accidents; we shall not much repine at a loss" (3:94). Epictetus promises that "you will not be disturbed"; Johnson

---

[26] Cf. *Rambler* 3:23, 35, 96; 4:228; 5:184, 234; *Idler* 2:251.

[27] Cf. *Rambler* no. 33; *Rambler* no. 47, 3:256.

[28] Cicero's Latin terms—*voluntatem, gaudium,* and *cautio*—render the Greek Stoic *boulesis, eulabeia,* and *eulogos eparsis;* see Martha Nussbaum, 398–401.

would protect only against too much dejection or disturbance. Johnson professedly aims his ethics not at the "heights of wisdom," but the "lower degrees of constancy necessary to common virtue" (*Idler* 2:39).

Johnson approved of the basic therapy of Stoicism—and approved it none the less for its being in accord with common sense. In *Rambler* no. 52, Johnson maintains that the central advice of Lipsius, "the great modern master of the Stoic philosophy," finds its echo in "the common voice of the multitude uninstructed by precept, and unprejudiced by authority." We are thus taught to moderate our passions not only by moralists, but more simply by "the . . . comforts which one neighbour administers to another" (*Rambler* no. 52, 3:280).

A third means of regulating the passions, prophylactic rather than con-solatory, is the code of polite behavior. The rules of politeness, promul-gated by *The Spectator* earlier in the century, institutionalize moderation in a most effective way: "[T]hose little civilities and ceremonious delica-cies . . . inconsiderable as they may appear to the man of science, and difficult as they may prove to be detailed with dignity, yet contribute to the regulation of the world, by facilitating the intercourse between one man and another. . . . Wisdom and virtue are by no means sufficient without the supplemental laws of good breeding to secure freedom from degenerat-ing into rudeness, or self-esteem from swelling into insolence" (4:161). Polite behavior restrains certain passions from running to excess in ordi-nary social life; politeness is, in effect, mediocrity socialized.

The creed of salubrious mediocrity derives not only from the authority of Addison, one's neighbors, and the ancients; Johnson also invokes its grounding in "experiment." Thus, Shakespeare, who according to John-son "caught his ideas from the living world, and exhibited only what he saw before him . . . knew, that any . . . passion, as it was regular or exorbi-tant, was a cause of happiness or calamity" (*Shakespeare* 7:63–64). And thus Johnson avers in *Rambler* no. 25 that worldly experience alone, with-out books or precept, will tend to correct the excess of a passion: "Pre-sumption will be easily corrected. Every experiment will teach caution, and miscarriages will hourly shew, that attempts are not always rewarded with success."

Yet while presumption by its very nature assays those experiments which will tame it, cowardice must first be exhorted to experiment at all. Unrea-sonable hopes will tend to be disappointed through experience; unrea-sonable fears may never be uprooted, as the experience that might dispel them is precisely what is feared. Johnson writes, "[T]imidity is a disease of the mind more obstinate and fatal; for a man once persuaded, that any im-pediment is insuperable, has given it, with respect to himself, that strength and weight which it had not before. He can scarcely strive with vigour and perseverance, when he has no hope of gaining the victory; and since he never will try his strength, can never discover the unreasonableness of his fears" (*Rambler* 1:137–38).

Thus it is the moralist's particular task to warn against false fears, and to point out, to the best of his knowledge, which fears are truly reasonable. "Fear is implanted in us as a preservative from evil; but its duty, like that of other passions, is not to overbear reason. . . . When fear is discovered to be groundless, it is to be eradicated like other false opinions" (*Rambler* 4: 307–9). In 1770, Johnson wrote "The False Alarm," a political pamphlet arguing that, notwithstanding the popular outcry, "liberty" was not endangered by John Wilkes's having been expelled, as a convicted criminal, from Parliament; the pamphlet opens:

> One of the chief advantages derived by the present generation from the improvement and diffusion of philosophy, is deliverance from unnecessary terrours, and exemption from false alarms. The unusual appearances, whether regular or accidental, which once spread consternation over ages of ignorance, are now the recreations of inquisitive security . . . . The advancement of political knowledge may be expected to produce in time the like effects. (*PW* 317–18)

Hopes and fears, Johnson tells us in the *Adventurer*, "ought to be proportioned to evidence or probability," although he is not without sympathy for the courageous man's tendency "to indulge hope beyond the warrant of reason" (2:392–94).

What reason warrants, however, is sometimes difficult to determine. On certain issues Johnson will vacillate, or entertain opposing sides. How reasonable is it, for example, to hope for literary fame? Neglect is a fate "every man who dares to write has reason to fear" (3:13). Yet in a slightly later *Rambler,* Johnson is more hopeful: "False hopes and false terrors are equally to be avoided. Every man, who proposes to grow eminent by learning, should carry in his mind, at once, the difficulty of excellence, and the force of industry; and remember that fame is not conferred but as the recompense of labour, and that labour, vigorously continued, has not often failed of its reward" (3:140). Johnson here asks us to balance reasonable fear against reasonable hope, but flatters hope in his final clause and his final word. The hope for fame is diluted in a later essay, however, when we are told that even once it is ours, "the utmost which we can reasonably hope or fear is to fill a vacant hour with prattle, and be forgotten" (4:85). (All in all, the Romantic temperament found Johnson insufficiently encouraging: William Hazlitt complained in 1819, "Johnson is . . . a complete balance-master in the topics of morality. He never encourages hope, but he counteracts it by fear; he never elicits a truth, but he suggests some objection in answer to it" [263]).

Although it might prove difficult in practice to distinguish a reasonable from an unreasonable passion, in theory the distinction is clear: a moderate or regular passion is appropriately directed toward either a good that is probably or at least possibly attainable, or an evil that is probably or at least possibly avoidable. In keeping with the Stoic analysis of the passions, Hume and Johnson assume that all passions take objects, even when, as Johnson explains in the case of the sorrow of mourning, the object is irrecoverably absent.

> Of the passions with which the mind of man is agitated, it may be observed, that they naturally hasten towards their own extinction by inciting and quickening the attainment of their objects. . . . Sorrow is perhaps the only affection of the breast that can be excepted from this general remark. . . . Sorrow is properly that state of mind in which our desires are fixed upon the past, without looking towards the future, an incessant wish that something were otherwise than it has been. (*Rambler* 3:253–54)

Johnson here anticipates what philosophers after Franz Brentano often call the "intentionality" of emotions: that is, their directedness toward objects which may or may not exist. One can hope for heaven; fear a bogeyman; feel sorrow for what did or did not transpire, or what may or may not have transpired, in the past.

Yet a regulated passion must determine its appropriate objects—the good and the evil—not with reference to itself alone, but to the whole individual of which the passion is but a part, and, furthermore, to the whole community of which the individual is a member. As Johnson reminds us in *The Patriot* (1774), the hopes of an individual are finally tied to those of a broader political community: the true patriot will "animate the reasonable hopes of the people"; the false patriot will "raise false hopes to serve a present purpose" (*PW* 394). That an appropriate wish or desire must be based on an all-things-considered reason may be illustrated by one of Hume's paradoxical assertions to the contrary. "Where a passion is neither founded on false suppositions, nor chuses means insufficient for the end, the understanding can neither justify nor condemn it. 'Tis not contrary to reason to prefer the destruction of the whole world to the scratching of my finger" (*T* 416). Hume later contends, "Actions may be laudable or blameable; but they cannot be reasonable or unreasonable" (458).

Hume's attempt here to drive a wedge between reason and passion results in an evident absurdity. For in common as well as philosophical parlance, a passion is surely "unreasonable" that pursues an aim that will result not in its satisfaction but its curtailment, along with the extinction of all the other passions and inclinations that constitute our consciousness. The passion itself—or, to accede to Hume's preferred form, the judgment accompanying the passion—is unreasonable because it evinces a neglect of necessary consequences: "the destruction of the whole world" entails the ruin of the very finger I (or my self-love) would keep from being scratched. Hence it is contradictory, contrary to reason, to prefer the destruction of the world to the scratching of my finger. And, despite Hume's eagerness to do so, it is impossible to separate judgment from passion in a complex comparative/evaluative concept such as "prefer."

Elsewhere in the *Treatise* Hume displays a wholesome disregard for the paradoxes he develops in his section about the passions. His own practice demonstrates quite as well as the criticisms leveled at him by later philosophical detractors that his strict theoretical division between the faculties of passion and reason cannot be maintained.[29] Hume attests to the untenability of his stated position in three ways. First, in the introduction to the *Treatise* Hume makes the following claim, explaining why the mind can rest content in its necessary ignorance of "the ultimate principles of the soul": "[N]othing is more certain, than that despair has almost the same effect upon us with enjoyment, and that we are no sooner acquainted with the impossibility of satisfying any desire, than that the desire itself vanishes" (xvii-iii). Hume here acknowledges that what we can only call the unreasonableness of a passion (or its root, desire), once perceived, will extinguish that passion; he thereby treats passion not as an "original existence" or brute fact (415) but as a mental event with intentionality, an opinion susceptible to correction. (The notion that desires vanish instantly—"we are *no sooner acquainted*"—upon recognition of their groundlessness might have amused Johnson, who had a fine appreciation for the persistence of unreasonable desires; Johnson also might have smiled at Hume's early theory of belief [*Treatise* 1.3.7], in which truths are necessarily more vivid to us than fantasies.)[30]

The second and more important way in which Hume dissolves the barrier he had earlier erected between passion and reason is by redefining much of what we commonly call "reason" as several "calm passions," such as "benevolence and resentment," or "the general appetite to good, and aversion to evil" (*T* 417-18; cf. 437). Accordingly, reason is not just the slave of the passions: reason, as we often think of it in daily life, is a subset of the passions. Hume later declares, magisterially, that what we usually call "*reason* . . . we have found to be nothing but a general calm determination of the passions, founded on some distant view or reflexion" (583). But the necessary corollary of this is that the passions are themselves re-

---

[29] Among Hume's later critics are Jerome Neu, 63–67; Cheshire Calhoun and Robert Solomon in their introductory essay to *Emotion*, 6, 17, 22, 31–32; Terence Penelhum, "Hume's Moral Psychology," 128, 139–40.

[30] Johnson portrays the ways in which desire and imagination readily become more vivid than truth in *Rasselas*, chaps. 32 and 49.

flexive and calculating: in other words, they themselves reason concerning causes and effects. Were this not the case—were the "determination" of the passions not a self-determining—then the passions would be determined by reason, traditionally understood, and thus reason could not be recategorized as a set of passions.[31]

Hume's third illustration of the collapse—or philosophical "deconstruction"—of the opposition reason/passion consists in his enactment of scenarios in which the passions do indeed perform the instrumental reasoning classically attributed to reason: that is, they "reflect" on chains of probable causes and effects and steer the will toward action appropriate to the realization of their own satisfaction. The imagery of the passion as a purposive agent is also to be found in Johnson: "It is the fate of almost every passion, when it has passed the bounds, which nature prescribes, to counter-act *its own purpose*" (*Rambler* 3:286, emphasis mine). Hume goes further, granting passion not only a telos, or purpose, but also powers of reflection and adaptability. We may see this most clearly in the progress of avidity that Hume envisions at the foundational moment of justice.

V. Passion and the Foundation of Justice

"Justice," for Hume, has three components: the stability of private property, its transference by consent only, and fidelity to oaths and contracts (*T* 541, 567).[32] Without justice, there could be no extended society (although there is always society, at least at the familial level [493]), and accordingly no public happiness, which requires "safety and commodity" (271–72, 499–500). Hume explains both the origin and the basis of justice with the following tale:

---

[31] See William Walker on the crucial ambiguity of the term *determination* in the psychological writings of Locke, Hume, and Fielding.

[32] Hume sometimes calls the fundamental rules of justice the "the laws of nature," employing a Stoic term of art, but without the metaphysical baggage the term carried for Stoics and their Christian heirs. Hume clarifies in the second *Enquiry* that such laws are simply a necessity of mankind, something internal to the human form of life (195, 307). (Hume comments on the ambiguities inherent in the term *nature*, LG 30–31; on Hume's complicated relation to modern or Grotian natural jurisprudence, see Haakonssen, "The Structure of Hume's Political Theory," 184–91, 199–201.) The law lectures that Johnson coauthored accept Hume's fundamental rules of justice, calling them "natural law, or as some writers call it, the law of reason" with little less qualification than Hume: these rules are discovered "by observing their consequences, and concluding, a posteriori, those actions to be good, the effects of which are good." These rules "may be considered as the will of the Creator," but then, they may not: our obligation to obey the rules is not dependent on their metaphysical status (*English Law* 85). In his own political writings, Johnson has no patience with appeals to "laws of Nature"—such as American colonists were apt to make—when these oppose the authority of positive law: "cant about nature and Providence would prove that no human legislature has a right to make any prudential laws"; "The laws of Nature . . . have been thundered in our ears, sometimes by interested faction, and sometimes by honest stupidity" (*PW* 174, 418).

This avidity alone, of acquiring goods and possessions for ourselves and our nearest friends, is insatiable, perpetual, universal, and directly destructive of society. There is scarce any one, who is not actuated by it; and there is no one, who has not reason to fear from it, when it acts without any restraint, and gives way to its first and most natural movements. . . . There is no passion, therefore, capable of controlling the interested affection, but the very affection itself, by an alteration of its direction. Now the alteration must necessarily take place upon the least reflection; since 'tis evident, that the passion [of avidity] is much better satisfy'd by its restraint, than by its liberty, and that by preserving society, we make much greater advances in the acquiring possessions, than by running into the solitary and forlorn condition, which must follow upon violence and an universal licence. (*T* 492)

Hume's rationale for justice appears to be an elaboration on Glaucon's speech in Plato's *Republic,* 2:359—a speech paraphrased by Johnson in *Idler* no. 89:

Of justice one of the heathen sages has shewn, with great acuteness, that it was impressed upon mankind only by the inconveniences which injustice had produced. "In the first ages," says he, "men acted without any rule but the impulse of desire, they practiced injustice upon others, and suffered it from them in their turn; but in time it was discovered, that the pain of suffering wrong was greater than the pleasure of doing it, and mankind, by a general compact, submitted to the restraint of laws, and resigned the pleasure to escape the pain." (2:276–77)

Men, who naturally seek pleasure and avoid pain, calculate from experience that more pain is avoided than pleasure incurred by submitting to a general rule to refrain from the goods and possessions of others. Hume tells basically the same story, but note the subtle differences between his telling and Johnson's paraphrase of Plato. In Plato, individuals determine their own fate through inductive reasoning; in Hume, a passion that operates through individuals, avidity, seeks its own satisfaction and discovers through experience that its purpose is served better by indirection than rapine. The passion of avidity redirects itself, simply by reflecting on itself: "[T]he passion of self-interest . . . itself alone restrains it" (*T* 492). It learns cunning. "The same self-love, therefore, which renders men so incommodious to each other, taking a new and more convenient direction, produces the rules of justice" (543).

Johnson's own analyses of the origin and basis of justice tend simply to elaborate on his paraphrase of Glaucon's speech from *The Republic*. In the law lectures Johnson composed for, and in association with, Sir Robert Chambers, we find Glaucon updated for the age of Newton:

[T]he experience of many ages has taught every civilized nation that as in the physical disposition of the universe every planet is detained in its orbit by an exact equipoise of contrary tendencies, so in the economy of the moral world contrary passions debilitate each other. Every man desires to retain his own in proportion as he desires to seize what is another's, and no man can be allowed to rob, where none are willing to be robbed; we therefore mutually agree to protect and be protected, and every invader of property is opposed by the whole community, at least by all that part of it which has any thing to lose.

The same account may be given of the means by which the *irascible* passions are restrained. Every man would at some time be willing to hurt another but that he is afraid of being hurt himself. (*English Law* 1:306–7)[33]

Thus people learn to restrain anger from fear of retribution and to restrain avidity through fear of rapine. The passions are operative here, although Johnson does not follow Hume in conspicuously effacing the individuals through whom they work: "every man" tolls throughout this passage, a small reminder that the will is not wholly determined by suprapersonal forces.

The difference is nice but perhaps not insignificant: for Johnson, the impetus to justice arises from every man's interested balancing of passions; for Hume, it arises from the impersonal passion of interest reflecting on itself. Yet in both cases justice marks the limit of self-love's free reign. Justice exemplifies self-love reasonably bound. Hutcheson, a complete moral sentimentalist, had maintained that the natural or instinctive virtues were sufficient for life in society; Butler responded, however, that they could not account for our duty to adhere to justice.[34] Prompted by Butler, Hume maintained that the natural virtues need to be supplemented by the "artificial virtue" of justice. This virtue is not, like benevolence, based immediately on a feeling of approval or pleasure, but rather on a rational calculation that a more or less strict adherence to the rules of justice is ultimately useful or beneficial both to oneself and to society.

Reason is not necessary in order for us to approve simple acts of benevolence such as—to take an example from Wordsworth's poem "Simon Lee" (1798)—ridding a plot of arable soil of a dead tree-root for an old man too feeble to do it for himself. However, some reflection is required if we are properly to assess acts of justice that might not seem immediately pleasing: for instance, shackling a poor man for taking coins from the pocket of a man who may be so rich as not to notice the loss. Justice is thus

---

[33] Johnson offers an expanded version of this account of justice in *Sermon* no. 18, which he concludes with a warning against avidity in its modern guise, commercial fraud. He offers an ethical defense of private property in *Sermon* no. 27. Johnson urges in both sermons that religion is a necessary supplement to nature and reason in the maintenance of society—a point befitting his genre. See also *The Vision of Theodore* (in *Rasselas* 179–212).

[34] The debate is concisely covered by Schneewind, 351–52. On Hume's debt to Butler, see 363–73.

a means of regulating, or reasoning with, the passions—the passion of benevolence, as well as those of anger and revenge. Justice is the adherence to rules that ultimately, if not always immediately, serve the general welfare.

VI. Passion and the Morality of Justice

It is the moralist's goal, however, to account for how or why we come to view justice not simply as a necessity, but as a good. To do so, Hume introduces the mechanism of sympathy; Johnson himself, to a large extent, appeals to the natural facts of fellow-feeling and the other-directed passions. The rational calculation of interest, even group interest, does not in itself entail a moral obligation. Hume grounds the morality of justice on what he calls our intuitive "sympathy" with what others feel. Hume argues in the *Treatise* that we morally approve the rules of justice because we sympathetically partake of the uneasiness of those who suffer from injustice:

> We partake of their uneasiness by *sympathy;* and as every thing, which gives uneasiness in human actions, upon the general survey, is call'd Vice, and whatever produces satisfaction, in the same manner, is denominated Virtue; this is the reason why the sense of moral good and evil follows upon justice and injustice. . . . *Thus self-interest is the original motive to the* establishment *of justice: but a* sympathy *with public interest is the source of the* moral approbation, *which attends that virtue.* (*T* 499–500)

He elaborates in the second *Enquiry* on the utility of justice, but notes that "[u]tility is only a tendency to a certain end; and were the end totally indifferent to us, we should feel the same indifference towards the means. It is requisite a *sentiment* should here display itself, in order to give a preference to the useful above the pernicious tendencies. This sentiment can be no other than a feeling for the happiness of mankind, and a resentment of their misery" (*ECPM* 286).

That justice was useful Johnson held to be self-evident: "Indeed so manifest is the tendency of justice, and other social virtues to promote the happiness of the whole, and of every individual, that no one however ignorant can help assenting to the position that principles which are productive of such effects, must be beneficial to mankind in general" (*English Law* 85).[35]

---

[35] Johnson and Hume both expressed a moral theory akin to what after Mill we call "rule utilitarianism": the notion that we ought to follow those general rules—and to cultivate those character types—that are of greatest utility to society as a whole. "What is of most use is of most value," writes Johnson in 1750 (*Rambler* 3:321); at roughly the same time, Hume declares, "In all determinations of morality, this circumstance of public utility is ever principally in view" (*ECPM* 180). James Crimmins argues persuasively that utilitarianism was developed by eighteenth-century Christian authors such as Warburton and John Brown; it was not until Bentham that utilitarianism took on a distinctly secular character (550). F. B. Kaye defends projecting some notion of utilitarianism back into the seventeenth and eighteenth

But what obliges us to care about the happiness of mankind? Here Johnson gives two possible answers. First, he clearly maintains a role for God in transforming the dictates of prudence or our moral sentiments into authoritative laws, backed by sanctions. Thus the above quotation on the utility of justice concludes that justice, being beneficial to mankind, is "therefore pleasing to God: an inference which can hardly be denied without impeaching *his* goodness, who is goodness itself." Johnson, in his 1757 review of Soame Jenyns's *Free Inquiry*, concurs with Jenyns that the happiness of humans is "conformable to the will of their creator"; happiness must be pursued "in pursuance of our belief in God, and in obedience to his commands." Johnson here subscribes to a morality of obedience: one is obliged to do what one is authorized to do by a higher power.

But Johnson's second answer for why we are obligated to pursue the good of the whole is a naturalistic one and compatible with Hume's morality of human self-governance. For at one point Johnson follows Jenyns in simply eliding the distinction between what we ought to do and the obligation to do it: "Morality obliges men to live honestly and soberly, because such behaviour is most conducive to public happiness, and consequently to their own" (*MW* 537–38). This conflation of practical benefit and moral duty is characteristic of utilitarian ethics. Elsewhere, however, Johnson at least suggests the Humean position that moral obligation derives from a sentiment. Johnson offers as a rich epigram that "all *reasonable* beings *naturally* love justice" (*Shakespeare* 8:704, emphasis mine). Justice is here linked to the sympathetic approval or love that all, and presumably only, reasonable beings feel toward it. All natural beings love, but only reasonable beings, capable of adherence to general rules even when their immediate results are unlovely, naturally love justice.

Justice can indeed require some tough love. Hume and Johnson both acknowledge that natural benevolence may sometimes be given reign locally—in the family or the neighborhood—but reflective acts or customary habits of justice are required for the benefit of the state as a whole.[36] On the public level, beneficence can be a dangerous game: Johnson notes that some acts of charity, such as contributing to hospitals for the working poor, "the mind can most securely review with unabated plea-

---

centuries in order to distinguish the type of ethical theory one may find in Mandeville from the "rigorist" ethics of both rationalists and many Christians, in which virtue resides only in motivation by right principle (*Fable of the Bees* 1:xlviii).

[36] Two recent commentators—one on Hume, one on Johnson—address this dichotomy between private benevolence and public justice. David Kaufmann argues that Hume invented this theoretical division as a solution to the chief problem of eighteenth-century political economy, "the conflict between commutative rights and distributive justice" (viii, 65–71). Thomas Reinert maintains that Johnson was the first to address, as Hume did not, the tension between the private sphere of benevolence and the public sphere of larger utilitarian aims; according to Reinert, Johnson grapples with the problems posed to traditional, individual-oriented moral instruction in the modern world of the effacing crowd (18–24).

sure"; but "of some kinds of charity the consequences are dubious" (*Idler* 14). Johnson notes, for example, that gifts to the poor, while seemingly beneficent, may foster their dependency and indolence, while money spent on luxuries creates employment for them (*Life of Johnson* 3:55–56). Beggars may receive one's coin only to spend it on gin.[37] Our inability to forecast consequences is what ought to make us wary of venturing beyond the rules of justice into action prompted by impulse, even virtuous impulse.

The sphere of justice thus marks the outer limit of Johnson's and Hume's ability to approve any prereflective passion, be it acquisitive or generous. Justice proves that the passions are, in fact, amenable to reason—or, as Hume sometimes suggests, themselves capable of reasoning. As we shall see in the next chapter, the passions of both self-love and benevolence, sometimes checked by justice from immediate gratification, find new routes to satisfaction in the recognition and moral approval of others.

---

[37] When others offered this argument against charity, Johnson—often the contrarian— was capable of taking the opposite position. "What signifies, says some one, giving halfpence to common beggars? they only lay it out in gin or tobacco. 'And why should they be denied such sweeteners of their existence (says Johnson)? it is surely very savage to refuse them every possible avenue to pleasure, reckoned too coarse for our own acceptance'" (*Miscellanies* 1:204–5).

CHAPTER FIVE

Self-Love and Community

In acts of sympathy, we foremost think of ourselves—on this, Hume and Johnson agree. Hume first introduces sympathy into his philosophy to explain why we seek fame: "Our reputation, our character, our name are considerations of vast weight and importance; and even the other causes of pride; virtue, beauty and riches; have little influence, when not seconded by the opinions and sentiments of others" (*T* 316). He later elaborates on sympathy's centrality to all our various pursuits: "Whatever other passions we may be actuated by; pride, ambition, avarice, curiosity, revenge or lust; the soul or animating principle of them all is sympathy; nor wou'd they have any force, were we to abstract entirely from the thoughts and sentiments of others" (*T* 363). For Hume, sympathy is a mode of perception that undergirds every passion[1]—in all we pursue, we are ultimately pursuing a way of being beheld by others. Without at least the image of other people who behold us and feel something of our feelings, we would be entirely without the motivation normally supplied by the passions.

Hume, then, stresses the importance of our sympathetic participation with others who sympathize with us; this circuit generates our very sense of self. By contrast, Johnson understands sympathy as something a rela-

---

[1] In Hume's philosophy, sympathy, as John Stewart puts it, "is part of a process of perception, a process by which feelings are shared; it is not a particular feeling, and, of course, is not to be confused with either compassion (pity) or benevolence. Sympathy relieves us from perceptual isolation" (116). For a thorough analysis of sympathy in its Humean sense, see Pall Árdal, 44–54. Antony Pitson treats Hume's account of sympathy as a rejection of Cartesian dualism, concluding "our acceptance of others as the subjects of mental states forms part of that response to experience for which nature itself is ultimately responsible" ("Sympathy and Other Selves" 267).

tively independent self feels toward others: indeed, for Johnson we only really care about others inasmuch as we imagine, however imperfectly or momentarily, that they *are* us. "All joy or sorrow for the happiness or calamities of others is produced by an act of the imagination, that realises the event however fictitious, or approximates it however remote, by placing us, for a time, in the condition of him whose fortune we contemplate; so that we feel, while the deception lasts, whatever motions would be excited by the same good or evil happening to ourselves" (*Rambler* 3:318–19). Accordingly, sympathy affords a powerful if not the sole motive to relieve or preserve others (*Life of Johnson* 2:469). It is only by imagining another as oneself that a person can reach out, morally or aesthetically. In his remarks on sympathy, Johnson treats the other as a simple mirror of the self; Hume's sense of the self as that which must at least try sympathetically to understand the response of others (even if a response to oneself) seems quite expansive by comparison.[2]

Despite their differences, Johnson and Hume share the basic premise that behind any or all other motives lies self-love. Building a social theory from this premise leads them to pose the questions—with whom will the self-regarding self (most readily) sympathize? Whose esteem will the self seek? Their answers to these questions are colored, finally, by their peculiar concerns as men of letters—and by their common reading of Cicero. The self-love or pride of the common person will seek a reputation and often excellence within the face-to-face community in which she lives and works; for the man of letters, however, as for the patriot and the sage of antiquity, the desire for local or even national recognition is finally eclipsed by the passion for enduring, cosmopolitan fame.

I. The Morality of Pride

Both Hume and Johnson participate in the Enlightenment project of vindicating self-love or, in a positive sense, pride—that basic habit we have of taking pleasure in the good, including the material goods, associated with our proper names; of feeling pain at whatever lessens us in our own eyes, especially when we see through the eyes of others. Theologically, the rehabilitation of self-love starts in England after the Restoration with Latitudinarian divines, and culminates in Joseph Butler's popular *Sermons* (1723). Butler argued that a person's self-love, properly understood, is not a particular passion, but "a general desire of his own happiness"—a "cool

---

[2] Jennifer Herdt deftly contrasts Hume's *hermeneutic* principle of "sympathetic understanding" (6–7) with the more immediately self-referential conceptions of sympathy found in Johnson and Adam Smith (143–56).

principle" by which we order and discipline our particular passions and affections according to a calculation of long-term self-interest (*Sermon* no. 11, 485–86). So defined, self-love is not incompatible with, but rather conducive to genuine benevolence and all its attendant virtues (491–92).

Both Johnson and Hume would have concurred with this statement of Butler's thesis—it was, indeed, little more than the argument of Cicero's *De Officiis*, newly dressed to refute the "selfish" systems of Hobbes and Mandeville. Butler, however, is led into an apparent contradiction by his nod to Christian ethics: although he holds that enlightened self-interest is sufficient to produce virtuous acts, he also maintains that truly virtuous acts must be motivated or at least sanctioned by Conscience, an "absolute authority" wholly distinct from personal interest (*Sermon* no. 3). The thought of Johnson and Hume is finally more Ciceronian—which is to say, more modern—than that of Butler. To appreciate this, we must first review the notion of pride to which Butler objected, and which he attempted to reformulate. Mandeville, developing Hobbes's egoistic interpretation of the passions, reduced all passional motivation to a single motive: the pleasure of self-gratification. This "vicious" pleasure is what lies behind all the ostensible virtues of society; even in self-sacrifice we seek to shine before others. Mandeville quips, "[T]he Moral Virtues are the Political Offspring which Flattery begot upon Pride" (*Fable* 1:51). Hume would later point out that Mandeville's "selfish hypothesis" is counterintuitive, contrary to "common language and observation" (*ECPM* 298; cf. *T* 486–87). Hume adduces the tendency of maternal tenderness to outweigh even the impulse to self-preservation: "What interest can a fond mother have in view, who loses her health by assiduous attendance on her sick child, and afterwards languishes and dies of grief, when freed, by its death, from the slavery of that attendance?" (300).

Yet Hume does not fully understand Mandeville. Mandeville would counter that the mother acting on fondness still does not act disinterestedly, but as selfishly as the next sinner. As Bernard Harrison notes, for Mandeville virtue and self-reference are radically incompatible, so that no one "can be counted virtuous for doing what he enjoys or for acting to protect what he loves, even though his act in itself might be considered morally right in the circumstances" (74). Mandeville thus anticipates Kant, whose purely formal requirements for moral action raise the possibility that no moral act ever has been or will be performed.

Neither Johnson nor Hume, by contrast, maintain that moral action must arise from some peculiarly or exclusively moral motive, such as Butler's Conscience or Kant's Categorical Imperative. For both men, that an act is motivated by pride does not necessarily make it a vice; on the contrary, they morally evaluate an act—or type of act—not in terms of the motive or intention that lies behind it, but according to the practical, social effect it is likely to produce. They are, to use a currently fashionable term, *pragmatic* moralists, and hence more modern than their closest predecessors.

Why is pride a good? Fundamentally, for Hume as for Johnson, pride is a pleasurable sensation, and the value of pleasure is, as Christopher Berry maintains, "a Newtonian 'ultimate' in the 'science of man'" (206). For Hume, "pride is a pleasant sensation, and humility a painful; and upon the removal of the pleasure and the pain, there is in reality no pride or humility. Of this our very feeling convinces us; and beyond our feeling, 'tis here in vain to reason or dispute" (*T* 286). Johnson similarly asserts, "[I]t is vain to labour for forms of argument, to evince that which sensation or intuition will inform us" (*Sermons* 287). While Johnson rightly observes to Boswell that "pleasure is a word of dubious import" (*Life of Johnson* 3:388), he is convinced that understood prima facie, in terms of a calculus of sensation, all life consists in seeking "pleasure" and avoiding "pain"; morally, "every pleasure is of itself a good. . . . unless counter-balanced by evil" (3:327).

Now, as pride is a pleasant and humility a painful sensation, Hume and Johnson concur that pride merits approbation insofar as its expression does not entail pain to others. Both view as not only praiseworthy but necessary to human endeavor a due degree of pride, "assurance," or, as Hume phrases it in his second *Enquiry,* "sentiment of conscious worth" (314). Conversely, neither writer is apt to recommend the humility of earlier Christian moralists. Johnson and Hume were well read in authors who urged humility. Hume, for his part, confessed to Boswell that he had been unusually pious as a boy, given to examining his character against the list of vices he found in *The Whole Duty of Man* (a popular devotional manual, probably written by Richard Allestree, d. 1681). Boswell records that the young Hume would "try if, notwithstanding his excelling his schoolfellows, he had no pride or vanity" (*Private Papers* 12:227–28). Johnson seems not to have read *The Whole Duty of Man* until much later in life (*Diaries* 306–7), but its strictures against pride were standard fare; in the words of one of Johnson's favorite seventeenth-century divines, Jeremy Taylor: "Entertain no fancies of vanity and private whispers of this devil of pride" (quoted in Alkon, 105).

Johnson's acceptance, even encouragement, of due pride is far afield from Taylor. Even in his one standard homily against the sin of pride, *Sermon* no. 6, Johnson limits his strictures to "an *immoderate degree* of self-esteem, or an over-value set upon a man by himself" (*Sermons* 67, emphasis mine), and his praise of humility is limited to a short closing paragraph on the life of Christ (73). The "pride" addressed in this sermon, as well as in *Rambler* no. 185 (published, significantly, on a Christmas eve) pertains only to that which issues in violence, revenge, oppression, tyranny. The pride Johnson deplores is that which "produce[s] effects equally injurious to others, and destructive to itself" (*Sermons* 68); that which, in its very tyranny over others, constitutes "the lowest and most ignominious slavery" to the "opinion of others" *(Rambler* 5:209). For Hume, the immoderately proud man or woman is criminal for harboring a "delicacy of passion," an "extreme sensibil[ity] to all the accidents of life"; the remedy for all such delicacy lies in philosophy and the arts, which promise to usher in a countervailing "delicacy of taste" and the "cool and sedate temper" that attends it *(Essays* 3–5).

Johnson and Hume condemn pride only when it gives rise to passions that have precipitous, unmeasured or unjust violence—not violence per se—as their object. Envious pride will often provide a motive for malice, a passion that may be more natural to us than its structural opposite, pity.[3] The most common violent passion, however, is not settled malice but simply anger. Anger, in Aristotle's sterling definition, is "an impulse, accompanied by pain, to a conspicuous revenge for a conspicuous slight directed without justification towards what concerns oneself or towards what concerns one's friends" *(Rhetoric* 1378a). With Aristotle—and Butler *(Sermon* no. 8, "Upon Resentment")—both Johnson and Hume assume that anger is, in certain instances and in proper degree, a valuable passion.[4] It can be a correct way of evaluating a situation: for example, in the case of the anger we feel toward someone whom we see abusing a friend; or the anger felt toward a stage or screen villain who imperils the hero or heroine with whom we sympathize. For Hume, anger recognizes the importance of the communal ties that bind us, as family, as citizens, and as humans: "We are not . . . to imagine that all the angry passions are vicious. . . . The want of them, on certain occasions, may even be a proof of weakness and imbecility." It is only when "these angry passions rise up to cruelty" that "they form the most detested of all vices" *(T* 605). Johnson evidently shares Hume's notion that some anger is good. The true patriot he describes in his late political writing knows that "to resent encroachments" is "reasonable" *(PW* 394).

The moral philosopher seeks only to restrain or regulate anger; to keep it, in Aristotelian fashion, from running to excess. The dispositionally angry man is the slave of a passion; the just man ought only "to retain his

---

[3] Hume, for his part, notes that animals—whose psychology is typically offered, throughout the *Treatise,* as analogous to our own—naturally possess more more envy and malice than pity, for enmity requires "less effort of thought and imagination" *(T* 398). If we too naturally possess a good deal of malice, it is offset at some stage of childhood by pity, for Hume also maintains that "children are most subject to pity, as being most guided by that faculty [imagination]" (370). Johnson concurs with Hume on natural malice, but not on childhood's access to pity: "Pity is not natural to man. Children are always cruel. Savages are always cruel. Pity is acquired and improved by the cultivation of reason. We may have uneasy sensations from seeing a creature in distress, without pity; for we have not pity unless we wish to relieve them" *(Life of Johnson* 1:437).

[4] Cicero, in a mood of Stoic anti-Aristotelianism, denounces the general temper of irascibility in *Tusculans* 4.43–54, 77–80; it does not appear, however, that even here Cicero opposes all instances of anger: see especially section 50.

resentment, till he has a full conviction of the offence, to proportion his anger to the cause, or to regulate it by prudence, or by duty"—only in such restraint is there "security" (*Rambler* 3:60). Practically, Johnson would regulate anger by urging a due degree of self-love: "Pride is undoubtedly the origin of anger: but pride, like every other passion, if it once breaks loose from reason, counteracts its own purposes. A passionate man, upon the review of his day, will have very few gratifications to offer his pride, when he has considered how his outrages were caused, why they were borne, and in what they are likely to end at last" (3:58–59). Johnson thus encourages the very "interest" which is evidently limited by anger as a principle of motivation—he does so not to play the Hobbist, but to strike an equilibrium of forces, a balance of countervailing passions: interest and anger, each in due measure.

II. An Honest and Useful Emulation

Pride and the pleasure of praise are positive goods in Johnson's system, constituents not only of individual but of the general happiness. Healthy self-love, or amour propre, inspires individuals with a love for their trades and professions, and that love in turn contributes to the development of the arts and sciences—to the manufacture and refinement, Johnson adduces, of goods such as glass, transparent windows, corrective lenses (*Rambler* no. 9). Our partiality to ourselves and hence to our professions "excites ingenuity, and sometimes raises an honest and useful emulation or diligence" (3:49). "An honest emulation," rooted in a "self-love" that inspires us "to think highly of ourselves in comparison with others," is the source of all achievement, all greatness: "the philosopher's curiosity may be inflamed by a catalogue of the works of Boyle and Bacon, as Themistocles was kept awake by the trophies of Miltiades" (*Adventurer* 401–2). Again we should recall Pope: "*Envy*, to which th' ignoble mind's a slave, / Is *emulation* in the learned or brave" (*Essay on Man* 2.191–92; cf. Cicero, *Tusculans* 4.17).

The necessity of "emulation" to a beneficent progress is a, perhaps the, great theme of the Enlightenment in Britain, shared alike by Hobbes, Mandeville, and Shaftesbury, Hume and Johnson.[5] It pervades Johnson's

[5] In the terms of Hobbes's "comparison of the life of man to a race," "[t]o endeavour to overtake the next, [is] emulation," "[c]ontinually to be out-gone is misery," "[a]nd to forsake the course is to die" (*Human Nature* 59–60). Johnson adopts this analogy in *Sermons* 239. On the theme of emulation as a prod to the arts and sciences, see Mandeville, *Fable of the Bees* 1:42–47; Shaftesbury, 1:155. Cf. James Thomson, *Liberty*, book 3, l. 80; book 5, ll. 270, 498; Oliver Goldsmith, "An Account of the Augustan Age of England," *Works* 1:498. The eighteenth-century theme of emulation is surveyed by Isaac Kramnick, *Republicanism and Bourgeois Radicalism* 6–18; Weinbrot, *Britannia's Issue* 99–113.

Idler essays still more than his *Rambler*. The "renaissance of letters" that, according to standard eighteenth-century wisdom, began in fourteenth-century Italy is itself a product of emulation: "[T]he European world was rouzed from its lethargy; those arts which had been long obscurely studied in the gloom of monasteries became the general favourites of mankind; every nation vied with its neighbour for the prize of learning; the epidemical emulation spread from south to north, and curiosity and translation found their way to Britain" (*Idler* 214).[6] Emulation is responsible for "elegance" of building, clothing, food (116); "commerce has kindled an universal emulation of wealth" (227).

Johnson and Hume agree that the fire that animates both the fine and practical arts and the sciences "is not kindled from heaven. It only runs along the earth; is caught from one breast to another; and burns brightest, where the materials are best prepared" (*Essays* 114; the metaphor derives from Longinus's *On the Sublime* chap. 13). The theme of emulation is omnipresent throughout Hume's *Essays* and *History of England*—its responsibility for the enlightenment of both ancient Greece and modern Europe ("Of the Rise and Progress of the Arts and Sciences," *Essays* 119–21); the birth and refinement of all arts and sciences, mechanical arts and manufactures (*Essays* 135–36; *History* 3:229, 328; 4:216; 6:149). Writing of Henry VII's reign, Hume reiterates the beneficial effects of "refinement in the arts," sometimes misnamed "luxury." Producing and acquiring commercial manufactures is, in Hume's eyes, "a more civilized species of emulation" than engaging retainers and waging war, the chief sports of the feudal period (*History* 3:76)—and this truth will hold, we might add, "as long as men are actuated by the passions of ambition, emulation, and avarice, which have hitherto been their chief governing principles" (*Essays* 370–71). While no friend to warfare, Hume nonetheless recognized that even the most civilized nations need to maintain the means of self-defense. Thus, the author of *Sister Peg*—whom, as David Raynor argues, may well be Hume—eloquently concludes a speech in favor of establishing a Scottish militia in these terms: "Your wisest establishments, when confined to a part, may perish for want of that emulation, which, when all are equally engaged, must kindle the ardor and spirits of generous minds" (103).

A certain faith in the new age brought about through emulation and by progress gives Hume's political and historiographical works their fundamental if cautious buoyancy, a headiness that must look more than a bit suspect to us in the crowded and naturally depleted globe that the Enlightenment has in part bequeathed us. But neither Johnson nor Hume— and here they differentiate themselves from a Mandeville or a Shaftes-

[6] Cf. *Idler*, 116, 206, 216.

bury—believed in the virtue of emulation wholeheartedly. They saw keenly that emulation was not always, in Johnson's phrase, "an honest emulation"—that is, one untainted by class envy or ugly nationalism. Johnson opines that the surest way to limit the turbulence of emulation in society is to maintain hereditary rank and wealth, or "subordination" (*Sermons* 291; *Life of Johnson* 1:447–48). Hume was also, for similar reasons, a great friend to subordination, as the fury of his *History of England* chapters on the Puritan Revolution amply attests. In the months leading up to Charles's execution, emulation runs amok, overturning society: Hume is aghast at the spectacle of "a base populace exalted above their superiors" (5:521).[7] Johnson is still more direct in attributing the revolution to "'strife' proceeding from 'envy'": "It was a war of the rabble against their superiors; a war, in which the lowest and basest of the people were encouraged by men a little higher than themselves, to lift their hands against their ecclesiastical and civil governours" (*Sermons* 246–47).

Hume saw that the dark side of emulation, between as well as within nations, is belligerence. "We may observe, that the ancient republics were almost in perpetual war, a natural effect of their martial spirit, their love of liberty, their mutual emulation" (*Essays* 404). It is from being "possessed with the ancient GREEK spirit of jealous emulation" that Britain's wars with France "have always been too far pushed" (339). Hume does, however, approve of offensive wars that are not de trop: he vindicates as a motive to naval war with the Dutch in 1653 "an honourable emulation" between two powers each desirous of "remaining sole lords of the ocean" (*History* 6:66).

Most intellectuals today would show far less latitude than Hume—or Johnson, another great admirer of Admiral Blake's—in determining the limits of just war or honorable emulation. Nonetheless, Annette Baier is right to emphasize that Hume is not simply a throwback to Hobbes or, to move from ocean to market, a precursor of Ayn Rand; on the contrary, an aspect of his thought was, as we would say today, deeply "communitarian," committed to the values of benevolent coexistence and cooperation. Baier writes of the *Treatise*, 3.3.2: "Partnership and common 'interest' reinforce the sort of more spontaneous sympathy and passion-sharing that Hume takes to be natural to us. What can interfere with it are rivalry and blurred vision" (*Progress of Sentiments* 151). In much the same vein, Isobel Grundy

---

[7] Throughout chapter 59 of the *History*, Hume sarcastically reminds us of the class origins of every Puritan soldier he singles out: for example, "Joyce, who had once been a taylor by profession" (5:497), "colonel Pride, formerly a drayman" (531), "Colonel Harrison, the son of a butcher" (533). Yet by the time that Hume came to write his Plantagenet volumes, he had become rather more dispassionate toward the threat of leveling. He concludes of Wat Tyler's 1381 rebellion: "[O]f all the evils incident to human society, the insurrections of the populace, when not raised and supported by persons of higher quality, are the least to be dreaded: The mischiefs, consequent to an abolition of all rank and distinction, become so great, that they are immediately felt, and soon bring affairs back to their former order and arrangement" (2:293).

contends that while Johnson acknowledged the central role of emulation in human psychology, he saw "community, the dependence of human beings on each other for their most important satisfactions, . . . as inescapable a truth as competitiveness" (*Scale of Greatness* 113). Accordingly, Johnson laments the dispersal of Scottish Highlanders throughout America after the Jacobite uprising of 1745 in terms of community lost; in going each in quest of his private fortune, "It may be thought that they are happier by the change . . . but they must want that security, that dignity, that happiness, whatever it be, which a prosperous community throws back upon individuals" (*Journey* 131–32).

III. Concentric Communities

In the communities we physically inhabit, sympathy radiates outward in concentric circles of diminishing intensity. We feel most strongly with those family members nearest to us, somewhat less strongly with our constellation of friends and colleagues, and still less with our more general acquaintance; yet, however diminished, sympathy extends to the circumference of the nation, and outward, however faintly, to the rest of the world. Hume writes that although there is a potential or dimly realized sympathy "among all human creatures," "we find, that where, beside the general resemblance of our natures, there is any peculiar similarity in our manners, or character, or country, or language, it facilitates the sympathy. The stronger the relation is betwixt ourselves and any object, the more easily does the imagination make the transition, and convey to the related idea the vivacity of conception, with which we always form the idea of our own person" (*T* 318). In the essay "Of National Characters" (1748), Hume maintains that the distinctive characteristics of different peoples are due not to any natural causes such as the air or climate of a nation, but to the sympathetic "contagion" of sentiments, passions and inclinations among any "number of men . . . united into one political body" (*Essays* 202).

Thus the laws of justice, which we morally affirm through sympathy, are far stronger within a single nation than between different nations.

Hume's basic view of the just human community derives from Cato's exposition of Stoic ethics in Cicero's dialogue *De Finibus,* book 3.[8] The first circle is drawn around the self: "[I]mmediately upon birth . . . a living creature feels an attachment for itself, and an impulse to preserve itself and to feel affection for its own constitution and for those things which tend to

---

[8] Cf. a passage preserved from Hierocles, a Stoic of the first and second centuries C.E.: "Each of us is as if surrounded by a series of concentric circles" (trans. Martha Nussbaum, 342). The Stoic theory of *oikeiosis*—"the tendency we have both towards developing self-concern and towards developing other-concern"—is presented and defended by Julia Annas, 262–76.

preserve its constitution" (sec. v). The next circle encompasses our parents, whom we first love as useful to our own preservation, and finally for their own sake (v). This impulse of fellow-feeling ripples outward into the further circles of "unions, societies and states"; and since justice places the safety of all above the safety of any individual, "it becomes us to love our country more than ourselves" (cf. *De Officiis* 3.21–26). The cosmopolis is mentioned, too—"the universe . . . is a city or state of which both men and gods are members"—but no ethical consequences are explicitly drawn from this premise; for all intents and purposes, we are to act as patriots rather than as citizens of the world.

Cicero's Cato upholds a radiating model of benevolence over a universal benevolence in which everyone counts the same as everyone else. His patriotic Stoicism opposes the thoroughgoing cosmopolitanism of the Cynics: Diogenes renounced his allegiance to the polis altogether, but Cato urges his wise man to cultivate "private property," "to engage in politics and government, and also to live in accordance with nature by taking himself a wife. . . . Even the passion of love when pure is not thought incompatible with the character of the Stoic Sage" (xx). Cato's model of benevolence receives its finest eighteenth-century expression in Pope's famous lines from *An Essay on Man:*

> God loves from Whole to Parts: but human soul
> Must rise from Individual to the Whole.
> Self-love but serves the virtuous mind to wake,
> As the small pebble stirs the peaceful lake;
> The centre mov'd, a circle strait succeeds,
> Another still, and still another spreads,
> Friend, parent, neighbour, first it will embrace,
> His country next, and next all human race,
> Wide and more wide, th' o'erflowings of the mind
> Take ev'ry creature in, of ev'ry kind;
> Earth smiles around, with boundless bounty blest,
> And Heav'n beholds its image in his breast.
> (4:361–72)

The radiating benevolence found in Pope and Cicero enters not only into Hume's notion of concentric circles of moral sympathy, but also into Johnson's social theory, especially as he expresses it in *Rambler* no. 99 (4: 164–69). Self-love is our first and foremost impulse (cf. *Rambler* 5:119); love radiates outward from self to our sexual unions, our private friendships, those who share our professions, the various levels of society we inhabit, and only lastly to "the great community of mankind." Johnson recognizes the Christian duty to universal benevolence, but shies away from a strong version of that doctrine:

To love all men is our duty, so far as it includes a general habit of benevolence, and readiness of occasional kindness; but to love all equally is impossible; at least impossible without the extinction of those passions which now produce all our pains and pleasures; without the disuse, if not the abolition of some of our faculties, and the suppression of all our hopes and fears in apathy and indifference.[9]

Our concern for others moves outward along widening circles of sympathy or love. Johnson quotes John Dennis's formulation of the principle:

> Of all our countrymen which do we love most, those whom we know, or those whom we know not? And of those whom we know which do we cherish most, our friends or our enemies? And of our friends, which are the dearest to us, those who are related to us, or those who are not? And of all our relations, for which have we most tenderness, for those who are near to us, or for those who are remote? And of our near relations which are the nearest, and consequently the dearest to us, our offspring or others? Our offspring, most certainly; as nature, or in other words Providence, has wisely contrived for the preservation of mankind. ("Addison," *Lives* 2:136)

Thus, Dennis concludes, it is absurd that the Cato of Addison's tragedy (in contrast to the Cato of Cicero's dialogue) should cry for the fate of Rome, but not for the death of his son:

> [D]oes it not follow . . . that for a man to receive the news of his son's death with dry eyes, and to weep at the same time for the calamities of his country, is a wretched affectation, and a miserable inconsistency? Is not that, in plain English, to receive with dry eyes the news of the deaths of those for whose sake our country is a name so dear to us, and at the same time to shed tears for those whose sakes our country is not a name so dear to us?

IV. The Esteem of Ages

We can see now the degree to which Hume's essay "The Stoic"—which we first observed above, in chapter 4—borrows from Cicero's characterization of Cato; and also to what extent it serves as a précis of Hume's own ethical writing.[10] Hume's Stoic is no toy of Fortune and retains always his

---

[9] The last great eighteenth-century statement of radiating benevolence was Burke's: "To be attached to the subdivision, to love the little platoon we belong to in society, is the first principle (the germ as it were) of public affections. It is the first link in the series by which we proceed to a love to our country and to mankind" (135; cf. 315). The French revolutionary asks, by contrast, that we love from whole to parts, like God.

[10] That Hume expresses his own view of human excellence in "The Stoic" has also, since the completion of my book, been argued by Donald Livingston, *Philosophical Melancholy and Delirium* 138–41.

"security" beyond the reach of chance and the ignoble passions that seek indolent and luxurious pleasures (*Essays* 149–50); nonetheless, he indulges his social passions, and his sympathy irradiates outward from family members and friends and neighbors to the nation as a whole:

> See the triumph of nature in parental affection! What selfish passion; what sensual delight is a match for it! Whether a man exults in the prosperity and virtue of his offspring, or flies to their succour, through the most threatening and tremendous dangers?
>
> Proceed still in purifying the generous passion, you will still the more admire its shining glories. What charms are there in the harmony of minds, and in a friendship founded on mutual esteem and gratitude! What satisfaction in relieving the distressed, in comforting the afflicted, in raising the fallen, and in stopping the career of cruel fortune, or of more cruel man, in their insults over the good and virtuous! But what supreme joy in the victories over vice as well as misery, when, by virtuous example or wise exhortation, our fellow creatures are taught to govern their passions, reform their vices, and subdue their worst enemies, which inhabit within their own bosoms?
>
> But these objects are still too limited for the human mind . . . It views liberty and laws as the source of human happiness, and devotes itself, with the utmost alacrity, to their guardianship and protection. Toils, dangers, death itself carry their charms, when we brave them for the public good, and ennoble that being, which we generously sacrifice for the interests of our country.
> (*Essays* 152–53)

Industriousness is, as Cicero stressed, natural to us (*De Finibus* 5.55–57), and "the great end of all human industry," Hume's Stoic knows, "is the attainment of happiness." The path to happiness, personally and nationally, lies in "the cultivating of our mind, the moderating of our passions, the enlightening of our reason" (148–49). And the happiness of the individual in society and in the nation is the end of Hume's ethics, man-as-he-ought-to-be.

Johnson would agree with most of the Stoic's program, with two key reservations: he would not limit happiness to this side of the grave, nor find perfect comfort in the Stoic's heroic profession, "Death itself loses its terrors, when he [the sage and patriot] considers, that its dominion extends only over a part of him, and that, in spite of death and time, the rage of elements, and the endless vicissitudes of human affairs, he is assured of an immortal fame among all the sons of men" (*Essays* 154). Johnson certainly knew the love of fame, and admired fame's power of translating one from any political community into the transhistorical community of the learned; he did not, however, find the prospect of fame capable of effacing the fear of death. (Boswell repeatedly notes that death and divine judgment terrified Johnson; Johnson himself maintained that in the face of death, "the dictates of Zeno" will not do: "[S]urely there is no man who, thus afflicted, does not seek succour in the Gospel" [*Idler* 2:131].) In all other regards, however, Hume's Stoic voices Johnson's own ethical ideal: Stoicism made compatible with a just and rational sympathy, the tear shed at scenes of affliction, industriousness, genuine patriotism, and albeit not as an ultimate recompense, the love of fame.[11]

"Fame" is indeed a double-edged term: Hume uses it to refer both to one's local reputation in one's own lifetime (for Hume, "bad fame or reputation" is synonymous with "shame," *T* 571), and also to one's posthumous fame—the "immortal fame among all the sons of men" for which Hume's Stoic thirsts (*Essays* 154). Hume himself in the autobiographical essay he wrote shortly before his death cites "love of literary fame" as "my ruling passion" ("My Own Life," *Essays* xi). Johnson tends, although not consistently, to reserve "fame" for that which will outlast us.[12] "The love of fame" is the "desire of filling the minds of others with admiration, and of being celebrated by generations to come with praises which we shall not hear" (*Rambler* 3:265).

This fame has no necessary temporal or geographical boundaries; its nature is cosmopolitan and extensive. It involves people whom we do not know, and who bear no necessary contiguous relation to us. Its very separation from any immediate social context renders it potentially suspect: might not the conquering hero sacrifice his fellows to amaze distant lands and future ages? Johnson evaluates the love of fame in *Rambler* no. 49, in which he evokes a felicific calculus: does the passion "promote the happiness, or increase the misery of mankind?" Ought it, consequently, to be cultivated or suppressed?

Johnson first surveys the arguments, and mimics the language, of both those who praise and those who condemn the love of fame. "The advo-

---

[11] For Cicero, as later for Adam Smith, the love of fame, inasmuch as it leads to virtuous action, is an acceptable motive, albeit a less excellent one than the sage's pure love of virtue; see Cicero, *De Finibus* 5.69, *Tusculans* 1:109–10, *De Officiis* 1:64–68; Smith, *Theory of Moral Sentiments* 7.2.4.10. Hume blurs this distinction in "The Stoic." The eclecticism of Hume's Stoic, and of Hume's own philosophy, contrasts with Smith's more pristine Stoic doctrine; however, Athol Fitzgibbons errs in presenting Hume as a systematic foil to Smith's Stoic vision of ethics and polity. At this point in my argument, Fitzgibbons's thesis needs only to be seen to be disbelieved: "Whereas Hume rejected the past completely . . . Smith proposed a modified Stoic[ism]"; "Smith countered Hume's nihilistic version of a liberal society, which eventually would lead to decadence and social degeneration, with a moral vision of the liberal state" (15–16).

[12] "Praise" or "celebrity" is what we seek in our contiguous communities: "Praise is so pleasing to the mind of man, that it is the original motive of almost all our actions. . . . Every man pants for the highest eminence within his view; none, however mean, ever sink below the hope of being distinguished by his fellow-beings, and very few have, by magnanimity or piety, been so raised above it, as to act wholly without regard to censure or opinion" (*Rambler* 5:244). *Rambler* no. 146 uses "praise," "celebrity" and "renown" interchangeably; the "hope of fame" seems at first to accord with this reference to a present audience, but Johnson adds that fame "sometimes . . . begins when life is at an end" (5:16–17).

cates for the love of fame" loom large in eighteenth-century life—they include, as A. O. Lovejoy notes, most major eighteenth-century writers.[13] As a schoolboy Johnson wrote in a Latin exercise, "An unsubdued and invincible desire of honour and praise is planted in our hearts, which I would believe wise Nature (for she does nothing in vain) has instilled in us to spur us on to praiseworthy deeds" (*MW* 39). In *Rambler* no. 49, Johnson assumes an air of greater impartiality, noting only that fame's advocates "allege in its vindication, that it is a passion natural and universal; a flame lighted by heaven, and always burning with greatest vigour in the most enlarged and elevated minds." At the same time, however, Milton's orthodox Christian sentiment from *Lycidas* dismissing fame as "that last infirmity of Noble mind" continued to issue from pulpits. Johnson thus avers that "[t]his ardour has been considered by some, as nothing better than splendid madness, as a flame kindled by pride, and fanned by folly" (3:265–66).

Johnson finally throws his weight, with due qualification, on the side of those who praise the love of fame: "Upon an attentive and impartial review of the argument, it will appear that the love of fame is to be regulated, rather than extinguished; and that men should be taught not to be wholly careless about their memory, but to endeavour that they may be remembered chiefly for their virtues, since no other reputation will be able to transmit any pleasure beyond the grave" (266). Johnson's final clause carries a double edge: first, one's virtuous reputation will transmit pleasure to those who outlive and succeed one on earth; second, it alone will steer one's departed soul toward an eternal home of pleasure rather than pain. Finally, Johnson's goal as a moralist is not only to secure us as much as possible from the slings and arrows of fortune in this life, but to remind us of and to anticipate a place where fortune plays no role—an afterlife in which each is given his or her due, in perfect justice. Still, Johnson cast an eye toward his earthly remembrance and hoped that his writing would by its virtues endure. Oliver Goldsmith, who knew Johnson well, presents him alongside Hume as an eager candidate for immortality on earth. In 1759, Goldsmith published an allegorical reverie in which, among the many contemporary authors who clamor for admittance onto the stagecoach of fame, Johnson and Hume are two of only three men of letters who gain admission (*Works* 1:444–50).[14]

---

[13]*Reflections on Human Nature*, 152–93. Lovejoy includes among those who approved the love of fame Mandeville, Pope, Edward Young, Butler, William Melmoth, Voltaire, Christian Wolff, Hume, Adam Smith, and Kant.

[14] The third is the Scottish-born novelist Tobias Smollett (1721–1771).

CHAPTER SIX

Necessity and Tragedy

I. Physics and Ethics

We have seen that the core of Johnson's and Hume's social theory derives ultimately from Cicero's version of Stoic philosophy. But to the Stoic, social harmony is but one instance of the providential design of the cosmos as a whole. Ethical order as we know it proves but one aspect or manifestation of the rational order of the universe.[1] Stoicism, like the other Hellenistic schools, sought to ground its ethics in a postulated physics; it would underwrite ethical obligation with the authority of a rationally discernible cosmic purpose. The providentialism of Stoic physics enjoyed a widespread revival throughout the seventeenth and earlier eighteenth centuries, supplying as it did a secular and universal defense for a proposition accepted by many Deists and Christians alike: "Whatever IS, is RIGHT" (Pope, *Essay on Man* 1:294).

Johnson, however, dismissed the Stoic physics of Chrysippus as dark and unintelligible; thinking of it as much the same thing, he elsewhere satirizes Pope's "Leibnitian reasoning" (*Lives* 3:243).[2] Chrysippus taught that the world was as good as it could be given the constraints imposed on a benevolent God by the passive principle of matter—a tenet revived in the "cosmic optimism" popularized by Pope's *Essay on Man,* and by lesser lights such as Soame Jenyns. Johnson concludes his review essay of Jenyns's *Free*

[1] See Cicero, *De Natura Deorum* book 2, especially secs. 45–58, 73–97, 164–67.
[2] Cf. Edinger 52–62 on Johnson's general opposition to the eighteenth-century poetic vogue of cosmological speculation.

Inquiry into the Nature and Origin of Evil: "[W]e are devolved back into dark ignorance, and all our effort ends in belief that for the evils of life there is some good reason, and in confession that the reason cannot be found. This is all that has been produced by the revival of Chrysippus's untractableness of matter, and the Arabian scale of existence [i.e., the "Great Chain of Being"]" (*MW* 542–43).

In entirely the same vein, Hume judges speculative physics to be ethically useless. In the following passage from the first *Enquiry* both his initial drollery and final stinging remark have a Johnsonian ring:

> There are many philosophers who, after an exact scrutiny of all the phenomena of nature, conclude, that the WHOLE, considered as one system, is, in every period of its existence, ordered with perfect benevolence; and that the utmost possible happiness will, in the end, result to all created beings, without any mixture of positive or absolute ill and misery. . . . From this theory, some philosophers, and the ancient *Stoics* among the rest, derived a topic of consolation under all afflictions, while they taught their pupils that those ills under which they laboured were, in reality, goods to the universe; and that to an enlarged view, which could comprehend the whole system of nature, every event became an object of joy and exultation. But though this topic be specious and sublime, it was soon found in practice weak and ineffectual. You would surely more irritate than appease a man lying under the racking pains of the gout by preaching up to him the rectitude of those general laws, which produced the malignant humours in his body, and led them through the proper canals, to the sinews and nerves, where they now excite such acute torments. (101; cf. "The Sceptic," *Essays* 173)

In Hume's *Dialogues concerning Natural Religion,* the reality of pain is again invoked to undermine the theoretical negation of natural and moral evil; although "*Leibniz* has denied it," "the united testimony of mankind, founded on sense and consciousness" confirms the fact of human misery (194). This last line belongs to the orthodox theist Demea, a character who resembles Johnson not a little; in part 10 of the *Dialogues,* Demea and the sceptic Philo concur that the misery and wickedness apparent in human life bear down the optimist's a priori belief that this is the happiest of all possible worlds. Demea speaks one altogether Johnsonian line: "So anxious or so tedious are even the best scenes of life, that futurity is still the object of all our hopes and fears" (193). At the end of part 11, Philo distances himself from his former ally, maintaining that Christian moralists are apt "to exaggerate all the ills and pains that are incident to men" precisely to turn the mind toward religion; this remark—along with Philo's argument that judging from created nature a posteriori, we can infer no more than a creator who is morally neutral—finally prompts Demea to depart (213). Yet Demea is not, to Hume, a character simply to be dismissed.[3] The provisional alliance between orthodoxy and possible infidelity lies in a shared rejection of the "specious and sublime" notion that the universe is an ideally good organism or orchestration. Although Johnson isn't simply Demea, nor Hume Philo, we cannot but help to see in each writer the scepticism of those characters toward an optimistic physicotheology.

Johnson and Hume did, however, accept what they viewed as the *experimental* physics of Newton. Hume's Newton in particular was less a metaphysician than any ancient physicist had been:

> In Newton this island may boast of having produced the greatest and rarest genius that ever arose for the ornament and instruction of the species. Cautious in admitting no principles but such as were founded on experiment; but resolute to adopt every such principle, however new or unusual . . . He was from these causes long unknown to the world; but his reputation at last broke out with a lustre, which scarcely any writer . . . had ever before attained. While Newton seemed to draw off the veil from some of the mysteries of nature, he shewed at the same time the imperfections of the mechanical philosophy; and thereby restored her ultimate secrets to that obscurity, in which they ever did and ever will remain. (*History* 6:542)

(James Noxon remarks, "No-one, I think, allows that [Newton] was as content as Hume with restoring the ultimate secrets of the nature to perpetual obscurity" [*Hume's Philosophical Development* 71–72].) Like Hume, Johnson accepted the Newtonian worldview and the logic underlying that worldview as the provisional starting points for his own naturalistic psychology and ethics. Neither man thought science capable of explaining ultimate principles, or even the practice of science itself; rather, as Nicholas Capaldi claims for Hume, "all understanding and all explanation must originate in a human cultural context" ("Dogmatic Slumber" 122). Johnson and Hume both admired, and sought to introduce into the study of human nature, the modesty and precision of Newton's focus on efficient causes.

II. Human Nature Demands a Newton

The "science" of mind in the eighteenth century deserves that name only in the sense that its central metaphors derive from popularizations

---

[3] The Demea of part 10 is, as Dorothy Coleman points out (185), an advocate of what Hume in *The Natural History of Religion* calls "vulgar religion," in which hope and fear bolster the desire to ascertain the nature of unknown causes. Demea's arguments here and in part 9 are not, however, without force; see James Dye's probing essays, "A Word on Behalf of Demea" and "Demea's Departure."

of Newton's science of physical bodies in rest and motion.[4] The elements of mind corresponding to Newton's bodies typically consist of "ideas" and "impressions"—especially the passions, reflective impressions whose operations seemed, of all mental events, the most law-governed. This trend culminates in Kames's immensely popular *Elements of Criticism* (a work begun, according to Kames, in 1753 [1:313], first published in 1762, and reaching a sixth, corrected edition in 1785). The *Elements* illustrates psychological principles—chiefly, the association of ideas and "the economy of the human passions" (1:193)—through examples drawn from the arts, chiefly literature. Kames's Newtonianism is salient: "[B]etween a passion and its object there is a natural operation resembling action and reaction in physics: a passion acting upon its object, magnifies it greatly in appearance; and this magnified object reacting upon the passion, swells and inflames it mightily" (2:121).

This type of aperçu is enabled by the epistemology of Hume and Johnson. Each sought to present the motions of the mind according to the implicit or explicit model of Newtonian physics. That each did so has by now received wide comment and extensive acknowledgement; yet no one has, to my knowledge, remarked on this debt to the new science as a common bond between the two men's moral philosophy. In 1948, W. K Wimsatt concluded his magisterial study of Johnson's philosophic style: "Johnson's *Ramblers,* as a plausible outcome of the very abstraction, simplification, and systematization of the world seen by the mechanical science, exhibit perhaps the most concentrated use in English literature of mechanical imagery turned inward to the analysis of the soul" (*Philosophic Words* 104). Thus, for example, we find: "All attraction is encreased by the approach of the attracting body. We never find ourselves so desirous to finish, as in the latter part of our work, or so impatient of delay, as when we know that delay cannot be long" (*Rambler* 5:312; cf. *Adventurer* 2:344). And as Newton discovered that "the distinct and primogenial colours are only seven," so the moralist recognizes that "the passions of the mind, which put the world in motion . . . are very few; but those few agitated and combined, as external causes shall happen to operate," afford us life's rich and ever changing pageant (*Adventurer* 428–29).

One year after Wimsatt alerted us to Johnson's debt to mechanical science, Norman Kemp Smith related Hume's psychological principle of the association of ideas and impressions (including passions) back to New-

---

[4] There is a large literature on the ways in which Newton's science was extended into the moral sphere; see, for instance, the bibliographical note in Haakonssen, *Natural Law and Moral Philosophy* 3–4. Jerome Schneewind is correct, I think, in claiming that Newton's influence on modern moral philosophy is significant but not radical; the root causes of the morality of self-governance that develops in the seventeenth century are rather the wars of religion that curtailed or compromised traditional modes of obedience (7).

tonian physics, particularly the theory of gravitational attraction (71–76, 184–85). Pall S. Árdal subsequently observed that "the influence of Newtonian mechanics . . . is evident" in Hume's understanding of the passions as opposed and mutually canceling forces: "The passions are opposed to each other in the same way as opposing gravitational forces. The more complex model of the emotional life common at the present time allows the possibility of, for example, loving and hating a person at one and the same time, and the result is tension and inner turbulence and not [as Hume would have it] equilibrium" (24). Details of Hume's psychology are evidently indebted to Newton, but Norman Kemp Smith also sparked a scholarly debate over the nature and extent of Newton's overall methodological influence on Hume. Smith suggested that the subtitle of Hume's *Treatise—An Attempt to Introduce the Experimental Method of Reasoning into Moral Subjects*—refers to Newton's conception of method; Smith quotes from the *Opticks:* "Hypotheses [a priori assumptions] are not to be regarded in experimental Philosophy. And although the arguing from Experiments and Observations by Induction be no Demonstration of general Conclusions; yet it is the best way of arguing which the Nature of Things admits of" (Kemp Smith, 56–57).

In the wake of Wimsatt and Kemp Smith a train of commentators have variously assessed Hume's debt to Newton and natural philosophy, and Johnson's debt to the same sources.[5] It is a common source of analogy, that, like their common debts to Cicero and Addison, draws together the two men's moral thought. It also forces each to consider the relationship between the necessity of mechanical law, and the freedom of the human will.

III. Necessity and Liberty

The mechanics of impressions and ideas implies a type of determinism or necessity that is potentially at odds with the moralist's therapeutic aims, which must assume the liberty or freedom of the will. Both Hume and Johnson would, however, show that the doctrine of necessity, or "fate," is compatible with human freedom and responsibility.

Hume offers a compatibilist argument in the *Treatise* 2.3.1–2, and a modified version of that argument in section 8 of the first *Enquiry*, "Of Liberty and Necessity." In both versions, he defines "necessity" as the necessary cause-and-effect connection between motive (i.e., instinct, passion, reflective passion, disposition) and action. In the *Enquiry*, he reserves the

---

[5] On Hume, see Passmore, *Hume's Intentions* 42–64; Noxon, *Hume's Philosophical Development* 32–75; Peter Jones, 11–19; Penelhum, "Hume's Moral Psychology," 120–29. On Johnson, see Alkon, 6–9, 209–14; Schwartz, 27–29, 59–93.

term *liberty* for what he had called in the *Treatise* the "liberty of *spontaneity*," or freedom from external constraint, as distinguished from the illusory "liberty of *indifference*," or freedom from any antecedent determination. Hume argues that, given these definitions, necessity is perfectly compatible with both the liberty of, and our responsibility for, our actions. Moreover, Hume "venture[s] to affirm that the doctrines, both of necessity and liberty, as above explained, are not only consistent with morality, but are absolutely essential to its support":

> The only proper object of hatred or vengeance is a person or creature, endowed with thought and consciousness; and when any criminal or injurious actions excite that passion, it is only by their relation to the person, or connexion with him. Actions are, by their very nature, temporary and perishing; and where they proceed not from some *cause* in the character and disposition of the person who performed them, they can neither redound to his honour, if good; nor infamy, if evil. . . . According to the principle, therefore, which denies necessity, and consequently causes, a man is as pure and untainted, after having committed the most horrid crime, as at the first moment of his birth, nor is his character anywise concerned in his actions, since they are not derived from it, and the wickedness of the one can never be used as a proof of the depravity of the other. (*ECHU* 97–98).

Every event is determined by causal laws, but that determination is not incompatible with human freedom and moral responsibility. Hume's compatibilist account of our practical freedom is referred to, after William James, as one type of "soft determinism." Another type of soft determinism, by which I believe Hume to have been inspired, is that of the Stoics, later revived by Spinoza.[6] The Stoics, too, believed in fate as an all-embracing causal network, but nonetheless affirmed that we feel and are free to act morally and thus ought to be blamed or praised for our actions. "In the Stoic view," writes Terence Irwin, "my action has a series of causes, each of which is made inevitable by its cause, and which together make the action causally inevitable. But sometimes my choice contributes to the result; and my choice depends on appearance and assent" (172). To think that fate obviates the exercise of rational agency is to fall prey to the so-called "lazy argument," a practical defense of not choosing famously confuted by Chrysippus. The lazy argument is presented by Cicero in *De Fato:*

> Nor will we be blocked by the so called "Lazy Argument" (the *argos logos,* as the philosophers entitle it). If we gave in to it, we would do nothing whatever

---

[6] Sophie Botros analyzes the ways in which the Stoic account of human freedom does and does not resemble that of contemporary soft determinists (288–89). That Hume can legitimately be called a soft determinist—"if not . . . a paradigm example of the orthodox version of soft determinism"—has recently been reaffirmed by Don Garrett (119–29).

in life. They pose it as follows: "If it is your fate to recover from this illness, you will recover, regardless of whether or not you call the doctor. Likewise, if it is your fate not to recover from this illness, you will not recover, regardless of whether or not you call the doctor. And one or the other is your fate. Therefore it is pointless to call the doctor." (sec. 38, trans. Long and Sedley, 339–40)

Chrysippus's rejoinder, also presented by Cicero (secs. 55–62), is developed by Larry Becker: as opposed to either a "categorical" fatalism ("Whatever will be, will be, no matter what"), or—although here the opposition is less clear—a "conditional" fatalism ("if such and such happens, then so and so happens"), the Stoic insists that "agency is the determinate product of antecedent events and its exercise has determinate outcomes" (63–64). Agency is not only a link in a causal chain, but a contribution to that chain.

As we've seen, the earliest Stoics held a cosmic, providential view of fate that Hume rejected. To him, fate is simply secular necessity, and necessity is only the more or less constant conjunction, as revealed through experience and historical record, between certain motives or dispositions and certain events:

> The same motives always produce the same actions: The same events follow from the same causes. Ambition, avarice, self-love, vanity, friendship, generosity, public spirit: these passions, mixed in various degrees, and distributed through society, have been, from the beginning of the world, and still are, the source of all the actions and enterprises, which have ever been observed among mankind. . . . Mankind are so much the same, in all times and places, that history informs us of nothing new or strange in this particular. (*ECHU* 83)

According to this account, historical records "are so many collections of experiments, by which the politician or moral philosopher fixes the principles of his science."

Hume's appeal in the first *Enquiry* to history as a guidebook to causal laws might serve as the epigraph to a poem Johnson published the following year, *The Vanity of Human Wishes*. We will turn to that poem in the next section. First, however, I would show that Johnson did in practice accept secular necessity, and the doctrine of compatibilism, as Hume defines them—his own thinking in this regard influenced probably by Cicero and certainly by the Stoically inflected Latin poem on which he based *The Vanity of Human Wishes*.[7]

---

[7] Johnson was influenced as well by the Renaissance neo-Stoic Justus Lipsius; the Christian accent that Lipsius gave Stoic compatibilism—see Schneewind, 173–74—would no doubt have appealed to Johnson.

When the wide-eyed young prince Rasselas announces as his goal the rational and unconditioned *"choice of life,"* the more worldly wise Imlac responds: "Very few . . . live by choice. Every man is placed in his present condition by causes which acted without his foresight, and with which he did not always willingly co-operate" (*Rasselas* 67). Who we are involves our choices, but is certainly not dependent on them alone: Imlac here offers a thumbnail sketch of soft determinism. Johnson correspondingly rejected a hard determinism, or categorical fatalism, and he does so on the same grounds as Hume: it potentially negates individual moral responsibility. *Rambler* no. 113, written in the voice of a young man seeking a suitable marriage partner, describes "the deep-read Misothea," a secular hard determinist of the scariest sort:

> Misothea endeavoured to demonstrate the folly of attributing choice and self-direction to any human being. It was not difficult to discover the danger of committing myself for ever to the arms of one who might at any time mistake the dictates of passion, or the calls of appetite, for the decree of fate; or consider cuckoldom as necessary to the general system, as a link in the everlasting chain of successive causes. I therefore told her, that destiny had ordained us to part; and that nothing should have torn me from her but the talons of necessity. (4:239)

In evincing our ability to manipulate the *discourse* of fate, Johnson's speaker offers, in effect, a sufficient refutation of the "lazy argument." At least sometimes, our fate is what we say it is.

In addition to the secular necessity of which we have been speaking, there is of course theological necessity or predestination—a topic on which Johnson was as loath to speculate as Hume. For Hume, viewing the Deity as "the mediate cause of all the actions of men" appears to imply that He is also "the author of sin and moral turpitude": but, "[t]hese are mysteries, which natural and unassisted reason is very unfit to handle. . . . Happy, if she be thence sensible of her temerity, when she pries into these sublime mysteries; and leaving a scene so full of obscurities and perplexities, return, with suitable modesty, to her true and proper province, the examination of common life" (*ECHU* 103). Johnson's court of appeal is also common life. Boswell was attracted to predestination: "The argument for the moral necessity of human actions is always, I observe, fortified by supposing universal prescience to be one of the attributes of the Deity." Johnson, in response, appeals to common experience to validate at least the liberty of spontaneity: "You are surer that you are free, than you are of prescience; you are surer that you can lift up your finger or not as you please, than you are of any conclusion from a deduction of reasoning." Johnson then proffers one of his very rare theological speculations, suggesting that God's prescience differs only in degree from our own prescient ability to make inferences based on constant conjunctions: "If I am well acquainted with a man, I can judge with great probability how he will act in any case, without his being restrained by my judging. GOD may have this probability increased to certainty" (*Life of Johnson* 3:290–91). God, that is, shares our (Humean) understanding of moral necessity, with the difference that He is fully cognizant, as we are not, of the exceptionless causal laws that govern all behavior. We are fallible students of human nature; He is the infallible the ideal to which our science imperfectly aims. Lo, the Enlightenment God!

In addition to the hoary doctrine of predestination, Johnson also opposed theological necessity in its updated, eighteenth-century form: the doctrine of the divinely implanted "ruling passion." This doctrine, most famously expounded by Pope in his philosophical poetry, holds that each individual is assigned at birth one ruling passion or passional disposition, such as fearfulness or hopefulness, avarice or extravagance. These several counterbalancing dispositions are the means by which God effects an elaborate division of mutually complementary human labors, and thus secures the harmonious working of the world.[8] (This God would later reappear as the "Invisible Hand" that orchestrates divergent interests in Adam Smith's marketplace.)

In 1742, Johnson published an annotated translation of Crousaz's *Commentary on Mr. Pope's Principles of Morality, or Essay on Man*.[9] In one of his annotations, Johnson objects to Pope's "system of a Ruling Passion interwoven with the original constitution and perpetually presiding over its motions, invariable, incessant, and insuperable." The first objection consists of an appeal to his own experience: "The author may perhaps be conscious of a Ruling Passion that has influenced all his actions and designs. I am conscious of none but a general desire of happiness, which is not here intended, so that there appears equal evidence on both sides." People do have, at various times in their lives, various "predominant inclinations . . . but perhaps if they review their early years and trace their ideas backwards, they will find that those strong desires were the effects either of example or instruction, the circumstances in which they were placed, the objects which they first received impressions from, the first books they read, or the first company they conversed with." Johnson's second objection, then, is that if one does have a certain passional disposition it might not be innate, but acquired; Johnson sounds here like a social constructionist, an exponent of nurture over nature.

[8] See Pope, *An Essay on Man* 2:133–248, and *Epistles to Several Persons* 2 ("To a Lady"):207–18; 3 ("To Bathhurst"):155–78.

[9] See *Life of Johnson* 4:494–96. Jean Pierre de Crousaz had recently published in French a commentary on the aesthetic and philosophical merits and demerits of Pope's internationally famous poem, although he knew only Du Resnel's French verse translation of the poem. (Kant, incidentally, came to love the poem in German verse.) Johnson, in turn, translated and annotated Crousaz's commentary in order to criticize both Du Resnel's misrepresentations of Pope and Crousaz's own failings as both a close reader and as a moral philosopher.

He will admit only that the changing circumstances of different stages of life facilitate the expression of different passions: "Every observer, however superficial, has remarked that in many men the love of pleasures is the Ruling Passion of their youth, and the love of money that of their advanced years." (Hume, in an essay he later withdrew, remarked precisely this progress of the passions.) [10] But the theory that we each have one innate and immutable ruling passion is not only contrary to common experience; it may also have pernicious ethical consequences: "[I]t is not proper to dwell too long on the resistless power and despotic authority of this tyrant of the soul, lest the reader should, as it is very natural, take the present inclination, however destructive to society or himself, for the Ruling Passion, and forbear to struggle when he despairs to conquer" (*MW* 91–92). Innate, necessary traits are not susceptible to therapeutic treatment, and believing one has them may make one incorrigible.[11]

Although Johnson rejected the theory of the ruling passion along with other types of divine necessity, he did not think the will undetermined by antecedent causes. However, his animadversions against the ruling passion, added to a few quips against the doctrine of "fatality," has led some critics to claim that Johnson opposed all determinism. Once we have seen the error of this claim, we need not be troubled by the deterministic spectacle of his great historical poem, *The Vanity of Human Wishes*.[12] The poem is simply a variation on Johnson's usual compatibilism. In it, his determinism takes the harder form of a *conditional* fatalism (if so and so, then so and so). The disasters that befall the historical personages of the *Vanity* do so because they indulge exorbitant passions. Johnson's lesson is that if one follows such passions, then such a fate will follow.

IV. The Vanity of Exorbitant Wishes

The Latin work on which Johnson bases his poem—Juvenal's Tenth Satire—might itself be titled "Rational and Irrational Wishing." Juvenal

---

[10] In "Of Avarice" (1741), Hume asserts that avarice is the strongest passion because it is the passion of old men left with no other remaining passions "to counter-balance, in some degree, its predominant inclination" (*Essays* 571); Hume does not, however, explain why avarice should be coincident with, or the effect of, age. The general perception that different passions predominate at different stages in a man's life goes back at least to Aristotle's *Rhetoric* book 2, secs. 12–14. Johnson treats the theme again in *Rambler* no. 151.

[11] Cf. Johnson's "Life of Pope," *Lives* 3:165. Johnson also criticizes the notion of a ruling passion in *Rambler* no. 43 and satirizes it in the voice of a "virtuoso," *Rambler* no. 82. Hume, by contrast, will use the psychology of the "ruling passion" when he comes to write his *History* (and "My Own Life"), although it is unclear whether or not he accepts the metaphysical baggage that the phrase carried after Pope.

[12] Voitle views Johnson as an antideterminist and so worries over "the uniquely fatalistic tone of *The Vanity of Human Wishes*" and its "anomalous determinism" (25–28, 40–46). Cf. Damrosch, *Fictions of Reality* 49.

satirizes unreasonable desires, the pursuit of objects that cannot be attained without disaster. The poem opens,

> Search every land, from Cadiz to the dawn-streaked shores
> Of Ganges, and you'll find few men who can distinguish
> A false from a worthwhile objective, or slash their way through
> The fogs of deception. Since when were our fears or desires
> Ever dictated by reason? . . .
> What you ask for, you get. The Gods aren't fussy, they're willing
> To blast you, root and branch, upon request.
>
> (ll. 1–8, trans. Green)

The poem then surveys seven "false objectives": great riches; pomp and ceremonial importance; great political power; overflowing eloquence; military conquest; long life; physical beauty. In each section, Juvenal adduces the exemplary fate of figures from Greco-Roman history: for example, Sejanus's abrupt fall from political power; Hannibal's inglorious defeat and death in exile.

The poem concludes with a brief list of "worthwhile objectives," or things for which one might reasonably wish or pray:

> For a sound mind in a sound body, a valiant heart
> Without fear of death, that reckons longevity
> The least among Nature's gifts, that's strong to endure
> All kinds of toil, that's untainted by lust and anger,
> That prefers the sorrows and labours of Hercules to all
> Sardanapalus' downy cushions and women and junketings.
> What I've shown you, you can find by yourself: there's one
> Path, and one only, to a life of peace—through virtue.
> Fortune has no divinity, could we but see it: it's we,
> We ourselves, who make her a goddess, and set her in the heavens.
>
> (ll. 357–66)

As E. Vernon Arnold notes, Juvenal, although professedly of no school, "expounds much of the ethical teaching of Stoicism with more directness and force than any professed adherent of the system" (402).[13]

Johnson apparently concurs with Juvenal that you ride the wheel of fortune only if you allow certain passions to motivate you unreflectively. *The Vanity of Human Wishes* opens with a voice more solemn than Juvenal's, an unperturbable voice that issues from some Archimedean point above the scene of worldly strife:[14]

---

[13] In his edition of Juvenal, John Ferguson notes that *Satire* 10 is indebted to two Stoic works, Seneca's *On Tranquillity of Mind* and Persius's *Satire* 2 (254).

[14] E. J. Hundert (146–50) traces the Epicurean line of this *theatrum mundi* device through to Bacon, Du Bos, Addison and Mandeville. "In the revived Epicurean tradition, the metaphor of society as theatre served not so much to expose the vanity of human aspirations from

> Let Observation with extensive View,
> Survey Mankind from *China* to *Peru;*
> Remark each anxious Toil, each eager Strife,
> And watch the busy Scenes of crouded Life;
> Then say how Hope and Fear, Desire and Hate,
> O'erspread with Snares the clouded Maze of Fate,
> Where wav'ring Man, betray'd by vent'rous Pride,
> To tread the dreary Paths without a Guide;
> As treach'rous Phantoms in the Mists delude,
> Shuns fancied Ills, or chases airy Good.
> How rarely Reason guides the stubborn Choice,
> Rules the bold Hand, or prompts the suppliant Voice.
>
> (ll. 1–12)

Reason, sound philosophy, is our proper guide; it rarely directs the will, but its ability to do so is inscribed in the very tone of these opening lines— their steeliness, their air of security. To borrow Nekayah's judgment on domestic discord (*Rasselas* chap. 26), unreflective motivation "is not inevitably and fatally necessary; but yet is not easily avoided."

Johnson preserves Juvenal's overarching theme that in wishing for certain airy goods we are willing our own destruction, and doing so, as Juvenal archly maintains, wittingly. Mankind being so much the same, in all times and places, Juvenal's Sejanus easily becomes Johnson's Wolsey; Johnson's task is to find a way of re-creating in English Juvenal's rendition of the overreaching man's fate. As William Hutchings notes, Juvenal uses the subjunctive mood (*esset*) to imply that Sejanus's building of airy towers was purposive: he intended them to rise and fall. (Juvenal's final lines on Sejanus read: "unde altior esset / casus et inpulsae praeceps inmane ruinae" [106–7].) Johnson finds an English equivalent in the interrogative phrase "why did":

> For why did *Wolsey* near the Steeps of Fate,
> On weak Foundations raise th'enormous Weight?
> Why but to sink beneath Misfortune's Blow,
> With louder Ruin to the Gulphs below?
>
> (ll. 125–28)

Johnson's poem bespeaks the danger of wishes that are "impetuous" or "restless" (ll. 17, 20, 105). The poem's satiric norm is the "humble peace" at which a Wolsey will ever chafe:

---

a celestial perspective as to highlight the distance between genuine knowledge and mere appearance in the minds of social actors themselves" (147).

Speak thou, whose Thoughts at humble Peace repine,
Shall *Wolsey*'s Wealth, with *Wolsey*'s End be thine?
Or liv'st thou now, with safer Pride content,
The wisest Justice on the Banks of *Trent?*

(ll. 121–24)

The Trent is the chief river of Johnson's native Staffordshire, a place the speaker here invokes as a reasonable arena for anyone's ambition; being a justice of the peace on the Trent sounds all the more satisfying when set against Juvenal's corresponding lines about being a magistrate in some run-down towns in Latium, "inspecting weights, giving orders for the destruction/ Of short-measure pint-pots" (99–102). Juvenal's caustic point is that even a dreary fate is preferable to what comes of Sejanus's excessive ambition. Johnson's opposing point is that, if our pride is properly moderated, we may flourish anywhere. Humble peace is what we ought, reasonably, to wish for—and if we do, it is what we may be able to achieve.

At moments in his poem, Johnson suggests, as a counterpoint to his therapeutic aims, a rather more dark and all-encompassing fatalism: "Fate wings with ev'ry Wish th'afflictive Dart, / Each Gift of Nature, and each Grace of Art" (ll. 15–16); "Nor think the Doom of Man revers'd for thee" (l. 156). This minatory imagery is, however, clearly hyperbolic, inserted to unsettle the complacent reader; we would do well not to yoke it to philosophical service. Indeed, directly after asserting the fatality of "ev'ry" wish and "each" gift and grace, Johnson considerably limits his claim through his illustrations: "impetuous courage" (as distinct from reasonable courage) and "restless fire" come to a bad end (ll. 17–20). Gifts prove fatal only when used unwisely. As Johnson everywhere insists in his moral and sermonic writings, "if we languish under calamities, they are brought upon us, not by the immediate hand of Providence, but by our own folly and disobedience; . . . happiness will be diffused, as virtue prevails" (*Sermons* 14:46). Our freedom to exercise our rational agency is compatible with a proper understanding of necessity.

However, at the end of *The Vanity of Human Wishes* Johnson departs from his Latin source to assert that man cannot achieve happiness purely by his own efforts: "Implore . . . [God's] Aid, in his Decisions rest, / Secure whate'er he gives, he gives the best" (ll. 355–56). Yet even here Johnson concedes, paradoxically, that happiness can be achieved through one's (specifically religious) efforts: entreaty and prayer may garner love, patience, and faith, and "[w]ith these celestial Wisdom calms the Mind, / And makes the Happiness she does not find" (367–68). Even here, Johnson's focus is not the Christian search for meaning in the universe, but—with Juvenal and the Stoics—the quest for happiness in this world.

Johnson's lesson in the *Vanity* accords with Juvenal's, and with Hume's implicit lesson in "Of Liberty and Necessity": the only way to be forearmed against misfortune is to regulate one's imagination by reality; to see things as they are, rather than as one could simply want them to be; practically, to make inferences based on the more or less constant conjunction of events revealed by experience or history. The historical record is key to establishing the causal links that allow us to make correct inferences about character and the course of events. As Johnson declared in his pamphlet on the Falkland Islands, echoing a sentiment that goes back at least to Dionysius of Halicarnassus, "The history of mankind does not want examples that may teach caution to the daring, and moderation to the proud" (*PW* 372). The type of "examples" that Johnson here has in mind are the exempla of Latin literature and historiography, stories of past characters and events that may serve as a warning or encouragement to those in the present—the type that Juvenal uses in his Tenth Satire.[15]

Hume's own vindication of historiography is the eighteenth-century standard: "History, the great mistress of wisdom, furnishes examples of all kinds; and every prudential, as well as moral precept, may be authorized by those events, which her enlarged mirror is able to present to us" (*History* 5:545). In fact, Hume's *History of England,* especially in its pre-Tudor volumes, offers a series of exempla not dissimilar to Johnson's or Juvenal's. There are few bona fide villains in Hume's history (St. Dunstan and St. Odo of Canterbury, and perhaps Cromwell, are exceptions); rather, the vicious characters in the *History* are presented as slaves to their passions, fools to improper human wishes. What history teaches is not the way things must be, do what one will, but rather, the way things will be if those involved act in such and such a manner. Brashness and precipitancy—a blind willingness to ride the rising tide of Fortune—generally result in personal and sometimes public disaster. As Hume understands it, history would teach caution both to impudence and imprudence; it would also, however, teach courage to undue fear or indolence.[16]

The Stuart volumes of Hume's *History*—the chronological end of a history Hume wrote backward, and so published first—present as the overarching lesson of the English civil wars the simple need for prudence.

> From the memorable revolutions, which passed in England in this period, we may naturally deduce the same useful lesson, which Charles himself, in his later years, inferred; that it is dangerous for princes, even from the appearance of necessity, to assume more authority, than the laws have allowed them.

[15] Quintilian characterized Roman writing as abounding in exempla to the same extent as Greek writing abounded in precepts (10.2.29–30).

[16] The best example of a king who requires courage comes, however, not in Hume's *History* but in its aftermath. In the years leading up to Louis XVI's beheading, French Royalists pointed out Stuart parallels to recent events in France "to rouse the French to more vigorous action" on behalf of the monarchy; Louis, however, accepted the "lazy argument" of fatedness, with disastrous consequences (Bongie 101, 123).

But, it must be confessed, that these events furnish us with another instruction, no less natural, and no less useful, concerning the madness of
the people, the furies of fanaticism, and the danger of mercenary armies.
(5:545–46)

What Charles needed, earlier in his career, was greater princely prudence;
especially in his dealings with Scotland, Charles was guilty of "indiscretion
and imprudence" (257). Charles's peculiar misfortune was to lack prudence precisely in an age when enthusiasm eclipsed prudence among his
subjects:

> In any other age or nation, this monarch had been secure of a prosperous
> and happy reign. But the high idea of his own authority, which he had im-
> bibed, made him incapable of giving way to the spirit of liberty, which *began*
> to prevail among his subjects. . . . And above all, the spirit of enthusiasm
> being universally diffused, disappointed all the views of human prudence,
> and disturbed the operation of every motive, which usually influences soci-
> ety. (221)

It was a place and age, in other words, in which the causal laws that naturally operate in the social and political world were obscured by the willingness of masses of people to affect artificial lives.[17] Hume's entire *History*,
in its aspect as a manual for princes or what the Renaissance called a
"mirrour for magistrates," inculcates the lesson that in general, or under
normal circumstances, prudence is the chief virtue, and its efficacy
demonstrable.[18]

As Hume worked backward into pre-Tudor history—into "barbarous
ages" that he found increasingly "unentertaining and uninstructive" (2:
518)—he increasingly relied on the adornment of short and conventional
exempla. Hume consistently treats the lives of great men and women as

[17] Hume concludes of the ability of religious superstition or enthusiasm to disrupt natural
language and moral patterns: "When men depart from the maxims of common reason,
and affect these *artificial* lives . . . no one can answer for what will please or displease them"
(*ECPM* 343).

[18] Thus, working backward in history, we see that James II lost his throne through imprudence and insolence, while William gained his through prudent conduct (chaps. 70 and 71,
passim); the Restoration was effected by the exalted prudence of General Monk (6:125–26,
130, 157); James I was governed not by prudence but by temper and inclination (5:5, 13,
32); prudence was Elizabeth's chief attribute, while Cecil was "the most vigilant, active, and
prudent minister ever known in England" (4:3, 9, 126, 195); Henry VIII was governed by
"passion and humour," not by prudence (3:227, 261). Edward IV was "a prince more splendid and showy, than either prudent or virtuous . . . and less fitted to prevent ills by wise pre-
cautions, than to remedy them, after they took place, by his vigour and enterprize" (2:493).
Henry IV is the only prince that Hume finds prudent in an unsavory way (2:316). Finally,
Richard II lost a kingdom through imprudence (2:315), and the great territorial gains made
during the early years of Edward III's reign are owing chiefly to that monarch's prudence
(2:234, 242, 271).

examples of either good or ill, and—as we shall see below, in chapter 9—
he often stages their dying scenes as set pieces for our instruction. He also
offers reflections of a still more conventionally moral sort on the vanity of
human wishes and the limits of human knowledge and power. In his Tudor and especially in his medieval volumes, Hume most fully becomes the
moral painter he had claimed in the 1730s not to be.

Several of his examples are meant to be inspiring. What now keeps
an individual from accomplishing, in an age of leisure and refinement, a
small part of what scholar-hero-kings such as Alfred, Henry I, and his
grandson Henry II achieved in ages of ignorance, warfare, and barbarity!
Hume acknowledges that there were several giants on the earth in those
days, and we would be wise to use our allotted time so well.[19] Later, we find
useful lessons in the chivalry of the Plantagenets. Hume renders with
glowing detail the young Edward III's "moderation and humanity" toward
the defeated John, king of France: "He came forth to meet the captive king
with all the marks of regard and sympathy; administered comfort to him
amidst his misfortunes; paid him the tribute of praises due to his valour;
and ascribed his own victory merely to the blind chance of war or to a
superior providence, which controls all the efforts of human force and
prudence." There may be no such thing as either chance or providence,
but there are occasions when to invoke them is not only good breeding,
but "real and truly admirable heroism"—"for victories are vulgar things
in comparison." Hume concludes the scene, "It is impossible, in reflecting
on this noble conduct, not to perceive the advantages, which resulted
from the otherwise whimsical principles of chivalry, and which gave men,
in those rude times, some superiority even over people of a more cultivated age and nation" (2:251–53).[20]

But Hume's examples chiefly concern the vanity of exorbitant wishes.
Such examples are intended, in Johnson's phrase, to teach caution to the
daring, and moderation to the proud. Hume first trots out kings and
conquerors who wisely recognize the limits of human achievement. The
Danish king Canute, who ascended to the throne of England in 1017, is
granted a Joblike wisdom:

> Canute, the greatest and most powerful monarch of his time, sovereign of
> Denmark and Norway, as well as of England, could not fail of meeting with
> adulation from his courtiers. . . . Some of his flatterers breaking out, one day,
> in admiration of his grandeur, exclaimed that every thing was possible for
> him: Upon which the monarch, it is said, ordered his chair to be set on the
> sea-shore, while the tide was rising; and as the waters approached, he com-

---

[19] On Alfred, see 1:74–81; on Henry I, 1:276–77; on Henry II, 1:370.

[20] On Hume's "increasingly favorable estimation of chivalry's civilizing, hence moralizing,
power," see Siebert, "Chivalry and Romance in the Age of Hume" (70).

manded them to retire, and to obey the voice of him who was lord of the ocean. He feigned to sit some time in expectation of their submission; but when the sea still advanced towards him, and began to wash him with its billows, he turned to his courtiers, and remarked to them, that every creature in the universe was feeble and impotent, and that power resided with one Being alone, in whose hands were all the elements of nature; who could say to the ocean, *Thus far shall thou go, and no farther;* and who could level with his nod the most towering piles of human pride and ambition. (1:125)[21]

Amusingly, Hume reserves such expressions of wisdom in his history of England for rulers who are not English. He greatly admires Saladin, twelfth-century sultan of Egypt and foe of the Crusaders, noting "the advantage indeed of science, moderation, humanity, was at that time entirely on the side of the Saracens." To Saladin he attributes a self-deprecating wit that contrasts, even as it evokes, the boasting, shattered monuments of Lucan's Pompey or Shelley's Ozymandias: "It is memorable, that, before he expired, he ordered his winding-sheet to be carried as a standard through every street of the city; while a crier went before, and proclaimed with a loud voice, *This is all that remains to the mighty Saladin, the conqueror of the East.* By his last will, he ordered charities to be distributed to the poor, without distinction of Jew, Christian, or Mahometan" (1:393). One of Hume's later wise men, the Holy Roman Emperor Charles V, observes that such religious distinctions are both inalterable and morally inconsequential. During the bloody religious wars that racked the sixteenth century, Charles resigns his crown, seeking "in the tranquillity of retreat, for that happiness, which he had in vain pursued, amidst the tumults of war, and the restless projects of ambition." There, "[h]aving amused himself with the construction of clocks and watches, he thence remarked how impracticable the object was, in which he had so much employed himself during his grandeur; and how impossible, that he, who could never frame two machines that would go exactly alike, could ever be able to make all mankind concur in the same belief and opinion" (3:445–47).

Not all conquerors are so wise. Hume also paints those who do not, or do not fully, or do not in a timely manner recognize the vanity of all human grandeur. William the Conqueror apprehends this vanity only on his remorse-torn deathbed; it is a lesson he perhaps learns, and that Hume would certainly teach us, through the casual and bathetic way he receives his mortal wound on the fields of France:

[21] Hume's source for this story is Henry of Huntingdon's *Historia Anglorum* (1135), book 6. Hume significantly omits from his telling Henry's Christian conclusion to the tale: "From thenceforth King Canute never wore his crown of gold, but placed it for a lasting memorial on the image of our Lord affixed to a cross, to the honour of God the almighty King" (199).

> [H]e led an army into L'Isle de France, and laid every thing waste with fire and sword. He took the town of Mante, which he reduced to ashes. But the progress of these hostilities was stopped by an accident, which soon after put an end to William's life. His horse starting aside of a sudden, he bruised his belly on the pommel side of the saddle; and being in a bad habit of body, as well as somewhat advanced in years, he began to suspect the consequences . . . He discovered at last the vanity of all human grandeur. (1:224)

The Conqueror's son, William Rufus, ironically meets his own death by a ricocheting arrow while hunting in the new royal forest that his father had ruthlessly cleared of its inhabitants; no one bothers to attend his funeral. "And all men, upon the king's fate, exclaimed, that, as the Conqueror had been guilty of extreme violence, in expelling all the inhabitants of that large district, to make room for his game, the just vengeance of heaven was signalized, in the same place, by the slaughter of his posterity" (1: 245–46).

Whether or not Hume believes in the moral order of the universe, its supposition affords the historian a tidy narrative device. It supplies as well the lesson that one's moral obligation to society is backed with at least the threat of transcendent sanctions. English history allows Hume to teach this lesson again, in the fate of the conquering hero Henry V and his son, an "infant prince [who] seemed to be universally regarded as the future heir" of both England and France:

> But the glory of Henry, when it had nearly reached the summit, was stopped short by the hand of nature; and all his mighty projects vanished into smoke. He was seized with a fistula. . . . [After making arrangements for his brothers to act as his son's regents should he die,] He next applied himself to his devotions, and ordered his chaplain to recite the seven penitential psalms. When that passage of the fifty-first psalm was read *build thou the walls of Jerusalem;* he interrupted the chaplain, and declared his serious intention, after he should have fully subdued France, to conduct a crusade against the infidels, and recover possession of the Holy Land. So ingenious are men in deceiving themselves, that Henry forgot, in those moments, all the blood spilt by his ambition; and received comfort from this late and feeble resolve . . . He expired in the thirty-fourth year of his age and the tenth of his reign. (2:376–77)

Hume's following two chapters detail the piecemeal loss of France; his son's "slender capacity"; and the civil disasters that put an end to the Lancastrian line.

V. Tragedy

Are Hume's or Johnson's examples of the vanity of exorbitant wishes satiric, or are they tragic? With respect to Johnson's *Vanity of Human Wishes,* the question has long been debated.[22] The terms of the debate, although not always clear or consistent, seem to be as follows: tragic action is necessary or fated, and our proper response to the tragic character is pity combined with a fearful recognition that a similar fate may lie in store for us. By contrast, we satirize characters whom we hold morally responsible and hence blameable for untoward, obnoxious or pernicious actions; satire is typically justified as a corrective of human vice and folly. Yet this contrast between the two terms would not have occurred to Johnson, who did not believe in any necessity incompatible with free will and moral responsibility. In fact, Johnson did not consider tragedy to be a (categorically) fatalistic genre, but rather an efficacious, therapeutic genre akin to satire. Note how well *The Vanity of Human Wishes*—and Hume's *vanitas* sketches—conform to Johnson's understanding of Aristotle's analysis of tragedy:

> [Boswell:] 'But how are the passions to be purged by terrour and pity?' (said I, with an assumed air of ignorance, to incite him to talk . . .). JOHNSON. 'Why, Sir, you are to consider what is the meaning of purging in the original sense. It is to expel impurities from the human body. The mind is subject to the same imperfection. The passions are the great movers of human actions; but they are mixed with such impurities, that it is necessary they should be purged or refined by means of terrour and pity. For instance, ambition is a noble passion; but by seeing upon the stage, that a man who is so excessively ambitious as to raise himself by injustice, is punished, we are terrified at the fatal consequences of such a passion. In the same manner a certain degree of resentment is necessary; but if we see that a man carries it too far, we pity the object of it, and are taught to moderate that passion.' (*Life of Johnson* 3:39)

Johnson supplies the perfect critical gloss on the intent and tragic purpose behind Johnson's *Vanity,* as well as Hume's *vanitas* sketches. Tragedy is a means of regulating or moderating the passions of an audience, especially those passions such as ambition that tend towards extravagance.

I would offer here a few words on Hume's and Johnson's taste in stage tragedy. Among the moderns, Hume preferred Racine while Johnson championed Shakespeare, but both based their preferences on a similar underlying assumption: in order to fulfill its purgative role, tragedy must accurately represent the natural laws by which a predominant passion operates, and it must do so in such a way as to seize and *not let slip* an audience's sympathetic interest. The only aesthetic experience that might

[22] The question arises especially with regard to Johnson's portrait of Charles XII of Sweden (lines 191–222)—I examine this portrait below, chapter 9, sec. 3. Leo Damrosch (*Samuel Johnson and the Tragic Sense* 144–49) argues that Charles's fate is more tragic than satiric; the point is also argued by Howard Erskine-Hill, who sees Charles XII as a type of Bonnie Prince Charlie after the '45 (*Poetry of Opposition and Revolution* 159–64). Alternatively, Donald Greene ("Johnson, Stoicism, and the Good Life") and Thomas Jemielity maintain that the portraits in Johnson's poem are not tragic but satiric.

serve to moderate a passion in common life is that of following an un-bridled passion to its utmost consequence on the stage, or in silent read-ing, and feeling that passion as our own.

Hume thought this experience most readily available in the tragedies of Racine. In 1754 he advised the dramatist John Home, "For God's sake, read Shakespeare, but get Racine and Sophocles by heart" (*HL* 1:215). If Hume were to bestow the palm upon one of his two favorite dramatists, it would probably be awarded to the Frenchman (*Essays* 91). Hume's pref-erence for Racine over Shakespeare may be partly explained by his own Francophilia and his probable distrust of "Bardolatry" as an emerging ex-pression of nationalist sentiment in England.[23] But a far greater reason, I think, has to do with Racine's representation of the passions—Racine's drama, as Paul Bénichou notes, replaced the external fatality of the an-cients with "la fatalité passionnelle"[24]—in a "classical" form designed to engage the passions of an audience. Racine's plays conform to the so-called "tragic unities" of action (the play presents a single engaging ac-tion), place (the action of the play occurs in one place), and time (the ac-tion of the play elapses during the course of no more than one twenty-four hour period). Aristotle found in unity of action the very essence of tragedy (*Poetics* 1450b–1451c); the two other unities were recommended along Aristotelian lines by Italian and French critics of the sixteenth and seven-teenth centuries.[25] Hume stressed the psychological importance of the Aristotelian unity of action in section 3 of the first *Enquiry:*[26]

The spectator's concern must not be diverted by any scenes disjoined or sep-arated from the rest. This breaks the course of the passions, and prevents that communication of the several emotions by which one scene adds force to an-other, and transfuses the pity and terror which it excites upon each succeed-ing scene until the whole produces that rapidity of movement which is pecu-liar to the theater. How must it extinguish the warmth of affection to be

[23] For a highly readable summary of the eighteenth-century rise of "Bardolatry" and its nationalist, anti-Gallic context, see Jonathan Bate, 73–86, 157–86.

[24] From Bénichou, *Morales du Grand Siècle* (1948), quoted in *Phèdre,* ed. Drouillard and Canal, 191.

[25] For the sources Hume was most likely to have known, see, in Elledge and Schier's *The Continental Model,* the selections from d'Aubignac, 80–100; Corneille, 101–15; and Boileau, 235.

[26] This discussion of aesthetics does not appear in the revised version of the first *Enquiry* published posthumously in *Essays and Treatises on Several Subjects,* 1777; it is therefore not re-tained in the Oxford edition of Hume's *Enquiries.* Fortunately, Charles Hendel does include it in his edition of *An Inquiry concerning Human Understanding;* the following quotation is from pp. 36–37 of Hendel's text. An abbreviated version of this quotation, and a slightly different version of the larger section in which it appears, may be found in Hume's second *Enquiry,* Oxford ed. pp. 221–24 (sec. 5, part 2); this redundancy is presumably the reason Hume cut his discussion of aesthetics from the first *Enquiry,* where it indeed appears as something of an excursion from his main topics.

entertained on a sudden with a new action and new personages no way related to the former; to find so sensible a breach or vacuity in the course of the
passions, by means of this breach in the connection of ideas?

Transgressing the unities opens a "vacuity in the course of the passions":
the problem, it seems, is a mechanical one. Newton maintained, in opposition to Epicurean physics, that gravity does not operate across a void;
similarly, Hume maintains that the motion of the passions cannot cross a
void or gap. Hume applied this analogical reasoning to epistemological as
well as aesthetic matters, and did so, perhaps, to the detriment of both: his
aesthetics are as a result narrowly neoclassical; logically, he is unable to admit "gappiness" into either the structure of personal identity or the laws of
the universe.[27] Adam Smith, Hume's successor in aesthetics as in ethics,
demanded articulated continuity in all narration, declaring "the very notion of a gap makes us uneasy." Connecting all phenomena in an uninterrupted "chain" is the glory not only of narration but of "didactic writing"
as well. Didactic unity of action, which finds its perfection in Newton, but
may also be found in Descartes, who "does not perhaps contain a word of
truth," but nonetheless affords "one of the most entertaining Romances
that has ever been wrote" (*Lectures on Rhetoric* 100, 146).[28]

Hume's trouble with Shakespeare's plays stems from their flagrant disregard of the unity of action (or of time or place); they abound in scenes
that are (at least superficially) "disjoined or separated from the rest." What
Johnson wrote of a later-seventeenth-century playwright applies to Shakespeare as well: "[H]e mixes comick with tragick scenes," and so "intercepts
the natural course of the passions" (*Idler* 2:187). By contrast, the virtue of
Racine's drama lies in continuity: in the case of his great tragedy *Phèdre*, we
follow and to some degree feel along with the heroine as her obsessive love
engenders self-loathing, criminal jealousy, and finally suicide. The sub-
plot, involving Hippolyte's own interdicted passion, complements but is
clearly subordinated to the main plot; it affords complexity without de-
tracting from a basic unity of purpose and emotional effect.

Johnson also read and had some appreciation for Racine, the only
French dramatist in his private library; he quotes *Athalie* in *Rambler* no. 172.
Yet for Johnson, the mythological setting of the Phaedra story detracted
from its believability, and thus its ability to communicate passion; as Johnson writes of Edmund Smith's English version of the tragedy, "The fable is
mythological, a story we are accustomed to reject as false, and the manners

---

[27] That Hume ought to have admitted "gappiness" in his account of personal identity is
argued by R. T. Herbert; in his account of physical laws, by Alasdair MacIntyre ("Hume, Miracles," 96–99).

[28] Cf. Kames, 1:22–30: the "principle of order" in every breast disapproves the divagations
of Homer and Pindar; interruption makes "the reader lose his ardor."

are so distant from our own that we know them not from sympathy, but by study" (*Lives* 2:16). Like Hume, Johnson's criterion for the success of stage characters is our ability to sympathize with the course of their passions; the difference between the two lie in what interrupted the course of their respective responses.

Johnson agreed that "[t]he mind is refrigerated by interruption" (*Shakespeare* 7:111), but his mind could brook a somewhat more expansive notion of continuous dramatic action than could Hume's. Thus Johnson famously rejected the restraints of the two tragic unities that continental critics added to Aristotle's unity of action. Johnson did not, however, seek to impeach the unity of action. Shakespeare, in his tragedies and comedies, "has well enough preserved the unity of action. . . . [H]is plan has commonly what Aristotle requires, a beginning, a middle, and an end; one event is concatenated with another, and the conclusion follows by easy consequence" (7:75). And yet, "[t]here are perhaps some incidents that might be spared": Johnson cautiously concedes that complaints about Shakespeare's excrescencies are not unfounded. More damning is Johnson's admission that, "[w]hat he does best, he soon ceases to do. He is not long soft and pathetick without some idle conceit, or contemptible equivocation. He no sooner begins to move, than he counteracts himself; and terrour and pity, as they are rising in the mind, are checked and blasted by sudden frigidity" (74). Shakespeare is thus indeed, moment by moment if not in his overall impact, too interruptive of the course of the passions; worst of all, a number of his history plays fail to "affect the passions" at all.[29] Johnson sounds, at moments such as these, not very different from Shakespeare's neoclassical detractors.

However, Johnson subsumed Shakespeare's faults into a greater unity. Shakespeare's plays, all in all, will move the passions more than French plays because, in their very excesses and imperfections, their mixed modes and impurity, they supply a more credible "mirrour of manners and of life" than the fabulous, equable, and meticulous plays of the French and their eighteenth-century English imitators.[30] "His persons act and speak by the influence of those general passions and principles by which all minds are agitated, and the whole system of life is continued in motion." "This therefore is the praise of Shakespeare, that his drama is the mirrour of life . . . from which a hermit may estimate the transactions of the world, and a confessor predict *the progress of the passions*"—that is, their necessary progress, the causal laws by which, when unchecked, they always and every-

[29] See Johnson's condemnations of *Richard II* (7:452) and *Julius Caesar* (8:836).
[30] Cf. *Rambler* no. 125: "That perpetual tumour of phrase with which every thought is now expressed by every personage, the paucity of adventures which regularity admits, and the unvaried equality of flowing dialogue, has taken away from our present writers almost all that dominion over the passions which was the boast of their predecessors" (4:305).

where operate (7:62–65, emphasis mine). In his explanatory notes to Shakespeare's plays, Johnson often has occasion to comment on the ways in which passions naturally progress; for example, he comments on Constance's line from *King John:* "I will instruct my sorrows to be proud; / For Grief is proud, and makes his owner stout" (3.1.68):

> In *Much Ado About Nothing,* the father of Hero, depressed by her disgrace, declares himself so subdued by grief that "a thread may lead him." How is it that grief in Leonato and Lady Constance, produces effects directly opposite, and yet both agreeable to nature. Sorrow softens the mind while it is yet warmed by hope, but hardens it when it is congealed by despair. Distress, while there remains any prospect of relief, is weak and flexible, but when no succour remains, is fearless and stubborn; angry alike at those that injure, and at those that do not help; careless to please where nothing can be gained, and fearless to offend when there is nothing further to be dreaded. Such was the writer's knowledge of the passions. (7:415)

One last question remains: Why do Johnson and Hume take pleasure (and believe that we take pleasure) in seeing the course of the passions uninterrupted in the theater? Why should the spectacle of sorrow hardened by despair, or anger turned cruel, please on stage, when it would not please off the stage? Hume observes in the second *Enquiry* that "all kinds of passions, even the most disagreeable, such as grief and anger, are observed, when excited by poetry, to convey a satisfaction" (259). Similarly, Johnson responds with pleasure to all that communicates vibrations to the heart, including that which he finds terrible. Jean Hagstrum (137–44) is wrong to limit Johnson's appreciation of passion in Shakespeare too narrowly with "the pathetic," or the tender and gentle feelings—on the contrary, Johnson likes best the play whose bleak ending troubled him most: "The tragedy of Lear is deservedly celebrated among the dramas of Shakespeare. There is perhaps no play which keeps the attention so strongly fixed; which so much agitates our passions and interests our curiosity" (8:702). And the tragedy of obsessive love, *Antony and Cleopatra,* "keeps curiosity always busy, and the passions always interested. The continual hurry of the action, the variety of incidents, and the quick succession of one personage to another, call the mind forward without intermission from the first act to the last" (8:873).

Why do we eagerly await the disastrous consequences we would strive to avert outside the theater? Johnson and Hume agree that it is because we are always at least half-aware of being in the theater. A character on stage (as distinct, for Johnson, from the player on stage) is supposed to feel the untrammeled force of a passion that we feel, as it were, in quotations. "If there be any fallacy, it is not that we fancy the players, but that we fancy ourselves unhappy for a moment; but we rather lament the possibility than suppose the presence of misery, as a mother weeps over a babe, when she remembers that death may take it from her. The delight of tragedy proceeds from our consciousness of fiction; if we thought murders and treasons real, they would please no more" (7:78). But Johnson here equivocates, for while the consciousness of fiction may be a necessary condition for theatrical pleasure it surely cannot be a sufficient condition. Why should a representation and not the reality of murder please?

Without plumbing the depths of our psyches very deeply, Johnson does suggest one other aesthetic consideration: "The truth is, that the spectators are always in their senses . . . They come to hear a certain number of lines recited with just gesture and elegant modulation" (77). Hume's essay "Of Tragedy" spells out that which Johnson strongly implies: a passion that would be painful to us in real life is experienced with pleasure when its force is "smoothed, and softened, and mollified" by our countervailing delight in "the force of imagination, the energy of expression, the power of numbers [poetic meter], the charms of imitation" (*Essays* 222–23). It is not only that we are conscious of fiction, but that the pleasures of art predominates over our sympathy with a painful passion. Johnson recognized that, conversely, one way of relieving our painful passions in real life is to subordinate them to the pleasure of their own expression: thus Prince Rasselas, in his early captivity, comes "to receive some solace of the miseries of life, from consciousness of the delicacy with which he felt, and the eloquence with which he bewailed them" (*Rasselas* 14).

Our passionate identification with theatrical characters—or indeed with anyone, including ourselves, who can speak artfully!—is always to some degree subjunctive. We feel with them as though we were really or fully feeling. And thus the stage is itself, in some ways, a mirror for the moralist's own art: both offer forums in which emotion may be cured of vehemence, and taught its proper bounds. The proper office of tragedy, like that of the moralist, is to deter the passions from seeking inappropriate means to their own ends. For Johnson, Shakespeare was morally the greatest dramatist because he displayed the tragic effects of pursuing *any* passion beyond its reasonable satisfaction:

> Upon any other stage the universal agent is love, by whose power all good and evil is distributed, and every action quickened or retarded. . . . But love is only one of many passions, and as it has no great influence upon the sum of life, it has little operation in the dramas of a poet, who caught his ideas from the living world . . . He knew, that any other passion, as it was regular or exorbitant, was a cause of happiness or calamity. (7:63–64) [31]

---

[31] Working in a Johnsonian tradition, Lily Campbell has persuasively written on Shakespeare's four great tragedies—*Hamlet, Othello, Lear,* and *Macbeth*—as studies of the causes and effects of four respective passions: grief, jealousy, wrath, and fear.

This is the knowledge that Johnson would convey in *The Vanity of Human Wishes,* and that Hume would teach in the *vanitas* exempla of his *History of England.* For Johnson as for Hume, the *vanitas* theme straddles that which we call "tragic" or necessary, and that which we think of as satiric or aimed at faults we're at liberty to correct. Satire and tragedy—like liberty and necessity—are related to each other not as opposites, but within a dialectic. A passion may prove fatal if one indulges it unduly; as in dominos, the fatal progress of the passions must first be set in motion by some act, at once determined and determinate, of the will.

VI. Coda: Chance and Authority

Johnson and Hume each believed that the will is at once determined and determining. Neither, strictly speaking, believed in chance events. The point requires argument because Johnson was apt to use "chance" in a nonphilosophical way—indeed, he famously quipped, "Hume is a Tory by chance, as being a Scotsman" (*Tour* 238–39).[32] Johnson's meaning, in Boswell's original version of the remark, is clear: Hume is a Tory not out of rational deliberation, but because of his nativity as a Scotsman, and his consequent feelings of loyalty to the Stuarts.[33] "Chance" in this instance simply means "causes external to one's own will."

In the *Treatise,* Hume philosophically defines chance as "the negation of a cause" (125). Are there chance events in the human world? Hume sometimes treats something we might be tempted to call "chance" as an agent in history—for example, Charles I's "chance" refusal, early in his reign, to allow a Puritan group that included Oliver Cromwell to emigrate (*History* 5:241–42). Yet Donald Livingston persuasively argues that for Hume, "to talk of chance is always to talk about our ignorance of causes relative to some system of determination" (*Hume's Philosophy* 228). Livingston usefully distinguishes between two different models of causal explanation: a "covering-law model," which includes "the thesis that what serves to explain an event could have served, if presented earlier, to have predicted it," and a nonpredictive moral model, which can rationally account for actual occurrences that appear irregular or extraordinary relative to some set of covering laws (187–96). Hume—and Johnson—assume that a covering-law model of causal explanation can in most cases account for "the progress of the passions." But the field of human history, as distinct from human nature, presents a wealth of individual actions that could not be predicted, but are not for that reason uncaused or unaccountable. So,

[32] Cf. *Life of Johnson* 4:194, where the explanatory second clause is deleted.
[33] Johnson elsewhere opposes "chance" to "deliberation": see *Life of Johnson* 1:365, 2:22.

for example, although Charles I's action in not allowing a ship of Puritans to emigrate in 1637 cannot be accounted for by any covering laws, it is not for that reason a random or uncaused action.

It was to this nonpredictive moral model of causal explanation that Johnson referred in his second nonphilosophical use of "chance." Johnson applies the term to historical events that cannot be accounted for according to a covering-law model of causal explanation—especially when those events, notably the distant origins of particular governments, are clouded by time. For Johnson, "chance" events could not have been predicted and hence cannot be reduced to a regular design. "A little knowledge of history," Johnson writes in *Idler* no. 11, suffices to show that "forms of government are seldom the result of much deliberation, they are framed by chance in popular assemblies, or in conquered countries by despotick authority" (2:37). In "The False Alarm" (1770), Johnson asserts, "Governments formed by chance, and gradually improved by such expedients, as the successive discovery of their defects happened to suggest, are never to be tried by a regular theory" (*PW* 328). Governments, that is, are not to be judged according to an a priori notion of either popular sovereignty and social contract theory, or on the other extreme, old Tory notions of the transcendent origins and authorization of princely power. Indeed, Johnson here employs the term *chance* rhetorically, as a loaded counterweight to the untenable causal claims made both by Whigs (government from contract) and old Tories (government from God).

Although the founding moment of any institution lacks "legitimacy" in a Lockean (or, more recently, Rawlsian) sense, it does not necessarily follow—and certainly neither Johnson nor Hume would have maintained—that the ongoing life of that institution lacks legitimacy.[34] In the next short paragraph of "The False Alarm" Johnson derives from the "chance" origins of governments this injunction: "Laws are now made, and customs are established; these are our rules, and by them we must be guided." If Johnson falls short of saying whatever is, is right, he clearly communicates that whatever is ought not be taken lightly, as there is no court of appeal other than "ongoing expediency." Government rests not on a rational or divine scheme, but on the long-standing bonds of duty and loyalty, "the sanction of antiquity"; thus, "long prescription is a sufficient argument in favour of a practice against which nothing can be alleged; nor is it sufficient to affirm that the change may be made without inconvenience, for change itself is an evil" (*PW* 85–86, 98).

In these sentiments, Johnson concurred with Hume. "Of the Original Contract" (1752)—a reworking of the *Treatise* 3.2.8—rejects both divine

---

[34] Thus Thomas Reinert strains to label Johnson's scepticism into the origins of government a "radical" insight, "which his conservatism tries to contain and repress" (144).

right and contract theories of the basis of government. The first is easily dismissed: since the Deity gave rise to government "not by any particular or miraculous interposition, but by his concealed and universal efficacy; a sovereign cannot, properly speaking, be called his vice-regent, in any other sense than every power or force, being derived from him, may be said to act by his commission" (*Essays* 467). Hume then argues at greater length, on both historical and philosophical grounds, against the contract theory then fashionably espoused by the ascendant Whig party. Philosophically, the artificial virtues of allegiance and fidelity presuppose society, and thus cannot be the original basis of society (480–81). Historically, there is no evidence for any social contract: "Almost all the governments, which exist at present, or of which there remains any record in story, have been founded originally, either on usurpation or conquest, or both, without any pretence of a fair consent, or voluntary subjection of the people" (471). Nor does any notion of a social contract enter into popular opinion: "[T]he people . . . imagine not, that their consent gives their prince a title: But they willingly consent, because they think, that, from long possession, he has acquired a title, independent of their choice or inclination" (475).

Hume earlier wrote in "Of the First Principles of Government" (1741), "as FORCE is always on the side of the governed, the governors have nothing to support them but opinion. It is, therefore, on opinion only that government is founded. . . . Antiquity always begets the opinion of right" (32–33). Hume's conclusion, like Johnson's, is that no alteration of the government should disrupt all sense of continuity with the past, for it is largely on the perception of continuity that the legitimacy of a government rests.[35] Institutions derive their right to power not from their founding moments, but through their historical endurance.

It is to the examination of history and its causal laws that next we turn. How do institutions arise? How do they endure? And how long may they be expected to endure? These are the questions that guide both Johnson and Hume.

[35] The point is reiterated in Hume's *History,* 5:544 (on the execution of Charles I) and 6:389–90 (on the Exclusion Bill controversy).

Chapter Seven

The Passions and Patterns of History

Voltaire noted in his 1764 review of Hume's *History* that the philosopher-historian seeks, therapeutically, to "treat weaknesses, errors, and barbarities as a doctor treats epidemic diseases" (*Oeuvres* 25:472). Like tragedy, Hume's history-writing would purge us of the dangerous excesses of passion. Yet the pages of history allow for a greater passionate identification with character than does the stage—except, perhaps, the staging of a history play. Historiography was, in Johnson and Hume's day, commonly thought to be the most absorbing type of writing. Thus Hume writes in his *Treatise* with the breeziness of a commonplace: "If one person sits down to read a book as a romance, and another as a true history, they plainly receive the same ideas, and in the same order"; but

> The latter has a more lively conception of all the incidents. He enters deeper into the concerns of the persons: represents to himself their actions, and characters, and friendships, and enmities: He even goes so far as to form a notion of their features, and air, and person. While the former, who gives no credit to the testimony of the author, has a more faint and languid conception of all these particulars; and except on account of the style and ingenuity of the composition, can receive little entertainment from it. (*T* 97–98; cf. *ECPM* 223)

Johnson concurs that "history will always take stronger hold of the attention than fable: the passions excited by . . . [it] are the pleasures and pains of real life" ("Life of Pope," *Lives* 3:227). History alone satisfies "that ardent love of truth which nature has kindled in the breast of man, and which remains even where every other laudable passion is extinguished"

("Review of Duchess of Marlborough's *Memoirs,*" *Major Works* 113). History is the very ground of that knowledge or truth which is experimental, so-cial, incremental—and which Johnson no less than Hume advocated over a priori rationalism. We can little doubt that Johnson would have con-curred with Hume's pronouncement in 1770: "I believe this is the histor-ical Age and this the historical nation" (*HL* 2:230).[1]

In this chapter I will attempt to determine to what degree Johnson and Hume may be said to share a "philosophy of history." They would have conceived of such a philosophy, I believe, as answering a set of three dis-crete if related questions. First, how if at all does history operate on human character, and conversely, how do the passions of character act on history? Second, what causes gave rise to a civilization, and what may cause it to fall? Finally, insofar as the progress of civilizations may be causally explained by covering law models, what lies in store for British civilization? What point or stage of its overall story does eighteenth-century Britain occupy?

I will focus on Hume's *History of England* and, to a lesser degree, his *Nat-ural History of Religion,* as these works represent a more focused historio-graphical achievement than Johnson's. Nonetheless, Donald Greene is right to call attention to Johnson's own "substantial and serious historiog-raphy" (*PW* 126), a body of work beginning with the "Introduction to the Political State of Great Britain" and related pieces from 1756 written for the political journal the *Literary Magazine,* and continuing through his four great political pamphlets of the 1770s—"The False Alarm," "Thoughts on the Late Transactions Respecting Falkland's Islands," "The Patriot," "Taxation No Tyranny"—and *A Journey to the Western Islands of Scotland* (1775).

I. Character in History

The starting point for all twentieth-century discussions of Hume's work is still J. B. Black's *The Art of History,* first published in 1926. In Black's

---

[1] John Vance amply documents the extent of Johnson's own interest in history and histo-riography—and his concurrence with Hume on matters of both general method and the as-sessment of particular historical periods ("Johnson and Hume: Of Like Historical Minds"). Hume's pronouncement about "the historical Age and . . . the historical nation" was occa-sioned, first, by belated but brisk sales of the quarto edition of his own complete *History;* sec-ond, by William Robertson's history of Scotland (1759), and the history of Spanish America Robertson was then writing. Edward Gibbon, whose own monumental history would begin to appear six years later, referred to Hume and Robertson as "Le Tacite et le Tite Live de l'Ecosse" (Gibbon, *Letters* 2:107). A considerable part of Hume's achievement was, as Philip Hicks demonstrates, to have written the first history of England, and the first history in English, that merited comparison to the admired "general histories" of the Greco-Latin tradition—of the type that Polybius, Livy, and Velleius Paterculus had written. Hume was also praised for reviving historiographical qualities associated with Tacitus: a seamless and rapid narration of events, and subtle investigation of historical cause and effect.

elegant amble through eighteenth-century historiography, Hume is applauded for his moralist's ability to draw apt lessons from great historical events, such as the death of Charles I. He receives no praise, however, as a historian. Black indeed crystalizes the charge, never fully rebutted, that Hume has no real historical sense.[2] And the root of Hume's unhistorical view of things is, according to Black, his "false and mechanical psychology." Black explains,

> To Hume, character appears in the light of an assemblage of virtues and vices, in the same way as an object is the sum of its qualities. The modern psychologist would take a very different view. He would insist upon unity as a *sine qua non;* he would point out that personality always acts as an organized unit, albeit under the influence of one or more dominating motive or motives; and the consequence is that whereas Hume regards the human soul as reproducing the same or similar acts, from one end of the historical epoch to the other, the modern philosopher would assert that it continually brings fresh phenomena to the light. (98)

If we share or can for a moment adopt the perspective of Black's "modernity," then we may allow his assessment of Hume to be, in general, quite apt and incisive. As Black contends, Hume's historical personages are not very individuated, nor is their motivation, for the most part, specific to their historical circumstances. Yet while Black is quite precise in observing these aspects of Hume's *History of England,* he misreads the text in one crucial regard, because for Hume character is not primarily an assemblage of "virtues and vices"; it is, rather, a congeries of human *passions.* This is a fine distinction but not one without a difference. Moral approval and disapproval are directed toward the dispositional characteristics inferred from behavior, and so the passions are indeed subject to moral judgment as virtues and vices. But there is still an important difference in tone between revealing character in terms of motivating passions, from which moral evaluations must be inferred, and presenting it in terms of the author's own direct evaluations. This difference corresponds to that between the anatomist and the painter—and in their depictions of character, both Hume *and* Johnson tend to assume the anatomist's part.

The description of character according to a sliding balance of virtues and vices had been raised to a fine art in Clarendon's *History of the Great*

---

[2] In the mid-1970s, S. K. Wertz and Duncan Forbes led the vanguard of those opposing the long list of historians who had made Black's view of Hume's *History* "the standard interpretation." Forbes insists that for Hume, "human nature . . . is in fact socially plastic and variable" (108), and that the character and assumptions of a given people change dramatically over time. I would counter that while Hume admits a people's "ruling passion" may indeed change over time, and/or acquire a greater or lesser amount of reflectiveness, he has little sense of the *Historism* that now defines our own historical sense (see Womersley, 1–6, 33–34).

Rebellion (published 1704–7).[3] Clarendon's model clearly informs Hume's early essay, "A Character of Sir Robert Walpole," originally published in the second volume of his *Essays: Moral and Political,* January 1742, and withdrawn by Hume in 1770 from all future edition of his *Essays*. This early character-sketch, hardly distinguishable from other sketches of Walpole such as Chesterfield's (*Characters,* published 1778), is built up of poised sentences that in large part balance the great man's vices against his virtues.[4] However, as Hume progressed in writing his *History of England,* he largely abandoned this style of character portrayal.[5] He developed instead a less overtly moralistic and more mechanistic analysis of character in terms of passional motivation. Witness, as a first example, Hume's description of Cromwell's anxious last days: "Of assassination likewise was he apprehensive, from the zealous spirit, which actuated the soldiers . . . Fleetwood, his son-in-law, actuated by the wildest zeal, began to estrange himself from him. . . . [Cromwell's] fatal ambition had betrayed him. . . . All composure of mind was now forever fled from the protector" (6:104–5).

Johnson also painted historical character in terms of conflicting or dominant passions. Of James I, Johnson writes:

> He was a man of great theoretical knowledge, but of no practical wisdom; he was very well able to discern the true interest of himself, his kingdom, and his posterity, but sacrificed it, upon all occasions, to his present pleasure or his present ease; so conscious of his own knowledge and abilities, that he would not suffer a minister to govern, and so lax of attention, and timorous of opposition, that he was not able to govern for himself. ("Introduction to the Political State," *PW* 133)

James is defined by a particular admixture of insight and indolence, fear and pride. Although Johnson vigorously attacked the notion of a "Ruling Passion," he nonetheless believes that certain passions "predominate" in given men, or at least in given men in certain circumstances: for instance, in Johnson's early "Life of Sir Francis Drake," Johnson writes of Drake's crew during a 1572 invasion of Nombre de Dios: "Some, whose fear was their predominant passion, were continually magnifying the numbers and

---

[3] See, for example, Clarendon's famous "characters" of Charles I (book 11, secs. 239–43) and Cromwell (book 15, secs. 147–56). Martine Brownley traces Clarendon's debts in character writing to Plutarch and Tacitus (148, 162–65).

[4] "His virtues, in some instances, are free from the allay of those vices, which usually accompany such virtues: He is a generous friend, without being a bitter enemy. His vices, in other instances, are not compensated by those virtues which are nearly allyed to them; His want of enterprise is not attended with frugality. The private character of the man is better than the public: His virtues more than his vices: His fortune greater than his fame" (*Essays* 575–76).

[5] The earlier style is still apparent in parts of his *Stuart* volumes: see especially the character of Charles I, chap. 59 (5:542–44).

courage of their enemies, and represented whole nations as ready to rush upon them; others, whose avarice mingled with their concern for their own safety, were more solicitous to preserve what they had already gained, than to acquire more; and others, brave in themselves, and resolute, began to doubt of success in an undertaking in which they were associated with such cowardly companions" (*Works* 10:70). Fear, courage, avarice: endlessly combined and recombined, such passions supply the stuff of history.

The transhistorical—or ahistorical—nature of the passions is of course a commonplace of the age. Hume announces in no uncertain terms in his first *Enquiry:* "Ambition, avarice, self-love, vanity, friendship, generosity, public spirit: these passions, mixed in various degrees, and distributed through society, have been, from the beginning of the world, and still are, the source of all the actions and enterprises, which have ever been observed among mankind. Would you know the sentiments, inclinations, and course of life of the Greeks and Romans? Study well the temper and actions of the French and English: You cannot be much mistaken in transferring to the former *most* of the observations which you have made with regard to the latter" (83). Johnson writes much the same in his translation of Brumoy's *Dissertation upon the Greek Comedy:* "The passions of *Greece* and *France* do not so much differ by the particular characters of particular ages, as they agree by the participation of that which belongs to the same passion in all ages" (*Works* 3:37).

What moved mankind once will move it ever again, and in at least roughly the same way. This assumption of human constancy is crucial for both Hume and Johnson's moral theory, as well as their aesthetics. Since our basic untutored feelings of approbation and disapprobation rely on a process of sympathy that is itself predicated on a similarity between ourselves and others, that which we share irrespective of time or place is the cornerstone of all ethics, of all standards of art. For Johnson as for Hume, man is essentially a social creature, but a *particular* social setting does not constitute his nature. Rather, historically invariable passions do.

II. A History of Passions

The motivational psychology of the passions is of course not an eighteenth-century invention; Thucydides and the Roman historians often presented passions as the animating force of both great individuals and whole peoples. What is arguably novel in the historiography of Hume and Johnson is the emphasis placed on the passions as agents, and the sheer variety of passions addressed. Earlier historians are neither so insistent nor so broad in their treatment of the passions. In Roman historiography, as D. S. Levene argues, "fear . . . is perhaps the single most important influence on the behaviour of individuals and states."[6] Fear as a central passion also finds its way into one of Hume's favorite seventeenth-century histories, Enrico Davila's *History of the Civil Wars of France* (1630). Davila draws dynastic events with a very limited palette of motives: princes and great men feel "emulation" or "jealousy" toward one another, but are moved chiefly by their "fear of falling from their greatness" (9). Voltaire's *Siècle de Louis XIV*, a work to which Hume's *History* was often compared (Hicks 200–01), contains only passing insights into the psychology of the passions.[7]

Hume and Johnson each built on this foundation, working earlier insights about the passions in history into a veritable history of the passions. Hume and Johnson saw the world in which they wrote as one that had, by admitting the passions for what they are, enabled them to become what they ought, logically, to be: self-restraining and directed toward (at least a negative conception of) the general welfare. As Philo asks in the *Dialogues:* "What more useful than all the passions of the mind, ambition, vanity, love, anger? But how often do they break their bounds, and cause the greatest convulsions in society?" (210). Hume wrote his *History*, and Johnson his political pamphlets and sermons, that the passions might be taught their proper bounds, and that we might cherish those bounds with watchfulness.

When Hume came to write history—from his speculative *Natural History of Religion* (1757) to his textually grounded *History of England* (1754–62)—he focused primarily on three sets of basic passions: hope and fear, pride and humility, love and hatred. Of these three pairs, hope and fear name our reactions, respectively, to anticipated pleasure and anticipated pain. These are the most primitive passions, and hence, according to Hume, the chief passions of the most primitive peoples. Thus, in the *History of England,* hope and fear are what actuate the Celts of pre-Roman Britain: "They dwelt in huts, which they reared in the forests and marshes, with which the country was covered: They shifted easily their habitation, when actuated either by the hopes of plunder or the fear of an enemy" (1:5). In the *Natural History of Religion,* hope and fear actuate the "barbarous, necessitous animal (such as man is on the first origin of society)" who

---

[6] Levene, "Pity, Fear and the Historical Audience: Tacitus on the Fall of Vitellius," in *The Passions in Roman Thought and Literature*, ed. Braund, 128–49. Levene's detailed analysis of the pitiable fearfulness of Vitellius's last days could serve as a model for close reading Hume's account of Cromwell's decline.

[7] See, for example, Voltaire's portrait of Cardinal Mazarin as one who, though happily free from Richelieu's dominant passions of "pride and vengeance," is unhappily more eager for wealth than for the public good (chap. 6, 120–21); his delicate consideration of whether King William of England inspired in Parisians greater fear or hatred (chap. 15, 254–55); and his analysis of the various passions that animate the Quietists and their ecclesiastical opponents (chap. 38, 764–84).

first "entertain[ed] some groveling and familiar notion of superior powers" (24).[8] Whereas in the eighteenth century believer and nonbeliever
alike tended to agree that the perception of unitary design in the universe would afford, or help to confirm, a conviction of a unitary Designer,
Hume maintained, to the contrary, that "the more regular and uniform,
that is, the more perfect nature appears, the more is he [man] familiar-
ized to it, and the less inclined to scrutinize and examine it." It is only "a
monstrous birth," an event out of the ordinary, that "excites his curiosity,
and is deemed a prodigy. It alarms him from its novelty; and immediately
sets him a trembling, and sacrificing, and praying" (25). Both the Scrip-
tures and the writings of Deists from Toland to Tindal agreed that the original religion of all peoples was monotheistic—and thus correct; Hume, on
the contrary, argues:

> [I]f . . . we trace the footsteps of invisible power in the various and contrary
> events of human life, we are necessarily led into [original] polytheism and to
> the acknowledgment of several limited and imperfect deities. Storms and
> tempests ruin what is nourished by the sun. The sun destroys what is fostered
> by the moisture of dews and rains. War may be favorable to a nation, whom
> the inclemency of the seasons afflicts with famine. . . . In short, the conduct
> of events . . . is so full of variety and uncertainty, that, if we suppose it imme-
> diately ordered by any intelligent beings, we must acknowledge a contrariety
> in their designs and intentions, a constant combat of opposite powers, and
> a repentance or change of intention in the same power, from impotence or
> levity. . . . We may conclude, therefore, that, in all nations . . . the first ideas of
> religion arose not from a contemplation of the works of nature [i.e., an over-
> arching design in the universe], but from a concern with regard to the events
> of life, and from the incessant hopes and fears, which actuate the human
> mind. (27)

Polytheism was thus the first religion of mankind, and the purpose of that
religion was to understand present calamity and influence future events.
    Early man—who is always also, in Enlightenment usage, the man still
deep inside us—shows no interest in the past, or in the regular, recurrent
patterns of either past or present; in this, Johnson agrees with Hume. "In
nations, where there is hardly the use of letters, what is once out of sight is
lost for ever. They think but little, and of their few thoughts, none are
wasted on the past, in which they are neither interested by fear nor hope"
(*Journey* 65). And little short of monstrous births can interest the unlettered in the present: "When the Islanders [inhabitants of the Western Is-

---

[8] In the *Natural History of Religion*, Hume writes the type of "conjectural history" (in Dugald
Stewart's later phrase) popularized by Rousseau's two *Discourses*. He tells a story, drawing inferences from human nature, about what (may have) happened in the past; it is an attempt
at anthropology, but hindered by a lack of data.

lands of Scotland] were reproached with their ignorance, or insensibility of the wonders of Staffa [an island famous for its caves and unusual basaltic formations], they had not much to reply. They had indeed considered it little, because they had always seen it; and none but philosophers, nor they always, are struck with wonder, otherwise than by novelty" (141–42). Dispassionate curiosity is not natural to us. Their agreement on this point suggests that Johnson, like Hume, would have little truck with the theological argument from design. And it is perhaps no mere coincidence that Hume sounds like Johnson when in his *Dialogues concerning Natural Religion* the character Demea speaks against the design argument on experiential grounds: "It is my opinion . . . that each man feels, in a manner, the truth of religion in his own breast; and from a consciousness of his imbecility and misery, rather than from any reasoning, is led to seek protection from that Being, on whom he and all nature is dependent" (193).

Yet with the rise of more stable social relationships than the earliest peoples are presumed to know, hope and fear recede in the breast, and the two pairs of indirect or social passions come to the fore: pride and humility (feelings directed toward ourselves according to our relation to others), and love and hatred (feelings directed toward other persons or socially constituted things). The passions of love and hatred, like those of hope and fear, each have several branches according to their several objects: thus Hume in his *History* speaks, for example, of the love of "revenge" and of "intemperance" which he describes as the "ruling inclinations" of the English Saxons (1:27). He speaks too of the "ardour for military enterprises" which he attributes as a "ruling passion" to the Crusaders. The Crusader's other ruling passion is the complex passion of "superstition," which may be reduced to its simple elements of humility and fear (1:237). Conversely, the complex passion of religious "enthusiasm" that so governed the Puritans during the English civil wars is reducible to the elements of pride and hope. (In "Of Superstition and Enthusiasm" (1741), Hume traced the two complex passions to their elemental sources: "Weakness, fear, melancholy, together with ignorance, are, therefore, the true sources of SUPERSTITION"; "Hope, pride, presumption, a warm imagination, together with ignorance, are . . . the true sources of ENTHUSIASM" [*Essays* 74].) The enthusiasm of the Puritans was steadily aggravated, according to Hume, through an ignoble "emulation of ghostly gifts"—that is, the competitive striving for more and more marvelous or singular signs and assurances of personal inspiration (*History* 6:87).

During the Tudor period, Hume traces the relative peace and prosperity of Henry VII's reign to that monarch's "ruling passion," "avarice," or the love of money, which "made him averse to all warlike enterprizes and distant expeditions" (3:29). The love of money is, for both Hume and Johnson, the root of all civility. Johnson presents as a historical counterpoint the pacific Dutch "love of money" and "the boundless ambition of the house of Bourbon" (*PW* 144–46); there is little doubt as to where his sympathies lie. By the same standard of utility, Hume prefers the halcyon avarice of Henry VII to the ambitious extravagance of Henry VIII. The turbulent history of early-sixteenth-century England derives ultimately from the capriciousness of a monarch ruled alternately by love and hatred, by furious pride and humble superstition (3:210–59). He little knew his own interest.

III. A Government "Happily Established"

Long before Hegel lectured on the "cunning of reason"—reason's ability to develop and perfect itself in history through the instrumental activity of people who follow their own "passions" or "private interests"[9]— Hume argued, in a logically similar though more evidently secular manner, that the empire of reason is built up precisely by the passion of interest.[10] The passion of self-interest becomes a virtue once it seeks its fulfillment not through rapine or any extraordinary form of domination over others, but through its own regulation first by the convention of justice, and finally by positive laws. Thus passion becomes reasonable when it discovers in its apparent restraint the conditions for its realization over time. As Hume argues in the *Treatise*, "Instead of departing from our own interest, or from that of our nearest friends, in abstaining from the possession of others, we cannot better consult both these interests, than by such a convention; because it is by this means that we maintain society, which is so necessary to their well-being and subsistence, as well as to our own" (489). This must occur to us, Hume concludes, "upon the least reflection" (492).

This reflection could never occur, however, to "rude and savage men" (488). It is the purpose of *The History of England* to demonstrate, against popular Whig appeals to supposed Saxon freedoms and the "ancient constitution," that property was not fully secure nor justice fully equal until the Glorious Revolution. Hume consistently contends that while the articles of the Magna Charta of 1215 "involve all the chief *outlines* of a legal govern-

---

[9] "We assert then that nothing has been accomplished without interest on the part of the actors; and—if interest be called passion [*die Leidenschaft*], inasmuch as the whole individuality, to the neglect of all other actual or possible interests and claims, is devoted to an object with every fibre of volition, concentrating all its desires and powers upon it—we may affirm absolutely that nothing great in the World has been accomplished without passion" (*The Philosophy of History* 23). "This may be called the cunning of reason—that it sets the passions to work for itself, while that which develops its existence through such impulsion pays the penalty, and suffers loss" (33).

[10] My following discussion of Hume's treatment of the reasonable passions is indebted to Albert Hirschman, 20–66.

ment, and provide for the equal distribution of justice, and free enjoyment of property" (1:445, emphasis mine), "a civilized nation, like the English, who have happily established the most perfect and most accurate system of liberty that was ever found compatible with government, ought to be cautious in appealing to the practice of their ancestors, or regarding the maxims of uncultivated ages as certain rules for their present conduct" (2:525). Hume concludes his history with the settlement of the crown on William and Mary, emphasizing, "The revolution forms a new epoch in the constitution" (6:351). The law lectures coauthored by Johnson similarly deflate popular Whig assumptions about the ancient roots of modern liberty. We know little of the Saxon Witenagemote (*English Law* 128–30), and little more about the Norman Great Council, before or after King John and the Magna Charta: "Our political historians too often forget the state of the age they are endeavouring to describe, an age of tyranny, darkness and violence, in which perhaps few of the barons to whom the contrivance of this wonderful system of government is ascribed, were able to sign their names to their own treaties, and in which therefore there could be little foresight of the future because there was little knowledge of the past" (133–34). The modern constitution outlined in part 1 of the *Lectures* is grounded lagely on texts from Sir Edward Coke to the statutes of William and Mary.

The history of England is the story of the passions slowly, gradually narrowing themselves into the civilized interests, in and through groups and individuals who need hardly reflect, or not reflect at all, on the process. This process may be called, in a modification of Hegel, the cunning of the passions. It might also be denominated the cunning of the Enlightenment historiographer, for the less civilized passions—along with their dramatic attendants, destruction, dereliction, dismay—are always still potentially with us. A key note in Johnson's historiography is that the unreflective, violent passions have never stopped erupting, even among nations generally ruled by enlightened interest. Thus Johnson avers of William III's policy against the French: "When the necessity of self-preservation had impelled the subjects of James to drive him from the throne, there came a time in which the passions, as well as the interest of the government, acted against the French, and in which it may perhaps be reasonably doubted, whether the desire of humbling France was not stronger than that of exalting England" (*PW* 142–43). Interest is nonetheless, in Johnson's (prescriptive) opinion, the main stream of modern English society, and the violent passions mere eddies. He begins his pamphlet against the resolutions of the American Continental Congress of 1774:

> In favour of this exemption of the Americans from the authority of their lawful sovereign, and the dominion of their mother-country, very loud clamours

have been raised, and many wild assertions advanced . . . and what is strange, though their tendency is to lessen English honour, and English power, have been heard by English-men with a wish to find them true. Passion has in its first violence controlled interest, as the eddy for a while runs against the stream. (*PW* 412)

Johnson proceeds to define the irrational, unjust passions animating certain Englishmen as pity for supposed American woes, and terror of supposed American strength (413–14, 449–51). Johnson's goal in the pamphlet is to dispel these passions by revealing their objects to be unreal. The nation need no longer be blinded to its own interest—nor ought it be, for in the case of its quarrel with the American Congress, Britain's interest is also justice (*PW* 419).

Johnson portrays immediate interest as the natural current, and enlightened interest as the proper current, of civilized motivation. Yet neither he nor Hume presumed that the current could not change. The story that has led to Britain's civility is neither providential nor irreversible. The same holds true for the history that has established Britain's modern constitution, with its celebrated balance between the separate interests of commons, lords, and king. That government, as Hume puts it, has been "*happily* established"—not only fortunately, but also haply, without guarantee for future performance. British civilization and the post-Settlement British government are both in a constant, if often quiet, state of jeopardy.

Accordingly, we hear a note of urgency in Hume's concluding reflections on English history before the Tudor period:

Thus have we pursued the history of England through a series of many barbarous ages; till we have at last reached the dawn of civility and sciences. . . . Nor is the spectacle altogether unentertaining and uninstructive, which the history of those times presents to us. The view of human manners, in all their variety of appearances, is both profitable and agreeable; and if the aspect in some periods seems horrid and deformed, we may thence learn *to cherish with the greater anxiety* that science and civility, which has so close a connexion with virtue and humanity, and which, as it is a sovereign antidote against superstition, is also the most effectual remedy against vice and disorders of every kind. (2:518–19, emphasis mine)

The lesson Hume offers his readers is that they ought not to take eighteenth-century science and civility, and their spread, for granted; now is the time for watchfulness; the barbarous ages wait like a thief in the night. Hume's very next sentence in the *History* illumines his chief source of anxiety: "The rise, progress, perfection, *and decline* of art and science, are curious objects of contemplation" (519, emphasis mine). Here necessity enters our picture: there are indubitable laws to which the course of arts and sciences—and perhaps civility and government as well—must all adhere. Those laws dictate constant change. As Hume ruminates elsewhere, in a Lucretian vein: "Nothing in this world is perpetual. Every being, however seemingly firm, is in continual flux and change: The world itself gives symptoms of frailty and dissolution" (*Essays* 597, cf. *De Rerum Natura* 2.1170–74).

IV. Decline and Fluctuation

The threat and reasonable fear of decline is what most sharply distinguishes eighteenth-century British historiography from that of Hegel or Marx—these later historians offer narratives that preclude the very possibility of retrogression.[11] Hume and Johnson both subscribed to the cyclical theory of history elaborated by the ancients, and particularly associated with the name of Velleius Paterculus, whose *Roman History* dates from circa 30 C.E. Velleius's history was a part of Hume's personal library, as it was of Johnson's. Although Hume does not cite Velleius in his essay "Of the Rise and Progress of the Arts and Sciences" (1742), his argument may nonetheless be summarized by these sentences from Velleius: "Genius is nourished by emulation . . . and it is natural that that which is cultivated with greatest zeal rises to the highest point of perfection. Yet to stay at the point of perfection is difficult, and naturally that which cannot go forward recedes" (translated in Harry Caplan, 181). Johnson, echoing these same lines, maintains that "nothing terrestrial can be kept at a stand"; "if it is not rising . . . [it] will be falling" (*Rambler* 4:83). Applying this principle to politics, Johnson frames the history of any state as a circular movement with only one revolution guaranteed: "Such is the general revolution of affairs in every state; danger and distress produce unanimity and bravery, virtues which are seldom unattended with success; but success is the parent of pride, and pride of jealousy and faction; faction makes way for calamity, and happy is that nation whose calamities renew their unanimity" ("Life of Blake," *Works* 10:49–50). Having once attained and fallen from perfection, a body politic can rebound—though Johnson suggests as the greater possibility its ceasing to be.

[11] Christopher Berry focuses on the crucial difference between Hume and Hegel's arguments about history: "For Hume, freedom is a contingent feature of the historical record. It is a corollary of the growth of cultivation (knowledge), leisure and commerce. There is nothing guaranteed about their continuance; Man has not changed—knowledge . . . affects the 'temper' not the constitution of man. For Hegel, on the contrary, the growth of freedom is identical with *Geist*'s process of self-completion. . . . For Hegel there can *actually* be no retrogression" (184). In our own day, Francis Fukuyama has revived the Hegelian perception of an "end of history," but with an important difference: he claims not that there could not be, but only that there probably will not be a retrogression from liberal democracy and technological capitalism.

Velleius postulated that, as in the natural world, so in the world of human history, there can be no stasis: things go forward to recede, or mature to decay (the label "maturism" is often applied to Velleius's theory).[12] Hume develops Velleius's two inchoate metaphors, presenting us with two clearly defined images—historical institutions as either *plants* that flourish, decay, and pass away; or as *shorelines* that abide, but are subject to a tide, a flux and reflux, a series of successive alternations. "Of the Rise and Progress of the Arts and Sciences" offers a sustained example of the former, organic analogy. It promulgates laws such as these: *"That though the only proper* Nursery *of these noble plants be a free state* [as it is conducive to emulation], *yet may they be transplanted into any government; and that a republic is most favourable to the growth of the sciences, a civilized monarchy to that of the polite arts"* (*Essays* 124). "Law . . . once taken root, is a hardy plant, which will scarcely ever perish through the ill culture of men, or the rigour of the seasons," but "the arts of luxury, and much more the liberal arts, which depend on a refined taste and sentiment, are easily lost; because they are always relished by a few only" (124). Hence, *"when the arts and sciences come to perfection in any state, from that moment they naturally, or rather necessarily decline, and seldom or never revive in that nation, where they formerly flourished"* (135).

Elsewhere, in speculating on the probable causes for the various forms of government and of religion—human institutions that in themselves are more durable than the arts and sciences—Hume employs the metaphor of tidal fluctuation. In answer to his title inquiry—"Whether the British Government Inclines More to Absolute Monarchy, or to a Republic" (1741)—Hume ventures, "The tide has run long, and with some rapidity, to the side of popular government, and is just beginning to turn toward monarchy" (*Essays* 51). Even as forms of government change with a tide-like regularity, so too do forms of religion: "It is remarkable, that the principles of religion have a kind of flux and reflux in the human mind, and that men have a natural tendency to rise from idolatry [polytheism] to theism, and to sink again from theism into idolatry" (*NHR* 46–47). For Hume, then, arts and sciences grow to ripeness only once before exhausting a particular soil; by contrast, peoples will always have governments and religion, but their forms will fluctuate.

The tide of British government was of particular interest to both Hume and Johnson in the 1760s and 1770s. What they awaited and sought to hasten was the tide's halfway point between populism and absolutism—the proper Polybian balance of king, commons, and lords that formed the perfection of Britain's mixed government. When the tide turns too force-

---

[12] The classical sources for "maturism" are discussed by Harry Caplan, 177, 181–82, 194–95. On Velleius's influence on eighteenth-century notions of history, see Walter Jackson Bate, *The Burden of the Past and the English Poet* 80–84; Erskine-Hill, *The Augustan Idea* 350–53.

fully toward the people, civility and at least some degree of civil liberty are at risk. Wholly popular governments are conducive neither to politeness nor, ultimately, to personal freedom—such is the lesson of the English civil wars, and the lesson, too, of ancient Greek history.[13] On the other hand, when the tide turns toward absolutism, political liberties are lost by definition. For Johnson and for Hume, the ideal balance of the post-Settlement order contains a healthy balance of civil liberty and political liberty, but should either have to choose, their choice would be for civil liberty—the liberty that derives from the obedience to just laws, whether or not the people are called on to frame those laws.[14]

Thus Johnson and Hume each expressed an inclination for a strong monarchical power in government, and each grew increasingly impatient with opposition cries for the political "liberty" of the people. Opposition platforms throughout the century tended to call for the greater accountability of MPs to their constituencies, including the tendering of "instructions"; more frequent parliamentary elections; and the territorial extension of the franchise. Certainly after 1742, Johnson and Hume resolutely opposed such innovations. Even in 1741, Hume maintained that "were the members [of Parliament] obliged to receive instructions from their constituents, like the DUTCH deputies," or were parliamentary elections made too frequent, the crown's power would be wholly diminished, an alteration that "would soon reduce it [our government] to a pure republic." Although Hume can, in Walpole's last months, still entertain the notion that a republic in Britain might be, given its dispersed electorate, no "inconvenient" thing, he nonetheless concludes cautiously: "But it is needless to reason any farther concerning a form of government, which is never likely to have place in GREAT BRITAIN. . . . Let us cherish and improve our ancient government as much as possible, without encouraging a passion for such dangerous novelties" (*Essays* 35–36).

Twenty-seven years later, writing to Turgot in the wake of the "Wilkes and Liberty" riots of 1768,[15] Hume contends that it is an excess of political liberty in England that will check "the perpetual Progress towards Per-

---

[13] Hume animadverts against the "want of politeness" fostered by republics ancient and modern in "Of the Rise and Progress of the Arts and Sciences," *Essays* 127–34; excessively democratic government, such as that of Athens, proves destructive of civil liberty as well ("Of Some Remarkable Customs," *Essays* 366–70). Johnson's most memorable assessment of Athenian democracy is recorded by Boswell: "Demosthenes, Madam [Mrs. Thrale], spoke to an assembly of brutes; to a barbarous people" (*Life of Johnson* 2:211).

[14] The distinction between civil and political liberty, the subject of Hume's essay "Of Liberty and Despotism" (1741), is clarified by Hume's French admirer and popularizer, Jean-Baptiste Suard: philosophers "know how to distinguish civil liberty, which consists in obeying only the laws, from political liberty, which calls each citizen to the formation of the laws; they know that civil liberty is the only one which contributes to the happiness of men and that it can be found in a monarchy as in a republic" (translated by Daniel Gordon, 173).

[15] On John Wilkes's public career and the "Wilkite" turbulence of the late 1760s, see George Rudé, as well as Linda Colley, 101–17.

fection" dreamed of by the *philosophes* and usher in "the usual Returns of Barbarism and Ignorance." The English "roar Liberty, tho' they have apparently more Liberty than any People in the World; a great deal more than they deserve; and perhaps more than any men ought to have. . . . There is too little difference between the Governors and Governed" (*Letters* 2:180).[16]

Johnson expresses a wholly similar view of the significance of the Wilkes affair in his pamphlet "The False Alarm" (1770). Johnson here defends the Commons's right to debar Wilkes, who was elected to Parliament in 1768 by the country of Middlesex while serving a prison sentence for seditious libel and obscenity. More than simply responding to Wilkite grievances, Johnson effectively questions the very importance of parliamentary representation in an age of corrupt, self-seeking voters; within a constitution that wisely provides for "virtual" rather than direct representation (Johnson emphasizes this point in "Taxation No Tyranny," *PW* 426–27, 436); and under "a king [George III] who knows not the name of party, and who wishes to be the common father of all his people" (*PW* 344). Johnson indeed contends—for rhetorical effect—that the Wilkite cries for liberty represent the ne plus ultra of popular government, the lowest ebb from which the tide can only rise. Note how Johnson traces this historical decline in three carefully chosen instances: "The civil war was fought for what each army called and believed the best religion, and the best government. The struggle in the reign of Anne, was to exclude or restore an exiled king [i.e., the Old Pretender]. We are now disputing, with almost equal animosity, whether Middlesex shall be represented or not by a criminal from a jail. The only comfort left in such degeneracy is, that a lower state can be no longer possible" (*PW* 343).

For Johnson as for Hume the current ebb of British government was clearly not a happy one. Both men were generally more sanguine, however, about the condition of the arts and sciences in the Europe, if not always in the England, of their day.[17] But this optimism must again be

---

[16] Hume's letters of the late 1760s and 1770s are replete with laments that "[l]icentiousness, or rather the frenzy of liberty, has taken possession of us" (*HL* 2:191); cf. 2:210 ("Our Government has become an absolute Chimera: So much Liberty is incompatible with human Society"), 2:216–18, 261 ("the English Government is certainly happy, though probably not calculated for Duration, by reason of its excessive Liberty"), 306. On the "troublesome and odious" Wilkites, see also 2:235, and David Raynor's "Hume on Wilkes and Liberty: Two Possible Contributions to the *London Chronicle*."

[17] The proliferation of bad literature in England was by the mid eighteenth century a satiric commonplace. Dryden (*Mac Flecknoe*), Swift (*The Tale of a Tub*), and Pope (*The Dunciad*) had all satirized the effects of a burgeoning print culture, in which authors increasingly catered to readers from an increasingly broad social spectrum; all saw in the literary hackwork of their day a threat to the dignity of the classical tradition and the authority of a learned elite. In France, Voltaire similarly lamented the inundation of "frivolous books and, what is worse, serious books that are useless" (*Siècle de Louis XIV* chap. 32, 646). Johnson's own laments over "the continual multiplication of books" may be found in *Idler* nos. 85 and 94:

understood within their conception of cyclical history. Johnson is every bit as Velleian as Hume in his assumption that the arts and sciences, civility and knowledge, grow to perfection in any nation only to decline. The year after Hume published his "Of the Rise and Progress of the Arts and Sciences," Johnson wrote his "Account of the Harleian Library"—an introduction to the five-volume sale catalog of the great library amassed by the earls of Oxford—in which he concludes,

> Nor is the use of catalogues of less importance to those whom curiosity has engaged in the study of literary history, and who think the intellectual revolutions of the world more worthy of their attention than the ravages of tyrants, the desolation of kingdoms, the rout of armies, and the fall of empires. Those who are pleased with observing the first birth of new opinions, their struggle against opposition, their silent progress under persecution, their general reception, *and their gradual decline, or sudden extinction* [note that Johnson offers no third option]; those that amuse themselves with remarking the different periods of human knowledge, and observe how *darkness and light succeed each other* . . . (*Major Works* 119, emphases mine)

As England's great lexicographer, as well of course as a careful student of "dead languages," Johnson was especially aware of the cycles of linguistic birth, maturity, and decline. His own humble expectations as a lexicographer, as expressed in the Preface to his *Dictionary* (1755), are not to stave off the natural and inevitable decay of the English language—"corruption and decay" attend languages no less certainly than mortal beings (*Major Works* 324)—but only to retard decline and cherish the perfection of English with the greater anxiety:

> If the changes we fear be thus irresistible, what remains but to acquiesce with silence, as in the other insurmountable distresses of humanity? It remains that we retard what we cannot repel, that we palliate what we cannot cure. Life may be lengthened by care, though death cannot ultimately be defeated: tongues, like governments, have a natural tendency to degeneration; we have long preserved our constitution, let us make some struggles for our language. (326–27)

In *Idler* no. 63, Johnson once again acknowledges the Velleian course of language, declaring quite simply, "Language proceeds, like every thing else, thro' improvement to degeneracy" (2:197). In his earlier Preface, he located the perfection of the English tongue, from which decline was already perceptible, in the writings of English Renaissance authors from Philip Sidney (d. 1586) to Francis Bacon (d. 1626) and Charles I (d. 1649).

---

for example, "It is observed that 'a corrupt society has many laws'; I know not whether it is not equally true, that 'an ignorant age has many books'" (2:265).

These authors Johnson declared "*the wells of English undefiled* . . . the pure sources of genuine diction," before the language began to deviate toward "Gallic structure and phraseology" (319).[18]

Hume, for his part, had no qualms about French influence. And far from finding the perfection of the English language in authors who lived before the Restoration, Hume seems to think of his own prose as approaching the perfection of the English language. Of Johnson's great touchstone, English Renaissance literature, Hume writes: "Learning, on its revival in this island, was attired in the same unnatural garb, which it wore at the time of its decay among the Greeks and Romans" (*History* 5:150); in Shakespeare, "it is in vain we look either for purity or simplicity of diction" (151). "English prose, during the reign of James, was written with little regard to the rules of grammar, and with a total disregard to the elegance and harmony of the period" (152). Indeed, Hume confidently claimed in 1741, "The first polite prose we have, was writ by a man who is still alive"—that is, Jonathan Swift (*Essays* 91). That Hume sought to make his own prose exemplary is attested by the extraordinary care he took in finessing and endlessly correcting it from edition to edition. In 1771 Hume wrote, quite characteristically, to his publisher William Strahan: "I know not whether the former purchasers [of earlier editions of his complete *History*] may complain of my frequent Corrections; but I cannot help it, and they run mostly upon Trifles; at least they will be esteemed such by the Generality of Readers, who little attend to the extreme Accuracy of Style. It is one great advantage that results from the Art of printing, that an Author may correct his works, as long as he lives" (*Letters* 2:246–47).

Johnson issued corrected and revised editions of the works he considered his major contributions to literature—his *Rambler, Idler,* and, above all, *Dictionary.* He never did so, however, with a vanity of authorship that equaled Hume's; he does not suggest, in letters or elsewhere, that his writing represents "extreme Accuracy," the ripeness of the art, the point from which there can be but decline. Hume's confidence in his own literary-historical place harkens back to claims made by many English literary critics from the 1680s to 1720s that the language had reached perfection in their own lifetimes; Jonathan Kramnick, who surveys these earlier claims (1088–89), sees Johnson as straddling their historical narrative of improvement and, antithetically, a narrative that emerges in the mid-eighteenth century of literary and linguistic decline from an apex of Renaissance models (1095–99). Thus, the man who proclaimed Renaissance English an undefiled well could also remark to Boswell in 1778 of

---

[18] On the contexts of Johnson's praise of the Elizabethan lexicon and distrust of French influence, see my article "'The Structure of His Sentences Is French': Johnson and Hume in the History of English."

a prose work written in 1702: "It is sad stuff, Sir, miserably written, as books in general then were. There is now an elegance of style universally diffused" (*Life of Johnson* 3:243).

Johnson did not remark on the historical importance of his own manner of writing, but we ought not mistake this reticence for humility. In fact, his *Rambler* style was often viewed in his own day as a brash display—in 1767, Alexander Campbell criticized Johnson precisely for his affectation of singularity, his "vanity and self-sufficience" (74). Campbell cites the authority of Hume's "Of the Rise and Progress of the Arts and Sciences" in advancing the principle that "all human things" proceed through "a slow rise and progression from a weak and infirm state, to that degree of maturity and perfection their nature is capable of, and thence a gradual decline, and total dissolution at last"; Campbell's conclusion, however, would have pleased neither Hume nor Johnson: "Swift himself, and his contemporaries . . . brought our Prose to the highest pitch of excellence it ever will attain to"; the subsequent decay of the art is necessitated by a "universal law of nature" and evident in "the vile affected Lexiphanick style in Prose of Mr. J——n, and his followers and imitators" (153–57). More congenial to Hume, at least, would have been the conclusion of Carlo Denina's *Essay on the Revolutions of Literature,* published in English in 1763: "The Scotch, as they form but one nation with the English, and write the same language, conceal . . . from the observation of the neighboring nations that sensible decline in the literature of England, which would otherwise be conspicuous to all Europe."[19] The Scottish rise to maturity follows hard on English decline, and so British literature retained its reputation—for the moment.

---

[19] Denina was professor of eloquence and belles-lettres in the Royal School of Turin; his essay is quoted in Mossner, *Life of Hume* 388–89.

CHAPTER EIGHT

Enthusiasm and Empire

Johnson and Hume were apt to agree that were civilization in Britain to decline or fall, the two most likely causes would be religious and political upheaval. "Superstition" and the still more diabolic "enthusiasm" constitute the potential corruptions of a civilized theism—which for Johnson, and to some degree for the mature Hume, means, in English history since the Tudors, Anglican Christianity. Meanwhile, a secular threat to Britain's civilized political and economic order came after 1756 from Parliament's—and especially the elder Pitt's—policy of militaristic, mercantile imperialism.

I. Enthusiastic Destruction

Johnson afforded Addison's moral writing his highest praise: "As a teacher of wisdom he may be confidently followed. His religion has nothing in it enthusiastick or superstitious" (*Lives* 2:148). "Superstition" is defined by Johnson as "unnecessary fear or scruples in religion; observance of unnecessary and uncommanded rites or practices; religion without morality." For Protestants, "superstition" tends practically to denote the perceived taints of medieval and Catholic Christianity: their mummery and saint-worship, sensual excesses and excessive austerities. The true-born Briton uses the term patriotically, as a slur upon various servile, "priest-ridden" peoples, particularly the French and Spanish. Addison sets the tone: "[T]he *Roman* Catholick Religion is one huge overgrown Body of childish and idle Superstition" (*Spectator* 2:289).

The only "superstition" generally recognized as an internal threat to eighteenth-century Britons was, in Johnson's phrase, the irrational, "unnecessary fear" that can prey on the melancholy temper. Unlike their forebears from Macbeth's time to the reign of James I, eighteenth-century Britons were no longer afraid of witches and goblins and things that go bump in the night—Johnson is careful, in his explanatory notes to *Macbeth,* to consign all such "credulity" to his countrymen's distant past (*Shakespeare* 8:752–55). But superstition abides in England in the gloomy temper that harbors unreasonable religious fears—this is the temper that Addison addresses in *The Spectator* no. 494, and that Johnson's friend Elizabeth Carter seeks to cure in *The Rambler* no. 44. Carter's essay recounts a dream-vision in which the allegorical figure of Superstition appears "drest in black," her looks "filled with terror and unrelenting severity, and her hands armed with whips and scorpions"; she is chased away by (true) Religion, at whose "approach, the frightful spectre, who had before tormented me, vanished away, and with her all the horrors she had caused. The gloomy clouds brightened into chearful sun-shine, the groves recovered their verdure, and the whole region looked gay and blooming as the garden of Eden." Religion, "the offspring of Truth and Love, and the parent of Benevolence, Hope and Joy," teaches that the world ought to be the site of "moderate enjoyment, and grateful alacrity" (*Rambler* 3:237–42).

In Hume's essay "Of Superstition and Enthusiasm" (1741), superstition preys upon the timorous disposition, and "renders men tame and abject, and fits them for slavery." By contrast, the hopeful, proud, presumptuous disposition affords fertile ground for religion's opposite excess, enthusiasm (*Essays* 73–79). Johnson's primary definition of enthusiasm is "[a] vain belief of private revelation; a vain confidence of divine favour or communication."[1] Hume and Johnson alike judged enthusiasm to be the

---

[1] Johnson's *Dictionary* illustration comes from Locke's chapter "Of Enthusiasm" (*Essay,* 4.19): according to Locke, enthusiasm is "founded neither on Reason, nor Divine Revelation, but rising from the Conceits of a warmed or over-weening Brain, works yet, where it once gets footing, more powerfully on the Perswasions and Actions of Men, than either of those two, or both together" (699). The theme of enthusiasm's evils tolls like a bell throughout the elite literature of eighteenth-century Britain. Addison explains that the deportment of the modern British gentleman, loath to display *any* piety, derives from a reaction to the excesses of the Interregnum: "Those Swarms of Sectaries that over-ran the Nation in the time of the great Rebellion, carried their Hypocrisie so high, that they converted our whole Language into a Jargon of Enthusiasm; insomuch that upon the Restoration Men thought they could not recede too far from the Behaviour and Practice of those Persons, who had made Religion a Cloak to so many Villanies" (*Spectator* 4:117). Church of England satires on "enthusiasts" from John Calvin to John Knox, from the seventeenth-century English Puritans to eighteenth-century Methodists, flourish in high literature between the Restoration and the American Revolution: some well-known examples include Samuel Butler's *Hudibras* (1663–78); Dryden's *Religio Laici* (1682); Swift's allegorical account of "Jack" and "the Aeolists" (inspirationalists) in *A Tale of a Tub* (1704); and Henry Fielding's *Shamela* (1741). The transformation of "enthusiasm" into a term of aesthetic approbation begins with Edward Young's *Conjectures on Original Composition* (1759); see Robert Griffin, 50–52.

characteristically British vice—unleashed during the seventeenth-century civil wars, and perhaps not yet chained for good.

Johnson thus characterizes "enthusiasts" in a biographical piece on Francis Cheynel, a Presbyterian controversialist and soldier who flourished in the 1640s:

> He then [Cheynel, c. 1642] retired into Sussex, to exercise his ministry among his friends, *in a place where,* he observes, *there had been little of the power of religion either known or practiced.* As no reason can be given why the inhabitants of Sussex should have less knowledge or virtue than those of other places, it may be suspected that he means nothing more than a place where the presbyterian discipline or principles had never been received. We may now observe that the methodists, where they scatter their opinions, represent themselves as preaching the gospel to unconverted nations. And enthusiasts of all kinds have been inclined to disguise their partial tenets with pompous appellations, and to imagine themselves the great instruments of salvation. (*Major Works* 479).

As they proceed beyond hypocrisy, such imaginings are so many steps toward madness—as Paul Alkon observes (92–94), Johnson like Locke distrusts enthusiasm as a perturbation of mind. It is thus not a little ironic that Johnson wrote his Cheynel biography for *The Student, or Oxford and Cambridge Miscellany* (1751), edited by his friend Christopher Smart, who was later confined in a madhouse for displaying a maniacal enthusiasm.[2]

In analyzing the psychology of enthusiasm, Johnson has recourse to charges of both hypocrisy and delusion: "[E]nthusiasts of all kinds have been inclined to *disguise* their partial tenets . . . and to *imagine* themselves" instruments of salvation (emphases mine). A similar balance or double vision animates Hume's analysis of the religious enthusiast; in the enthusiast or zealot, one finds a concentrated example of the "sophistry, which attends all the passions" (*History* 6:357). Those who claim religious sanctions for their great deeds may generally, or largely, think themselves following the dictates of faith and right reason, but all the while they are really prompted by passions working, so to speak, behind the scenes. Hume arrives at this principle through investigating complex characters such as Thomas à Becket, archbishop of Canterbury,

---

[2] Boswell repeatedly adduces Smart's madness in order to evince Johnson's powers of sympathy. Johnson is quoted, for example, as saying, "I did not think he ought to be shut up. His infirmities were not noxious to society. He insisted on people praying with him; and I'd as lief pray with Kit Smart as any one else. Another charge was, that he did not love clean linen; and I have no passion for it" (*Life of Johnson* 1:397). Johnson's sympathy with Smart may to some degree have been facilitated by similitude: according to Adam Smith Johnson himself had a mania for prayer (*Lectures on Rhetoric* 228). Johnson's feeling for Smart also illustrates that while he hated enthusiasts in general, he could not help but love individuals: cf. Swift's letter to Pope on the art of satire, "for instance I hate the tribe of Lawyers, but I love Councellor such a one, Judge such a one. . ." (Sept. 29, 1725, *Correspondence* 3:103).

a prelate of the most lofty, intrepid, and inflexible spirit, who was able to cover, to the world and probably to himself, the enterprizes of pride and ambition, under the disguise of sanctity and of zeal for the interests of religion. . . .[3] But no man, who enters into the genius of that age, can reasonably doubt of this prelate's sincerity. The spirit of superstition was so prevalent, that it infallibly caught every careless reasoner, much more every one whose interest, and honour, and ambition, were engaged to support it. . . . Throughout that large collection of letters, which bears the name of St. Thomas, we find, in all the retainers of that aspiring prelate, no less than in himself, a most entire and absolute conviction of the reason and piety of their own party, and a disdain of their antagonists: Nor is there less cant and grimace in their stile, when they address each other, than when they compose manifestos for the perusal of the public. The spirit of revenge, violence, and ambition, which accompanied their conduct, instead of forming a presumption of hypocricy, are the surest pledges of their sincere attachment to a cause, which so much flattered those domineering passions. (1:333–34)

In this dramatic passage, Hume actively searches for a judgment about Becket. He moves from the tentative proposition that Becket was "probably" able to cover his own pride and ambition to himself under the "disguise of sanctity," to the willful and thus doubtful verdict, "But no man . . . can reasonably doubt of this prelate's [religious] sincerity." In the space that separates these two assertions lies the space between Locke's equation of personal identity with self-consciousness and our own notion of unconscious motivation.[4]

History is ever spurred onward by the selfish passions—yet for much of English history those passions were often known, and almost as often sincerely knew themselves, as "zeal for religion." So Hume comprehends, among others, Joan of Arc, who "mistook the workings of passion for heavenly inspiration" (2:398); Mary Tudor, whose "obstinancy, bigotry, violence, cruelty, malignity, revenge, tyranny" were balanced by only one ostensible virtue, "sincerity" or fidelity in both promises and religious professions (3:461); the seventeenth-century Puritans, whose "insurmountable passion, disguised to themselves, as well as to others, under the appearance of holy fervours, was well qualified to make proselytes, and to seize the mind of the ignorant multitude" (5:285); and, finally, the villainous Cromwell, whose atrocious regicide "was to him covered under a mighty cloud of republican and fanatical illusions; and it is not impossible, but he might believe it, as many others did, the most meritorious action, that he could perform" (6:110). In the *Dialogues concerning Natural Reli-*

---

[3] Cf. Gibbon: ambitious churchmen "concealed from others, and perhaps from themselves, the secret motives of their conduct" (*Decline and Fall* chap. 15, 1:483).

[4] Cf. Hundert, 134, on unconscious motivation in Mandeville and the heritage of Jansenist moral psychology.

gion, Hume theorizes this fine line between religious hypocrisy and delusion in Philo's remark, "Many religious exercises are entered into with seeming fervour, where the heart, at the time, feels cold and languid: A habit of dissimulation is by degrees contracted: And fraud and falsehood become the predominant principle" (222).

Johnson shares Hume's conviction that public zeal for religion is typically a mask, wittingly or unwittingly worn, to cover a spirit of faction and ambition. Johnson also stresses, as Hume does in his depiction of the draymen and butchers that peopled Cromwell's army (*History* chap. 59), the role that envious hatred—or what we might call, after Marx, class antagonism—plays in many zealous professions, particularly those of the Puritans. In a sermon written for the thirtieth of January—the day established by Parliament in 1661 as commemorative of the martyrdom of Charles I— Johnson maintains that in "the ravages of religious enthusiasts, and the wars kindled by difference of opinions," "envy still operates, however various in its appearance, however disguised by specious pretences, or however removed from notice by intermediate causes" (*Sermon* no. 23, 240– 42). Similarly, Johnson writes of Milton that his republicanism—and by extension, his opposition to church government—"was, I am afraid, founded in an envious hatred of greatness, and a sullen desire of independence; in petulance impatient of control, and pride disdainful of superiority" (*Lives* 1:157). Such are the passions that comprise enthusiasm.

Johnson's most sustained critique of enthusiasm comes in his *Journey to the Western Islands of Scotland.* His literary account begins with a meditation on the wreckage wrought by "the tumult and violence of Knox's reformation" and the "epidemical enthusiasm" to which it gave rise (5–6). He presents as a casualty of enthusiasm the ruined cathedral of St. Andrews, and the nearby ruins of a once great Augustinian priory, the grotesque habitation of "an old woman, who claimed the right of abode there . . . she is now neglected, but spins a thread, has the company of her cat, and is troublesome to nobody" (8–9). "The ruins of the cathedral of Elgin afforded us another proof of the waste of reformation" (23–24). Nor are such ruins solely the memorial of "the tumultuous violence of Knox," but reminders too that eighteenth-century Britons need to preserve their own "monuments of sacred magnificence": "Our own cathedrals are mouldering by unregarded dilapidation. . . . we are in danger of doing that deliberately, which the Scots did not do but in the unsettled state of an imperfect constitution" (24).

Johnson laments the passing of cathedrals not as a historian of the church, still less as a student of architecture; for Johnson, these cathedrals, and the rites and ceremonies that once inhabited them, *are* history, indeed the only history an illiterate people have to bequeath. Enthusiasm did not simply destroy religious buildings, but effaced history itself:

In nations, where there is hardly the use of letters, what is once out of sight is lost for ever. . . . Their only registers are stated observances and practical representations. For this reason an age of ignorance is an age of ceremony. Pageants, and processions, and commemorations, gradually shrink away, as better methods come into use of recording events, and preserving rights.

It is not only in Raasay that the chapel is unroofed and useless; through the few [Hebridean] islands which we visited, we neither saw nor heard of any house of prayer, except in Sky, that was not in ruins. The malignant influence of Calvinism has blasted ceremony and decency together; and if the remembrance of papal superstition is obliterated, the monuments of papal piety are likewise effaced. (65)

Johnson's *Journey* is a print memorial to the effacement of memorials effected by violence and by time. Johnson recognizes that an age of print is an improvement over an age of ceremony, yet regrets the passing of "ceremony and decency" from the lives of an illiterate people: unless there comes a day when all people can read, and read well—in 1775 Johnson does not think this day coming soon—ceremony and ritual are the necessary preservatives of history and community, religion and knowledge. Historically, then, superstition has its benefits. As a corollary of his attack on the violence of enthusiasm, Johnson displays an appreciation for the virtues of ceremony, even though it include "papal superstition."[5]

The emotional climax of Johnson's journey comes in his visit to the moldering churches on Iona, "that illustrious island, which was once the luminary of the Caledonian regions, whence savage clans and roving barbarians derived the benefits of knowledge, and the blessings of religion" (148). (The monastery that St. Columba founded on Iona in 563 provided the center from which missionaries spread throughout Scotland and northern England.) Johnson laments Iona's decay from its former glory: "The island, which was once the metropolis of learning and piety, has now no school for education, nor temple for worship, only two inhabitants that can speak English, and not one that can write or read" (152). The ostensible absence of religion on the island—"I know not if they are visited by any minister"—is the natural aftermath of enthusiasm having run its course. It follows from "that laxity of practice and indifference of opinion, in which men, not sufficiently instructed to find the middle point, too easily shelter themselves from rigour and constraint" (6). Johnson's concluding hope—perhaps not a reasonable, but a heart-felt one—is that all that was lost through the outbreak of enthusiasm may yet be restored through the cyclical revolutions of time: "Perhaps, in the revolutions of

[5] Cf. Johnson's earlier remarks on the naturalness of ritual to religion in *The Rambler* no. 110: "Incorporated minds will always feel some inclination towards exterior acts, and ritual observances. Ideas not represented by sensible objects are fleeting, variable, and evanescent" (4:222).

the world, Iona may be sometime again the instructress of the Western Regions" (153).

When Johnson surveys the Highlands and finds negligence of religion where once enthusiasm had burned most brightly, he offers experimental confirmation of Hume's 1741 reflection: "When the first fire of enthusiasm is spent, men naturally, in all fanatical sects, sink into the greatest remissness and coolness in sacred matters" ("Of Superstition and Enthusiasm," *Essays* 77). In this early essay, Hume viewed enthusiasm as the lesser of two evils, both because it abates more naturally than superstition, and because at its zenith it fosters civil liberty and the destruction of priestcraft. But this early preference was expressed when Hume could still assume the republican style that prevailed in most corners of the literary world in the late days of Walpole's ministry. He came in later years to be far less enthusiastic about that "love of liberty" fostered by "enthusiasts, and zealous promoters of the passionate devotion, and of the inward life" (79). In the course of writing both a conjectural history of religion and a political history of England, Hume came to share Johnson's respect for necessary authority, in church as in state, and for those "rites," "ceremonies," and "observances" that ground individuals in "the common train of life" (78).

Donald Siebert finely observes that "implicit in . . . [*The Natural History of Religion*] and other works published later in . . . [Hume's] career is a growing appreciation of the power of religious rites and images to control or even neutralize the dangerous caprices of religious zeal. . . . Hume came to regard extreme Protestantism as the most pernicious form of religion" (*Moral Animus* 104). Rites and images of the sort denounced as "superstition" by the more austere Protestant sects are a useful prophylactic against the disease of an unsocial and unruly imagination. By focusing the minds of many on a shared, observable reality, "superstition" is more empirical than the inward religious life and serves to maintain basic social or group ties. Enthusiasm, by contrast, is along with unreflective pride and rapacity one of the centrifugal forces that threatens to dissolve society into, to borrow a phrase from Johnson, "a tumult of individuals" (*PW* 425).

Thus, among the ancient Britons, "the bands of government, which were naturally loose among that rude and turbulent people, were happily corroborated by the terrors of their superstition" (*History* 1:5–6). The Norman victory over the English at the Battle of Hastings is the effect, and the vindication, of their orderly religious practice: "[T]he aspect of things, on the night before the battle, was very different in the two camps. The English spent the time in riot, and jollity, and disorder; the Normans in silence and in prayer, and in the other functions of their religion" (1:156). Writing of the clerics of the thirteenth century, Hume acknowledges that though their religion may be called "superstition," "it served to unite together a body of men who had great sway over the people, and who kept the community from falling to pieces, by the factions and independant power of the nobles"; the clerics "still maintained, even amidst the shock of arms, those secret links, without which it is impossible for human society to subsist" (2:14). Despite his appreciation of the social utility of medieval Christianity, Hume cannot keep from remarking "the more generous superstition of the ancients" (2:410, with reference to Joan d'Arc's ungenerous condemnation by an ecclesiastical court). Hume's preference for the superior ethical effects of ancient polytheism—with regard to the fostering of courage, toleration, reasonableness—over those of medieval and Catholic Christianity is the burden of the second half of *The Natural History of Religion* (48–65).

But Hume mutes his Shaftesburian ideals in *The History of England;* as a historian of British church establishments, Hume sounds far more like Warburton or Johnson than like a pagan, ancient or modern. Nicholas Hudson has established the crucial influence of Warburton's *The Alliance of Church and State* (1736) on Johnson's own support of an established church in the interest of social order; Warburton argues, as Johnson would in *Sermon* no. 24, that ritual and ordinance were necessary to the moral influence of religion, because "a mere mental Intercourse with God which makes Religion only a divine Philosophy of the Mind is altogether unfit for such a Creature as Man in his present Station here" (quoted in *Samuel Johnson and Eighteenth-century Thought* 226–27). Compare Hume's arguments in favor of James I's attempts to "infuse a small tincture of ceremony into the national worship [of Scotland], and to introduce such rites as might, in some degree, occupy the mind, and please the senses":

> The fire of devotion, excited by novelty, and inflamed by opposition, had so possessed the minds of the Scottish reformers, that all rites and ornaments, and even order of worship, were disdainfully rejected as useless burthens; retarding the imagination in its rapturous ecstacies, and cramping the operations of that divine spirit, by which they supposed themselves to be animated. A mode of worship was established . . . [that] reposed itself entirely on the contemplation of that divine Essence, which discovers itself to the understanding only. This species of devotion, so worthy of the supreme Being, but so little suitable to human frailty, was observed to . . . confound all rational principles of conduct and behavior. The mind, straining for these extraordinary raptures, reaching them by short glances, sinking again under its own weakness, rejecting all exterior aid of pomp and ceremony, was so occupied in the inward life, that it fled from every intercourse of society, and from every chearful amusement, which could soften or humanize the character. (5:68)[6]

[6] Again, compare Gibbon: "The sages of Greece and Rome . . . supposed that any popular mode of faith and worship which presumed to disclaim the assistance of the senses, would, in proportion as it receded from superstition, find itself incapable of restraining the wanderings of the fancy and the visions of fanaticism" (chap. 16, 1:519).

Hume pictures enthusiasm in religion as the counterpart to Cartesianism in philosophy: here as at the end of book 1 of the *Treatise,* the inward turn breeds monsters of melancholy, gloom, and finally social disruption. Our salvation lies in the social instinct, and for philosophers, recognition of the passions that govern us all.

In terms quite similar to his support of James's (failed) attempt to reform the Church of Scotland, Hume also approved of Archbishop Laud's (frustrated) efforts, during the reign of Charles I, to introduce liturgical reform into the Church of England: "Even the English church, though it retained a share of popish ceremonies, may justly be thought too naked and unadorned, and still to approach too near the abstract and spiritual religion of the puritans. Laud and his associates, by reviving a few primitive institutions of this nature, corrected the error of the first reformers, and presented to the affrighted and astonished mind, some sensible, exterior observances, which might occupy it during its religious exercises" (5:459–60). Johnson's heroicizing of Laud—he is in *The Vanity of Human Wishes* the favorite of "Art and Genius" (lines 165–74), the modern counterpart to Juvenal's Cicero and Demosthenes—strongly suggests approval of his attempted reforms, presumably along Warburtonian lines. But as Donald Siebert notes, "[B]oth Johnson and Hume had rather High Church sympathies—Johnson, in theory and practice; Hume, only in theory" (*Moral Animus* 85).

Hume's own High Church sympathies, as distinct from Johnson's, derive in part from his conviction that only an established church can keep priests unambitious (*History* 3:134–36) and thus encourage a wholesome religious laxity among parishioners.[7] The statesman sets sound policy in establishing full civic control over the church. Hume's lack of sympathy with Johnson's wish to restore the Church of England's Convocation to its full powers is explained by Hume's "Idea of a Perfect Commonwealth" (1752): in such a state, "the magistrates name rectors or ministers to all

[7] Hume believed that such an atmosphere indeed prevailed in the centuries directly preceding the Protestant Reformation; in a passage from the first edition of his *History*'s first volume, later withdrawn, Hume wrote that before "the doctrine of Luther was promulgated. . . . the attachment to superstition, tho' without reserve, was not extreme; and, like the ancient pagan idolatry, the popular religion consisted more of exterior practices and observances, than of any principles, which either took possession of the heart, or influenced the conduct." "Learning and knowledge, as of old in Greece, [were] stealing in gradually," and would perhaps have corrected "the ecclesiastical abuses as were the grossest and most burdensome"; but, lamentably, the violence of "the enraged and fanatical reformers" was met with the violence of the counter-Reformation, and learning and liberty suffered the consequences (*History* 1:xvi–xvii). In thus rejecting a central assumption of what would later be called Whig historiography—that the Reformation represents a signal stage in the progress of liberty—Hume anticipates Herbert Butterfield's critique: "[W]hen we look at Erasmus and Machiavelli and the spirit of the Renaissance we must at least wonder whether freedom of thought and modern rationalism might not have had an easier course if Luther had never resuscitated militant religion" (80–81).

the parishes," and may "depose or suspend" them as they see fit (*Essays* 520). For should the reins of civil law be loosened in any way, the passions might once again express themselves in the religious professions of especially factious men and women.

Johnson believed that religion must *ultimately* be subservient to the needs of civil society—hence his objection to "the *inward light,* to which some methodists pretended": "it was a principle utterly incompatible with social or civil security. 'If a man (said he,) pretends to a principle of action of which I can know nothing, nay, not so much as that he has it, but only that he pretends to it; how can I tell what that person may be prompted to do? When a person professes to be governed by a written ascertained law, I can then know where to find him'" (*Life of Johnson* 2:126). (Elsewhere in the *Life,* Johnson expresses approval for the simple homiletic *style* of the Methodist preachers—but style and message are not here sanctioned together.) Johnson's respect for the civic function of the Church did not, however, persuade him that civil magistrates should "micromanage" its affairs. Johnson maintained that the practical matters of church government such as taxation and minor appointments ought to be decided within the church, and not by any magistrate. Hume's blindness or indifference to arguments in favor of the Convocation may be inferred from his insistence, throughout his *History,* that ecclesiastical offices and incomes ought to belong wholly to the discretion of the civil magistrate;[8] convinced of the necessity of an established church, Hume has no patience for scruples about the integrity of a specifically Christian church. Christianity is, for Hume, somewhat beside the point.

And so a mere three years after completing the *History,* Hume complained, in a letter of 1765—in an intellectual climate marked in England by the concurrent growth of Methodism and Warburton's reputation as a censor—that the English "are relapsing fast into the deepest Stupidity, Christianity & Ignorance" (*HL* 1:498).[9] Hume would repeat this lament to Gibbon in March 1776 (*Letters* 2:310), on the appearance of the first volume of the *Decline and Fall of the Roman Empire.* A reputation for derogatory references to Christianity is precisely what Johnson could not brook in Hume; it marks the boundary between Johnson's Enlightenment and that of Hume, Gibbon, and the French *philosophes.* Yet we must note that, like Cicero, Hume admits such references only in his correspondence,

---

[8] Witness the vehemence with which Hume supports the claims of the Holy Roman emperor Henry IV against Pope Gregory in their "investiture controversy" (1:215–16), or of the English king Henry I against Anselm, archbishop of Canterbury, and Pope Pascal II (1:262–68).

[9] In his 1751 annotated edition of Pope's *Dunciad,* Warburton added Hume, as the author of the *Enquiry concerning Human Understanding,* to Pope's legion of Dunces (*Dunciad* 3.224, n.).

never in his published work; in the latter, he always makes allowance for Christian faith.

II. The Costs of Empire

If civilization in Britain were not toppled by a resurgence of enthusiasm, it might be done in by Pitt's policy of imperial expansion. The 1760s were not only, as Hume lamented, an era of Christian revival; they also saw Britain's transformation, after the Seven Years' War, into a military-mercantile empire of ancient Roman proportions (Colley 101–02). Johnson and Hume both wrote against the costly acquisition and maintenance of this empire.[10] They also commented sardonically on the ethics of colonial imperialism.

Hume opposed colonial imperialism not only on economic but also on moral grounds; he censured it not only in his own day, but in all its historical instances. At the outset of his complete *History*, Hume writes dryly of "the Romans, in the reign of Claudius": "Without seeking any more justifiable reasons of hostility than were employed by the late Europeans in subjecting the Africans and Americans, they sent over an army . . . and made a considerable progress in subduing the inhabitants" (1:7–8). Hume similarly assesses the English conquest of King William (1:152) and the French conquest of Edward III (whose mercantilist policies stand him in particularly bad stead) (2:272–80). And Hume's portrait of Spanish, Portuguese, and English colonization of the Americas is Swiftian in its irony:

> When the courage and avarice of the Spaniards and Portuguese had discovered so many new worlds, that they were resolved to shew themselves superior to the barbarous heathens whom they invaded, not only in art and arms, but also in the justice of the quarrel: They applied to Alexander VI. who then filled the papal chair; and he generously bestowed on the Spaniards the whole western, and on the Portuguese the whole eastern part of the globe. The more scrupulous protestants, who acknowledged not the authority of the Roman pontiff, established the first discovery as the foundation of *their* title; and if a pirate or sea-adventurer of their nation but erected a stick or stone on the coast, as a memorial of taking possession, they concluded the whole continent to belong to them, and thought themselves intitled to expel or exterminate, as usurpers, the ancient possessors and inhabitants. It was in this manner that Sir Walter Raleigh . . . had acquired to the crown of England a claim to the continent of Guiana, a region as large as the half of Europe. (5:75–76)

[10] Anthony Pagden (156–77) provides a broad context of other British and French critics of empire in the eighteenth century.

Satirizing the same European claims in more solemn tones, Johnson attributes this oration to an Indian chief in the wake of the fall of Quebec (1759):

> Many years and ages are supposed to have been . . . passed in plenty and security; when at last, a new race of men entered our country from the great ocean. . . . Those invaders ranged over the continent, slaughtering in their rage those that resisted, and those that submitted, in their mirth. . . . and when the sword and the mines have destroyed their natives, they supply their place by human beings of another colour, brought from some distant country to perish here under toil and torture. (*Idler* no. 81, 2:252–53)

Johnson complains vehemently against the inhumanity of Europe's colonial endeavors in his "Introduction to the Political State of Great Britain" (1756) and his long preface to *The World Displayed* (1759–61), a two-volume collection of travel accounts; in the latter, he summarily presents the advances in European navigation as affording "a new world to *European* curiosity and *European* cruelty" (*Prefaces* 236).[11]

Although, as I have argued in chapters 3 to 5, Johnson and Hume share a uniform conception of human happiness or flourishing—reason ought to be enlightened, the passions sifted and moderated—they simultaneously maintain a pluralistic notion of social or political flourishing. Hume sought to reconcile the possible contradiction between these two positions in his allegory about a country called "Fourli," modeled on his understanding of ancient Athens. The inhabitants of Fourli, although motivated by the same moral sentiments and, abstractly, the same notion of happiness as cultured eighteenth-century Europeans, nonetheless sanction practices repugnant to many in Hume's day, including pederasty, infanticide, and suicide. Hume carefully explains that these practices are, at bottom, reasonable responses to the particular physical and social circumstances of Fourli—that is, Athens. So, for example, male homoeroticism seems the natural (and morally indifferent) effect of the strict sexual segregation of social spaces, and the habit of exercising nude in the palestra (*ECPM* 324–43).

The good of communities, and thus of individuals considered as members of those communities, need not conform to one ideal template. Rather, a community vindicates itself, in an important way, by the very fact of its endurance or survival—by the "plenty and security," to recall John-

---

[11] Steven Scherwatzky persuasively argues that Johnson's masterpiece *Rasselas* (1759) is itself an allegory against empire: "[W]hen we consider that . . . [it] appeared at a time when England was once more engaged in a war over territorial rights, a time when these exploits were justified through images of paradise and opportunity in distant lands, then perhaps we can offer yet another reason why the Happy Valley is not so happy, and why Rasselas' journeys fail to provide the satisfaction that he seeks" (112).

son, that accumulates over "many years and ages." Modern European institutions, while serving Europeans more or less well, are not necessarily a good to be exported—certainly not exported by any means necessary.

Dispossessing "barbarous heathens" (in Hume's ironic phrase) is wrong in principle; in practice, such usurpations have also proved calamitously expensive to the usurpers. Empire in general, in Hume's as in Johnson's eyes, was priced exorbitantly. The foreign wars that secured Britain's empire incurred a massive national debt. Johnson typically expresses his horror at this debt in the context of denouncing the Hanoverians' military policies. The Continental entanglements of the first two Georges drained "the wealth of England," thereby "neglecting futurity . . . the liberty and welfare of ages to come"—then as now, a national debt is an intergenerational burden (*PW* 27, 32). Writing in 1771 in defense of Lord North's avoidance of war with Spain—and against the hawkish clamors of Pitt—Johnson generalizes: "The wars of civilized nations make very slow changes in the system of empire. The publick perceives scarcely any alteration but an increase of debt; and the few individuals who are benefited, are not supposed to have the clearest right to their advantages" (371). This final clause drips with irony, as Johnson proceeds to delineate the nature of these few who reap advantage from war and national debt: "paymasters and agents, contractors and commissaries." Hume praised these lines of Johnson's.[12]

Yet Hume shrewdly analyzes the wartime benefits that accrue not chiefly to paymasters and agents, but to public stockholders—in his view, the first global capitalists:

> In this unnatural state of society, the only persons, who possess any revenue beyond the immediate effects of their industry, are the stock-holders, who draw almost all the rent of the land and houses, besides the produce of all the customs and excises. These are men, who have no connexions with the state, who can enjoy their revenue in any part of the globe in which they chuse to reside, who will naturally bury themselves in the capital or in great cities, and who will sink into the lethargy of a stupid and pampered luxury, without spirit, ambition, or enjoyment. Adieu to all ideas of nobility, gentry, and family. ("Of Public Credit" [1752], *Essays* 357–58)

---

[12] The quotation is from Johnson's "Thoughts on the Late Transactions Respecting Falkland Islands" (1771), a pamphlet Hume applauded: "One sees that he speaks from the Heart, and is moved with a cordial Indignation against these Ruffians" (the war party of Lord Weymouth, Pitt, Junius et al.). Hume finds fault only with Johnson's relative moderation towards Pitt: Johnson had called Pitt's martial speeches "feudal gabble" (*PW* 367), but Hume elaborates, "What other Talent indeed has he, but that of reciting with tolerable Action and great Impudence a long Discourse in which there in neither Argument, Order, Instruction, Propriety, or even Grammar?" Pitt was, in short, far from the stylistic and ethical ideal Hume had enshrined in "Of Eloquence," and that Johnson embodied in the parliamentary orations he wrote for *The Gentleman's Magazine*. Hume finally dismisses Pitt as "our Cut-throat" (*HL* 2:240–42).

Hume speaks against the public debt ("credit") with an uncharacteristic tone of indignation, indeed of apocalypticism: "It must, indeed, be one of these two events; either the nation must destroy public credit, or public credit will destroy the nation" (360–61). Hume never wavered in this stance—indeed, in his *History of England* he traces the origins of the debt to the reign of Henry VI, and comments dryly, "The ruinous effects of it are now become apparent, and threaten the very existence of the nation" (2:454).[13] By 1769 Hume was positively gleeful about the prospect of purifying collapse: "Notwithstanding my Age, I hope to see a public Bankruptcy, the total Revolt of America, the Expulsion of the English from the East Indies, the Diminution of London [as the "great city" that battens on public stock] to less than a half, and the Restoration of the Government to the King, Nobility, and Gentry of this Realm" (*HL* 2:210).

The empire Britain sought to establish would serve only to increase the nation's crushing debt; America, as a large and increasingly wealthy territory across the sea, would inevitably win its independence. Looking back at the Seven Years' War, Hume complains in 1771 that "the wise and virtuous Minister, Pitt, could contract more Incumbrances, in six months of an unnecessary War, than we have been able to discharge during eight Years of Peace . . . I can foresee nothing but certain and speedy Ruin either to the Nation or to the public Creditors"; Hume further laments that although British agriculture has improved, "our Manufactures do not advance; and all depends on our Union with America, which, in the Nature of Things, cannot long subsist" (*HL* 2:237). Hume elaborates in a 1775 letter to William Strahan on the reasons why "our Union with America . . . cannot long subsist":

> that a forced and every day more precarious Monopoly of about 6 or 700,000 Pounds a Year of Manufactures, was not worth contending for; that we should preserve a greater part of this Trade even if the Ports of America were open to all Nations; that it was very likely, in our method of proceeding, that we should be disappointed in our Scheme of conquering the Colonies; and that we ought to think beforehand of how we were to govern them, after they were conquer'd. . . . Let us, therefore, lay aside all Anger; shake hands, and part Friends. Or if we retain any anger, let it only be against that wicked Madman, Pitt; who has reducd us to our present Condition. (2:300–301)[14]

We tend to think of Johnson, despite his general aversion toward empire, as a staunch opponent of American independence, largely because of his presumed antipathy toward Americans themselves as "a race of con-

---

[13] John Christian Laursen and Greg Coolidge situate Hume's fears of the debt within both their historical context and subsequent British history.

[14] On Hume's attitudes toward American independence, see J. G. A. Pocock, "Hume and the American Revolution: The Dying Thoughts of a North Briton," in *Virtue, Commerce, and History* 124–42; Donald Livingston, *Philosophical Melancholy and Delirium* 290–313.

victs" (*Life of Johnson* 2:312). Taken out of context, his most-often-cited pronouncement on the matter is, "[H]ow is it that we hear the loudest yelps for liberty among the drivers of negroes?" (*PW* 454). Yet quotation out of context is, as we have seen, particularly apt to misrepresent Johnson or Hume. Johnson's line comes near the end of his pamphlet "Taxation No Tyranny" (1775), written in response to the "resolves" published by the American Continental Congress of 1774, largely as a vindication of Britain's sovereign right to tax American colonists. Johnson's famous line on American as hypocritical yelpers for liberty who presumably deserve to be subdued directly precedes one of his characteristic "Buts": "But let us interrupt a while this dream of conquest, settlement, and supremacy. Let us remember that . . . we may possibly be checked in our career of reduction. We may be reduced to peace on equal terms, or driven from the western continent." Johnson then proceeds, quite calmly, to delineate his hopes for fair trade agreements with the independent Americans, and for sparing English settlers in America who have given "an oath of allegiance to the reigning powers" from the indignity of "an oath of abjuration" (454–55). Donald Greene is, I believe, correct to suggest that it is "significant . . . that in fact he concludes . . . by contemplating American independence with no particular symptoms of alarm," and to note that Johnson had earlier written, in a *Literary Magazine* review of 1756, of the inevitability of American independence: "This great country, for which we are so warmly incited to contend, will not be honestly our own though we keep it from the French" (*PW* 407). Johnson appears to have agreed with Hume that "in the Nature of Things, our Union with America . . . cannot long subsist."

One signal difference between Johnson and Hume's critique of mercantile imperialism, however, is that Johnson would preserve British mercantilism sans empire, while Hume as reformist seeks the end of both policies. Johnson, like most of his contemporaries who opposed Pitt's program, supported a "little Englander" mercantilism in his pamphlet "Further Thoughts on Agriculture" (1756) and his undated manuscript, "Considerations on Corn": Britain ought, in Johnson's view, to remain economically independent through governmental support for surplus production in agriculture and pasturage. People "must feed upon bread, and be cloathed with wool; and the nation that can furnish these universal commodities, may have her ships welcomed at a thousand ports, or sit at home and receive the tribute of foreign countries, enjoy their arts, or treasure up their gold" (*PW* 124). Johnson's last phrase—"treasure up their gold"—suggests that a nation's wealth lies in its accumulation of specie; Hume aims at disproving precisely this assumption in his free-trade theory.[15]

[15] On Johnson's mercantilism, see Donald Greene, *The Politics of Samuel Johnson*, 237–39, 280–84, and *PW*, 116–20. Once again, it is easy to overstate the difference between John-

Hume generally opposed protective tariffs and other measures designed to insure a nation's favorable balance of trade. Hume's free trade credo—now generally accepted among economists—is that, so long as any nation produces commodities (a substantial percentage of which ought be "manufactures and mechanic arts"), its supply of gold and silver money at any one time is of no count.[16] Of Henry VII's misguided efforts to regulate prices and wages, and to prohibit the exportation of money, plate, bullion or horses, Hume concludes, "It is evident, that these matters ought always to be left free, and be entrusted to the common course of business and commerce" (*History* 3:78). Yet Hume would end his life without convincing the majority of his countrymen of the natural justice of free markets; this task was reserved for his heirs in political economy, Adam Smith and David Ricardo.

Their differences on economy aside, Hume and Johnson shared in their late years a premonition that Britain might enter upon a new era of decline: martial and mercantile imperialism, and the national debt it incurred, might precipitate another turn of Fortune's wheel; popular discontent and murmuring against authority, evident in the new enthusiasm of the Methodists and in the cries of the "Wilkes and Liberty" men, might put an end to civility as they knew it. Under such circumstances, heroism meant standing by one's commitment to the old order of church and nation; the hero, if heroes there be, must be seen as a "conservator"— defined by Johnson as "preserver; one that has the care or office of keeping any thing from detriment, diminution, or extinction."

---

son and Hume; as Andrew Skinner points out (242–44, 248–49), Hume himself could endorse economic protectionism when circumstances demanded it. Still, with regard to England's corn trade—the occasioning topic of Johnson's mercantilism essays—Hume advocated a policy of laissez-faire even during times of scarcity: see the 1758 Hume manuscript published by David Raynor in "Who Invented the Invisible Hand?"

[16] Hume sets forth his theory of how unimpeded trade will arrive at a "natural level" between a nation's industry and its money in "Of the Balance of Trade" (1752): the less money a nation has, the cheaper its labor and hence it exports; the cheaper its exports, the greater its influx of money; the greater its money, the more expensive its labor and commodities; cheaper imports will then issue in a outflow of money until the circle starts again (see *Essays* 311–12). In "Of Commerce," published in the same year, Hume argues that the employment of a large proportion of a nation's labor in the manufacture of commercial luxuries contributes to national happiness, industry, and military power, as such laborers "may be easily converted to the public service" in times of war.

CHAPTER NINE

Constancy

I. Sceptical Conservatism

Johnson and Hume both accept that, with regard to the morally indifferent or indeterminate aspects of life, the established rules and manners of a given place and time ought to be followed. Fundamental moral judgments apply universally, and entail obligations that may at times conflict with and transcend our local duties; but in most aspects of our political and social lives, we simply render to Caesar what is Caesar's. Positive institutions that have endured over time are justified precisely by *our* endurance. Those institutions may not be ideal, but then neither are we. Johnson and Hume shared—along with Voltaire, Robertson, Gibbon, and Burke—a sophisticated conception of the crucial importance of social and political continuity to a world in which the authority of institutions derived neither from God nor Reason, but only from opinions annealed through time. Opinions and practices need continually to be reformed, of course—either toward greater reasonableness, or toward greater conformity with the foundational authority of the past—but reform ought to proceed cautiously on abiding foundations.

The goal of totally restructuring society according to either a revealed or a rational scheme was repulsive to almost all British writers of the early to mid eighteenth century; such a goal, they maintained, could only be a madman's dream, the delusion of "Adam-wits," a mere prelude to bloodshed and tyranny.[1] Schemes of total reform—"revolutions," in our mod-

---

[1] "Adamwit" (not in the Oxford English Dictionary) is used by Dryden in his poem *Absalom and Achitophel* (1681) to characterize the fractious temper of his countrymen: "These

ern sense—cannot, according to the laws of history, succeed. So in the 1640s, the constitution as established under the Stuarts stood in need of limited reforms; of the popular uprising and military coup that ensued, any reader of Roman history could have foretold the results. Tyranny is and will be the immediate, antithetical consequence of popular upheaval; the regular plan of liberty established in 1689 is only a distant, unintended, and unpredictable consequence of the agitations of the 1640s.

"Liberty is the perfection of civil society; but still authority must be acknowledged essential to its very existence" (Hume, *Essays* 41). For Hume, the fundamental spectrum of political opinion lies not between "Whig" and "Tory," or any other such shifting labels, but between those "who love peace and order," and those "who are passionate lovers of liberty" (64). As Hume and Johnson matured, so each became a more ardent friend of order and authority, and opponent of "license" or "licentiousness." Although "conservatism" as a political ideology was not a part of Johnson's or Hume's vocabulary, it seems a useful term by which to distinguish their social and political temperament from the political utopianism and rational perfectibilism fashionable on the Continent and in some corners of America in the last quarter of the eighteenth century.[2] It seems quite natural to attribute to Johnson and Hume the "moderate conservatism" often associated with Cicero, and with men such as Justus Lipsius who sought to revive Roman Stoicism in the early modern era.[3]

Labeling Johnson and Hume "conservatives" is, in fact, a commonplace of their respective scholarly commentaries, with Johnsonians sometimes suspecting that Hume's conservatism was kindred to Johnson's, and Humeans occasionally suspecting that Johnson's might be similar to Hume's. Donald Greene suggested several decades ago, "On the whole, it seems to me, Johnson is . . . a type of what may be called the rational or skeptical conservative, of whom Hobbes, Hume, and Gibbon may be cited as other examples" (*Politics* 253). Unfortunately, Greene does not elaborate on the relation of Johnson's politics to Hume's. Donald Livingston does so, but without expertise in Johnson studies: while arguing that "Hume should be thought of as the first conservative philosopher," he recognizes Johnson's apparent claim to share the title, but dismisses it with the assertion that Johnson's conservatism is of that bastard variety—

Adam-wits, too fortunately free, / Began to dream they wanted libertie" (lines 51–52). William Hazlitt employs the phrase to advantage in his summary of the principles of the French Revolution: "The world was to be turned topsy-turvy; and poetry, by the good will of our Adamwits, was to share its fate and begin *de novo*" (216).

[2] Paine, Condorcet, Mirabeau, and Robespierre prominently modeled the fashion. For Johnson's opposition to utopian perfectibilism, see Richard Schwartz, chap. 6, "The Utopian Fallacy" (146–64); for Hume's opposition to Continental utopianism, see his correspondence with Turgot, *HL* 2:179–81.

[3] On moderate conservatism as a political ramification of Stoicism, see Mark Morford on Lipsius and his circle, esp. xii, 205–10.

shared by Joseph de Maistre, Coleridge, T. S. Eliot, Jacques Maritain, and others—that appeals "to a sacred ordering of things" (*Hume's Philosophy of Common Life* 310, 329). Taking a more ironic view on appeals to sacred orderings, Leo Damrosch sees both Johnson *and* Hume—as well as "every 'major' writer . . . between the 1680s and 1780s"—as invoking such order, "the 'natural' rightness of the current organization of things," but also recognizing the fictional status of that order (*Fictions of Reality* 12–13, 52–57). Jerry Muller begins his chronological anthology of conservative political thought with the writings of Hume, but while he finds room for de Maistre he neglects Johnson altogether.[4]

I trust that the reader will by now have seen in both Hume and Johnson the political outlook that, according to Livingston, lies at the heart of a valuable, philosophical conservatism: opposition to "the violent intrusion of . . . metaphysics into politics" (308), be those metaphysics theological, as with the seventeenth-century government of the saints, or rationalistic, as with a priori doctrines of natural liberty and the rights of man. Livingston considers the evils of the latter to be a logical outcome of Cartesian method: the seed that would in time bring Robespierre, Stalin and Pol Pot was planted when

> Descartes laid it down as a principle of method for thinking rationally about the world that all former opinions are to be treated as false unless they can be made to "conform to the uniformity of a rational scheme." . . . Descartes applied his revolutionary conception of reason to metaphysics, physics, and mathematics, but he was not unaware of its possible application to politics. The Cartesian conception of reason would appear to entail that the only way "to reform a state" is "by altering everything, and by overturning it throughout, in order to set it right again." (275–78)

For Livingston, Hume stands alone as the original, systematic anti-Cartesian; yet on the other side of an unfortunate disciplinary divide, Donald Greene saw that Johnson must share that mantle: "the essential feature" of Johnson's conservatism, he writes, "is distrust of grandiose a priori theory and dogma as the basis for political action" (*PW* xxix).

However bad Whig contractarians and Wilkite Bill-of-Rightsmen may have appeared to Johnson and Hume, both would agree that the worst blows the fabric of European society had yet suffered came from political

---

[4] If Muller thinks of Johnson at all, it is probably not as a conservative but, mistakenly, as an "orthodox" ideologue: "While the orthodox defense of institutions depends on belief in their correspondence to some ultimate truth, the conservative tends more skeptically to avoid justifying institutions on the basis of their ultimate foundations . . . What makes social and political arguments *conservative* as opposed to *orthodox* is that the critique of liberal or progressive arguments takes place on the enlightened grounds of the search for human happiness, based on the use of reason" (4–5).

theology. Each associated schemes of radical innovation chiefly with the seventeenth-century English saints whom they deplored. Hume's indignation at the rebellion of the enthusiasts is, as we have seen, inscribed throughout the Stuart volumes of his *History*. Johnson's "Life" of the royalist poet Samuel Butler offers a thumbnail indictment of the Puritan revolution in keeping with Hume's:

> It is scarcely possible in the regularity and composure of the present time, to imagine the tumult of absurdity, and clamour of contradiction, which perplexed doctrine, disordered practice, and disturbed both public and private quiet, in that age when subordination was broken, and awe was hissed away; when any unsettled innovator, who could hatch a half-formed notion, produced it to the public; when every man might become a preacher, and almost every preacher could collect a congregation.
>
> The wisdom of the nation is very reasonably supposed to reside in the parliament. What can be concluded of the lower classes of the people, when in one of the parliaments summoned by Cromwell it was seriously proposed, that all the records in the Tower should be burnt, that all memory of things past should be effaced, and that the whole system of life should commence anew? (*Lives* 1:214–15)

Yet Johnson's appeal to the peace of the British Augustans—"the regularity and composure of the present time"—appears brittle with hindsight. His description of the Puritan revolution anticipates the picture that only a decade later Burke would paint, in more glaring colors, of the French Revolution. Burke energetically responds to the French Revolution's English sympathizers: "[I]t is vain to talk to them of the practice of their form of a constitution, whose merits are confirmed by the solid test of long experience, and an increasing public strength and national prosperity. They despise experience as the wisdom of unlettered men; and as for the rest, they have wrought under-ground a mine that will blow up at one grand explosion all examples of antiquity, all precedents, charters, and acts of parliament" (*Reflections* 148).

The conservatism of Burke's *Reflections on the Revolution in France* does not, however, simply extend the political thought of Johnson and Hume. Threatened by French theory, Burke responds in part by praising the happy consequences of British anti-intellectualism. Johnson and Hume, by contrast, supported a more reflective, indeed philosophic political stance than did Burke in the 1790s; for the most part, neither would have sympathized with Burke's positive use of terms such as *prejudice* or even *custom*.[5] A "prejudice," according to Johnson's *Dictionary,* is first, a "judgment formed beforehand without examination"; but it is, second, "commonly

---

[5] Burke's famous defense of "prejudice" occurs on pp. 183–89, 194–95.

a bad thing." Hume defines it simply as "an unphilosophical species of probability . . . deriv'd from *general rules,* which we rashly form to ourselves" (*T* 146). Johnson and Hume have each been represented as proto-Burkean defenders of consecrated prejudice and habit;[6] such depictions, however, do not stand up under scrutiny.

"Prejudice" is always a pejorative in Johnson's moral essays; so too, to a surprising degree, are "custom" and "habit." The literary judgments of most critics are "corrupted by prejudices" (*Rambler* 3:14; cf. 3:18, *Idler* 2: 282, *Adventurer* 2:371); "We are blinded in examining our own labours by innumerable prejudices" (*Rambler* 3:120). Historical accounts or political reports are typically distorted by the "inveterate prejudice and prevailing passions" of the reporter (*Idler* 2:62). Great caution must be taken to se-cure young people "from unjust prejudices" (*Rambler* 3:21) The material advancement of mankind is based upon a continual overcoming of "preju-dice and censure," as "whatever has been effected for convenience or ele-gance, while it was yet unknown, was believed impossible" (4:325). Simi-larly, in the moral sphere, "the enchantments of custom" comprise a trap from which many need "to extricate themselves" (3:286; cf. *Idler* 2:85–86). Johnson will allow "some regard to prejudice" when it happens, on inspection, to coincide with what is true or at least socially beneficial, for example, the prejudices of Scottish Highland tenants concerning appro-priate rents (*Journey* 94); but in his *Journey to Scotland* as elsewhere, most prejudices are in effect "malignant prejudices" (104). "Freethinking," construed *in bono,* "is to be understood as implying only freedom from un-reasonable prejudice" (*Lives* 3:322).

Hume, all in all, is hardly less suspicious of prejudice than Johnson. Somewhat misleadingly, Hume wrote early in his career an essay, "Of Moral Prejudices," which criticizes "that grave philosophic Endeavour af-ter Perfection, which, under Pretext of reforming Prejudices and Errors, strikes at all the most endearing Sentiments of the Heart, and all the most useful Byasses and Instincts, which can govern a human Creature" (*Essays* 539). The prejudices that Hume endorses in this essay, however, are *only* those partialities we tend to possess in favor of our families and friends, and our generalizing biases in favor of the institutions of family and friendship. The essay largely consists of a character sketch of "Eugenius," the happy family man, juxtaposed to that of a French "Philosophical Hero-

---

[6] Paul Fussell, in his early and very influential synthesis *The Rhetorical World of Augustan Humanism,* implicated Johnson alongside Reynolds, Gibbon, and Burke in a "quasi-religious awareness of the dignity and value of long-practised, 'consecrated' human habits" (5). H. B. Acton fit Hume into a similar intellectual heritage, again culminating in Burke. More re-cently, however, David Bromwich has effectively questioned whether Hume *or* Burke is what was known in America and Britain duing the Cold War Era as a "Burkean Conservative" (55–67, 152–55).

ine" who coolly decides to have an out-of-wedlock child with a man chosen on grounds of eugenic desirability (540–44). Hume withdrew this 1742 essay from all subsequent editions of his *Essays*—possibly because his endorsement of "prejudice" in domestic affairs might be, and indeed by Acton has been, misinterpreted as a recommendation of prejudice *tout court*. (As an ironic consequence of withdrawing the essay, in the "hearth and home" Victorian era Hume was taken to task by Leslie Stephen for *not* paying proper regard to family pieties [2:101–02].)

In general, Hume's moral writing—as distinct from his metaphysics— is strenuously opposed to "prejudice" and "custom" as guides to life. Thus, while the observation that "men . . . [are] guided more by custom than reason" might have been a purely descriptive one in Hume's metaphysics, in *The History of England* it signals disapproval: men *ought* to have been— and by implication, to be—guided more by reason than unreflective habit. Hume refers here, specifically, to the medieval "custom" of choosing a foreign prince to adjudicate in a state's internal dissensions, a "perilous . . . expedient" (2:86–87); but in general, his *History* abounds with examples of custom's lamentable precedence over reason.[7] In Hume's epistemology, "custom," designating a way of knowing that we share with animals, serves as a humbling corrective to the pretensions of Cartesian rationalism. In Hume's historiography, however, "custom" represents a force that all too often impedes the introduction of sound philosophy, or simple reflection, into daily life.[8]

While "custom" thus has a double-edge in his writings, Hume is remarkably consistent in his pejorative use of "prejudice" and its more ardent variant, "bigotry" (defined by Johnson's *Dictionary* as "blind zeal; prejudice"). Ethnic—and, by extension, racial—prejudice is based on erroneous, albeit all-too-human, reasoning (*T* 146–48); Hume never strayed from this basic position, although he could not always avoid slipping into a rash generalization of his own.[9] Ethnic prejudices that Hume seeks to

[7] For example—of "the practice of challenges and duels" which became common in the sixteenth century, Hume writes, "[N]otwithstanding the severity of law and the authority of reason, such is the prevailing force of custom" that it is "far from being as yet entirely exploded" (*History* 3:169). While "custom and precedent" extricated Henry VIII from his unwanted marriage to Catherine of Aragon on the grounds that she was his brother's widow, "the principles of sound philosophy" ought to have declared their marriage legal and binding (3:191–92). Of Parliament's unreasonable parsimony towards Charles I in 1625, refusing to vote him the subsidies necessary for the conduct of a war that was "the result of their own importunate applications and intreaties," Hume laments, "Habits, more than reason, we find, in every thing, to be the governing principle of mankind" (5:157–59).

[8] I thus find Donald Livingston to be a somewhat prejudiced reader of Hume when he insists on Hume's parallel commitments, in his philosophical and historical work, to "the authority of the prejudices and customs that constitute the order of common life" (*Hume's Philosophy of Common Life* 6).

[9] Intellectuals of our own day who seek to give nineteenth- and twentieth-century American racism an illustrious Enlightenment lineage sometimes cite the essay "Of National Char-

dispel include those against the Islamic East, which he pointedly presents as far more civilized than Europe in the days of Richard the Lion Hearted (*History* 1:393), and those against Jews (1:483, 2:68–69, 77). Above all, however, Hume assails those violent prejudices harbored by religious and political factions against their perceived opponents—these are for Hume the greatest evil that history reveals.[10]

As a social and political thinker, Hume advocates a host of reasoned reforms in the Britain of his own day—in economic policy, religious attitudes, social codes (which still included "the point of honour" and the duel), and perhaps constitutional arrangement.[11] The reforms called for by Johnson sometimes coincide with those advanced by Hume: they share, for example, a critique of empire and its corollaries, war, debt, and slavery. Yet Johnson's proposed reforms are, in their general tenor, more "Tory" or paternalistic than Hume's, geared more toward social welfare than the wealth of nations. Hume could, of course, muster little sympathy for the reforms that Johnson sought in church government, such as the restoration of the Convocation to its pre-1717 powers. The modern temperament is apt to be little ruffled by the terms of this particular debate. But inasmuch as Johnson's traditional paternalism has been recast in the social

---

acters," in which Hume speculates in a footnote: "I am apt to suspect the negroes to be naturally inferior to the whites" (for examples of bringing this passage to the bar, see Winthrop Jordan, 252–54, and Henry Louis Gates, 17–19; Emmanuel Eze conveniently reproduces Hume's footnote alongside elaborations by Kant and Jefferson). Hume is surely injudicious here—he speaks without any real knowledge of sub-Saharan African culture, and without considering that among enslaved or manumitted blacks in European territories the institution of chattel slavery itself may explain perceived inequalities between the "races"; but with Annette Baier (*Moral Prejudices* 291–93) and Robert Palter I would offer in Hume's defense the sceptical tentativeness of both his assertion and supporting evidence. Hume's tone bears no relation to that of nationalist racism in the nineteenth century, with its glorification of the Saxon "race" and its civilizing mission; on the origins of this later discourse, see Nicholas Hudson, "From 'Nation' to 'Race'." I would also stress that Hume's sentiment in no way entailed condonement of slavery, an institution he denounces in "Of the Populousness of Ancient Nations," *Essays* 383–84.

[10] On religious prejudices, see 2:330; 3:407 (Queen Mary I), 437; 4:53 (Philip II of Spain); 5:31 (the Gunpowder Plot), 129, 164, 481, 526–27 (the reigns of James I and Charles I); 6:80 (Cromwell), 451 (James II). On the related prejudices of political party, see 5:248; 6:232, 356–57, 427, 532. Hume reserves the term *prejudice* for unreasonable and harmful beliefs; Joel Weinsheimer is thus misleading when he generalizes from a close reading of the essay "Of the Standard of Taste" that "Hume equates [all] historical particularity with prejudice, which is to say that prejudices are no more or less than manifestations of historicity" (*Eighteenth-Century Hermeneutics* 129). Weinsheimer is less interested here in getting Hume right than in winnowing his metaphysics for imperfect traces of the "antifoundationalism" of Gadamerian hermeneutics.

[11] See John B. Stewart, chap. 6, "Changing the British Mind," 224–317. Stewart's view of Hume as reformist differs in emphasis, but not in substance, from Donald Livingston's view of Hume as a principled conservative; Stewart elaborates on that which Livingston fully admits: "Reforms of all sort are possible. As Hume observes, the sacred character of common life is based on social utility and is not absolute and systematic as in philosophy and religion" (*Hume's Philosophy of Common Life* 334).

welfare policies of the twentieth century, present-day "liberals" are more likely to sympathize with Johnson's sentiments for reforms in penal law and educational policy than with Hume's call for an end to international trade restrictions.[12] The humbler areas of social life appear largely to have escaped Hume's notice. It is doubtful that he would have agreed with Johnson that "a decent provision for the poor, is the true test of civilization" (*Life of Johnson* 2:130).

Yet for all their differences, Hume and Johnson share a central commitment to a larger *philosophical* program of reform. By making the passions reflective, they would make men, individually and nationally, as happy as possible. Of course, the men and women imagined in their writings are, in accord with their own origins, the "middling sort" of people; Johnson, scorner of patrons and proud to the great, would hardly disagree with Hume's verdict that it is the "middle station" that is chiefly "susceptible of Philosophy," the rich being too immersed in pleasure and the poor too busy in fending off pain (*Essays* 546). Middling life is for them (and perhaps for us) common life. The ideal to which both writers appeal is common life pruned of its prejudices and errors; both attempt, in Johnson's phrase, "the regulation of common life," in the tradition of the sages of antiquity (*Rambler* 3:57). Neither seeks wholly to strip life, domestic or public, of what Burke calls its "pleasing illusions" (171), but their occasional regard for certain prejudices is typically accompanied by a careful and explicit calculation of social utility.[13] In this sense both Johnson and Hume's conservatism, should we call it that, is distinctly rational, enlightened, reformist. Neither man would have much sympathy for the unreflective forces of conservation celebrated in Burke's depiction of the vast majority of British subjects as "thousands of great cattle, reposed beneath the shadow of the British oak, [who] chew the cud and are silent" (181).

II. Heroic Conservatism

To some degree, sceptical conservatism renders suspect both the need for heroic action, of the type usually employed to effect some bold change or "revolution" of the political wheel, and indeed the very heroism of any given individual, once his or her true motives are properly examined.

---

[12] Johnson argues against the death penalty for theft in *Rambler* no. 114; he denounces debtor's prisons in *Idler* no. 22 and no. 38. His most vehement plea for economic and educational opportunities for the poor comes in his review of Soame Jenyns, *Major Works* 526–29.

[13] As Hume writes of Charles I's execution, "That illusion, if it be an illusion, which teaches us to pay a sacred regard to the persons of princes, is so salutary, that to dissipate it by the formal trial and punishment of a sovereign, will have more pernicious effects upon the people, than the example of justice can be supposed to have a beneficial influence upon princes, by checking their career of tyranny" (*History* 5:545).

Hume's historiography analyzes the passions that unite *us;* it does not, for the most part, pay homage to the heroic wills of great men, but rather takes notice of the passions that work through kings and commoners alike. In this regard, Hume's historiography is in keeping with Johnson's "leveling" dicta on the illusion of inequality: "[I]f it be true which was said by a French prince, 'that no man was a hero to the servants of his chamber,' it is equally true that every man is yet less a hero to himself" (*Idler* no. 84, 2:262–63; cf. no. 51). "A little more than nothing is as much as can be expected from a being who with respect to the multitudes about him is himself little more than nothing" (no. 88, 2:274–75). It is perhaps not surprising that Johnson harped most on this theme in his essays written during the pivotal days of the Seven Years' War, when reports of martial heroism were steadily awaited.

Hume does, however, recognize one kind of hero in his *History of England:* the man or woman who risks life for the defense of an old order whose sanctity is etched upon the heart and confirmed by the understanding. Hume's greatest respect is reserved for individuals such as Thomas More, the marquess of Montrose, and Charles I, who stake their honor and their lives on protecting institutions that they believe in—and that Hume at least half believes in—against the prospect of violent, radical change. What these individuals possess is *magnanimity,* one of the four cardinal virtues of Cicero's *De Officiis.*[14]

Magnanimity is, according to Hume, "greatness of mind or dignity of character . . . elevation of sentiment, disdain of slavery, and . . . that noble pride and spirit, which arises from conscious virtue" (*ECPM* 252). Hume is reluctant wholly to espouse the magnanimity of the ancients, as it is in Homer and "among all uncultivated nations" too closely tied to an aggressive, "martial temper"; yet even in its most destructive aspects, Hume contends, magnanimity "engages the affections" (*ECPM* 254–55). Similarly, Johnson, certainly no friend of invasive or imperial campaigns, cannot help but admire the "plebeian magnanimity" of the English common soldier in the Seven Years' War, the noble emulation that fires him to seek "the fame of courage" (*PW* 281–84). And it is with some ambivalence that, in his meditation on the passing of the Highlanders' accustomed way of life, he ponders the waning of their fierce military courage (*Journey* 91–92).

Still, Johnson found it difficult to single out military heroes. I will return to Johnson at the end of the next section; I would like now to focus on Hume. When he came to write his *History of England,* he found only one true magnanimous man who was also a great military hero—James Gra-

---

[14] The other cardinal virtues are wisdom, justice, and decorum. Cicero's ideal of *magnanimitas* was an adaptation of the Greek *megalopsychia;* see Aristotle, *Nicomachean Ethics* 4.3 (1123a–1125a).

ham, the first marquess of Montrose (1612–1650), "one of those heroes, of whom there are no longer any remains in the world, and who are only to be met with in Plutarch" (6:20). Montrose, the leading Royalist commander in Scotland after 1644, met with imprisonment and execution in Edinburgh the year after Charles I was beheaded. Of his character, Hume concludes,

> Thus perished, in the thirty-eighth year of his age, the gallant marquess of Montrose; the man whose military genius, both by valour and conduct, had shone forth beyond any, which, during these civil disorders, had appeared in the three kingdoms. The finer arts too, he had, in his youth, successfully cultivated; and whatever was sublime, elegant, or noble touched his great soul. Nor was he insensible to the pleasures either of society or of love. Something, however, of the *vast* and *unbounded* characterized his actions and deportment; and it was merely by an heroic effort of duty, that he brought his mind, impatient of superiority, and even of equality, to pay such unlimited submission to the will of his sovereign. (6:24–25)

The distance is immense between Hume's portrait of Montrose and the ideal of the "great man" as it evolved in the nineteenth century from Byron to Carlyle to Nietzsche. For the Romantics, the great man impresses his own creative, controlling will on his community, his nation, his world. Hume, on the contrary, recalls the Roman Stoics in conjuring a hero who submits his considerable passions and energies to the preservation of inherited institutions. As Cato submits his will, and finally lays down his life, for the Republic, so Montrose gives all for the Stuart cause. Montrose indeed embodies Hume's "Stoic": for all his independence of mind, he never loses sight of his abiding loyalties, and the social affections on which they are grounded; in the end, he merits the immortal fame for which the Stoic thirsts.

Montrose may prove Hume's one truly Plutarchan hero, but his *History* as a whole does not lack magnanimous *acts*. And although magnanimity is gendered as masculine, Hume never confuses gender and sex, as he presents a string of strong heroines possessed of "every manly virtue" (2:235). Hume here speaks of two opposed "heroic dames," Jane, countess of Montfort, and Jeann de Penthievre, heir of Bretagne and wife of Charles of Blois, near the outset of the Hundred Years' War (1337–1453). Hume's account of that war indeed abounds in heroines and their magnanimous deeds.[15] Philippa, queen of Edward III, proves more admirable than her

---

[15] And in doing so, amply disproves Leo Braudy's claim that as Hume worked his way back from the seventeenth century into earlier English history, he gradually lost his belief in the crucial importance of "great figures engaged in military and political events . . . the eruptions and idiosyncrasies of personality" (*Narrative Form in History and Fiction* 39, cf. 68).

husband both in her defense of England against the "barbarous ravagers" descending from Scotland, and in her clemency toward the "six heroic burgesses" who offered their lives for Calais (2:235–38). "This age was the reign of chivalry and gallantry," Hume declares, "And if anything could justify the obsequious devotion then professed to the fair sex, it must be the appearance of such extraordinary women as shone forth during that period" (236). The close of the Hundred Years' War does not bring an end to female magnanimity,[16] but it does bring its most shining moment in the conduct of Joan of Arc at her trial. Facing the unjust charges of an ecclesiastical court and "treated . . . with every mark of contumely," Joan "never betrayed any weakness or womanish submission"; "This admirable heroine, to whom the more generous superstition of the ancients would have erected altars, was, on pretence of heresy and magic, delivered over alive to the flames" (2:408–10).

III. Magnanimous Dying

Magnanimity ever culminates in the art of dying well. Hume includes "as a branch of magnanimity" the "undisturbed philosophical tranquillity, superior to pain, sorrow, anxiety, and each assault of adverse fortune" displayed by Socrates and Epictetus—two men the Stoics adduced as "sages" (*ECPM* 256). Socrates taught all philosophers how to die, and his example was reinforced for the eighteenth century through the title hero of Addison's widely acclaimed play, *Cato* (1713). By the opening scene of Act 5, Cato, the last great light of the Republican cause after its defeats at Pharsalus and Thapsus, has just witnessed the wreck of his own final plan to oppose Caesar's advancing troops from his north African stronghold in Utica. The stage direction for the scene reads: "CATO solus, sitting in a thoughtful posture: in his hand Plato's book on the immortality of the soul [*Phaedo*]. A sword drawn on the table by him." The lesson Cato draws from Socrates is a Stoic one:

> If there's a pow'r above us,
> (And that there is all Nature cries aloud
> Through all her works) he must delight in virtue:
> And that which he delights in must be happy.
> (5.1.15–18)

[16] Margaret of Anjou, wed to Henry VI, proves "a masculine, courageous spirit" (2:419). Queen Elizabeth's "ambition and masculine character was . . . well known" (4:81) and renders her still more admirable if less loveable than her cousin Mary, who "seemed to partake only so much of the male virtues as to render her estimable, without relinquishing those soft graces, which compose the proper ornament of her sex" (4:251). During the civil wars, the countess of Derby "displayed a manly courage" in her defense of the Isle of Man from the parliamentary armies (6:42).

Cato knows, however, to count no man happy until he is dead, a saw that goes back to Solon's speech to the Lydian King Croesus in Herodotus 1.32 (cf. Aristotle's elaboration in *Nicomachean Ethics* 1100a–b). Dryden employed it in his imitation of Juvenal's Tenth Satire:

> I hasten to our own; nor will relate
> Great Mithridates, and rich Croesus' fate;
> Whom Solon wisely counsell'd to attend
> The name of happy, till he know his end.
>   (used by Johnson to illustrate "attend,"
>   definition 12, *Dictionary*) [17]

Solon's wariness of calling any living person happy proceeds from an assumption succinctly expressed by Cicero: "[W]e usually speak of a life as a happy one not in reference to a part of it, but to the whole of a lifetime; indeed, 'a life' means a finished and complete life" (*De Finibus* 2.88). And while the Stoic sage may be assured of maintaining his happiness "uninterrupted to the pyre" (3.76), the rest of us mortals need to prepare for our final scenes with rather more circumspection.

An appropriate death is requisite to the ancients' whole-life frame of reference. Cato calmly prepares to take his own life, a fate much preferable to being taken "[a] slave, a captive, into Caesar's hands" (5.2.9). Socrates arguably committed suicide by drinking hemlock,[18] and Stoic philosophy—especially that which, as one character in *Cato* phrases it, "the *Romans* call . . . stoicism" (1.4.84, emphasis mine)—theorized the "decorum" of suicide, the situations in which it became an "appropriate action" or *officium*. Thus Cato, while preparing for his own suicide, assures his son, "thou may'st rely upon my conduct. / Thy father will not act what misbecomes him" (5.2.30–31). Indeed, Addison's hero vindicates taking his own life in terms borrowed from Cicero's apology for Cato: "[S]ince nature had assigned to Cato an extraordinary seriousness, which he himself had consolidated by his unfailing constancy . . . he had to die rather than look upon the face of a tyrant" (*De Officiis* 1.112). With the arrival of Caesar's troops imminent, Cato recognizes that his life is complete in its biographical, if not its biological arc. His story has come to its appropriate, "happy" ending. And the happiness of its ending lies precisely in the fact that it conforms to its beginning, that it is of a piece.

---

[17] Johnson's own version of these lines in *The Vanity of Human Wishes* is, I think, less happy: "From *Lydia's* Monarch should the Search descend, / By *Solon* caution'd to regard his End, / In Life's last Scene what Prodigies surprise, / Fears of the Brave, and Follies of the Wise?" (lines 313–16). Johnson is much more cogent in *Rambler* no. 21, where the advice "to defer to the end of life . . . [one's] estimate of happiness" is illustrated by a quotation from Ovid's *Metamorphoses* [3.135–37], rendered in English by Addison: "But no frail man, however great or high, / Can be concluded blest before he die."

[18] That Socrates' death constitutes a suicide is admirably argued by R. G. Frey.

This biographical principle is itself a conservative one, in that it prizes constancy over change, preservation over conversion. As a model for self-fashioning in eighteenth-century letters, Cato's life is opposed to that of St. Paul or Augustine, men who undergo radical renovation or rebirth. The Enlightenment ideal is typically the path of greatest *constantia.* Rousseau, as a sign and surety of breaking with his *philosophe* friends, announces his personal conversion on the road to Vincennes: "I beheld another universe and became another man" (book 8, *Confessions*). By contrast, Boswell begins his monumental biography of Johnson with every assurance that in the child lies the man: he was "eminent . . . from his cradle to his grave"; when he "was not quite three years old" he was already "the infant Hercules of toryism," applauding the principles of the High Church preacher Henry Sacheverell (1:38–39). With similar intent, Joshua Reynolds painted *The Infant Johnson* (1781–82), a child that gazes downward as though at a desk, with forehead and features no less meditative and somber than those of Johnson's maturity.[19] Johnson's death mask, preserved in England's National Portrait Gallery, is but the final installment of a story without significant interruption.

In the philosopher's life, death is denouement. And the philosopher's ability to see a happy ending in circumstances that less Stoic souls might see as tragedy or disaster is precisely what animates the dying heroes of Hume's *History,* from Joan of Arc onward. The scene of magnanimous dying is Hume's favorite set piece.[20] I will focus on two such scenes: let us first go to the block with Sir Thomas More. The "noble Instance" of More's dying was earlier adduced by Addison in *The Spectator* no. 349, his own essay on counting no man happy until his death. "This great and learned man was famous for enlivening his ordinary Discourses with Wit and Pleasantry, and, as *Erasmus* tells him in an Epistle Dedicatory [to *The Praise of Folly*], acted in all parts of Life like a second *Democritus. . . .* His Death was of a piece with his Life" (3:300). For Hume, More proved not only a second Democritus ("the laughing philosopher"), but the incarnation of "The Stoic" he had earlier drawn: "The austerity of this man's virtue, and the sanctity of his manners, had nowise encroached on the gentleness of his temper, or even diminished that frolic and gaiety, to which he was naturally inclined" (*History* 3:197). His life and dying prove seamless: "Not only his constancy, but even his chearfulness, nay, his usual facetiousness, never forsook him; and he made a sacrifice of his life to his integrity with the same indifference that he maintained in any ordinary occurrence. When he was mounting the scaffold, he said to one, 'Friend, help me up,

---

[19] The evidence for attributing this portrait to Reynolds is accepted by Brownell, 89–90.
[20] Cf. the deaths of Lady Jane Grey, 3:420–21; Archbishop Cranmer, 3:448–50; Sir Walter Raleigh, 5:74; Montrose, 6:22–25; Cornelius de Wit of Amsterdam, 6:269.

and when I come down again, let me shift for myself.'" (3:222).[21] Given Hume's disapproval of the cause for which More died—his own ideal, rather like Henry VIII's, was of a church yoked to state control—he feels compelled to cap the lengthy account of More's gallows humor that follows with the caveat: "Nothing was wanting to the glory of this end, except a better cause, more free from weakness and superstition." There follows, however, one of Hume's pivotal "Buts": "But as the man followed his principles and sense of duty . . . his constancy and integrity are not the less objects of our admiration."

More dies as a true philosopher. The death of Charles I is far more dramatic. Charles dies as the icon of the true king—indeed, as the Christ.[22] "The great source whence the king derived consolation amidst all his calamities, was undoubtedly religion; a principle, which, in him, seems to have contained nothing fierce or gloomy, nothing which enraged him against his adversaries, or terrified him with the dismal prospect of futurity" (5:518). With a reverence unique to Hume's writings, he renders Charles's death in the terms of an *imitatio Christi:*

> It is confessed, that the king's behaviour, during this last scene of his life, does honour to his memory; and that, in all appearances before his judges, he never forgot his part, either as a prince or as a man. Firm and intrepid, he maintained, in each reply, the utmost perspicuity and justness both of thought and expression: Mild and equable, he rose into no passion at that unusual authority, which was assumed over him. His soul, without effort or affection, seemed only to remain in the situation familiar to it. . . . Some of . . . [the soldiers] were permitted to go the utmost length of brutal insolence, and to spit in his face, as he was conducted along the passage to the court. To excite a sentiment of piety was the only effect, which this inhuman insult was able to produce upon him. (5:537)

The "sentiment of piety" Charles expresses is presumably a reference to Luke's rendering of Christ's words upon the cross: "Father, forgive them; for they know not what they do." This, at least, was the moral lesson that William Juxon, bishop of London, drew from Charles's own last words:

> It being remarked, that the king, the moment before he stretched out his neck to the executioner, had said to Juxon, with a very earnest accent, the

---

[21] Cf. Hume's account of "the integrity and virtuous intentions" of Lord Russel, and his expressions of "not only composure, but good humour" before being executed for his alleged part in the Rye House plot (1683), 6:434–35. Hume's respect for the constant man who jests with his last breath derives, in all probability, from Cicero, *Tusculans* 1:95–97, 100–102.

[22] The analogy is suggested by the frontispiece to *Eikon Basilike* (1649), in which Charles holds a crown of thorns and gazes upward to a crown of glory in heaven. Clarendon elaborates: Charles's execution is "the most execrable murder that was ever committed since that of our blessed Saviour" (book 11 sec. 238).

single word, REMEMBER; great mysteries were supposed to be concealed under that expression; and the generals vehemently insisted with the prelate, that he should inform them of the king's meaning. Juxon told them, that the king, having frequently charged him to inculcate on his son the forgiveness of his murderers, had taken this opportunity, in the last moment of his life, when his commands, he supposed, would be regarded as sacred and inviolable, to re-iterate that desire; and that his mild spirit thus terminated its present course, by an act of benevolence towards his greatest enemies. (5:542)

Charles's decorum is Christlike; it may also be described, in the Aristotelian-Ciceronian tradition, as supremely magnanimous.

A chief lesson of Renaissance Christian humanism had been to show the compatibility of classical ethics and Christian doctrine; their convergence is illustrated, according to Merritt Hughes, by Milton's depiction, in *Paradise Regained,* of Christ as Aristotle's great-souled man (*Complete Poems* 476–77). Johnson evidently saw Milton's Christ in this syncretic manner, as he culls from Milton's poem (2.481–83) his first *Dictionary* definition of "magnanimous": "to give a Kingdom hath been thought / Greater and nobler done, and to lay down / Far more magnanimous than to assume." To refuse an earthly crown had made the fame of many before and after Christ—Julius Caesar, Charles Martel, even Oliver Cromwell are among those who have showed such magnanimity. And yet, in the context of a dictionary in which Charles's *Eikon Basilike,* "The Portraiture of His Sacred Majesty in His Solitudes and Sufferings," is quoted almost 350 times, it is difficult not to associate the laying down of kingdoms with the fate of Charles I.[23] Charles proves far more magnanimous than those who took his kingdom from him.

But if we may infer that Johnson's illustration of "magnanimous" is meant to conjure Charles I, we need also acknowledge that it is perhaps the last time Johnson was willing to attribute a magnanimous death to anyone. Earlier in his career, Johnson had eagerly sifted history for magnanimous figures. His biographies written for *The Gentleman's Magazine* between 1738 and 1742 present heroes, men both of action and of humane and scientific learning, who live and die magnanimously—among them, Sir Francis Drake, a "heroick spirit" who "never suffered himself to be diverted from his designs by any difficulties" (*Works* 10:79); Admiral Blake, a man of "insuperable courage, and a steadiness of resolution not to be shaken" (10:43); the theologian, church historian, and Venetian patriot Paolo Sarpi; Dr. Herman Boerhaave, physician and professor at the Uni-

---

[23] A computation derived from Anne McDermott's CD-ROM version of Johnson's *Dictionary.* David Hume's judgment of "the *Icon Basilike*" is extremely favorable: "the best prose composition, which, at the time of its publication, was to be found in the English language" (5:548).

versity of Leyden. Isobel Grundy aptly remarks of these early biographical subjects:

> They experience death as a victory conferred almost without threat of defeat. Not content with enlarging the bounds of the humanly possible in their life-times, they assert the status of romance heroes by triumphing even in death. Johnson, taking leave of Drake while some years of his life remain, refuses to believe the story which had made him die of discouragement. His Sarpi dies with exemplary piety, more affectingly still than in Johnson's source; Boer-haave as he approaches death rises progressively above his 'exquisite tor-tures.' (*Samuel Johnson and the Scale of Greatness* 193)

All die, Grundy concludes, with "confidence and tranquillity." "Magna-nimity is here the keynote. Hero after hero despises difficulties, pain, dan-ger, and personal reward, though they may hanker after fame" (194). Johnson's endorsement of heroism during this period is summed up in his jingoistic sketch, in the poem *London*, of Edward III as a Christian warrior hero, presiding over "the Land of Heroes and of Saints" (l. 100)—a height from which modern Englishmen have declined, but to which they could will their return.

Johnson's later biographies, by contrast, are never panegyrical. Scepti-cism toward accounts of human greatness marks the mature Johnson—perhaps by the time of "The Live of Savage," certainly by *The Vanity of Human Wishes,* and all the more by the time of his *Lives.* Indeed, in a bio-graphical chiasmus, Johnson grew *more* sceptical of the well-crafted life as Hume grew *less* so. In counterpoise to the high-minded lives and deaths of both Johnson's early biographical subjects and Hume's historical heroes, Johnson takes pains in *The Vanity of Human Wishes* to deheroicize the deaths of great men, even when doing so runs counter to the historical record.

The best example lies in his treatment of Charles XII, king of Sweden and military adventurer (1682–1718):

> His Fall was destin'd to a barren Strand,
> A petty Fortress, and a dubious Hand . . .
> (ll. 219–20)

In fact, Charles was killed either by enemy cannon or musket during his siege of Fredericshall in Norway, "a strong and important place which was regarded as the key to the kingdom," as Voltaire describes it (*Histoire* 538). Johnson, who was almost certainly familiar with Voltaire's *History of Charles XII* (1731),[24] transforms Fredericshall into "a petty Fortress." In consign-

---

[24] See Howard Weinbrot, "Johnson, Jacobitism, and Swedish Charles."

ing Charles's death to "a dubious Hand," Johnson trucks with a rumor that he knew through Voltaire to be false, or at least unlikely—Voltaire flatly calls it "a calumny." Of Andre Siquier, the officer sometimes alleged to be the assassin of his king, Voltaire records: "[H]e said to me these very words: *I could have killed the king of Sweden; but such was my respect for this hero, that if I had wanted to, I would not have dared*" (545). Johnson took such testimony with more than a grain of salt. Later, Johnson openly declared his scepticism of Voltaire's heroic portraiture. In Johnson's portrait of Frederick II of Prussia, written some seven years after *The Vanity of Human Wishes,* we find: "The acquisitions of kings are always magnified. His [Frederick's] skill in poetry and in the French language has been loudly praised by Voltaire, a judge without exception, if his honesty were equal to his knowledge" (*Works* 10:225). Johnson refers here to Voltaire's *Histoire de la Guerre de 1741* (1755–56), of which he later adds (apropos a romantic tale Voltaire tells of Maria Theresa): "It is the great failing of a strong imagination to catch greedily at wonders" (10:246).[25]

Nor was Johnson's scepticism directed only at military figures and heads of state. Johnson's later literary lives are full of deaths as bathetic as Charles XII's: for example, the dramatist Thomas Otway, formerly acclaimed, ends in poverty, choking on the first mouthful of "a piece of bread which charity had supplied" (1:247). The scholarly poet Edmund Smith (who adapted *Phaedra* to the English stage) inadvertently poisons himself; overfull from meat and strong ale, he writes his own prescription for "a purge so forcible, that the apothecary thought it his duty to delay it till he had given notice of its danger. Smith, not pleased with the contradiction of a shopman, and boastful of his own knowledge, treated the notice with rude contempt, and swallowed his own medicine, which, in July, 1710, brought him to the grave" (2:17–18).

The deathbed becomes for Johnson, in Grundy's words, a "negation of distinctions of superiority"; "death in the end imposes a community not to be evaded" (9–10).[26] Johnson's scepticism toward human greatness arises both from his critical assessment of testimony, and his moralist's love of a memento mori. That there need be nothing peculiarly Christian in the latter is evidenced by Hume's equal attachment, as a historian, to the *vanitas* exemplum. As a safeguard against the possible ill consequences of our personal successes, the moralist's warning fulfills the role anciently assigned to the slave who, attending the Roman *triumphator* in his procession through the city, ritually chanted, "Remember you are mortal."

[25] Hume concurred with Johnson in his assessment of *Histoire de la Guerre de 1741:* "We find, that in his [Voltaire's] relations he is more singular than authentic, more credulous than well informed, and that he cannot quite lose the poet in the historian" (*Life of Hume* 201).

[26] See also Grundy's reading of Johnson's biographical sketch of "the admirable Crichton" in *Adventurer* no. 81 (113–19).

Of course, the triumph itself honored the aspiration to be more than one's fellow mortals. The Romans' healthy ambivalence toward greatness animates Hume's *History* and may also be found in the pages of the mature Johnson. Johnson came to admire Shakespeare (more than Hume ever would) for having "no heroes; his scenes are occupied only by men" (*Shakespeare* 7:64). But Johnson never wholly abandoned his ideals of heroic magnanimity: thus he pauses in his "Preface" to Shakespeare to glance toward Addison's drama, and praise the "dignity and force . . . [of] the soliloquy of *Cato*" (79). Cato's famous soliloquy is one in which, with the *Phaedo* and a sword before him, he decides not to be. (Pity Hamlet's all-too-human indecision!) Johnson presumably had Christian qualms about Cato's suicide—he is reported late in life to have been exasperated by Hume's posthumous essay in support of this ancient aspect of magnanimity.[27] But he nonetheless admires Cato's motives and professions. (Addison allayed disapproval of Cato's final deed by giving him some glimmer of Christian light in his dying moments.)[28] Cato's greatness makes him less interesting as a dramatic *character* in Johnson's eyes—"Cato is a being above our solicitude; a man of whom the gods take care, and whom we leave to their care with heedless confidence"—but Johnson hangs on the

[27] T. L. Beauchamp argues that Hume's "Of Suicide" is a point-by-point refutation of Aquinas's three arguments against suicide in the *Summa Theologica* (Part 2.2, Q. 64 Art. 5): for Hume, suicide is a crime *neither* against God, the social community, nor oneself. Hume's proof that "Suicide is no transgression of our duty to God" is predicated on the assumption of a "watch-maker God" who does not intervene in the ongoing life of the cosmos He set in motion (*Essays* 581–86). The logical premise of Johnson's own *Rambler* no. 32—that as God's particular providence is inscrutable to us, "we have a right to remove one inconvenience as well as another" (3:177)—would, if rigorously followed, lead to a *theological* sanction of suicide not unlike Hume's. Johnson, however, has a less nuanced sense of our *social* obligations than Hume—"every individual receives many benefits from the labours of others, which, by labouring in his turn for others, he is obliged to repay" (*Idler* no. 19, 2:59)—and these obligations imply an argument against suicide (cf. *Rambler* no. 48, *Adventurer* no. 126). In the tricky matter of the voluntary deaths of saints, Johnson implicitly defers to Augustinian orthodoxy: when Goldsmith asks whether martyrdom is not "voluntary suicide," Johnson's response suggests his belief that it is, and is thus only permissible through "a delegation from heaven" (*Life of Johnson* 2:250; cf. *City of God* book 1, secs. 21, 26). We may suspect that much of Johnson's disapproval of suicide, however, comes neither from philosophy nor church teaching, but from the gut. Thus his reported response to the argument of "Of Suicide" is a derisive reference to Hume as "a man who endeavoured to persuade his friend who had the stone to shoot himself" (*Miscellanies* 2:10). Johnson implies what the state and medical profession believe today—that suicide is less an act of reasoning than a mechanical effect of physical pain, poor spirits, etc. Johnson's exasperated tone may be rooted in his own morbid attraction to easeful death: according to one contemporary account, Johnson in his twenties "strongly entertained thoughts of suicide" (Walter Jackson Bate, *Samuel Johnson* 116). Bate speculates that the mysterious death of Johnson's brother Nathaniel in 1737 may have been a suicide (160–62). And, as Richard Holmes suggests, a mutual fascination with suicide was likely one of the bonds between Johnson and his friend Richard Savage (148, 155).

[28] "—And yet methinks a beam of light breaks in / On my departing soul. Alas! I fear / I've been too hasty! O ye powers that search / The heart of man, and weigh his inmost thoughts, / If I have done amiss, impute it not!—/ The best may err, but you are good, and— oh! (*Dies*)" (5.4.94–99).

poetry of every word that issues from his mouth: "[T]here is scarcely a scene in the play which the reader does not wish to impress upon his memory" ("Life of Addison," *Lives* 2 : 132–33).

Magnanimity is that which, as Charles I signaled to Juxon, ought to be remembered.

IV. Hume's Deathbed

We come now to the best-known period of Hume's own life—his protracted dying. With Boswell and Adam Smith as key witnesses, Hume sought to assure his personal fame by dying, like the sages of antiquity, with neither complaint nor great expectation in an afterlife.[29] For good measure, he would die with all the pleasantry of Thomas More. The chief critic of Hume's final scene was Johnson. His scepticism of magnanimity by now finely honed, Johnson sought beneath Hume's final show of serenity the agitation of human motives.

Hume's composure at the prospect of annihilation was brought to Johnson's attention, twice, by Boswell. Intrigued by Johnson's own sometime obsessive fear of death, Boswell introduced Hume's sentiments less to console his mentor than to aggravate him—and, above all, to incite him to oratory. Boswell first broaches the topic on 26 October 1769:

> When we were alone, I introduced the subject of death, and endeavoured to maintain that the fear of it might be got over. I told him that David Hume said to me, he was no more uneasy to think he should *not be* after this life, than that he *had not been* before he began to exist.[30] JOHNSON. 'Sir, if he really thinks so, his perceptions are disturbed; he is mad; if he does not think so, he lies. He may tell you, he holds his finger in the flame of a candle, without feeling pain; would you believe him? When he dies, he at least gives up all he has.'

Johnson's own thoughts of death, Boswell concludes, "were in general full of dismal apprehensions" (*Life of Johnson* 2 : 106). Johnson feared damnation—hence his ominous phrase, "[H]e *at least* gives up all he has." Conscious of his own remarkable talents, the gospel parable of the talents haunted Johnson throughout his life; to one whom so much had been given, much would be asked. Some mid-twentieth-century critics have further speculated that Johnson may have been a closet unbeliever, less afraid of punishment than of eternal nothingness.[31]

---

[29] On the tentative, hypothetical nature of Socrates' beliefs in the *Phaedo*, see John Herman Randall, 211–19.

[30] Cf. Lucretius, *De Rerum Natura* 3 : 830–977.

[31] A few years after Johnson's own death, the Reverend William Agutter delivered a sermon that defended Johnson's orthodox *timor mortis* against the insensibility or hypocrisy of "infidels" such as Hume and Voltaire: "On the Difference between the Deaths of the Righteous and the Wicked, Illustrated in the Instance of Dr. SAMUEL JOHNSON, and DAVID HUME, Esq.; A Sermon, preached before the University of Oxford, at St. Mary's Church, on Sunday,

Six and a half years after Boswell recorded this conversation with Johnson, he visited Hume on his deathbed in Edinburgh. "On Sunday forenoon the 7 of July 1776, being too late for church [a timing of ironic significance], I went to see Mr. David Hume, who was returned from London and Bath, just a dying. I found him alone, in a reclining posture in his drawing room. He was lean, ghastly, and quite of an earthy appearance." In the place of any literature of Christian consolation, "[h]e had before him Dr. Campbell's *Philosophy of Rhetorick.*" Like Cicero, who read Euripides while awaiting Antony's assassins, Hume set out to be studious to the last.[32] Boswell attempts to make him admit to a belief in a future state, or at least to some uneasiness concerning the prospect of annihilation. To Boswell's mortification, Hume "seemed to be placid and even cheerful" throughout their long and varied conversation on the soul's mortality or immortality; on "Wilkes and the Mob" as (facetious) evidence that the soul *ought* not be immortal; and on the durability, beyond any life, of Hume's *History of England.* Boswell interjects,

> In this style of goodhumour and levity did I conduct the conversation. Perhaps it was wrong on so aweful a subject. But as nobody was present, I thought it could have no bad effect. I however felt a degree of horrour, mixed with a sort of wild, strange, hurrying recollection of My excellent Mother's pious instructions, of Dr. Johnson's noble lessons, and of my religious sentiments and affections during the course of my life.

Boswell's journal entry concludes, "He said he had no pain, but was wasting away. I left him with impressions that disturbed me for some time" (*Private Papers* 12:227–32). Addison had famously summoned a young man "of very irregular life" to his deathbed, telling him "I have sent for you that you may see how a Christian can die" ("Life of Addison," *Lives* 2:11); Hume evidently intended, in Boswell's company as in Adam Smith's,[33] to show in

---

July 23, 1786" (London, 1800). Critics of the mid twentieth century, by contrast, relished Johnson's dismay at Hume's insouciance as a sign that he doubted the Christian consolations he professed. See Mossner, *The Forgotten Hume* 189–209; Gay, 401–19; Walter Jackson Bate, *Samuel Johnson* 450–52.

[32] The self-conscious defiance of Hume's deathbed reading is more clearly seen in relation to a journal entry of one Janet Schaw, traveling with a companion from Scotland to the Caribbean; recalling a terrifying gale, Schaw writes, "We were meeting death, like philosophers not Christians: with a Lord Kaims in our hands in place of a Bible" (quoted in Elizabeth Bohls, 369).

[33] Smith's letter to William Strahan dated 9 November 1776, and published early in 1777 along with Hume's *My Own Life,* widely publicized Hume's "magnanimity and firmness" during his last months of life (*HL* 2:450–52). Smith later remarked that this one letter had caused more furor than all his other works combined (*Life of Hume* 605). The public was entertained with "the most minute circumstances respecting . . . [Hume's] exit" by the minor poet Samuel Jackson Pratt in a pamphlet, *Supplement to the Life of David Hume, Esq., containing Genuine Anecdotes and a circumstantial Account of his Death and Funeral . . .* (London, 1777). Of the funeral, Pratt writes, "notwithstanding a heavy rain . . . multitudes of all ranks gazed at the funeral procession, as if they expected the hearse to have been consumed in livid flames, or encircled with a ray of glory" (43).

what peace a philosopher can die. He would prove himself, in the words of the Hume family motto and his own bookplate, "True to the End."

On 16 September 1777, three weeks after Hume's death, Boswell recalled the visit to Johnson:

> I mentioned to Dr. Johnson, that David Hume's persisting in his infidelity, when he was dying, shocked me much. . . . I said, I had reason to believe that the thought of annihilation gave Hume no pain. JOHNSON. 'It was not so, Sir. He had a vanity in being thought easy. It is more probable that he should assume an appearance of ease, than that so very improbable a thing should be, as a man not afraid of going (as, in spite of his delusive theory, he cannot be sure but he may go,) into an unknown state, and not being uneasy at leaving all he knew.' (*Life of Johnson* 3 : 153)

Johnson's assessment of Hume's public character is acute. It modestly anticipates Terence Penelhum's more wide-reaching conclusion that Hume's seeming "temperamental immunity to philosophical anxieties," his self-presentation as "the affable and corpulent gentlemanly loiterer," is "a deliberately assumed *persona*": presumptive proof of the ability of his "neo-Hellenistic" philosophy to protect us from anxiety, and the violence that religion does to our nature ("Hume's Moral Psychology," 118–20, 143–44).

Johnson's comments raise a further question, which I will address in my next chapter. How *can* we speak of an "unknown state" without a knowing tone? If, as Johnson charges, Hume's serenity assumes a knowledge he did not have, what would have been a more truly agnostic way of confronting, or representing, that which we do not know? If Hume was indecorous, what is the proper decorum of ignorance on a topic such as the consequences of death, on which the many have settled opinions? And what, finally, are the consequences of such decorum for our understanding of happiness?

Chapter Ten

The Spirit of Ending

The ending of Johnson's *Rasselas* ultimately addresses the same philosophical questions broached by the title of David Hume's essay "Of the Immortality of the Soul": What is the soul, and will it, whatever it is, outlast us? The *querelle* that surrounds this question is a familiar one, and we might expect Johnson and Hume to espouse opposing points of view. But despite their pat differences, Johnson and Hume's *methods* of exposition—and hence, I will argue, their underlying intentions—actually converge. That is, a similarly conceived ambiguity animates the discussion of the soul in both *Rasselas* and "Of the Immortality of the Soul." Neither text declares itself wholeheartedly for or against the prospect of immortality, much as many readers would be pleased to have them do so. And this decorum of Johnson's and Hume's writing says more about both writers than any compendium of their golden sayings.

The locus of ambiguity is the same for *Rasselas* and "Of the Immortality of the Soul"—both avoid making an authoritative statement on the immortality of the soul by refusing to end with any air of authority. Hume's last paragraph and Johnson's final chapter would indeed both seem, prima facie, to deviate from or to deconstruct the preceding logic of their works: for Hume ends his attack on the immortality of the soul with a fideistic retort, while Johnson follows his defense of the soul's immortality with a conclusion that's quite adrift. I would like in this final chapter to reflect on the problems posed by Johnson's and Hume's peculiar manner of ending their works. I will bear in mind two related questions: First, is it possible to determine to what extent Johnson or Hume is seriously committed to either confirming or subverting an orthodox faith in the immortality of the soul?

And second, assuming that either author possessed even a modicum of high seriousness, how may it be reconciled with the texts' arch inconclusiveness? That is, why do both Johnson and Hume discuss our mortal end in ways that render our sense of an ending uncertain?

I. Christian Integrity versus Secular Disintegration

The middle section of *Rasselas* focuses on decidedly sublunary concerns, as the young prince Rasselas and company canvas a variety of familiar occupations and professions in search of a stable and rational happiness. What they discover, however, is that unalloyed *contentment* is not to be found in life—unless, ironically, it may be found in a life of mortification. For the one "state of life" that Imlac praises to his young wards above all others is the "silent convent" of the monks of St. Anthony (chapter 47). Imlac conceives the monastic life to be graced by the one expectation that (at least in this life) will not be disappointed: "Their devotion prepares them for another state, and reminds them of its approach while it fits them for it. . . . There is a certain task to be performed at an appropriated hour; and their toils are cheerful, because they consider them as acts of piety by which they are always advancing towards endless felicity." But while Imlac expounds on the virtues of monasticism with an assurance as yet unprecedented in Johnson's tale, Rasselas's attention still wanders: his thoughts are hardly riveted by, as Imlac puts it, "the state of future perfection, to which we all aspire, [where] there will be pleasure without danger, and security without restraint" (*Rasselas* 164–67). Rasselas remains intent merely on sight-seeing, and it is indeed his somewhat jaded curiosity that brings the party, in the next chapter, to the catacombs outside Cairo.

This, the penultimate chapter of *Rasselas,* is, as W. K. Wimsatt aptly remarks, "the only place [in the tale] where it is impossible to find a smile" ("In praise of *Rasselas*" 129–30). In it, Imlac elaborates the so-called "metaphysical argument" for the immortality of the soul—an argument that can be traced back to the *Phaedo* and to Cicero's *De Senectute.* Imlac argues that the soul must be immortal by maintaining that "whatever perishes is destroyed by the [dis]solution of its contexture, and separation of its parts" (172). The soul, having no parts, just as the ideas it forms have none, must be "indiscerptible," and thus immortal. The following quotation contains Rasselas's initial bafflement at this argument, and his eventual comprehension:

> "I know not," said Rasselas, "how to conceive any thing without extension: what is extended must have parts, and you allow, that whatever has parts may be destroyed." "Consider your own conceptions," replied Imlac, "and the

difficulty will be less. You will find substance without extension. An ideal form is no less real than material bulk: yet an ideal form has no extension. It is no less certain, when you think on a pyramid, that your mind possesses the idea of a pyramid, than that the pyramid itself is standing. What space does the idea of a pyramid occupy more than the idea of a grain of corn? or how can either idea suffer laceration? As is the effect such is the cause; as thought is, such is the power that thinks; a power impassive and indiscerptible."

"But the Being," said Nekayah, "whom I fear to name, the Being who made the soul, can destroy it."

"He, surely, can destroy it," answered Imlac, "since, however unperishable, it receives from a superior nature its power of duration. That it will not perish by any inherent cause of decay, or principle of corruption, may be shown by philosophy; but philosophy can tell no more. That it will not be annihilated by Him that made it, we must humbly learn from higher authority." (173–74)

Robert Walker, while noting Johnson's debt to earlier metaphysicians such as Clarke and Wollaston, calls Imlac's speech "perhaps the most clear and most concise version [of the metaphysical argument] that the eighteenth century produced" (60). And perhaps the most compelling: Rasselas and Nekayah, at least, are convinced. Impressed by Imlac's rational theology, as well as his clinching appeal to "higher authority," they steadfastly determine thereafter to "think only on the choice of eternity" (*Rasselas* 175).

But it is not only the characters within *Rasselas* who respond to Imlac's wisdom. His discourse on the soul has subsequently been applauded by a long series of readers who believe that it lies at the heart of the tale. This camp of readers tends to claim that the tale is a unified text, generically a conversion narrative or, in Walter Raleigh's phrase, a Christian "apologue."[1] Thus, in a neat symmetry, readers who would conceive of the soul as integral correspondingly choose to read the text as integral. Boswell made such a choice; for him, *Rasselas* is a unified "moral tale" that intends, "by shewing the unsatisfactory nature of things temporal, to direct the hopes of man to things eternal" (*Life of Johnson* 1:342). Gwin Kolb waxes still more eloquent on the tale's moral: "The wise man . . . will accept submissively the essential grimness of life, seek no more lasting felicity than is given by a quiet conscience, and live with an eye on eternity, in which he may perhaps find, through the mercy of God, the complete happiness unattainable of earth" ("The Structure of *Rasselas*" 700). More recently, in his Yale edition of *Rasselas,* Kolb effectively indicates the centrality of chapter 48 ("Imlac Discourses on the Nature of the Soul") by weighting it with thirty-one lengthy footnotes that evoke the authority of Clarke, Wollaston,

---

[1] That Walter Raleigh was the first critic to call *Rasselas* an "apologue" (in *The English Novel,* 1894) is noted by Edward Tomarken, 13–14.

Richard Bentley, Ralph Cudworth, Sir Thomas Browne, et al. By contrast, four notes are devoted to chapter 49—"The Conclusion, in Which Nothing is Concluded."

The problem with readings such as Kolb's, however, is that they counterintuitively treat the text as if it ended with the penultimate chapter. Any reading of *Rasselas* as a religious apologue abuts against the simple fact that the "choice of eternity" is not given the last word in the text. In the final chapter, quite famously, "nothing is concluded": Rasselas and Nekayah maintain desires for achieving happiness in this world, however unattainable they may recognize them to be. Nekayah would "found a college of learned women in which she would preside," and Rasselas "desired a little kingdom, in which he might administer justice in his own person . . . but he could never fix the limits of his dominion, and was always adding to the number of his subjects." Similarly, Nekayah's attendant, Pekuah, "wished only to fill [the convent of St. Anthony] with pious maidens, and to be made prioress of the order." The tale ends, rather baldly, "Of these wishes that they had formed they well knew that none could be obtained. They deliberated awhile what was to be done, and resolved, when the inundation should cease, to return to Abissinia" (175–76). However inconclusive this chapter may otherwise be, it clearly depicts the characters' distinctly sublunary schemes of happiness.

Moreover, as Paul Fussell maintains, the final wishes of the travelers are "ironic" in that "each wish betrays the secret lust for power over others which, among decent, cultivated people like these, cloaks itself in proclaimed motives of beneficent intention" (*Samuel Johnson and the Life of Writing* 241). Indeed, Rasselas continues to express the same earnest idealism, ethical naiveté, and self-magnifying ambition that he has evidenced all along: he has learned nothing from either Imlac's governmental realism (chapter 8), or from his own briefly sobering examination of "high stations" (chapters 24 and 27). Rasselas's will-to-govern steadily and, as it were, inexorably develops from chapter 4, in which he daydreams of exercising his benevolence "in the relief of distress, the detection of fraud, the defeat of oppression, and the diffusion of happiness" (18); to chapter 8, in which he marvels that his father could allow any injustice in Abyssinia, fuming, "If I were emperour, not the meanest of my subjects should be oppressed with impunity" (32). Finally, in chapter 44, "The Dangerous Prevalence of Imagination," prince Rasselas confesses that his daydreams of administering "a perfect government" have led him to thoughts of parricide: "I start, when I think with how little anguish I once supposed the death of my father and my brothers" (153).[2] Recollection of this line cer-

---

[2] Cf. *Rambler* no. 8 on the danger of imaginatively entertaining passions that could prove dangerous in the real world.

tainly compromises the seeming innocence of Rasselas's final wish for an ever-expanding kingdom—in other words, for a kingdom that increasingly resembles the Abyssinian empire ruled by his father. And among the many lessons that Rasselas has failed to learn include that of the limited power and role of government, particularly its scarce ability to channel benevolence; as Johnson wrote in his concluding lines to Oliver Goldsmith's poem, "The Traveller", "How small, of all that human hearts endure, / That part which laws or kings can cause or cure" (lines 429–30). The true ironic twist of the last chapter, however, lies in the quiet change of heart that separates Nekayah's promise "to think only on the choice of eternity" from her ensuing wish to administer the rules of an institution wherein one may meditate on eternity. For Nekayah—as for Pekuah—the idea of religious seclusion segues into a fantasy of dominating a place of seclusion. The "choice of eternity" seems fairly forgotten.

Are we therefore to read *Rasselas*'s final chapter as undercutting Imlac's metaphysical consolations? The tale's end would seem both to ironize the otherwordly sentiments of the penultimate chapter and to highlight their incongruity with the strong and vivid account of our world that fills out the bulk of *Rasselas*. Is Imlac's rationalist theology, like the similarly rarified professions of the two Zenolike Stoic philosophers whom Rasselas meets earlier in the tale (chapters 18 and 22), simply irrelevant to us mere humans? Is Imlac's otherworldliness akin to the professed apathy of the first Stoic professor in being, finally, yet another untenable pretension of Reason? "He compared reason to the sun, of which the light is constant, uniform, and lasting; and fancy [the parent of passion] to a meteor, of bright but transitory lustre, irregular in its motion and delusive in its direction. He then communicated the various precepts given from time to time for the conquest of passion, and displayed the happiness of those who had obtained the important victory" (71–72). Expectably, in a world in which reason is and ought only be the educated guide (the Imlac, if you will) of the passions, the Stoic who claims not to be motivated by them is revealed as a liar: the death of his beloved daughter leaves him mired in inconsolable sorrow. To quote Rasselas on this all-too-human philosopher—are the technical cadences of the tale's penultimate chapter only another instance of "the emptiness of rhetorical sound, and the inefficacy of polished periods and studied sentences" (76)? And if so, doesn't the reader of *Rasselas* who seeks an assuring moral simply rehearse Rasselas's own doomed search to find assurance? And if such a reader should then recount his own supposed enlightenment, wouldn't we, in assenting to that reading, blindly enact a *mis-en-abyme* of metaphysical error?

Christianizing readers of *Rasselas* tend to avoid these heady questions, or indeed any indications that the tale may finally be an ironic fable. And they certainly may do so without any bad faith. For as Boswell suggests,

Christianizing *Rasselas* is of a piece with moralizing the biblical book of Ecclesiastes—and this latter task had, by Boswell's time, a long and familiar lineage. Indeed, when Boswell writes, "This Tale, with all the charms of oriental imagery, and all the force and beauty of which the English language is capable, leads us through the most important scenes of human life, and shews us that this stage of our being is full of 'vanity and vexation of spirit'" (*Life of Johnson* 1:341–42), he demonstrates that his sense of *Rasselas* is modeled on his understanding of Ecclesiastes. As Thomas R. Preston has more recently shown, the traditional patristic interpretation of Ecclesiastes holds that "the Preacher's futile quest for perfect happiness . . . teaches man that he should despise and reject this world to contemplate the world to come." Preston's own argument, however, is that Johnson actually abided by the "reformed" reading of Ecclesiastes, elaborated by Bishop Simon Patrick, which held that "Ecclesiastes . . . is designed to show that after choosing eternity, one can and should then partake of the limited goods of this world" (274, 280). Clearly—though Preston doesn't spell out the connection—this last point might provide a way of reconciling the worldliness of chapter 49 with the transcendent attitudes struck in the catacombs.

Other Christianizing readers have attempted more explicitly to effect this reconciliation. Earl Wasserman argues that by subverting comic closure in *Rasselas*'s last chapter, "Johnson has, in effect, rescued the original Christian pattern of the Fortunate Fall from the novelistic secularized version, which he has formally repudiated. Man does not leave Paradise Hall or the Happy Valley to repossess it securely through the acquisition of Wisdom; he acquires Heaven through the wisdom that the 'choice of eternity,' not the 'choice of life,' is essential" (25). Alternatively, Robert Walker attempts to maintain the "central" truths of Imlac's discourse by arguing that the final chapter, consisting of wishes that the travelers realize can never be satisfied on earth, effectively advances the so-called "argument from desire"—that is, the popular notion that, in William Wollaston's words, "the great expectation, which men have, of continuing to live in another state, beyond the grave, has . . . been commonly admitted as one proof, that they shall live." Walker concludes that chapter 49 "continues the argument from desire that runs throughout *Rasselas* and is thus a different path but to the same end as the chapter that precedes it" (28, 63). Clearly, there are viable grounds on which to advance a Christian reading of Johnson's tale.[3] The success of any such reading, however, fi-

---

[3] The references to revealed religion in chapter 48 are less than cryptic: Imlac's clinching appeal to "higher authority" is prefaced by his earlier opposition between "heathenism" and "our opportunities of clearer knowledge." Moreover, in chapter 12 Imlac narrates having spent three years in Palestine, which he calls "that country whence *our* religion had its beginning" (emphasis mine). And note, finally, that while Imlac's proofs for immortality in

nally lies in how well it can yoke the apparently secular coda of chapter 49 to the theological context of Imlac's discourse on the integrity and imperishability of the soul.

A second camp of readers—let us call them the secularists—are considerably less attentive to Imlac's discourse. Accordingly, they have fashioned a *Rasselas* very different from Boswell's. They see it as the testament of an author who was, somewhat despite himself, a religious sceptic; who possessed, for all his professions to the contrary, the Enlightenment style.[4] Richardson's friend Hester Mulso Chapone, who would have been happy to find an apologue in *Rasselas,* was disappointed that Johnson had published "such an ill-contrived, unfinished, uninstructive tale" (quoted in Hilles, 111). Readers closer to our own day, however, have been delighted rather than irritated with the unintegrated and, in any facilely moral sense, unprofitable nature of the tale. W. K. Wimsatt, who notes the "lumpy and bumpy," "episodic" nature of the text, goes on to praise it as a "descendental exercize" with affinities to the modern literature of the absurd. However much weight we give to its "saving theological clause in the catacombs" is finally a matter of taste ("In Praise of *Rasselas*" 115, 129–30). Joseph Wood Krutch is even less sympathetic to the wisdom of Johnson's penultimate chapter. In it, Johnson "pays to orthodoxy, as he always does, the tribute of a formal profession. But these formal professions . . . constitute only the formal rather than the effective moral." The effective moral is the "tragic sense of life" that accumulates from the discrete episodes of the text. Paying no heed to the episode in the catacombs, Krutch attributes no real sense of closure to *Rasselas,* but observes that the tale "does not so much end as break off"; Johnson "did not know what more to say" (182–83). Paul Fussell, equally apt to ignore the tale's theological momentum, characterizes *Rasselas* as "an accumulation of shining particles," set in the "secular wasteland" (*Samuel Johnson and the Life of Writing* 226–27).

These readings oppose Boswell's ideal of a text that coalesces in glorification of a soul without contexture. To read *Rasselas* as an essentially episodic, open-ended work is necessarily to render Imlac's discourse on the soul a merely formal tribute to orthodoxy, a mere part that can be excerpted without loss. It is as if Johnson had prefaced Imlac's metaphysics

---

chapter 48 are not originally Christian, Imlac offers them only as an admittedly weak supplement to the distinctly Christian devotion of the monks of St. Anthony.

[4] In an argument similar at points to my own, José Angel Garcia Landa observes that *Rasselas* allows for—and has indeed propagated—opposed camps of readers, from those who "find that its moral stance is concerned solely with human existence in this world," to those who "bring to the fore the role of religion in the tale" (87–88). Building on Charles Hinnant's reading of the tale in *Samuel Johnson: An Analysis,* Landa concludes that the final ambiguity of *Rasselas* reflects the tale's ongoing dissolution of binary oppositions.

with a request to the reader to "either pass over the following chapter altogether or read the whole connectedly," for Johnson's readers seem in fact to have done one or the other. Of course, this request derives not from Johnson but from the outset of Coleridge's twelfth chapter of the *Biographia Literaria*—a chapter in which he proceeds to expound on the thorny topic of the "SUM or I AM" and its necessary relation to "the eternal I AM." As Coleridge immediately adds to his prefatory remarks, "dissevering" a part will disrupt "the organic whole": it is ambiguous if "the whole" in question is simply the chapter at hand or the entire *Biographia*—or, indeed, the self whose transcendental unity Coleridge is about to assert (135). For in the *Biographia* as in *Rasselas,* to disrupt the organic unity of the text seems to deny the unity of the soul—and vice versa.

Of course, the reader of *Rasselas* who would treat chapter 48 as an alienable portion does not need a Coleridgean bit of advice to do so. Rather, this manner of reading corresponds to the Enlightenment style of writing, which is ever keen to the possibilities of aggregative rather than unified presentation. Indeed, the *philosophes* seem to have presupposed in much of their writing that the endings of tales or essays are indeed discerptible from the narratives or arguments that precede them. A sense of false endings is variously to be found in Voltaire's poem on the Lisbon earthquake and in *Zadig;* in Hume's "Of Miracles," "Of the Immortality of the Soul," and perhaps the last words of his *Dialogues concerning Natural Religion;* and in the tag lines of some of Blake's *Songs of Innocence,* particularly "The Chimney Sweeper." Most of these endings are rendered suspect by abruptly evoking an authority absent until that point; in context, the author's appeal to "duty" or "higher authority" rings less like a resolving chord than a discordant note.

The example most pertinent to my discussion is Hume's essay "Of the Immortality of the Soul," written in 1755. In the body of the essay Hume draws on Locke and Lucretius to refute sweepingly both metaphysical and moral arguments for the soul's immortality. He quickly dismisses the type of metaphysical argument found in *Rasselas:*

> Metaphysical topics are founded on the supposition that the soul is immaterial, and that it is impossible for thought to belong to a material substance.
>
> But just metaphysics teach us, that the notion of substance is wholly confused and imperfect, and that we have no other idea of any substance than as an aggregate of particular qualities, inhering in an unknown something. Matter, therefore, and spirit are at bottom equally unknown; and we cannot determine what qualities may inhere in the one or in the other.
>
> They likewise teach us, that nothing can be decided *a priori* concerning any cause or effect; and that experience being the only source of our judgments of this nature, we cannot know from any other principle, whether matter, by

its structure or arrangement, may not be the cause of thought. Abstract reasonings cannot decide any question of fact or existence. (*Essays* 591) [5]

Thus, if all we know of matter is "an aggregate of particular qualities," and if the soul for all we know may be material, it follows that the soul may indeed be but an accumulation of particles. As a contexture it will dissolve with the dissolution of the body.

This initial conjecture becomes fairly conclusive in the course of Hume's essay, which presents the immortality of the soul not simply as uncertain, but as rationally untenable. Hume writes, "*[P]hysical* arguments from the analogy of nature are strong for the mortality of the soul; and these are really the only philosophical arguments, which ought to be admitted with regard to this question, or indeed any question of fact." These "physical arguments," largely derived from book 3 of Lucretius, center on the reciprocity of soul and body: "The weakness of the body and that of the mind in infancy are exactly proportioned; their vigor in manhood; their sympathetic disorder in sickness; their common gradual decay in old age. The step farther seems unavoidable; their common dissolution in death" (596). Annihilation thus emerges as the unavoidable and incontestable end of Hume's logic. Indeed, his penultimate paragraph dryly mocks our pretensions to rationally conceive any posthumous fate of the soul. He asks, "By what arguments or analogies can we prove any state of existence, which no one ever saw, and which no wise resembles any that ever was seen? Who will repose such trust in any pretended philosophy, as to admit upon its testimony the reality of so marvellous a scene? Some new species of logic is requisite for that purpose; and some new faculties of the mind, which may enable us to comprehend that logic" (598). A strict philosophical empiricism clearly cannot abide the soul's immortality.

But the final twist of Hume's essay is that, after his exhaustive reasonings against immortality, he calmly accepts that a belief in immortality can trump the claims of rational inquiry. He offers in his final paragraph an orthodox assurance that the soul *is* indiscerptible, tersely concluding, "Nothing could set in a fuller light the infinite obligations, which mankind have to divine revelation; since we find, that no other medium could ascertain this great and important truth" (598). Hume thus appeals to a truth beyond experience. Illumination, he concedes, descends only when the light of sense goes out.

Just about no one, of course, believed that Hume meant what he said. Indeed, readers both sympathetic and antipathetic to an alleged Enlight-

---

[5] This curt dismissal of the doctrine of the immateriality and indivisibility of a thinking substance is far less ingenious than Hume's rebuttal of this doctrine in the *Treatise* (1.4.5), where he paradoxically equates it with Spinozan "atheism."

enment program have generally concurred in not taking his fideistic professions seriously. From eighteenth-century Christian apologists such as Warburton, Hurd and Campbell through to twentieth-century Humeans such as Norman Kemp Smith and Richard Popkin, most readers agree that Hume's codas tend to be patently ironic; that is, they pay to orthodoxy the tribute of a hollow profession. Warburton and Hurd noted that Hume's writings on religion, in Ciceronian spirit, take care to avoid public censure for the infidelity they promulgate (Remark XIII, 66–68). George Campbell, in "A Dissertation on Miracles" (1762), remarked of the fideistic coda of Hume's "Of Miracles," "An author is never so sure of writing unanswerably, as when he writes altogether unintelligibly" (234). More recently, Norman Kemp Smith, in his edition of Hume's *Dialogues concerning Natural Religion* dubs the closing Christian turnabout of the sceptic Philo a "conventionally required proviso" (74). Richard Popkin, in his edition of the *Dialogues* and Hume's two posthumously published essays, "Of Suicide" and "Of the Immortality of the Soul," maintains more generally, "Hume sprinkled fideistic remarks throughout his writings. His opponents interpreted these remarks as insincere efforts to avoid criticism. My own suspicion is that they were intended to be ironic, to make the reader realize how silly religious belief was" (xv). One may, in effect, dismiss them.

If its fideistic ending is indeed irrelevant and discerptible, then "Of the Immortality of the Soul" becomes a particularly well-wrought essay, whose form illustrates its argument: the essay itself provides a neat metaphor for death, understood as what happens when parts will not coalesce. As Lucretius observes, "Death does not put an end to things by annihilating the component particles but by breaking up their conjunction" (89).[6]

II. Contested Intentions

The attraction of reading Hume ironically is apparent, especially in our own sceptical age. But are we constrained to do so? Indeed, is Hume's ironic intent as obvious as is often imputed? What happens if we take him at his word? Norman Kemp Smith recognizes that Hume gives his reader the option of doing so. The reader "has still the alternatives before him, either to follow Hume in his thorough-going scepticism, or . . . to look . . .

---

[6] Like Hume, Johnson also tended to think of texts as analogous to souls: the most excellent writing, like the soul, is sempiternal by virtue of being simple and indiscerptible, while lesser writing is heterogenous and dissoluble, a passing thing. Johnson praises Shakespeare's "personages," built on the bedrock of "genuine passion," in terms of this metaphysics: "The accidental compositions of heterogeneous modes are dissolved by the chance which combined them; but the uniform simplicity of primitive qualities neither admits increase, nor suffers decay" (*Shakespeare* 7:69–70).

for instruction only in the *via negativa*—a discipline upon which theology . . . has itself found reason to insist" (*Dialogues* 75.) My own concern is to suggest what might have motivated Hume to allow for a sincere fideistic reading.

Johann Georg Hamann, for one, took the Christian fideism of Hume's endings quite seriously; for him, coda is closure, and the soul's immortality secure. Hamann's *Socratic Memorabilia* (1759) evokes Hume's authority in claiming that "faith is not a work of reason and therefore cannot succumb to any attack by reason; because believing happens as little by means of reason as tasting and seeing" (in Ronald Smith 182). Years later, Hamann wrote to F. H. Jacobi, "I studied Hume just before I wrote my *Socratic Memoirs,* and this is the source to which I am indebted for my doctrine of faith" (quoted in Terence German 110).[7] It is doubtful whether Hamann considered Hume a willing ally in fideistic orthodoxy, but finally the question seems not to matter. The irrelevance of reason to faith is something Hume's philosophic style allowed Hamann to see. In a letter to Kant dated 1759, Hamann quotes the fideistic coda of Hume's "Of Miracles" at length, and joyfully proclaims, "[D]espite all [Hume's] errors, he is like Saul among the prophets . . . one can preach the truth in jest and without knowing or desiring to do so, even if one were the greatest doubter and like the serpent doubted what God said" (in Ronald Smith 182–83).

As with readers of *Rasselas,* Hamann's desire to see the soul as integral is accompanied by a faith in the integrity of texts. For Hamann, Hume's essay remains whole, its last paragraph an essential part of its argument. And although we may be tempted to dismiss Hamann's reading as biased, we should first ask ourselves what a truly disinterested reading of this text might possibly be. Indeed, we only take note of Hamann's bias inasmuch as it differs from our own; and inasmuch as it does, it reveals the dubious grounds of our own assumptions concerning Hume. For Hume indeed speaks the prophets' truth at the end of "Of the Immortality of the Soul" and "Of Miracles," just as Johnson's last words afford him a place among the *philosophes*' party.

Still, at vexing moments such as these we tend to look to some larger context for clarification; in practice, we usually turn first to biography. But, ironically, the biographies of Johnson and Hume tend to reproduce rather than resolve our dilemma. For Boswell's Johnson, as we all know, was a staunch Anglican apt to appeal on all occasions—and especially on that

---

[7] For a concise account of Hamann's debt to Hume, see Philip Merlan, "From Hume to Hamann." The convergence of sceptical critique and negative theology in the mid eighteenth century has recently been remarked by Steven Lynn: see especially 95–97, on Johnson's relation to Hume.

of his mother's death—to the consolations of a "higher authority";[8] but we also know, according to Murphy, that as he contemplated "his own approaching end," he was wont to chant the lines from Shakespeare's *Measure for Measure* (3.1), "Ay, but to die, and go we know not where; / To lie in cold obstruction and to rot" (*Johnsonian Miscellanies* 1:439). Moreover, a curious moment of rhetorical heightening within his argument for the soul's immortality in chapter 48 of *Rasselas*—that ideas and thus minds "cannot *suffer laceration*" (my emphasis)—tends to weight the argument towards wish-fulfillment, especially in light of Johnson's later comment to Thomas Lawrence, "He that outlives a Wife whom he has longed loved" (Johnson's wife Tetty died in 1752) feels disjointed: "The continuity of being is lacerated" (*JL* 3:223).

And what of Hume? Although, as we know from Boswell, "positive in incredulity" on his deathbed, Hume nevertheless wrote or acted in such a manner as allowed Boswell to dream, nearly eight years later, that the philosopher "was in reality a Christian and a very pious man" (*Private Papers* 16:20–21). Hume is reported to have said to an Ayrshire minister, when "in the deepest affliction" for his own mother's death, "Though I threw out my speculations to entertain and employ the learned and metaphysical world, yet in other things I do not think so differently from the rest of mankind as you may imagine" (*Life of Hume* 173–74). Ernest Campbell Mossner notes that many of Hume's Scottish friends received this remark as "the great Infidel's" bashful profession of Christian faith. That they could do so may attest less to Hume's probable intention than to his flagrant ambiguity. His remark can be interpreted in any number of boldly antithetical ways: it can mean, for example, either "I, like you, believe in the Christian testament," or "you, like me, don't really believe." This latter sense is supported by Hume's deathbed comment to Boswell that no one believes in the Christian religion in the same way as he believes in the Glorious Revolution. Yet, as Diderot reports, Hume once remarked to the dogmatic atheist Baron d'Holbach that neither did he "believe in atheists, that he had never seen any." Diderot professes not to understand why— "for what purpose"—Hume injected this observation into their conversation (*Life* 483). Clearly, any interpretation of why Hume said what he did in the manner that he did, and for what purpose, remains yours, just as it does at the end of his essay on the soul, and as it does at the end of Johnson's *Rasselas*.

In short, judging from texts either by or about them, we have no better reason for reading Hume ironically than for reading Johnson integrally. In

---

[8] Boswell links the death of Johnson's mother in January 1759 with the composition of *Rasselas* (*Life of Johnson* 1:339–41); Robert Walker argues more explicitly that "the death of [Johnson's] mother . . . caused [him] to turn . . . to the doctrine of immortality, and . . . to embody it in the form of a moral apologue" (5).

Rasselas and "Of the Immortality of the Soul," both Johnson and Hume authorize two opposed readings, but sanction neither: and they do so similarly, by concluding their texts twice—which may be the same thing as not concluding at all.[9] By offering two endings of equal authority, both force their readers to decide which ending to choose; any integrity or splendid disunity the text may have therefore depends on an act of imputation.

III. The Manner of the Ancient Dialogists

As we have had ample opportunity to see throughout this study, Johnson and Hume shared a genius for presenting both sides of a complex issue; for presenting an argument and then pirouetting to present a counterargument. Both were masters of this "dialogic" mode of writing, as well as the verbal debate. "In conversation, the lively spirit of dialogue is agreeable," wrote Hume (*ECPM* 262), and contemporary reviewers found in Hume the writer, as Mark Box puts it, "an aggressive, cocky debater" ("How Disturbed Was Hume" 9). Boswell remarked that Johnson "could talk upon any side of a question" (*Life of Johnson* 1:465), and Johnson theorized the virtue of debate: "[T]he gay contention for paradoxical positions rectifies the opinion" (*Rambler* 4:108). It is a manner of writing not to be found in most of their immediate predecessors: among moralists, Addison often seems homiletic by contrast; among moral philosophers, Descartes, Hobbes, and Locke sought to give their ethical writing the deductive hardness of geometry or math, and hence supply their conclusions with absolute authority.[10]

On the contrary, Johnson and Hume each wrote in the spirit, and sometimes in direct imitation, of—to use the third earl of Shaftesbury's phrase—"the ancient dialogists" (1:129).[11] Hume owes a signal debt to the type of open-ended philosophic dialogue pioneered by Cicero, a form that greatly attracted Johnson as well, and that may lie behind the conversational give and takes of *Rasselas*.[12] Hume closely modeled his *Dialogues*

[9] For William Vesterman, *Rasselas* expresses "the constant need [Johnson] feels to rebel against and unbalance settled and balanced conclusions—even his own—the need to keep from choosing one attitude to the exclusion of others" (78). My particular notion that *Rasselas* eschews a stance of univocal authority through "concluding twice, and in opposed ways" draws on Fredric Bogel's fine reading of Johnson's *Life of Savage* (*The Dream of My Brother* 7–22).

[10] Hobbes's attraction to geometry's techniques of demonstration is well known; William Youngren traces Locke's own faith in the possibility of a demonstrative ethics to his acquaintance with the Cambridge Platonists.

[11] Michel Malherbe (201–13) recounts Shaftesbury's own debts to the ancient dialogists and his opposition to the rigged "theological dramas" popular among divines in his own day.

[12] Catherine Parke places *Rasselas* in dialogue with Carl Becker, Kenneth Burke, Richard Rorty et al. and finds in Johnson a commitment to education through ongoing conversation, and to history itself as an ongoing conversation, an ongoing give and take of different speakers and standpoints. Such a reading develops Carey McIntosh's earlier view of *Rasselas* as em-

concerning Natural Religion on Cicero's *De Natura Deorum*—a work that
Johnson once intended to translate. The virtue of Cicero's dialogic form,
as Peter Gay remarks, is "to defeat the claims of the absolute," to be "hos-
pitable to the varieties of experience" (172, 176)—or, at least, as Michel
Malherbe specifies, the varieties of speculative opinion (213–18).

Malherbe rightly observes that for Hume, dialogue is less appropriate
for moral debate—for the central moral truths can be empirically ascertained—than for metaphysical or religious debate, which is by its very
nature inconclusive, discursively open-ended. Thus Hume's several dialogues concerning moral principles are *merely* formal or rhetorical: one
speaker will eventually lead us to (what Hume considers) the ethical truth
(see *ECPM* 269–70; 324–43). By contrast, when Hume addresses religious principles or ultimate ends—the question of what will make our
lives happy or flourishing here and/or hereafter—he often uses a dialogue form in which no one speaker is given clinching arguments or a
definitive last word. (Indeed, in the *Dialogues concerning Natural Religion*
the sceptic Philo is given a last word—a professed belief in some type of
designing Deity—that appears to contradict many if not all of his former
objections to the theological argument from design.) Consequently, the
interpretive question traditionally asked of Hume's *Dialogues concerning
Natural Religion* has been who, of its three speakers, speaks for Hume?
After decades of wrangling, the current trend seems to be to accept stale-
mate: they all speak for Hume, to some degree; none do so fully.[13]

We could say much the same for Hume's other great philosophical dialogue, staged as a series of consecutive speeches: the quartet of essays once
commonly called "Four Philosophers"—"The Epicurean," "The Stoic,"
"The Platonist," and "The Sceptic."[14] Hume here follows Cicero's *De Finibus* in allowing for considerable latitude in debating final ends; as Hume
wrote in a public letter to one of his Edinburgh literary antagonists, "Let

bodying the Enlightenment ideals of "disinterestedness, commitment to the secular river of
life, a tireless interest in travel and talk, and an insatiable appetite for surveys of mankind"
(211). Michael Prince, who offers a valuable overview of eighteenth-century translations and
imitations of Ciceronian dialogue (108–11, 122–26), sees *Rasselas* as a series of philosophical dialogues framed by an Oriental tale; he concludes, however, that Johnson stages the *failure* of dialogue in order to dramatize "the need for absolute submission to sovereign authority" (232). Such a conclusion, deaf to the dialogic play of the tale's final two chapters,
follows from Prince's premise that the genre of the philosophical dialogue can and ought to
be clearly distinguished from a dialogic manner of writing (24–25).

[13] See, for example, Charles Hendel, *Selections* xxii; *Dialogues,* ed. Popkin, xv–xvi; Noxon,
"Hume's Agnosticism." With greater piquancy, Malherbe concludes the dialogue is "author-
less" (202, 218).

[14] On "The Four Philosophers" as an open-ended philosophical dialogue, see John
Immerwahr, "Hume's Essays on Happiness." Although Hume is sometimes identified by
other readers with his Sceptic, I have attempted to show throughout this study that his philosophical temperament is at least as closely allied to that of his Stoic.

us revive the happy times, when Atticus and Cassius the Epicureans, Cicero the Academic, and Brutus the Stoic, could, all of them, live in unreserved friendship together, and were insensible to all those distinctions, except so far as they furnished agreeable matter to discourse and conversation" (*Life of Hume* 296).

Hume also found the dialogue or debate form well suited to historical writing. His *History of England* re-creates over a dozen political controversies by presenting both sides of an issue in some depth. Differences that once inspired violent conflict may be calmly assessed with hindsight— and, Hume's method implies, many ongoing conflicts might be similarly defused by the ability sympathetically to understand one's opponent's position as well as one's own. Hume exemplifies and would so teach the lawyer's (and the courtier's) ability to argue both sides of a case: for example, he balances Yorkist and Lancastrian claims during the War of the Roses (2:435–39); he balances the viewpoints of Parliament and Charles I, 1625–27, over the proper extent of royal prerogative (5:156–81). Hume's efforts at achieving an equipoise of contrasting arguments becomes most apparent, and seems most admirable, when he argues cases he elsewhere argues forcefully against in propria persona. Thus, in presenting arguments for and against tolerating religious dissent, Hume gives those against toleration fair clarity and force (3:430–35), although elsewhere in the *History* he advocates toleration as "the true secret for managing religious factions" (4:352; cf. 4:123, 6:322). (Incidentally, parts of the argument against toleration retailed by Hume—particularly the importance of "public tranquillity" over "liberty of conscience"—reappear in Johnson's speeches to Boswell [*Life of Johnson* 2:249–54].) More impressively, Hume recounts the arguments in 1689 for establishing a regency versus those for changing the succession with evenhandedness (6:524–27), although he had recently argued the Whig side of the issue in his essay "Of the Protestant Succession" (1752).[15] Hume's general attitude toward most such debates is neatly summarized by his remark, "[A]midst these disputes, the wise and the moderate in the nation endeavoured to preserve, as much as possible, an equitable neutrality between the opposite parties" (5:95).

[15] For other re-created debates in the *History*, see 3:231–32 (Protestant arguments for and Catholic arguments against disseminating Bibles); 5:91–96 (James I's arguments with his Parliament over the nature of civil liberty); 5:192–202 (arguments for and against the Parliament's "petition of right"); 5:273–76 (Parliament's arguments for and against granting Charles supplies); 5:351–59 (arguments for and against Charles' assenting to the Parliament's Remonstrance); 6:18–20 (for and against Prince Charles's acceptance of the Scottish throne in 1650); 6:170–72 (for and against a "comprehension" between Presbyterians and Prelatists under Charles II); 6:293–94 (for and against the act of announcing the principles of passive obedience); 6:454–56 (for and against granting James II a revenue for life).

Johnson, we will recall, mastered the art of equitably presenting political debate early in his life of writing, in the parliamentary debates he wrote (largely through invention) for *The Gentleman's Magazine* and in another work he did for that magazine, *The Debate between the Committee of the House of Commons and Oliver Cromwell* (1741), an abridgement and rewriting of a formal debate from 1657 over whether or not Cromwell ought to take the title of king. In these works, Johnson hones the arguments on either side of a debate—he leaves us with no straw men. Walter Jackson Bate characterizes Johnson's work for *The Gentleman's Magazine* as "a drama of ideas," and "a prototype" for "the dialectical form of . . . [Johnson's] great moral writing" in the periodical essays and *Rasselas* (*Samuel Johnson* 205–07). In those later essays, Johnson often offers dialogues on aspects of society and manners, with different speakers or "correspondents" taking different sides of an issue: so, for example, in *Rambler* no. 147, a young scholar from the country scoffs at the emptiness of polite London conversation; ten numbers later, another young scholar come to London regrets his lack of conversational ease among the polite; in no. 159, Johnson's mouthpiece, Mr. Rambler, offers a mediating (but not conclusive) response.[16] Johnson's one caveat against the open-ended dialogue or form coincides with Hume's one limitation of the form: in *Rambler* no. 95, the character Pertinax warns against applying the ability to argue either side of an issue to *moral* matters.

But Bate's comment on "the dialectical form" of Johnson's great essays points to something other than the dialogue of different characters or voices. It points to something more intrinsic to Johnson's prose: his ability to offer a generalizing statement about human life, illustrate it, qualify it, relate it to alternative or opposed statements, and finally either to discard it or to subsume it into a new statement. This sort of "dialectic" is the voice of one conversing with oneself; it is the dialogue of a doubled self. To isolate this aspect of Johnson's writing we need only reduce his prose to its logical skeleton. For example, the first ten paragraphs of *Rambler* no. 1 proceed roughly as follows:

—opening premise: "The difficulty . . . is";
—an illustration prefaced with "Perhaps";
—proposition 1: a possible solution to the difficulty;
—a qualification prefaced with "But";
—a rejection of the qualification;
—an exception to the qualified proposition 1 marked with "yet";

[16] Cf. also *Idler* nos. 15 and 28 (the two sides of a marriage spat), and the debates staged within *Idler* no. 20 (the 1758 seige of Louisbourg told first from the English and then from the French point of view), *Rambler* no. 49 (the debate over the love of fame).

—an antithetical proposition (2) in the subjunctive mood;
—"It may . . . be", an illustration of proposition 2;
—a qualifying "But";
—a "maxim" that illustrates by analogy proposition 1;
—the analogy capped by an "If . . . Then" statement;
—the analogy rejected with a "But."

I will not try the reader's patience with inspecting the essay's following four lengthy paragraphs. It suffices to say that Paul Fussell's comment on *The Rambler* is exact: "To the attentive reader . . . these *buts* and *yets* become something like its very substance" (*Samuel Johnson and the Life of Writing* 163).[17]

In a parallel scholarly universe, David Marshall has noted that Hume, in his essay "Of the Standard of Taste," twenty-seven times "interrupts himself with a 'But' . . . which qualifies, complicates, or even challenges the assertion he has just made" ("Arguing by Analogy" 327). Hume's manner of proceeding, no less than Johnson's, depends on the swiveling "but." One can open his *History of England* to nearly any page to see this artistry at work: "but" allows Hume to offer a point of view, and then to supplement it (the accretive "but") to overturn it (the substitutive "but"), or to do something in between.[18]

I have suggested that this fine art of propositional counterpoint, this dialogic writing, derives from an understanding of Cicero's philosophical dialogues—a form Cicero himself theorized in his remarks on the deco-

---

[17] Also see Isobel Grundy's fine essay, "Samuel Johnson: Man of Maxims?"

[18] Take, for example, Hume's last pages on the reign of Edward I (2:140–44). His last battle is against Robert Bruce in 1307: "Bruce fought with the most heroic courage . . . *but* was at last obliged to yield to superior fortune." Here the conjunction signals, as it often does in narrative, the difference between an actor's merit and his fate; it plays its part in a sequence of events. But when Hume moves from narrative to reflection on Edward's character, the word serves rather as it does in Johnson's essays. Edward's enterprises "were more prudent, more regularly conducted, and more advantageous the solid interests of his kingdom, than those which were undertaken in any [earlier] reign"; apparently expecting some readers to object to his campaign to annex Scotland, Hume offers this supplement: "But Edward, however exceptionable his character may appear on the head of justice, is the model of a politic and warlike king." After a few sentences on Edward's military enterprises, Hume spins on a "but" that doesn't quite contradict, but does more than supplement the importance of those enterprises: "But the chief advantage, which the people of England reaped, and still continue to reap, from this great prince, was the correction, extension, and establishment of the laws." Two paragraphs describe Edward as "the English Justinian," before that image is similarly qualified: "But though Edward appeared thus . . . a friend to law and justice, it cannot be said, that he was an enemy to arbitrary power"; the paragraph that so begins ends, "He took care that his subjects should do justice to each other; but he desired always to have his own hands free in all his transactions." Finally, we learn that although ardent for the Crusades, Edward was "little infected with superstition, the vice chiefly of weak minds. But the passion for the Crusades was really in that age the passion for glory." Here "but" signals the substitution of one definition of the Crusades by another.

rum of conversation in *De Officiis* (1:134–137). And yet in Johnson's case (to employ a Johnsonian turn myself), especially in *Rasselas,* a debt to Ciceronian models is obscured by more evident borrowings from Ecclesiastes. Readers from Boswell to George Saintsbury to Harold Bloom have noted that *Rasselas* resembles Ecclesiastes; what they do not note is that from the eighteenth-century onward, Ecclesiastes has been identified as what I have been calling a dialogic work. Bishop Lowth characterizes the dialectic of Ecclesiastes in terms of "a person investigating a very difficult question, examining the arguments on either side, and at length disengaging himself from an anxious and doubtful disputation" (2:174). In our own era, Elias Bickerman has written that in Ecclesiastes, the speaker's "vision transcends and embraces the opposites of his interpreters" (153). We might note as well that Ecclesiastes appears to have a double-ending: its speaker (*koheleth,* "the preacher") concludes "Vanity of vanities, all is Vanity" (12:8), but a later sage infers or appends, "Let us hear then the conclusion of the whole matter: fear God and keep his commandments: for this is the whole duty of man" (12:13). Two points of view are perilously balanced; any conclusion is our own.

V. Making Allowances

But why does the reader have to choose? Can't she, rather, choose not to choose? Indeed, isn't the ground for valid choice precisely what's precluded by the endings of *Rasselas* and "Of the Immortality of the Soul"? The late literary theorist Paul de Man might answer that we are left in a "state of suspended ignorance"—a condition of uncomfortable (or only secretly delicious) cognitive paralysis (19).[19] This may indeed be a paralysis devoutly to be wished, merely the negative stage of a Pyrrhonian dialectic leading to serene indifference. Hume, for one, suggests such a scenario elsewhere in his writings: since "doubt, uncertainty, suspence of judgment appear the only result of our most accurate scrutiny," he suggests that we "happily make our escape into the calm, though obscure, regions of philosophy" (*NHR* 76).

But "Of the Immortality of the Soul" does not quite allow for such withdrawal. Here, not choosing involves at least a benign nod to those who choose belief. To leave the issue of the soul's immortality undecided is to recognize the limits of rational enquiry, and thus to allow for the fideism entertained in the essay's ending. Conversely, in *Rasselas* to leave the question of our proper course in life undecided is, for all of Johnson's reasoned

---

[19] On the ethical implications of de Man's sceptical hermeneutics, see J. Hillis Miller, "Reading Unreadability: de Man," in *The Ethics of Reading* 41–59.

arguments for belief, to acknowledge the limited effectiveness of rational inquiry. *Aporia* (the trope of doubt or undecidability) is not, in these works, an inroad to *apatheia,* but rather an access to sympathy—to making allowances for both sides of a choice that's beyond reason or at least, in *Rasselas,* what reason can reasonably claim to accomplish.

Neither Johnson nor Hume believe in unconditioned choices, nor would they deem an act of volition a thing apart from the passions. Yet one can be made conscious about one's choices, can be put in the unsettling position of being asked to choose in texts between options one never recognized as such in life. And to flounder for even a moment is already an exercise in sympathy. Hume offers as his credo: "I am convinced that, where men are the most sure and arrogant, they are commonly the most mistaken, and have there given reins to passion, without that proper deliberation and suspense, which can alone secure them from the grossest absurdities" (*ECPM* 278). Johnson concurs: "Doubts will produce disputes and disquisition, disquisition requires delay, and"—Johnson adds, ironically—"delay causes inconvenience" (*PW* 379).

In conclusion, neither *Rasselas* nor "Of the Immortality of the Soul" quite commits itself to either side of the oppositions we may expect texts to conform to: integral or disintegral, religious or secularist, apologetic or critical. The texts are dialogic; they entertain a vision of contraries. Of course, the perils of balanced form are evidenced by each texts' ability to accommodate the competing enthusiasms of partisan readers. For if dialogue allows for partisanship, partisanship rarely recognizes dialogue. Thus Hume, in later years, openly cautions against the *parti pris.* In a late footnote to the *Dialogues concerning Natural Religion,* he expressed the hope not only that dialogue over speculative matters might soften difference, but that some rigid philosophical oppositions might wither away altogether. He writes, "It seems evident, that the dispute between the sceptics and dogmatists is entirely verbal, or, at least, regards only the degrees of doubt and assurance, which we ought to indulge with regard to all reasoning" (219).

This book has hopefully demonstrated that Johnson's putative differences from Hume, the alleged dogmatist's from the sceptic's, have been of degree only, and often scarcely that. Johnson saw that even in disagreements about ends we ought always to be cautious against despising sentiments that differ from ours, as they may have once been or may someday become our own. "The enquirers after happiness" have, since Greek times, come to such opposite conclusions—is it to be found in this life, or not?—that "though they will not much assist our determinations, they may, perhaps, equally promote our quiet, by shewing that no absolute determination ever can be formed." And as we view both sides of an issue,

This inconstancy and unsteadiness, to which we must so often find ourselves liable, ought certainly to teach us moderation and forebearance towards those, who cannot accommodate themselves to our sentiments: if they are deceived, we have no right to attribute their mistake to obstinacy or negligence, because we likewise have been mistaken: we may, perhaps, again change our own opinion; and what excuse shall we be able to find for aversion and malignity conceived against him, whom we shall then find to have committed no fault, and who offended us only by refusing to follow us into error. (*Adventurer* no. 107, 2:444–45)

This is not relativism, for truth and error do exist; it is simply difficult, "with regard to questions, wherein we have most interest," to know where each lies.

Rightfully understood, the dialogism of both Hume and Johnson contests the history of bifurcated readings to which it has not inevitably given rise. The discourse of the Enlightenment, at its best, permitted and continues to permit disagreement over final things, over endings. One might choose one's happiness either fully here or partly hereafter. The choice is yours, critical reader.

Bibliography

Acton, H. B. "Prejudice." *Revue International de Philosophie* 6:3 (1952): 323–36.

Addison, Joseph. *Cato.* In *British Dramatists from Dryden to Sheridan,* ed. George H. Nettleton and Arthur E. Case, rev. George Winchester Stone. Boston: Houghton Mifflin, 1969.

Addison, Joseph, and Richard Steele. *The Spectator.* 5 vols. Ed. Donald F. Bond. Oxford: Clarendon Press, 1965.

Alkon, Paul Kent. *Samuel Johnson and Moral Discipline.* Evanston: Northwestern University Press, 1967.

Annas, Julia. *The Morality of Happiness.* New York: Oxford University Press, 1993.

Aquinas, St. Thomas. *Summa Theologica.* 3 vols. Trans. Fathers of the English Dominican Province. New York: Benzinger Brothers, 1948.

Árdal, Pall S. *Passion and Value in Hume's Treatise.* Edinburgh: Edinburgh University Press, 1966.

Aristotle. *Rhetoric and Poetics.* Trans. W. Rhys Roberts and Ingram Bywater. Oxford: Clarendon Press, 1908.

———. *Nicomachean Ethics.* Trans. Martin Ostwald. Indianapolis: Bobbs-Merrill, 1962.

Arnold, E. Vernon. *Roman Stoicism.* Cambridge: Cambridge University Press, 1911.

Baier, Annette. *A Progress of Sentiments: Reflections on Hume's "Treatise."* Cambridge, Mass.: Harvard University Press, 1991.

———. *Moral Prejudices: Essays on Ethics.* Cambridge, Mass.: Harvard University Press, 1994.

Baldwin, Anna, and Sarah Hutton, eds. *Platonism and the English Imagination.* Cambridge: Cambridge University Press, 1994.

Barnouw, Jeffrey. "Johnson and Hume Considered as the Core of a New 'Period Concept' of the Enlightenment." *Studies on Voltaire and the Eighteenth Century* 190 (1980): 189–96.

Bate, Jonathan. *The Genius of Shakespeare.* London: Picador, 1997.

Bate, Walter Jackson. *The Burden of the Past and the English Poet.* Cambridge, Mass.: Harvard University Press, 1970.

———. *Samuel Johnson.* New York: Harcourt Brace Jovanovich, 1975.

Bayle, Pierre. *Oeuvres Diverses, Volumes Supplémentaires: Choix D'Articles Tirés du Dictionnaire Historique et Critique* (1740 ed.). 2 vols. Ed. Elisabeth Labrousse. Hildesheim: Georg Olms Verlag, 1982.

Beattie, James. *An Essay on the Nature and Immutability of Truth; In Opposition to Sophistry and Scepticism.* Edinburgh, 1770.

Beauchamp, T. L. "An Analysis of Hume's Essay 'On Suicide'." *Review of Metaphysics* 30:1 (1976): 73–95.

Becker, Lawrence. *A New Stoicism.* Princeton: Princeton University Press, 1998.

Bender, John. *Imagining the Penitentiary: Fiction and the Architecture of Mind in Eighteenth-century England.* Chicago: University of Chicago Press, 1987.

Berland, Kevin. "Bringing Philosophy Down from the Heavens: Socrates and the New Science." *Journal of the History of Ideas* 47:2 (1986): 299–308.

———. "Dialogue into Drama: Socrates in Eighteenth-Century Verse Dramas." In *Drama and Philosophy,* ed. James Redmond, pp. 127–41. Cambridge: Cambridge University Press, 1989.

Berry, Christopher. *Hume, Hegel and Human Nature.* The Hague: Martinus Nijhoff, 1982.

Bickerman, Elias. *Four Strange Books of the Bible.* New York: Schocken, 1967.

Black, J. B. *The Art of History: A Study of Four Great Historians of the Eighteenth Century.* New York: F. S. Crofts, 1926.

Bloom, Harold, ed. *Dr. Samuel Johnson and James Boswell: Modern Critical Views.* New York: Chelsea House, 1986.

Bogel, Fredric V. *Literature and Insubstantiality in Later Eighteenth-Century England.* Princeton: Princeton University Press, 1984.

———. *The Dream of My Brother: An Essay on Johnson's Authority.* ELS Monograph Series no. 47. Victoria: University of Victoria, 1990.

Bohls, Elizabeth. "The Aesthetics of Colonialism: Janet Schaw in the West Indies." *Eighteenth-Century Studies* 27:3 (1994): 363–90.

Bongie, Laurence. *David Hume: Prophet of the Counter-Revolution.* Oxford: Clarendon Press, 1965.

Boswell, James. *Letters.* 2 vols. Ed. Chauncy B. Tinker. Oxford: Clarendon Press, 1924.

———. *Private Papers from Malahide Castle.* 18 vols. Ed. Geoffrey Scott and Frederick A. Pottle. Mount Vernon, N.Y.: privately printed (W. E. Rudge), 1928–34.

———. *Boswell in Extremes, 1776–1778.* Ed. Charles Weis and Frederick A. Pottle. New York: McGraw Hill, 1970.

Botros, Sophie. "Freedom, Causality, Fatalism and Early Stoic Philosophy." *Phronesis* 30 (1985): 274–304.

Box, Mark A. *The Suasive Art of David Hume.* Princeton: Princeton University Press, 1990.

———. "How Disturbed Was Hume by His Own Scepticism?" *1650–1850: Ideas, Aesthetics, and Inquiries in the Early Modern Era* 1 (1994): 295–316.

Braudy, Leo. *Narrative Form in History and Fiction: Hume, Fielding, and Gibbon.* Princeton: Princeton University Press, 1970.

———. "Penetration and Inpenetrability in *Clarissa.*" In *New Approaches to Eighteenth-Century Literature: Selected Papers from the English Institute,* ed. Phillip Harth, pp. 177–206. New York: Columbia University Press, 1974.

Braund, Susanna Morton, and Christopher Gill, eds. *The Passions in Roman Thought and Literature.* Cambridge: Cambridge University Press, 1997.

Bromwich, David. *Politics by Other Means: Higher Education and Group Thinking.* New Haven: Yale University Press, 1992.

Brown, Charlotte. "From Spectator to Agent: Hume's Theory of Obligation." *Hume Studies* 20:1 (1994): 19–35.

Brownell, Morris. *Samuel Johnson's Attitude to the Arts.* Oxford: Clarendon Press, 1989.

Brownley, Martine Watson. *Clarendon and the Rhetoric of Historical Form.* Philadelphia: University of Pennsylvania Press, 1985.

Burke, Edmund. *Reflections on the Revolution in France.* Ed. Conor Cruise O'Brien. Harmondsworth, England: Penguin, 1968.

Burton, John Hill. *Life and Correspondence of David Hume.* 2 vols. Edinburgh, 1846.

Butler, Joseph. *The Analogy of Religion, Natural and Revealed . . . and Fifteen Sermons.* London, 1878.

Butterfield, Herbert. *The Whig Interpretation of History.* 1931. New York: Norton, 1965.

Calhoun, Cheshire, and Robert C. Solomon, eds. *What Is an Emotion? Classic Readings in Philosophical Psychology.* New York: Oxford University Press, 1984.

Campbell, Alexander. *Lexiphanes, A Dialogue.* 2d ed. London, 1767.

Campbell, George. *A Dissertation on Miracles.* 3d ed. Edinburgh, 1796.

Campbell, Lily. *Shakespeare's Tragic Heroes: Slaves of Passion.* Cambridge: Cambridge University Press, 1930.

Cannon, John. *Samuel Johnson and the Politics of Hanoverian England.* Oxford: Oxford University Press, 1994.

Capaldi, Nicholas. "Hume's Theory of the Passions." In *Hume: A Re-Evaluation,* ed. Donald Livingston and James King, pp. 172–90. New York: Fordham University Press, 1976.

———. "The Dogmatic Slumber of Hume Scholarship." *Hume Studies* 18:2 (1992): 117–35.

Caplan, Harry. *Of Eloquence: Studies in Ancient and Medieval Rhetoric.* Ithaca: Cornell Universtity Press, 1970.

Chapin, Chester F. *The Religious Thought of Samuel Johnson.* Ann Arbor: University of Michigan Press, 1968.

———. "Samuel Johnson and the Scottish Common Sense School." *The Eighteenth Century: Theory and Interpretation* 20:1 (1979): 50–64.

Chesterfield, fourth earl of. *Characters.* Intro. by Alan T. McKenzie. Los Angeles: William Andrew Clark Memorial Library, 1990.

Chisick, Harvey. "David Hume and the Common People." In *The 'Science of Man' in the Scottish Enlightenment: Hume, Reid and Their Contemporaries,* ed. Peter Jones, pp. 5–32. Edinburgh: Edinburgh University Press, 1989.

Christensen, Jerome. *Practicing Enlightenment: Hume and the Formation of a Literary Career.* Madison: University of Wisconsin Press, 1987.

Cicero. *De Finibus Bonorum et Malorum.* Trans. H. Rackham. Cambridge, Mass.: Harvard University Press, 1931.

———. *Tusculan Disputations.* Trans. J. E. King. Cambridge, Mass.: Harvard University Press, 1945.

———. *De Natura Deorum / Academica.* Trans. H. Rackham. Cambridge, Mass.: Harvard University Press, 1951.

———. *On Duties [De Officiis].* Trans. M. T. Griffin and E. M Atkins. Cambridge: Cambridge University Press, 1991.

Clarendon, Henry Hyde, earl of. *The History of the Great Rebellion.* 6 vols. Ed. W. Dunn Macray. Oxford: Clarendon Press, 1888.

Clark, J. C. D. *Samuel Johnson: Literature, Religion and English Cultural Politics from The Restoration to Romanticism.* Cambridge: Cambridge University Press, 1994.

Clingham, Greg. *James Boswell: The Life of Johnson.* Cambridge: Cambridge University Press, 1992.

———, ed. *The Cambridge Companion to Samuel Johnson.* Cambridge: Cambridge University Press, 1997.

Coleman, Dorothy. "Interpreting Hume's *Dialogues.*" *Religious Studies* 25 (June 1989): 179–90.

Coleridge, Samuel Taylor. *Biographia Literaria.* Ed. George Watson. London: Dent, 1975.

Colley, Linda. *Britons: Forging the Nation, 1707–1837.* New Haven: Yale University Press, 1992.

Comer, Ronald. *Abnormal Psychology.* 3d ed. New York: W. H. Freeman, 1998.

Crimmins, James. "John Brown and the Theological Tradition of Utilitarian Ethics." *History of Political Thought* 4 (1983): 523–50.

Cunningham, J. S. "The Essayist, 'Our Present State,' and 'The Passions'." In *Samuel Johnson: New Critical Essays,* ed. Isobel Grundy, pp. 137–157. Totowa, N.J.: Barnes & Noble, 1984.

Damrosch, Leo. *Samuel Johnson and the Tragic Sense.* Princeton: Princeton University Press, 1972.

———. *Fictions of Reality in the Age of Hume and Johnson.* Madison: University of Wisconsin Press, 1989.

Davila, Enrico Caterino. *The History of the Civil Wars of France.* Trans. Roger L'Estrange. London, 1678.

De Man, Paul. *Allegories of Reading: Figural Language in Rousseau, Nietzsche, Rilke, and Proust.* New Haven: Yale University Press, 1979.

DeMaria, Robert. *Johnson's Dictionary and the Language of Learning.* Chapel Hill: University of North Carolina Press, 1986.

———. *The Life of Samuel Johnson.* Oxford: Blackwell, 1993.

Dowling, William C. *The Boswellian Hero.* Athens: University of Georgia Press, 1979.

Dryden, John. *Works of John Dryden.* Vol. 12. *Poems 1681–1684.* Ed. H. T. Swedenberg and Vinton A. Dearing. Berkeley: University of California Press, 1972.

Dye, James. "A Word on Behalf of Demea." *Hume Studies* 15:1 (1989): 120–40.

———. "Demea's Departure." *Hume Studies* 18:2 (1992): 467–81.

Edinger, William. *Johnson and Detailed Representation: The Significance of the Classical Sources.* ELS Monograph Series no. 72. Victoria: University of Victoria, 1997.

Elledge, Scott, and Donald Schier, eds. *The Continental Model: Selected French Critical Essays of the Seventeenth Century.* Ithaca: Cornell University Press, 1970.

Emerson, Roger L. "The "Affair" at Edinburgh and the "Project" at Glasgow: the Politics of Hume's Attempts to Become a Professor." In *Hume and Hume's Connexions,* ed. M. A. Stewart and John P. Wright, pp. 1–22. University Park: Penn State University Press, 1995.

Epictetus. *The Discourses as Reported by Arrian, The Manual, and Fragments.* 2 vols. Trans. W. A. Oldfather. Cambridge, Mass.: Harvard University Press, 1928.

Erskine-Hill, Howard. *The Augustan Idea in English Literature.* London: Edward Arnold, 1983.

———. *Poetry of Opposition and Revolution: Dryden to Wordsworth.* Oxford: Clarendon Press, 1996.

Eze, Emmanuel Chukwudi. *Race and the Enlightenment: A Reader.* Oxford: Blackwell, 1997.

Fielding, Henry. *Tom Jones.* 2 vols. Ed. Fredson Bowers, with an intro. and commentary by Martin Battestin. Oxford: Clarendon Press, 1974.

Fitzgibbons, Athol. *Adam Smith's System of Liberty, Wealth and Virtue: The Moral and Political Foundations of 'The Wealth of Nations'.* Oxford: Clarendon Press, 1995.

Fleeman, J. D., ed. *The Sale Catalogue of Samuel Johnson's Library.* ELS Monograph Series no. 2. Victoria: University of Victoria, 1975.

Flew, Anthony. *David Hume: Philosopher of Moral Science.* Oxford: Blackwell, 1986.

Forbes, Duncan. *Hume's Philosophical Politics.* Cambridge: Cambridge University Press, 1975.

Force, James E. "Hume and Johnson on Prophecy and Miracles: Historical Context." *Journal of the History of Ideas* 43 (1982): 463–75.

Fox, Christopher. *Locke and the Scriblerians: Identity and Consciousness in Early Eighteenth-Century Britain.* Berkeley: University of California Press, 1988.

Frey, R. G. "Did Socrates Commit Suicide?" *Philosophy* 53 (1978): 106–08.

Fukuyama, Francis. *The End of History and the Last Man.* New York: The Free Press, 1992.

Fussell, Paul. *The Rhetorical World of Augustan Humanism: Ethics and Imagery from Swift to Burke.* Oxford: Clarendon Press, 1965.

———. *Samuel Johnson and the Life of Writing.* New York: Harcourt Brace Jovanovich, 1971.

Gaarder, Jostein. *Sophie's World: A Novel about the History of Philosophy.* Trans. Paulette Moller. New York: Farrar, Straus and Giroux, 1994.

Garrett, Don. *Cognition and Commitment in Hume's Philosophy.* New York: Oxford University Press, 1997.

Gates, Henry Louis. *Figures in Black: Words, Signs, and the "Racial" Self.* New York: Oxford University Press, 1987.

Gay, Peter. *The Enlightenment: An Interpretation.* Vol. 1. *The Rise of Modern Paganism.* New York: Knopf, 1966.

Gerard, Christine. *The Patriot Opposition to Walpole: Politics, Poetry, and the National Myth, 1725–1742.* Oxford: Oxford University Press, 1994.

German, Terence J. *Hamann on Language and Religion.* Oxford: Oxford University Press, 1981.

Gibbon, Edward. *Letters.* 3 vols. Ed. J. E. Norton. London: Cassell, 1956.

————. *The History of the Decline and Fall of the Roman Empire.* 3 vols. Ed. David Womersley. London: Penguin, 1994.

Giddings, Robert. "The Fall of Orgolio: Samuel Johnson as Parliamentary Reporter." In *Samuel Johnson: New Critical Essays,* ed. Isobel Grundy, pp. 86–106. Totowa, N.J.: Barnes & Noble, 1984.

Goldgar, Bertrand A. *Walpole and the Wits: The Relation of Politics to Literature, 1722–1742.* Lincoln: University of Nebraska Press, 1976.

Goldsmith, Oliver. *Collected Works.* 5 vols. Ed. Arthur Friedman. Oxford: Clarendon Press, 1966.

Gordon, Daniel. *Citizens without Sovereignty: Equality and Sociability in French Thought, 1670–1789.* Princeton: Princeton University Press, 1994.

Greene, Donald. *The Politics of Samuel Johnson.* New Haven: Yale University Press, 1960.

————. "Johnson, Stoicism, and the Good Life." In *The Unknown Samuel Johnson,* ed. John J. Burke and Donald Kay, pp. 17–38. Madison: University of Wisconsin Press, 1984.

————. "The *Logia* of Samuel Johnson and the Quest for the Historical Johnson." *The Age of Johnson: A Scholarly Annual* 3 (1990): 1–33.

Griffin, Robert. *Wordsworth's Pope: A Study in Literary Historiography.* Cambridge: Cambridge University Press, 1995.

Grotius, Hugo. *The Rights of War and Peace* [*De Ivre Belli ac Pacis*]. Trans. Basil Kennet. London, 1738.

Grundy, Isobel. "Samuel Johnson: Man of Maxims?" In *Samuel Johnson: New Critical Essays,* ed. Isobel Grundy, pp. 13–30. Totowa, N.J.: Barnes & Noble, 1984.

————. *Samuel Johnson and the Scale of Greatness.* Athens: University of Georgia Press, 1986.

Haakonssen, Knud. "The Structure of Hume's Political Theory." In *The Cambridge Companion to Hume,* ed. David Fate Norton, pp. 182–221. Cambridge: Cambridge University Press, 1993.

————. *Natural Law and Moral Philosophy: From Grotius to the Scottish Enlightenment.* Cambridge: Cambridge University Press, 1996.

Habermas, Jurgen. *The Structural Transformation of the Public Sphere: An Inquiry into a Category of Bourgeois Culture.* Trans. Thomas Burger. Oxford: Polity, 1989.

Hagstrum, Jean H. *Samuel Johnson's Literary Criticism.* Chicago: University of Chicago Press, 1967.

Harpham, Geoffrey Galt. "Of Rats and Men; or, Reason in Our Time." *Raritan* 14:4 (1995): 88–114.

Harrison, Bernard. *Henry Fielding's Tom Jones: The Novelist as Moral Philosopher.* London: Chatto & Windus for Sussex University Press, 1975.

Hazard, Paul. *European Thought in the Eighteenth Century: From Montesquieu to Lessing.* Trans. J. Lewis May. London: Hollis & Carter, 1954.

Hazlitt, William. *Selected Writings.* Ed. Ronald Blythe. Harmondsworth: Penguin, 1970.

Hegel, G. W. F. *The Philosophy of History.* Trans. J. Sibree [1899]. New York: Dover, 1956.

Hendel, Charles, ed. *Selections from Hume.* New York: Scribner's, 1927.

———, ed. *Inquiry concerning Human Understanding* [Hume]. Indianapolis: Bobbs-Merrill, 1955.

Henry of Huntingdon. *The History of England, from the Invasion of Julius Caesar to the Accession of Henry II.* Trans. Thomas Forester. London: Bohn, 1853.

Herbert, R. T. "Gappiness and Personal Identity." In *Faith, Scepticism and Personal Identity.* Ed. J. J. MacIntosh and H. A. Meynell, pp. 199–210. Calgary: University of Calgary Press, 1994.

Herdt, Jennifer. *Religion and Faction in Hume's Moral Philosophy.* Cambridge: Cambridge University Press, 1997.

Hertz, Neil. "Dr. Johnson's Forgetfulness, Descartes' Piece of Wax." *Eighteenth-Century Life* 16:3 (1992): 167–81.

Hicks, Philip. *Neoclassical History and English Culture from Clarendon to Hume.* New York: St. Martin's Press, 1996.

Hilles, Frederick W. "*Rasselas,* an 'Uninstructive Tale'." In *Johnson, Boswell, and Their Circle: Essays Presented to Laurence Fitzroy Powell,* ed. Mary M. Lascelles et al. pp. 111–21. Oxford: Clarendon Press, 1965.

Hillman, James. *Emotion: A Comprehensive Phenomenology of Theories and Their Meanings for Therapy.* Evanston: Northwestern University Press, 1964.

Hinnant, Charles H. *Samuel Johnson: An Analysis.* New York: St. Martin's Press, 1988.

Hirschmann, Albert O. *The Passions and the Interests: Political Arguments for Capitalism before Its Triumph.* Princeton: Princeton University Press, 1977.

Hobbes, Thomas. *Leviathan Parts I and II.* Ed. Herbert W. Schneider. Indianapolis: Bobbs-Merrill, 1958.

———. *The Elements of Law, Natural and Politic: Part I, Human Nature: Part II, De Corpore Politico.* Ed. J. C. A. Gaskin. Oxford: Oxford University Press, 1994.

Hof, Ulrich Im. *The Enlightenment.* Trans. William E. Yuill. Oxford: Blackwell, 1994.

Holmes, Richard. *Dr. Johnson and Mr. Savage.* New York: Pantheon, 1993.

Horace. *Satires, Epistles, Ars Poetica.* Trans. H. R. Fairclough. Cambridge, Mass.: Harvard University Press, 1929.

Hudson, Deal. *Happiness and the Limits of Satisfaction.* Lanham, Md.: Rowman & Littlefield, 1996.

Hudson, Nicholas. *Samuel Johnson and Eighteenth-Century Thought.* Oxford: Clarendon Press, 1988.

———. "Three Steps to Perfection: *Rasselas* and the Philosophy of Richard Hooker." *Eighteenth-Century Life* 14:3 (1990): 29–39.

———. "From 'Nation' to 'Race': The Origin of Racial Classification in Eighteenth-Century Thought." *Eighteenth-Century Studies* 29:3 (1996): 247–64.

Hundert, E. J. *The Enlightenment's Fable: Bernard Mandeville and the Discovery of Society.* Cambridge: Cambridge University Press, 1994.

Hutcheson, Francis. *An Essay on the Nature and Conduct of the Passions and Affections* (3d Ed., 1742). Facsimile reprint with an intro. by Paul McReynolds. Gainesville, Fla.: Scholars Facsimilies, 1969.

Hutchings, William. "Johnson and Juvenal." Paper delivered at the Samuel Johnson and the Languages of Literature Conference, Birmingham, England, September 1997.

Ignatieff, Michael. *The Needs of Strangers.* New York: Viking Penguin, 1985.

Immerwahr, John. "Hume's Essays on Happiness." *Hume Studies* 15:2 (1989): 307–24.

———. "Hume on Tranquillizing the Passions." *Hume Studies* 18:2 (1992): 293–314.

Irwin, Terence. *Classical Thought.* Oxford: Oxford University Press, 1989.

Jemielity, Thomas. "Samuel Johnson, *The Vanity of Human Wishes,* and Biographical Criticism." *Studies in Eighteenth-Century Culture* 15 (1986): 227–39.

Jones, Emrys. "The Artistic Form of *Rasselas.*" *RES* n.s. 18 (1967): 384–401.

Jones, Peter. *Hume's Sentiments: Their Ciceronian and French Contexts.* Edinburgh: Edinburgh University Press, 1982.

Jordan, Winthrop. *White over Black: American Attitudes Towards the Negro, 1550–1812.* Chapel Hill: University of North Carolina Press, 1968.

Juvenal. *The 16 Satires.* Trans. Peter Green. Harmondsworth, England: Penguin, 1967.

———. *The Satires* [Latin]. Ed. John Ferguson. New York: St. Martin's Press, 1979.

Kames, Henry Home, Lord. *Elements of Criticism.* 2 vols. 6th ed. Edinburgh, 1785.

Kaufmann, David. *The Business of Common Life: Novels and Classical Economics between Revolution and Reform.* Baltimore: Johns Hopkins University Press, 1995.

Kenny, Anthony, ed. *The Oxford History of Western Philosophy.* Oxford: Oxford University Press, 1994.

Kenshur, Oscar. *Dilemmas of Enlightenment: Studies in the Rhetoric and Logic of Ideology.* Berkeley: University of California Press, 1993.

Kolb, Gwin. "The Structure of *Rasselas,*" *PMLA* 66:5 (1951): 698–717.

Kramnick, Isaac. *Bolingbroke and His Circle: The Politics of Nostalgia in the Age of Walpole.* Cambridge, Mass.: Harvard University Press, 1968.

———. *Republicanism and Bourgeois Radicalism: Political Ideology in Late Eighteenth-Century England and America.* Ithaca: Cornell University Press, 1990.

———, ed. *The Enlightenment: A Reader.* London: Penguin, 1995.

Kramnick, Jonathan Brody. "The Making of the English Canon." *PMLA* 112:5 (1997): 1087–1101.

Krutch, Joseph Wood. *Samuel Johnson.* New York: Henry Holt, 1944.

Lackington, James. *Memoirs of the First Forty-Five Years.* London, 1794.

Lamb, Jonathan. *The Rhetoric of Suffering: Reading the Book of Job in the Eighteenth Century.* Oxford: Clarendon Press, 1995.

Landa, José Angel Garcia. "Samuel Johnson's *Rasselas:* The Duplicity of Choice and The Sense of an Ending." *Revista Canaria de Estudos Ingleses* 19–20 (Nov. 1989/Apr. 1990): 75–99.

Langford, Paul. "Convocation and the Tory Clergy, 1717–61." In *The Jacobite Challenge,* ed. Eveline Cruickshanks and Jeremy Black, pp. 107–22. Edinburgh: John Donald, 1988.

Laursen, John Christian, and Greg Coolidge. "David Hume and Public Debt: Crying Wolf?" *Hume Studies* 20:1 (1994): 143–49.

Lipking, Lawrence. "Learning to Read Johnson: *The Vision of Theodore* and *The Vanity of Human Wishes.*" *ELH* 43 (1976): 517–37.

————. "M. Johnson and Mr. Rousseau." *Common Knowledge* 3:3 (1994): 109–26.

Livingston, Donald. *Hume's Philosophy of Common Life*. Chicago: University of Chicago Press, 1984.

————. *Philosophical Melancholy and Delirium: Hume's Pathology of Philosophy*. Chicago: University of Chicago Press, 1998.

Livingston, Donald, and Marie Martin, eds. *Hume as Philosopher of Society, Politics and History*. Rochester: University of Rochester Press, 1991.

Locke, John. *An Essay concerning Human Understanding*. Ed. Peter H. Nidditch. Oxford: Oxford University Press, 1975.

Long, A. A., and D. N. Sedley. *The Hellenistic Philosophers*. Cambridge: Cambridge University Press, 1987.

Lovejoy, A. O. *Reflections on Human Nature*. Baltimore: Johns Hopkins University Press, 1961.

Lowth, Robert. *Lectures on the Sacred Poetry of the Hebrews*. 1753. Trans. G. Gregory. 2 vols. London, 1787.

Lucretius. *On the Nature of the Universe*. Trans. R. E. Latham. Harmondsworth, England: Penguin, 1970.

Lynn, Steven. *Samuel Johnson after Deconstruction: Rhetoric and "The Rambler."* Carbondale: Southern Illinois University Press, 1992.

McDermott, Anne, ed. *A Dictionary of the English Language: On CD-ROM* (Johnson; incl. 1st ed., 1755, and 4th ed., 1773). Cambridge: Cambridge University Press, 1996.

McIntosh, Carey. *The Choice of Life: Samuel Johnson and the World of Fiction*. New Haven: Yale University Press, 1973.

MacIntyre, Alasdair. "Hume on 'Is' and 'Ought'." *Philosophical Review* 68 (1959): 451–68. Rptd. in *Hume: A Collection of Critical Essays*, ed. V. C. Chappell, pp. 240–64. Notre Dame: University of Notre Dame Press, 1968.

————. *After Virtue: A Study in Moral Theory*. 2d ed. Notre Dame: University of Notre Dame Press, 1984.

————. "Hume, Testimony to Miracles, the Order of Nature, and Jansenism." In *Faith, Scepticism and Personal Identity*, ed. J. J. MacIntosh and H. A. Meynell, pp. 83–99. Calgary: University of Calgary Press, 1994.

McKenzie, Alan T. *Certain Lively Episodes: The Articulation of Passion in Eighteenth-Century Prose*. Athens: University of Georgia Press, 1990.

Malherbe, Michel. "Hume and the Art of Dialogue." In *Hume and Hume's Connexions*, ed. M. A. Stewart and John P. Wright, pp. 201–23. University Park: Penn State University Press, 1995.

Mandeville, Bernard. *The Fable of the Bees*. 2 vols. Ed. F. B. Kaye. Oxford: Oxford University Press, 1924.

————. *A Treatise of the Hypochondriack and Hysterick Diseases*. 2d ed. London, 1730.

Manning, Susan. *The Puritan-Provincial Vision : Scottish and American Literature in the Eighteenth Century*. Cambridge: Cambridge University Press, 1990.

Marshall, David. *The Figure of Theater: Shaftesbury, Defoe, Adam Smith, and George Eliot*. New York: Columbia University Press, 1986.

————. "Arguing by Analogy: Hume's Standard of Taste." *Eighteenth-Century Studies* 28:3 (1995): 323–43.

Martin, Marie. "Hume on Human Excellence." *Hume Studies* 18:2 (1992): 383–99.

Mauzi, Robert. *L'Idée du Bonheur dans la Littérature et la Pensée Françaises au XVIIIe Siècle.* Paris: Armand Colin, 1960.

Melehy, Hassan. *Writing Cogito: Montaigne, Descartes, and the Institution of the Modern Subject.* Albany: State University of New York Press, 1997.

Merlan, Philip. "From Hume to Hamann." *The Personalist* 32 (Winter 1951): 11–18.

Miles, Geoffrey. *Shakespeare and the Constant Romans.* Oxford: Clarendon Press, 1996.

Miller, J. Hillis. *The Ethics of Reading.* New York: Columbia University Press, 1987.

Milton, John. *Complete Poems and Major Prose.* Ed. Merritt Y. Hughes. New York: Odyssey, 1957.

Moore, James. "Hume and Hutcheson." In *Hume and Hume's Connexions,* ed. M. A. Stewart and John P. Wright, pp. 23–57. University Park: Penn State University Press, 1995.

Moravia, Sergio. *Filosofia & Scienza Umane Nell'eta Dei Lumi.* Florence: Sansoni, 1982.

Morford, Mark. *Stoics and Neo-Stoics: Rubens and the Circle of Lipsius.* Princeton: Princeton University Press, 1991.

Mossner, Ernest Campbell. *The Forgotten Hume: Le Bon David.* New York: Columbia University Press, 1943.

Muller, Jerry Z. *Conservatism: An Anthology of Social and Political Thought from David Hume to the Present.* Princeton: Princeton University Press, 1997.

Neu, Jerome. *Emotion, Thought and Therapy: A Study of Hume and Spinoza and the Relationship of Philosophical Theories of the Emotions to Psychological Theories of Therapy.* Berkeley: University of California Press, 1977.

Norton, David Fate. *David Hume: Common-Sense Moralist, Sceptical Metaphysician.* Princeton: Princeton University Press, 1982.

———, ed. *The Cambridge Companion to Hume.* Cambridge: Cambridge University Press, 1993.

Norton, David Fate, and Mary J. Norton. *The David Hume Library.* Edinburgh: Edinburgh Bibliographical Society, 1996.

Noxon, James. "Hume's Agnosticism." In *Hume: A Collection of Critical Essays,* ed. V. C. Chappell, pp. 361–83. Notre Dame: University of Notre Dame Press, 1968.

———. *Hume's Philosophical Development: A Study of His Methods.* Oxford: Clarendon Press, 1973.

Nussbaum, Felicity. *The Autobiographical Subject: Gender and Ideology in Eighteenth-Century England.* Baltimore: Johns Hopkins University Press, 1989.

Nussbaum, Martha C. *The Therapy of Desire: Theory and Practice in Hellenistic Ethics.* Princeton: Princeton University Press, 1994.

Nuttall, A. D. *A Common Sky: Philosophy and the Literary Imagination.* Berkeley: University of California Press, 1974.

O'Brien, Karen. *Narratives of Enlightenment: Cosmopolitan History from Voltaire to Gibbon.* Cambridge: Cambridge University Press, 1997.

O'Shaughnessy, Toni. "Fiction as Truth: Personal Identity in Johnson's *Life of Savage.*" *SEL* 30 (1990): 487–501.

Outram, Dorinda. *The Enlightenment.* Cambridge: Cambridge University Press, 1995.

Pagden, Anthony. *Lords of All the World: Ideologies of Empire in Spain, Britain and France c. 1500–c. 1800.* New Haven: Yale University Press, 1995.

Palter, Robert. "Hume and Prejudice." *Hume Studies* 21:1 (1995): 3–23.

Parke, Catherine. "*Rasselas* and the Conversation of History." *The Age of Johnson: A Scholarly Annual* 1 (1987): 79–109.

Passmore, John. *Hume's Intentions.* 1952. 3d ed. London: Duckworth, 1980.

———. "Enthusiasm, Fanaticism and David Hume." In *The 'Science of Man' in the Scottish Enlightenment: Hume, Reid, and Their Contemporaries,* ed. Peter Jones, pp. 85–107. Edinburgh: Edinburgh University Press, 1989.

Patey, Douglas Lane. "Johnson's Refutation of Berkeley: Kicking the Stone Again." *Journal of the History of Ideas* 47:1 (1986): 139–45.

Penelhum, Terence. "Hume on Personal Identity." In *Hume: A Collection of Critical Essays,* ed. V. C. Chappell, pp. 213–39. Notre Dame: University of Notre Dame Press, 1968.

———. "Hume's Moral Psychology." In *The Cambridge Companion to Hume,* ed. David Fate Norton, pp. 117–47. Cambridge: Cambridge University Press, 1993.

Pettit, Alexander. *Illusory Consensus: Bolingbroke and the Polemical Response to Walpole, 1730–1737.* Newark: University of Delaware Press, 1997.

Pitson, Antony. "The Nature of Humean Animals." *Hume Studies* 19:2 (1993): 301–16.

———. "Sympathy and Other Selves." *Hume Studies* 22:2 (1996): 255–71.

Pocock, J. G. A. *The Machiavellian Moment: Florentine Political Thought and the Atlantic Republican Tradition.* Princeton: Princeton University Press, 1975.

———. *Virtue, Commerce, and History: Essays on Political Thought and History, Chiefly in the Eighteenth Century.* Cambridge: Cambridge University Press, 1985.

Pope, Alexander. *Complete Poems.* 10 vols. Gen. ed. John Butt. London: Methuen, 1939–1969.

Popkin, Richard, ed. *Dialogues concerning Natural Religion and the Posthumous Essays, Of the Immortality of the Soul and Of Suicide* [Hume]. Indianapolis: Hackett, 1980.

Porter, Roy. *The Enlightenment.* Atlantic Highlands, N.J.: Humanities Press, 1990.

Porter, Roy, and Mikulas Teich, eds. *The Enlightenment in National Context.* Cambridge: Cambridge University Press, 1981.

Potkay, Adam. "Johnson and the Terms of Succession." *SEL* 26 (1986): 497–509.

———. *The Fate of Eloquence in the Age of Hume.* Ithaca: Cornell University Press, 1994.

———. "Theorizing Civic Eloquence in the Early Republic: The Road from David Hume to John Quincy Adams." *Early American Literature* 34 (1999): 147–70.

———. "'The Structure of His Sentences Is French': Johnson and Hume in the History of English." Forthcoming in *Language Sciences* (2000).

Preston, Thomas R. "The Biblical Context of Johnson's *Rasselas.*" *PMLA* 84:2 (1969): 274–81.

Priestley, Joseph. *The Rudiments of English Grammar.* 2d rev. ed. London, 1769.

Prince, Michael. *Philosophical Dialogue in the British Enlightenment: Theology, Aesthetics, and the Novel.* Cambridge: Cambridge University Press, 1996.

Quennell, Peter. *The Pursuit of Happiness.* Boston: Little, Brown, 1988.

Quintilian. *Institutio Oratoria.* 4 vols. Ed. H. E. Butler. Cambridge: Harvard University Press, 1920–22.

Racine. *Phèdre.* Ed. Philippe Drouillard and Denis Canal. Paris: Larousse, 1990.

Randall, John Herman. *Plato: Dramatist of the Life of Reason.* New York: Columbia University Press, 1970.

Raynor, David. "Hume on Wilkes and Liberty: Two Possible Contributions to the *London Chronicle.*" *Eighteenth-Century Studies* 13 (1980): 365–76.

———. *Sister Peg: A Pamphlet Hitherto Unknown, by David Hume.* Cambridge: Cambridge University Press, 1982.

———. "Who Invented the Invisible Hand?: Hume's Praise of Laissez-Faire in a Newly Discovered Pamphlet." *TLS* August 14, 1998: 22.

Reddick, Allen. *The Making of Johnson's Dictionary, 1746–1773.* Cambridge: Cambridge University Press, 1990, rev. ed. 1996.

———. "Johnson Beyond Jacobitism: Signs of Polemic in the *Dictionary* and the *Life of Milton.*" *ELH* 64:4 (1997): 983–1005.

Reedy, Gerard, S.J. *The Bible and Reason: Anglicans and Scripture in Late Seventeenth-Century England.* Philadelphia: University of Pennsylvania Press, 1985.

Reid, Thomas. *Works.* 2 vols. 7th ed. Edinburgh: Maclachan and Stewart, 1872.

Reinert, Thomas. *Regulating Confusion: Samuel Johnson and the Crowd.* Durham: Duke University Press, 1996.

Richetti, John. *Philosophical Writing: Locke, Berkeley, Hume.* Cambridge, Mass.: Harvard University Press, 1983.

Rousseau, Jean-Jacques. *Les Confessions.* 2 vols. Ed. Michel Launay. Paris: Garnier-Flammarion, 1964.

———. *A Discourse on Inequality.* Trans. Maurice Cranston. Harmondsworth: Penguin, 1984.

Rudé, George. *Wilkes and Liberty: A Social Study of 1763 to 1774.* Oxford: Oxford University Press, 1962.

Ruhe, Edward. "Hume and Johnson." *Notes and Queries* (Nov. 1954): 477–78.

Sachs, Arieh. *Passionate Intelligence: Imagination and Reason in the Work of Samuel Johnson.* Baltimore: Johns Hopkins University Press, 1967.

Saintsbury, George. *The Peace of the Augustans.* 1916. Oxford: Oxford University Press, 1946.

Scherwatzky, Steven. "Johnson, *Rasselas,* and the Politics of Empire." *Eighteenth-Century Life* 16:3 (1992): 103–113.

Schlereth, Thomas J. *The Cosmopolitan Ideal in Enlightenment Thought: Its Form and Function in the Ideas of Franklin, Hume, and Voltaire, 1694–1790.* Notre Dame: University of Notre Dame Press, 1977.

Schneewind, Jerome. *The Invention of Autonomy: A History of Modern Moral Philosophy.* Cambridge: Cambridge University Press, 1998.

Schwartz, Richard B. *Samuel Johnson and the New Science.* Madison: University of Wisconsin Press, 1971.

Shaftesbury, third earl of, Anthony Ashley Cooper. *Characteristics of Men, Manners, Opinions, Times.* 2 vols. in 1. Ed. John M. Robertson. Intro. by Stanley Grean. Indianapolis: Bobbs-Merrill, 1964.

Sher, Richard. *Church and University in the Scottish Enlightenment.* Princeton: Princeton University Press, 1985.

Siebert, Donald. "Johnson and Hume on Miracles." *Journal of the History of Ideas* 36 (1975): 543–47.

———. *The Moral Animus of David Hume.* Newark: University of Delaware Press, 1990.

———. "Chivalry and Romance in the Age of Hume." *Eighteenth-Century Life* 21:1 (1997): 62–79.

Sitter, John. *Literary Loneliness in Mid-Eighteenth-Century England.* Ithaca: Cornell University Press, 1982.

Skinner, Andrew. "David Hume: Principles of Political Economy." In *The Cambridge Companion to Hume.* Ed. David Fate Norton, pp. 222–54. Cambridge: Cambridge University Press, 1993.

Smith, Adam. *The Theory of Moral Sentiments.* Ed. A. L. Macfie and D. D. Raphael. Oxford: Clarendon Press, 1979.

———. *Lectures on Rhetoric and Belles-Lettres.* Ed. J. C. Bryce. Oxford: Clarendon Press, 1983.

Smith, Norman Kemp. *The Philosophy of David Hume: A Critical Study of Its Origins and Central Doctrines.* London: Macmillan, 1949.

Smith, Ronald Gregor. *J. G. Hamann, 1730–1788: A Study in Christian Existence, with Selections from His Writings.* London: Collins, 1960.

Somerville, James. *The Enigmatic Parting Shot: What Was Hume's 'Compleat Answer to Dr. Reid and to That Bigotted Silly Fellow, Beattie'?* Aldershot, Hamptonshire: Averbury, 1995.

Spacks, Patricia. *Imagining a Self: Autobiography and Novel in Eighteenth-Century England.* Cambridge, Mass.: Harvard University Press, 1976.

Stephen, Leslie. *The History of English Thought in the Eighteenth Century.* 1876. 2 vols. New York: G. P. Putnam's Sons, 1927.

Stewart, John B. *Opinion and Reform in Hume's Political Philosophy.* Princeton: Princeton University Press, 1992.

Suwabe, Hitoshi. "Boswell's Meetings with Johnson: A New Count." In *Boswell: Citizen of the World, Man of Letters,* ed. Irma Lustig, pp. 246–57. Lexington: University of Kentucky Press, 1995.

Swift, Jonathan. *Correspondence.* 5 vols. Ed. Harold Williams. Oxford: Clarendon Press, 1963–65.

Taylor, Charles. *Sources of the Self: The Making of the Modern Identity.* Cambridge: Harvard University Press, 1989.

Thomson, James. *"Liberty"; "The Castle of Indolence"; and Other Poems.* Ed. James Sambrook. Oxford: Oxford University Press, 1981.

Tomarken, Edward. *Johnson, "Rasselas," and the Choice of Criticism.* Lexington: University of Kentucky Press, 1989.

Trumpener, Katie. *Bardic Nationalism: The Romantic Novel and the British Empire.* Princeton: Princeton University Press, 1997.

Vance, John A. *Samuel Johnson and the Sense of History.* Athens: University of Georgia Press, 1984.

———. Ed. *Boswell's Life of Johnson: New Questions, New Answers.* Athens: University of Georgia Press, 1985.

———. "Johnson and Hume: Of Like Historical Minds." *Studies in Eighteenth-Century Culture* 15 (1986): 241–56.

Vesey, Godfrey. *Personal Identity.* London: Macmillan, 1947.

Vesterman, William. *The Stylistic Life of Samuel Johnson.* New Brunswick: Rutgers University Press, 1977.

Voitle, Robert. *Samuel Johnson the Moralist.* Cambridge, Mass.: Harvard University Press, 1961.

Voltaire. *Oeuvres Complètes.* 52 vols. Paris: Garnier Frères, 1877–1885.

———. *Siècle de Louis XIV.* Ed. Emile Bourgeois. Paris: Librairie Hachette, n.d.

———. *Histoire de la Guerre de 1741.* Ed. Jacques Maurens. Paris: Garnier Frères, 1971.

———. *Histoire de Charles XII.* Ed. Gunnar Von Proschwitz. Oxford: Voltaire Foundation, 1996.

Walker, Robert. *Arguments for Immortality and Johnson's "Rasselas".* ELS Monograph Series no. 9. Victoria: University of Victoria, 1977.

Walker, William. "The Determination of Locke, Hume, and Fielding." *Eighteenth-Century Life* 20:2 (1996): 70–93.

[Warburton, William, and Richard Hurd.] *Remarks on Mr. David Hume's Essay on the Natural History of Religion: Addressed to the Rev. Dr. Warburton.* London, 1777.

Wasserman, Earl. "Johnson's *Rasselas:* Implicit Contexts." *Journal of English and Germanic Philology* 74:1 (1975): 1–25.

Weber, Max. *The Protestant Ethic and the Spirit of Capitalism.* Trans. Talcott Parsons. New York: Charles Scribner's Sons, 1930.

Weinbrot, Howard. *Britannia's Issue: The Rise of British Literature from Dryden to Ossian.* Cambridge: Cambridge University Press, 1993.

———. "Johnson, Jacobitism, and the Historiography of Nostalgia." *The Age of Johnson* 7 (1996): 163–211.

———. "Johnson, Jacobitism, and Swedish Charles: *The Vanity of Human Wishes* and Scholarly Method." *ELH* 64:4 (1997): 945–81.

Weinsheimer, Joel. *Imitation.* London: Routledge & Kegan Paul, 1984.

———. *Eighteenth-Century Hermeneutics: Philosophy of Interpretation in England from Locke to Burke.* New Haven: Yale University Press, 1993.

Wertz, S. K. "Hume, History, and Human Nature." *Journal of the History of Ideas* 36 (1975): 481–96.

Whelan, Frederick G. *Order and Artifice in Hume's Political Philosophy.* Princeton: Princeton University Press, 1985.

Willey, Basil. *The English Moralists.* London: Chatto & Windus, 1964.

Wimsatt, William K. *Philosophic Words: A Study of Style and Meaning in the Rambler and Dictionary of Samuel Johnson.* New Haven: Yale University Press, 1948.

———, and Cleanth Brooks. *Literary Criticism: A Short History.* New York: Knopf, 1957.

———. "In Praise of *Rasselas:* Four Notes Converging." In *Imagined Worlds: Essays on Some English Novels and Novelists in Honour of John Butt,* ed. Maynard Mack and Ian Gregor, pp. 111–36. London: Methuen, 1968.

Wind, Edgar. *Hume and the Heroic Portrait: Studies in Eighteenth-Century Imagery.* Ed. Jaynie Anderson. Oxford: Clarendon Press, 1986.

Wolff, Larry. "When I Imagine a Child: The Idea of Childhood and the Philosophy of Memory in the Enlightenment." *Eighteenth-Century Studies* 31:4 (1998): 377–401.

Womersley, David. *The Transformation of the Decline and Fall of the Roman Empire.* Cambridge: Cambridge University Press, 1988.

Wright, John P. *The Sceptical Realism of David Hume.* Minneapolis: University of Minnesota Press, 1983.

Yolton, John, et al., eds. *The Blackwell Companion to the Enlightenment.* Oxford: Blackwell, 1991.

Youngren, William. "Founding English Ethics: Locke, Mathematics, and the Innateness Question." *Eighteenth-Century Life* 16:3 (1992): 12–45.

Yung, Kai Kin, et al. *Samuel Johnson 1709–84.* London: The Herbert Press, 1984.

Index